Rural People and Communities in the 21st Century

We dedicate this book to our families, Nina Glasgow, Sarah and Joseph Brown, Annyce and Emmet Schafft, and Harry, Gretchen, and Soren Schafft.

Rural People and Communities in the 21st Century

Resilience and Transformation

DAVID L. BROWN AND KAI A. SCHAFFT

polity

First published in 2011 by Polity Press
Reprinted 2012, 2013, 2014 (twice), 2016

Polity Press
65 Bridge Street
Cambridge CB2 1UR, UK

Polity Press
350 Main Street
Malden, MA 02148, USA

ISBN-13: 978-0-7456-4127-0 (hardback)
ISBN-13: 978-0-7456-4128-7 (paperback)

A catalogue record for this book is available from the British Library.

Typeset in 9.5 on 12pt Utopia
by Servis Filmsetting Ltd, Stockport, Cheshire
Printed and bound in the United States by RR Donnelley

For further information on Polity, visit our website: www.politybooks.com

Contents

Figures and Tables

Figures

Tables

Acknowledgments

This book could not have been completed without the support, wisdom, advice, and input of many people. We would especially like to acknowledge the patience, guidance, and unflagging enthusiasm and encouragement of Jonathan Skerrett and Emma Longstaff at Polity Press. Emma encouraged us to embark on this adventure, and Jonathan facilitated our journey through to completion. We would also like to acknowledge the helpful comments we received from several anonymous reviewers on the book's prospectus and on the completed manuscript. Our colleague Leland Glenna provided thorough and invaluable feedback on the entire manuscript as it took its present shape. Our home departments, Development Sociology at Cornell and Educational Policy Studies at Penn State, have consistently provided supportive environments for scholarly accomplishment. In particular, we would also like to thank our students, past and present, at Cornell University, Penn State University, and Binghamton University's Decker School of Nursing, who have helped us refine our thinking and test out many of the ideas that appear in one form or another throughout this book. This book contributes to USDA multi-state research project W-2001: Population Dynamics and Change: Aging, Ethnicity, and Land Use Change in Rural Communities. Writing this book brought us back together as scholarly partners after nearly a decade of working on other projects either alone or with other collaborators. It has been a pleasure.

PART I

THINKING ABOUT RURAL PLACES IN METROPOLITAN SOCIETY

1 Rurality in Metropolitan Society

In 2008, the United Nations announced that for the first time in history, more than half of the world's population lived in urban environments (U.N. Department of Economic and Social Affairs/Population Division 2007). While the share of population living in urban areas is higher in more developed nations, the United Nations projects that less developed nations will also surpass the 50 percent urban threshold by 2019. If the world is so highly urbanized, why should we care about rural people and communities, particularly in metropolitan societies such as the United States? In the following section we discuss reasons why rural people and places matter in the twenty-first century, even in the context of overwhelming urbanization. These issues will provide the substantive framework shaping our analysis of persistence and change in rural society that is contained in the remaining chapters. However, prior to examining these contemporary issues, we need to acknowledge that concern about rural people and places did not develop overnight. The intellectual legacy of rural studies began over one hundred years ago with the profound societal transformations that gave rise to sociology and other social sciences. We briefly review this legacy before turning to a discussion of the reasons why rural people and places matter in contemporary society.

The Development of Social Scientific Thought about Rurality

Interest in the social effects of the transformation from rural to urban society traces to the very beginnings of systematic social science. Concern about the perceived negative outcomes of modernization, in particular of industrialization and urbanization, represented one of the central questions driving the new discipline of sociology during the latter part of the nineteenth century. Two influential titans of classical European sociology, Ferdinand Toënnies and Emile Durkheim, shared a concern for the social outcomes of the transformation from rural agrarian to urban industrial society. Both scholars observed that the nature of social relationships is fundamentally altered in larger, denser, more diverse urban places compared with their rural counterparts. Toënnies wrote of the transformation from *Gemeinschaft* (community) to *Gesellschaft* (society), while Durkheim used the terms mechanical and organic solidarity to describe the social relationships characterizing urban and rural communities. "What brings men together," he wrote, "are mechanical causes and impulsive forces, such as affinity of blood, attachment to the same soil, ancestral worship, community of habits, etc." (Durkheim 1964 [1933]: 278). They also both argued that industrialization and changes in the organization of agriculture resulted in communities where more distant relationships replaced the primary social ties characteristic of villages and the agrarian countryside. Durkheim, in particular, worried that this alteration of the fundamental nature of social relationships would separate people from the institutions and interpersonal influences that regulate social behavior and produce social solidarity. Another early sociologist who contributed to understanding the origin of urban–rural differentiation was Pitirim Sorokin, a Russian-American scholar who founded the department of sociology at Harvard University. His work focused more on demographic and occupational attributes of differentiating urban and rural communities than on the relational issues discussed by Toënnies and Durkheim (Sorokin & Zimmerman 1929).

In the United States this concern was most clearly articulated by Louis Wirth (1938) who felt that urban life released people from social controls and alienated them from their neighbors. He saw urban areas as "communities of limited liability" where increased population size and density reduced community attachment, and family and community ceased being the building blocks of society. We will explore these and other sociological concerns about urban and rural community in greater depth in Chapters 2 and 3. For now it is sufficient to acknowledge that interest in rural (and urban) places and populations has a rich legacy in the history of social thought.

What is Rural in a Metropolitan Society?

Like many terms in common usage, the meaning of *rural* is somewhat ambiguous. Even within the social sciences there is disagreement about the meaning and exact definition of rural. The strongest disagreement is between scholars who consider rural to be a type of socio-geographic locality and those who see rural as a social construct. Let's examine these two approaches in order to understand their similarities and differences.

The Location or "Place" Approach to Defining Rural

Social scientists, policy-makers and program administrators typically define rural as a particular kind of socio-geographic place that is distinguished by certain attributes. While scholars, policy-makers, and statistical agencies often concentrate on one or another defining characteristic such as population size or dependence on farming, most acknowledge that rurality is a multidimensional concept that entails a combination of social, demographic, economic, and/or cultural aspects.

The Social Constructivist Approach to Defining Rural

Other social scientists consider rural to be a social construction. Keith Halfacree (1993: 34), for example, has observed that "the rural as space and the rural as representing space" must be distinguished. He contends that a contrast should be drawn between a largely "material" understanding of rural, based on physical space, geographic characteristics and population density, and a *dematerialized* concept that places rural within the realm of imagination (Halfacree 2004). Instead of trying to identify social, demographic, environmental, and economic attributes that define rural places and distinguish them from their urban counterparts, this approach emphasizes symbols and signs people imagine when they think about rurality.

As Cloke and Milbourne (1992: 360) have observed, rurality becomes a matter of determining how people "construct themselves as being rural," that is, of understanding rurality as a socially constructed state of mind. In other words, the social constructivist position contends that mental constructs are an element of culture that helps to determine what people consider as "rural." Woods (2006: 11) has observed, this "shifts attention from the statistical features of rural areas to the people who live there . . ." Hence, places are rural not because of their structural and/or environmental characteristics, but because people who live there think of themselves as being rural with respect to a set of social, moral, and cultural values (Bell 1992; Cloke & Milbourne 1992), an idealized or idyllic landscape (Boyle & Halfacree, 1998), and/or a lifestyle more attuned to organic community life than to a more bureaucratic and rationalized form of social organization (Short 1991).[1]

In this book we will treat these two perspectives as complementary rather than competitive, yet our approach will most often be in line with the locality perspective; *we will treat rural areas as places where people live, work, and visit and as spatially delimited natural environments.* Following this approach, the next section examines four distinguishing dimensions of places: demographic and ecological, economic, institutional, and socio-cultural – comparing rural versus urban areas on a number of attributes contained in the respective domains. You will see that rural areas can be defined in terms of what they are and what they are not, in terms of their intrinsic characteristics, or as a critique of urban.

A Multidimensional Approach to Defining Rural Places

Population & Settlement Structure and Landscape

Demographic and ecological attributes such as population size and density are most commonly used to distinguish rural from urban with the general consensus that rural places are smaller and less dense than their urban counterparts. Rural areas are also thought to be geographically and socially isolated from centers of power and influence which are thought to emanate from urban complexes. Finally, rural areas are considered to be "natural" environments while urban environments are seen as being constructed. As shown in Figure 1.1, while rural areas are found throughout the U.S, areas with the highest degree of rurality, as indicated by small population size and spatial separation from metropolitan centers, are concentrated in the Great Plains, the Midwest, the Ozarks and Appalachia.

Economy

Rural areas can also be distinguished by their economic activities, and in particular by the kinds of goods and services that are produced. Traditionally, rural economies have been characterized by heavy dependence on primary industries such as farming, fishing, forestry, and mining, and these are the types of activities that comprise most people's images of rural places. As will be shown in Chapters

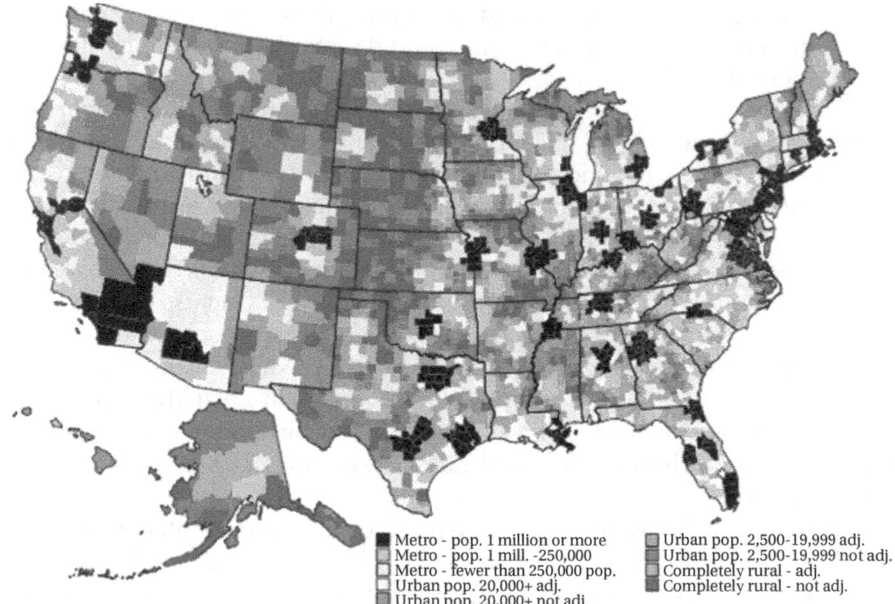

Source: USDA Economic Research Service

Figure 1.1 Urban–Rural Comparisons, 2003

5, 8, and 9, however, rural economies have undergone fundamental changes in the past fifty years, and rural workers now obtain their living from a different array of jobs, some local, and some located at a distance.

Rural economies are not simply distinguished by the nature of their economic activities, but also by the number of establishments they contain and the size of those establishments, by the diversity of economic activities or lack thereof, and by whether economic activity is controlled locally or from a distance. With respect to these economic dimensions, rural areas are typically thought to have a small number of jobs and firms, to be comprised of small-scale establishments, to lack economic diversity, and to be controlled by external interests.

Institutions

Rural and urban areas also differ with respect to the complexity and capacity of their institutional spheres. This difference is especially marked with respect to local government and the public sector. While urban governments typically have strong managerial and technical capacity, rural governments are limited and challenged with respect to public management and technical expertise. We will examine local government capacity in some detail in Chapter 4. Urban governments also typically exceed rural governments in the ability to raise financial resources in support of public services and other responsibilities, but fiscal capacity is quite variable among urban governments as well. Rural areas are characterized by more limited choices in other institutional realms such as religious denominations, clubs, associations, and service organizations in which to participate.

Socio-Cultural

Finally, rural areas are thought to differ from their urban counterparts with respect to a number of socio-cultural domains, but evidence supporting this claim is not convincing. While some aspects of socio-cultural differentiation can be documented, many of the socio-cultural attributes that comprise popular images of rurality have now diminished if they ever existed, and other aspects are being muted by ongoing processes of social, demographic and technological change. Rural–urban differences in social attitudes are probably most persistent and best supported by empirical analysis. There is convincing evidence, for example, that rural people are more socially conservative. For example, research shows that rural voters provide decisive support for socially conservative candidates in many parts of the United States.

Rural areas are also thought to be more homogeneous with respect to race and ethnicity, although, as we show in Chapter 7, this is truer in some regions than in others. Moreover, recent immigration trends in the U.S. have distributed foreign born persons more widely than in the past, thereby diversifying many rural populations (Kandel & Cromartie 2004; Kritz & Gurak 2005; Jensen 2006). It is also thought that rural communities are more likely to be characterized by close personal relationships while urban social interaction is more likely to occur within organizational and associational networks. Similarly, some observers believe that social order in rural areas is typically maintained via informal control while formal controls and third-party enforcement are required to maintain order in urban communities. As we demonstrate in Chapter 3, empirical evidence does not support these preconceptions of rural versus urban differences in social structure.

Critiquing the Location Approach

The location approach to defining rural places and comparing these geographic entities with places that are not rural suffers from a number of inadequacies which, while not fatal, must be kept in mind as we use this framework in succeeding chapters to describe persistence and change in rural structure and examine rural versus urban differences in economy and society during recent decades.

First and foremost, this approach assumes that urban and rural places are grouped into dichotomous categories, that is that they can be discretely and unambiguously differentiated. This is simply not true. Regardless of which characteristics one uses to examine rural–urban differentiation – demographic, economic, political, or some other attribute – the boundary dividing the two categories is always somewhat arbitrary. Of course, this criticism could be leveled against almost any social science category. How old is elderly? Which jobs are professional? Who is an African American; an American Indian?

In our own classes in community and rural sociology at Cornell and Penn State, we often display a set of pictures of settlements and ask our students to indicate which are urban and which are rural. Without exception, students agree on the extremes but give variable responses in categorizing the places in between. Rurality, then, is a variable, not a discrete category, and various indicators can be used to array places as to their degree of rurality (or urbanity), not its presence or absence. Moreover, seeing rurality as a variable implies that there is an interstitial zone of settlement between what is clearly urban and unmistakably rural. As you will see in later chapters (especially Chapters 2, 3, 5, and 8) political contention over land use, landscape management and economic development is particularly acute in these rapidly urbanizing spaces located in the urban periphery.

A related criticism of the "either/or" approach is that while the urban category is fully theorized, the rural category is simply a residual. In other words, rural becomes everything that is not urban with no attention given to the intrinsic characteristics that contribute to a place's rurality. As Halfacree (2004: 285) has observed, "we must move away from considering rural as necessarily a 'residual' and see it instead as an integral part of such settlement systems." Unfortunately, the residual approach to identifying rural areas is an almost universal practice in national statistical systems throughout the world.

Social scientists create analytical categories so that they can study social differentiation and social change within and between geographically based populations and over time. Their analytical goal is to minimize the variability (in population size and composition, economy, political process, and so on) within categories, while maximizing variability between categories. Be that as it may, social categories are not homogeneous, and this is certainly true of urban and rural. The U.S. government's classification of counties into metropolitan and nonmetropolitan areas is a case in point. Even within our home states, New York and Pennsylvania, the metropolitan category groups together mega cities such as New York City and Philadelphia with Ithaca and State College (both metropolitan areas of about 100,000 population whose undiversified economies are dominated by Cornell and Penn State Universities). Obviously, the metropolitan category is hugely diverse with respect to demographics, economics, institutions and socio-cultural characteristics, but the nonmetropolitan sector is similarly diverse. Consider New York's *North Country*, the part of the state that forms its Northern border with Canada. All seven counties in this relatively isolated region are non-metropolitan, but they are not all the same. Hamilton County, for example, has a population of 5,162 while Jefferson County is home to over 114,000 residents. Or consider employment. One in ten jobs in Lewis County are in agriculture, which is almost three times the North Country's (and the state's) dependence on farming (Gavurnik 2008). In other words, urban versus rural differences are important, but they often mask important diversity within the rural and urban categories themselves. Finally, as discussed earlier in this chapter, it is important to remember that the location or place-based approach to defining and conceptualizing rural is only one approach, and many scholars put equal or greater store in rurality as a social and symbolic construction.

What Images and Attitudes Do People Have About Rural People and Places in Metropolitan Societies?

North Americans and Europeans hold favorable opinions about rural areas, opinions that are not always consistent with the material reality of rural places. In the U.K. for example, the British Attitudes Survey revealed that only five percent of people would choose to live in a big city if they had a free choice while 65 percent would live in small cities or country villages (Parkinson et al. 2006: 199). These positive views can influence people's migration and employment decisions, and they can affect their political support of public programs that are designed to assist rural people and communities.

Beginning in the 1970s, social scientists in the United States began systematically to examine people's size of place preferences.[2] This issue was especially salient at the time because as will be discussed in Chapter 2, the nation's long-term trend of urban–rural population redistribution had begun to switch from urban concentration to deconcentration in the 1970s. Accordingly, researchers wanted to understand why the long-term trend of population concentration reversed. Was this "population turnaround" strictly motivated by economic factors, or were social factors and community amenities also involved? Research by Glenn Fuguitt and James Zuiches (1975) showed a strong public preference for rural areas and small towns, especially if the rural area is located within commuting distance of a larger city. Their national study showed that 75 percent of Americans would prefer to live in a place of less than 50,000 population even though only 56 percent actually lived in places of that size at the time of the survey. In addition, they demonstrated that persons who expressed a preference for rural living were drawn to perceived rural amenities and rebuffed by the negative aspects of urban environments while economic opportunities were much more closely associated with preferences for large cities.

More recent research has shown that preferences for small towns and rural areas have remained stable since the 1970s even though the direction of urban–rural migration changed during the twenty years studied (Fuguitt & Brown 1990; Brown et al. 1997). Furthermore this research showed that while most people prefer the size of place they currently live in, those who do not are almost twice as likely to prefer smaller rather than larger settings (Brown et al. 1997).

Many scholars have observed that preferences for small towns and rural areas are a mixture of pro-rural and anti-urban attitudes (Fuguitt & Zuiches 1975). In other words, while persons respond positively to what they perceive as intrinsic rural attributes, their residential preferences also contain a critique of what they consider to be negative aspects of urban living and urban environments. Willits and her colleagues (1990) dug into this issue by asking respondents to a Pennsylvania survey to agree or disagree with thirty-five statements about the positive and negative aspects of urban and rural life. They found that the same respondents who agreed with positive images of rural life held negative appraisals of urban life, and rejected negative images of rurality. Positive rurality was comprised of statements about the quality of family and community relationships, neighborliness, and closeness to nature, while anti-urbanism was comprised of statements focusing on the fast pace and high stress of urban living, the remoteness of urban relationships, the materialistic focus of urban life, and the poor quality and danger of urban environments. They found that people who agree with one pro-rural or anti-urban statement are highly likely to agree with others. In other words, individual responses to specific urban and rural attributes group together in ways that reflect global attitudes about rural and urban living with the overwhelming sentiment favoring rural and rejecting urban.

It should be noted that pro-rural and/or anti-urban attitudes are not always consistent with the material reality of urban and rural communities, partly because people tend to form these attitudes from afar, not through actual experience (Logan 1996). As Logan commented, ". . . these 'facts' do not much matter, A large share of what we value is the mythology and symbolism of rural places rather than their reality" (p. 26).

What Logan is referring to is called the *rural mystique* in the U.S. or the *rural idyll* in Britain. The mystique is composed of treasured or almost sacred elements. It is an idealized form of community that stands in contrast to urban life. It is the antithesis of the modern urban world, somehow more moral, virtuous, and simple. In other words, rurality reflects what people feel has been lost in the transformation from rural to urban society. Similarly, the British rural idyll represents a balance between people and nature. As represented in poetry and painting, the idyll ignores the misery of rural poverty and presents emotional and sometimes sentimental renderings of people and landscapes in harmonious unity.

Resource economists have developed a framework for deconstructing the "value of rurality" into five dimensions of public goods which provide insights into why people are willing to spend their own money and/or support public policies for rural areas and environments.[3] Using this framework, economists contend that rural environments have natural resource, nostalgia, existence, option, and bequest value. Natural resource value means that persons are willing to pay more for access to rural landscapes. For example, they are willing to pay for a "room with a view." Nostalgia value means that people will spend their own money, or support public spending, to preserve visual reminders of the nation's heritage. As William Howarth (1996) has observed, rural areas are seen as a well of permanence and continuity which stems the fear of cultural loss. He contends that people cling to nostalgia more strongly during periods of rapid social and technological change. Paradoxically, they seek change but at the same time resist it. Existence value means that people simply value the knowledge that rural areas exist, regardless of their intentions to live, work, or visit. This logic is similar to laws that protect endangered species. Option value means that people who have never experienced rural environments as residents, visitors and/or workers place value on the option to do so in the future. Similarly, bequest value means that people are willing to support current expenditures to protect rural environments so that future generations will have the option of living, working, and/or visiting such places. This aspect of rural value is closely associated with notions of sustainability that will be discussed in Chapter 5.

How Do People Acquire Pro-Rural and Anti-Urban Attitudes?

Obviously, people are not born with innate predilections toward rural living and against urban environments. Moreover, while the majority of Americans and Britons may hold pro-rural and anti-urban attitudes, a significant minority disagree. Also, while rural communities are preferred locations in the U.S., U.K., and many other developed nations, the reverse is true in many parts of the developing world. Pro-rural attitudes have a long history in the United States. While early colonists tended to favor cities, pro-rural attitudes began to solidify during the American Revolution as an aspect of Enlightenment thought, and as a way of differentiating the United States from England. From the beginning, rural areas were mainly valued for what they are not, that is, not England, not urban, and not industrial (Danbom 1996). Jefferson (1955), and other Enlightenment thinkers, praised rural areas as being more authentic and natural.[4] Moreover, as Danbom (1996: 20) observed, "the new republic's ruralism became an essential part of its identity, and in Enlightenment terms, a sign of its superiority to England."

As discussed earlier, residential attitudes are not typically formed through direct experience (Logan 1996). Rather, as Howarth (1996) has shown, vivid images of urban and rural life are contained in art, music, popular culture, and literature. The rural idyll is expressed in works by literary giants such as Tennyson, Wordsworth, Goethe, and Sandburg while anti-urban messages are contained in works by the likes of T.S. Eliot, Upton Sinclair, Henri Lefebvre, and Jane Jacobs. In other words, since most Americans and Europeans do not experience rural communities on a daily basis, rural images are a cultural construction, not an experiential reality.

However, it would be a mistake to discount completely the importance of personal experiences in the production of pro-rural attitudes. As Gottfried (1996: 14) has said, "the image of a place is the thing most people are aware of on a daily basis. It derives from conscious and unconscious perception through the bodily senses, and it becomes embedded in human memory through experience and interaction." Further, he observes that part of the symbolic value of the rural derives from the collective memory of sensations about the land.

Why Rural People and Places Matter in Urbanized Society

Why should we be concerned with rural people and places? First, while only 15–30 percent of the population lives in the rural parts of most developed nations, this is a large minority. In the United States for example, the rural population share, about 17 percent in 2006, accounts for almost sixty million persons, which is a large population in its own right. Moreover, the U.S. rural population exceeds the size of other important subgroups such as Hispanics (43.2 million, 14.7 percent), African Americans (40.2 million, 13.7 percent), or persons age 65 and older (37 million, 12 percent) (U.S. Census Bureau 2006). Accordingly, problems and opportunities associated with living and working in rural environments merit attention. While the rural population is socially, demographically, and politically diverse, it can be mobilized toward perceived collective ends. Such mobilization tends to reflect rural "identity" with respect to an agenda of social beliefs rather than the rural population's particular economic interests.

Survey research in the United States has shown that rural people hold more conservative attitudes toward abortion, sex education, homosexuality, and other social issues (Beale 1995), and rural voters have been shown to support more conservative candidates in local and national elections. Many political analysts in the U.S. contend that rural voters are a key component of the conservative voting base, and candidates tend to spend a disproportionate share of resources courting them. For example, Hamilton (2006) showed that rural voters played an important role in re-electing George W. Bush as President of the United States in 2004, and the rural impact on voting persisted even after race, region and other characteristics of urban and rural voters were considered in his analysis.

Rural people and communities also merit attention based on claims of territorial equity. As will be shown later in Chapters 8, 10, and 11, rural and urban economies contain different opportunity structures, different arrays of occupations and industries. A main result is that rural people have less access to good jobs and secure incomes, so that living in a rural area has a negative impact on opportunities and life chances. Many rural workers, especially those with high educational attainment, face a difficult dilemma in order to make a good living. They must either move to the city to find a good job that is matched to their education and experience, or commute long distances to urban opportunities. To complicate the picture, access to education also tends to be lower in rural areas so rural youth tend to have lower human capital than their urban counterparts (Gibbs 1998). Hence, even the presence of well-paying jobs nearby does not insure that rural workers with low education will be able to make a secure living close to home.

Where a person lives is important because it contributes to one's personal identity. When asked *who they are*, most people respond with a list of personal attributes including perceived characteristics of *where they live*. For example, we both live in college towns – Ithaca, New York, and State College, Pennsylvania – where the permanent residents proudly don "Ithaca is Gorges" and "I'm Happy to be in Happy Valley" hats, T-shirts, and other garb. As David Hummon (1990) has shown, this is not simply parochialism or local boosterism, but rather an important component of identity, one that influences personal decisions and choices in a wide range of social and economic situations over one's life course. For example, strong associations with or attachment to place partly explains why poor people stay in lagging regions. In contrast, a discontinuity between where one lives and where one would prefer to live is one factor contributing to migration and population redistribution. This issue will be examined more fully in Chapter 2.

Even though rural areas may only contain 15–30 percent of a nation's population they typically contain most of its land, water, and mineral resources. As a result, the bulk of a country's food, fiber, and energy sectors are located in rural environments. In an era where food and energy supplies are increasingly insecure, and where environmental sustainability challenges social sustainability, rural environments take on added value and meaning. In highly urbanized societies, rural areas depend on their metropolitan counterparts for a multitude of social, economic, and political goods and services but, since we live in an interdependent world, the reverse is also true when it comes to supplying the essential inputs that make urban industry and communities possible.

As indicated earlier, 70–85 percent of population is concentrated in urbanized environments in North America, Western Europe, and in other highly developed regions of the world. Ironically, while population is highly concentrated, most settlements – towns, villages, and cities – remain dispersed throughout rural regions. In the United States, for example, 62 percent of 3,100 counties are officially designated as nonmetropolitan areas, and the majority of sub-national units of local government are located in these counties. While serving relatively small populations, each of these rural places manages public business, collects and disperses revenues, delivers services, and plans for the future. Given their small size and limited capacity, this is a significant challenge that we will discuss in Chapter 4.

Finally, it should be noted that most of a nation's physical infrastructure (locks and dams, roads, railroads, bridges, ports, energy transmission lines, aqueducts, wind turbines, cellular towers, etc.) is primarily located in rural environments. A nation's social and economic wellbeing, its economic efficiency and competitiveness, and its ability to mobilize resources toward national priorities is contingent on transportation and communication systems that are managed and maintained by local governments many of which are located in rural areas.[5]

In summary, while we live in an urban world, rural areas continue to contribute to a nation's economic and social wellbeing, and to its energy and food security. Where one lives affects one's life chances as well as one's personal identity. This book examines persistence and change in rural economy and society in the United States and other highly metropolitan societies during the twenty-first century. By the end of the book we hope that you will agree with us that rural people and communities merit consideration in a wide range of social, economic, and environmental discussions at all levels of society from local to national.

Notes

1 Short's use of "organic" differs from Durkheim's use as discussed earlier. For Durkheim, organic solidarity is based on a complex division of labor. Short's usage focuses more on cohesion that is produced by consensus on values cultivated by socializing institutions such as the school and family (Johnson 1995).

2 A number of public opinion polls asked size of place preference questions as early as 1948, and showed a strong preference for small towns and rural areas even at that time during a period of strong urbanization (Roper cited in Fuguitt & Zuiches (1975). Similarly, Roper Polls conducted in Britain showed that 2/3 of British persons preferred the countryside to the city as early as the 1930s. Systematic scientific study of residential preferences in the U.S. began in 1971 with research by Zuiches and Fuguitt conducted for the President's Population Commission (Zuiches & Fuguitt 1972).

3 Public goods are said to be non-rivaled and non-excludable. Consumption of a public good by one individual does not reduce availability of the good for consumption by others; and that no one can be effectively excluded from using the good. Of course this definition is an ideal type, and no goods are purely public in reality. Public goods have economic value, but their value is not necessarily determined in the market.

4 Some scholars are skeptical about the origins of Jefferson's favorable view of farmers. Thompson (2000) contends that Jefferson's view was based on his observation that many businessmen fled to Canada during the American Revolution while farmers were more likely to fight the British. Hence, his view of rural people is more concrete and pragmatic than metaphysical.

5 Towns, villages, and small cities are part of a complex intergovernmental system. Sometimes they operate on their own, but partnerships with state and national government is also an important aspect of rural government. This is discussed in Chapter 4.

References

Beale, C. 1995. Noneconomic Value of Rural. Paper presented at the USDA Experts' Conference on the Value of Rural America. Washington, D.C., U.S. Department of Agriculture-Economic Research Service.

Bell, M. 1992. The Fruit of Difference: The Rural–Urban Continuum as a System of Identity. *Rural Sociology.* 57(1), 65–82.

Boyle, P. & Halfacree, K. 1998. *Migration Into Rural Areas: Theories and Issues.* Chichester, Wiley.

Brown, D.L., Fuguitt, G., Heaton, T., & Waseem, S. 1997. Continuities in Size of Place Preferences in the United States, 1972–1992. *Rural Sociology.* 62(4), 408–428.

Cloke, P. & Milbourne, P. 1992. Deprivation and Lifestyles in Rural Wales: II Rurality and the Cultural Dimension. *Journal of Rural Studies.* 8, 359–371.

Danbom, D. 1996. Why Americans Value Rural Life. *Rural Development Perspectives.* 12(1), 19–23.

Durkheim, E. 1964 [1933] . *The Division of Labor in Society.* New York, The Free Press.

Fuguitt, G. & Brown, D.L. 1990. Residential Preferences and Population Redistribution, *Demography.* 27(4), 589–600.

Fuguitt, G. & Zuiches, J. 1975. Residential Preferences and Population Distribution, *Demography.* 12(3), 491–504.

Gavurnik, J. 2008. The North Country in Statistical Profile. *CaRDI Report* No. 5. Ithaca, Community & Rural Development Institute.

Gibbs, R.M. 1998. College Completion and Return Migration Among Rural Youth, pp. 61–80. In Gibbs, R.M., Swaim, P.L., & Teixeira, R. (eds) *Rural Education and Training in the New Economy.* Ames, Iowa State University Press.

Gottfried, H. 1996. Corridors of Value: Rural Land in Rural Life. *Rural Development Perspectives.* 12(1), 1–18.

Halfacree, K. 1993. Locality and Social Representation: Space, Discourse and Alternative Representations of the Rural. *Journal of Rural Studies.* 9(1), 23–37.

Halfacree, K. 2004. Rethinking Rurality, pp. 285–304. In Champion, T. & Hugo, G. (eds) *New Forms of Urbanization: Beyond the Urban–Rural Dichotomy.* Aldershot, Ashgate.

Hamilton, L. 2006. Rural Voting in the 2004 Election. Durham, NH, Carsey Institute.

Howarth, W. 1996. The Value of Rural Life in American Culture. *Rural Development Perspectives.* 12(1), 6–12.

Hummon, D. 1990. *Common Places: Community Ideology and Identity in American Culture.* Albany, SUNY Press.

Jefferson, T. 1955. *Notes on the State of Virginia*: Chapel Hill, University of North Carolina Press.

Jensen, L. 2006. New Immigrant Settlements in Rural America: Problems, Prospects and Policies. *Reports on Rural America.* 1(3), Durham New Hampshire, Carsey Institute.

Johnson, A. 1995. *The Blackwell Dictionary of Sociology.* Malden Massachusetts, Blackwell.

Kandel, W. & Cromartie, J. 2004. New Patterns of Hispanic Settlement in Rural America. Rural Development Research Report No. 99. Washington D.C., United States Department of Agriculture.

Kritz, M.M. & Gurak, D.T. 2005. Immigration and a Changing America, pp. 259–301. In Farley, R. & Haaga, J. (eds) *The American People: Census 2000.* New York, Russell Sage Foundation.

Logan, J. 1996. Rural America as a Symbol of American Values. *Rural Development Perspectives.* 12(1), 24–28

Parkinson, M., Champion, T., Simmie, J., Turok, I., Crookston, M., Katz, B., Park, A. 2006. *The State of English Cities.* London, Office of the Deputy Prime Minister.

Short, J. 1991. *Imagined Countryside.* London, Routledge.

Sorokin, P. & Zimmerman, C. 1929. *Principles of Rural–Urban Sociology.* New York, Henry Holt.

Thompson, P. 2000. Thomas Jefferson's Agrarian Philosophy, pp. 118–139. In Thompson, P. & Hilde, T. (eds) *The Agrarian Roots of Pragmatism.* Nashville, Vanderbilt University Press.

United Nations Department of Economic and Social Affairs/Population Division. 2007. *World Urbanization Prospects: The 2007 Revision.* New York, United Nations.

U.S. Census Bureau. 2006. *Current Population Survey.* Annual Social and Economic Supplement, 2006, Ethnicity. Washington, D.C., U.S. Census Bureau.

Woods, M. 2006. *Rural Geography.* London, Sage.

Willits, F., Bealer, R., and Timbers, V. 1990. Popular Images of 'Rurality': Data From a Pennsylvania Survey. *Rural Sociology.* 55(4), 559–578.

Wirth, L. 1938. Urbanism as a Way of Life. *American Journal of Sociology.* 44(1), 3–24.

Zuiches, J. & Fuguitt, G. 1972. Residential Preferences: Implications for Population Redistribution in Nonmetropolitan Areas, pp. 617–630. In Mazie, S. (ed.) *Population, Distribution, and Policy.* Research Reports of the Commission on Population Growth and the American Future, vol. V. Washington, D.C., USGPO.

2 Urbanization and Population Redistribution

Urbanization refers to the social and economic processes that concentrate populations, resulting in the formation and growth of cities. Urbanization began around 3000 B.C. when the development of settled agriculture produced a big enough food surplus so that large segments of the population could pursue activities outside of farming. Urbanization proceeded relatively slowly until the Industrial Revolution in late eighteenth-century Europe. Since then, urbanization has been very rapid, affecting all regions of the world. In the United Kingdom, for example, about one quarter of the population lived in cities in 1800. One hundred years later, in 1900, this figure had increased to 77 percent (Davis 1967). According to the United Nations Population Division (2008), 75 percent of persons in more developed regions live in urban places, and 45 percent are urban in less developed regions. But, urbanization is about more than population concentration. It reflects profound transformations in the organization of human social life.

In this chapter we will compare and contrast a number of different frameworks used by scholars to examine urbanization, and we will explore how statistical agencies use these conceptual frameworks to measure the extent and pace of urbanization as well as its impact on the wider society. The second part of the chapter examines the forces that promoted urbanization in North America, Europe and other highly developed regions and asks whether these same forces are responsible for stimulating urbanization in today's developing world. The chapter's final section explores whether urbanization is a strictly linear, one-way process, or whether it can be interrupted and reversed. We view this question through the lens of "counter-urbanization" in the U.S., U.K., and other highly developed nations.

Conceptualizing and Measuring Urbanization

Two Perspectives for Conceptualizing Urbanization

Many scholars see urbanization as a strictly demographic process. Hope Tisdale (1942), for example, conceptualized urbanization as a process of population concentration – a process that builds cities. According to Tisdale, cities are defined by two demographic characteristics – population size and population density. Accordingly, urbanization proceeds through multiplication of the number of cities and through population growth of existing cities. Nations urbanize when the share of their population living in urban places increases, and the share living in rural areas decreases. In other words, urbanization occurs when urban rates of population growth exceed rural rates. However, as Charles Tilly (1974) and others have pointed out, urbanization does not mean that rural populations are necessarily declining or even growing slowly. It simply means that the rate of urban population growth exceeds that of its rural counterparts. As we will see shortly, this strictly demographic perspective has influenced the ways in which official statistical agencies delineate urban and rural populations and measure the level and rate of urbanization.

While not disputing the importance of population concentration, other scholars contend that urbanization involves more than simply assembling large populations in high density locations. According to Tilly (1974) and others, urbanization involves a broad-scale social change where societies are transformed from localized, small-scale, homogeneous activities and organizational forms to large-scale, differentiated and coordinated institutions and activities. As a result, urban communities and economies come to dominate societies because geographic concentration of differentiated and coordinated activities is efficient. Economies of scale[1] are realized, and productivity enhanced when complementary functions are integrated in complex divisions of labor. In addition, many urban scholars have recognized that cities not only grow in proportion to a nation's total population, they also come to dominate their surrounding peripheries (Bogue 1949; Duncan et al. 1960; Hawley 1950; McKenzie 1933; Tilly 1974). As urbanization advances, so does the strength and extensiveness of social, economic and political relationships binding cities with their hinterlands. City and periphery, rather than being independent social and economic spaces, are transformed into integrated social and economic systems. City-hinterland interdependence becomes a defining characteristic of highly urbanized societies. Moreover, in the contemporary world, large metropolises extend far beyond their national boundaries to become world cities which dominate hinterlands that are often global in scope. Doreen Massey (2007), Saskia Sassen (2006) and others have observed that world cities are now the major nodes through which global economic relations are managed and controlled. As Sassen (2006: 122) has written, "cities are strategic places that concentrate command functions, global markets, and . . . production sites for the advanced corporate service industries." A global city may be contained by national borders, but socially, economically and demographically global, such as New York, Los Angeles or Beijing.

Measuring Urbanization.

As discussed in Chapter 1, urban and rural are social constructions that can be approached as either sets of cultural elements that affect how persons imagine community, or as material constructions defined by concrete place-based attributes. While these two perspectives are complementary, we deploy the materialistic place approach in this chapter and elsewhere in this book because the availability of social, demographic, economic, and natural resources data for various types of geographic places permits us to use quantitative empirical analysis to examine rural persistence and change, and to compare and contrast urban and rural places and populations. However, even though we will depend on statistical analysis to examine urban and rural structures and change in many parts of this book, we will also examine the more subjective aspects of rurality and of rural social change.

While we stressed that rural and urban are multidimensional concepts involving demographic, geographic, economic, cultural and social structural domains, statistical agencies typically either follow Tisdale's advice and focus exclusively on population size and/or density, or they deploy an economic concept of urbanization by demarcating the city's zone of economic interaction with its hinterland.[2] Rural, in almost all statistical systems, is treated as a residual, what is left over after urban areas have been defined. And, statistical agencies seldom if ever use any cultural, natural resource, or social structural indicators to delineate urban and rural populations. We illustrate these statistical practices by examining how government agencies in the United States define urban and rural areas, thereby providing the basis for measuring urbanization. The fact that rural is treated as an undifferentiated residual in most data systems is another reason why we have attempted to use both statistical analysis and a more constructivist approach to examining rural structure and change.

Defining Urban and Rural in the United States

The United States uses two separate methods to measure urbanization: urban versus rural and metropolitan versus nonmetropolitan. The U.S. Bureau of the Census, employing Tisdale's (1942) conceptualization, differentiates urban places from their rural counterparts by using population size and density thresholds. The second approach, employed by the U.S. Office of Management and Budget (OMB), uses both demographic and economic criteria to identify metropolitan regions. Similar to the urban–rural distinction, nonmetropolitan areas are treated as residuals, that is, they are defined by what they are not, not what they are.

Urban versus Rural

Urban areas include urban clusters and urbanized areas. *Urban clusters* are defined as central places and adjacent territory with at least 2,500 people and an overall density of 1,000 persons per square mile. *Urbanized areas* are a special sub-set of urban cluster with 50,000 or greater population. The distinction between urban clusters and urbanized areas is important because, as will be shown below, metropolitan areas must be organized around an urbanized area.

Metropolitan versus Nonmetropolitan

Metropolitan areas are urban regions comprised of a central county plus adjacent counties that are highly integrated with the center. Central counties contain the urbanized area that gives the area its name.[3] Outlying counties qualify for inclusion in the metropolitan area if they have a sufficient rate of in- and out-commuting with the central county's urbanized area. The city-hinterland concept discussed above was influential in shaping this statistical practice.

Nonmetropolitan areas are counties that neither have an urbanized area of 50,000 people nor are integrated by workforce commuting with a metropolitan central county. About two-thirds of U.S. counties (2,151 of 3,141) were classified

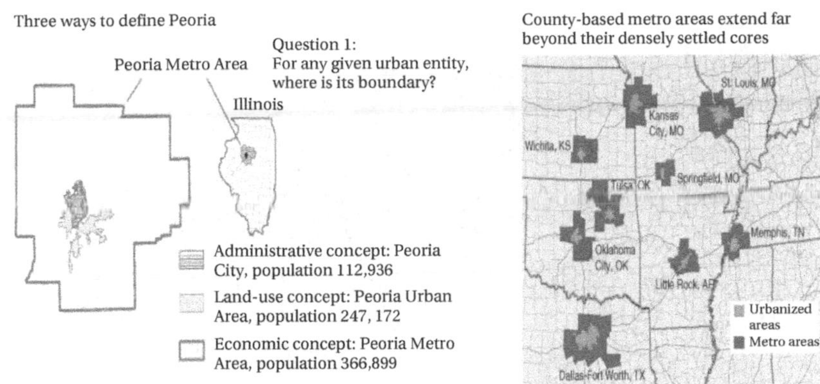

Source: USDA Economic Research Service

Figure 2.1 Three Ways of Measuring Urban Population

as nonmetropolitan after the 2000 census, but these areas contain only 17 percent of the nation's population (see Figure 2.1) (United States Department of Agriculture-Economic Research Service 2007). Scholars have criticized this system not only because the nonmetropolitan population is a residual, but even worse an undifferentiated residual (Brown & Cromartie 2003). As early as 1975, the USDA observed that the nonmetropolitan sector was extremely diverse and recommended that it be disaggregated by combining the urban–rural classification with the metropolitan–nonmetropolitan delineation (Hines et al. 1975). Following the 2000 census, the OMB finally responded to this critique by creating a statistical system in which nonmetropolitan counties are grouped into two types of core-based statistical areas. Micropolitan areas are organized around an urbanized area of 10,000 to 49,999 persons, while "non-core" based areas are counties lacking even one place with 10,000 population (Brown et al. 2004). For the first time, the U.S. government is now displaying nonmetropolitan data in a way that compares unambiguously rural counties with more highly urbanized micropolitan areas.

Critiquing Conventional Statistical Practice

The urban–rural categorizations described above have obvious utility for describing and comparing populations, for examining challenges and opportunities facing various types of communities, and for targeting public assistance to communities, establishments and/or households. However, the measurement of urban–rural settlement in the United States and in most other nations has a number of weaknesses that should be kept in mind when using demographic data for research, educational and/or policy purposes. First, thresholds of population size, population density, inter-county commuting or other social, economic or demographic attributes are somewhat arbitrary. What may seem large for some purposes, for determining the location of a major trauma hospital for example, may far exceed the necessary threshold for determining the optimal location of social welfare offices. Clearly, no one would contend that every location regardless of size, location, or other characteristics should have these facilities, but if

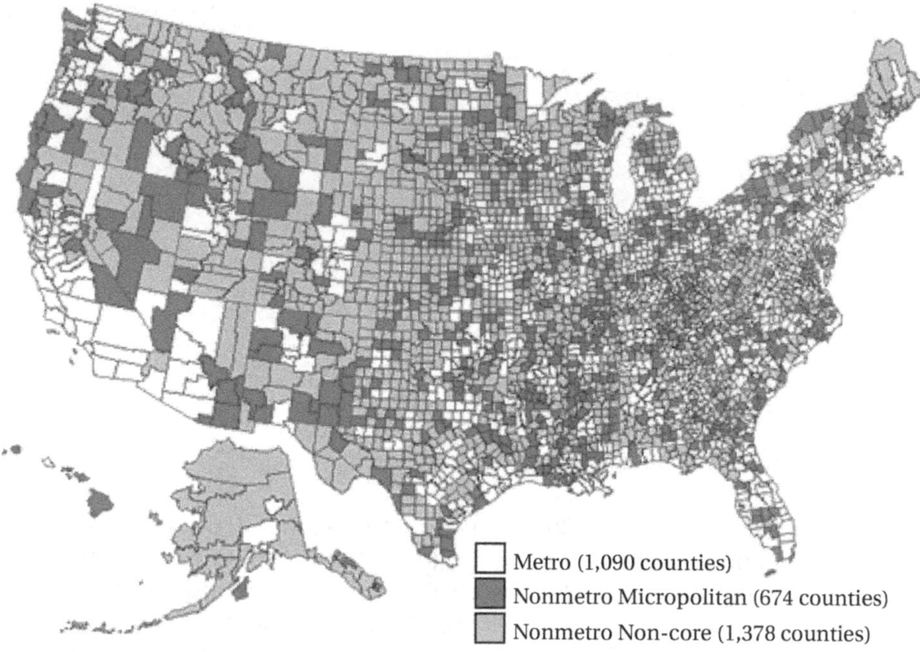

Source: Prepared by ERS using data from the census bureau

Figure 2.2 Metropolitan, Micropolitan, and Non-core Counties, 2003

eligibility is determined by being an "urban" place, then what is urban for major trauma centers is not the same as the minimum size or density needed to house offices that are tasked with the direct administration of social programs.

Disagreement on appropriate and scientifically accurate thresholds of population size and density for differentiating urban and rural populations is reflected in the wide variety of statistical practice employed throughout the world. In Europe alone, the minimum urban size threshold ranged from 1,500 (Ireland) to 20,000 (Switzerland) (United Nations 2008). However, as Champion (2004) has shown, only 98 of the world's 228 nations use population size and/or density to define urban places. In contrast, the modal approach (109 nations) is to define urban places by administrative criteria regardless of their size, density or other attributes.

Second, the process of urbanization should be conceptualized and measured as a variable characteristic of places, not as a set of discrete categories. Accordingly, places can be arrayed on a continuum that ranges from clearly rural locations, those identified as "non-core based places" in the U.S statistical system, to global mega cities such as New York, London, Paris, or Beijing. Places located in between these extremes are not unambiguously urban or rural. From a rural perspective, these intermediate locales are of particular interest because they tend to be where growth and change are occurring and where decisions over land use, the proper scale and content of education and other community issues are particularly contentious. Moreover, these areas are often located at the urbanizing periphery of expanding metropolitan areas, and hence are experiencing dramatic transformations of their social and economic lives (Cromartie 2006).

Third, all measurement systems, including those in social science, seek to maximize between category differences while minimizing within category variability. In other words, social science categories, such as those designed to measure the level and pace of urbanization, are not unitary or homogeneous. As discussed in Chapter 1, New York City and Ithaca are both official metropolitan areas as determined by the U.S. OMB, even though New York is over two hundred times larger than Ithaca (18.8 million versus 100,000). Similarly, the nonmetropolitan category is highly diverse including counties with small cities of 20,000 or greater population and counties that lack even one place with 2,500 residents.

Finally, while most scholars agree that urbanization involves demographic, economic, institutional and socio-cultural dimensions, statistical practice is typically dominated by demographic and economic measures. Even if suitable data were available to measure urban and rural areas in a fully theorized multidimensional manner, the cost of doing so would be prohibitive (Brown & Cromartie 2004). Other interests such as racial and ethnic groups are stronger competitors for the federal statistical budget than settlement structure, spatial inequality, or rural and urban affairs. Accordingly, it is unlikely that urban–rural measurement will gain additional depth in the future. While the lack of multidimensional measures of urban and rural limits the nature of research on urbanization and rural social change, scholars can use other kinds of data to conduct more nuanced studies that help us interpret the findings of research conducted with official statistics. In addition, it is imperative that scholars and policy-makers are aware of the limitations of official statistical categories such as urban and rural or metropolitan and nonmetropolitan when using research based on these data to make decisions.

Why Population Concentrates in Urban Places

Most scholars believe that urbanization and industrialization are inseparable processes. This may have been true during industrialization in North America, Western Europe, and other highly developed world regions, but is it true in today's developing countries? In this section we develop a conceptual model for examining the determinants of urban population concentration in more developed regions, and compare this framework with what is happening today in other less developed yet rapidly urbanizing parts of the world.

The Demographic Equation

The explanation of urban population redistribution begins with the demographic balancing equation since population concentration results when urban places as a category grow faster than their rural counterparts. This simple equation, shown below, indicates how two component processes fully account for differences in the rate of population change between urban and rural or other types of geographic areas.

Population growth = f (natural increase + net migration)[4]

In other words, the demographic equation shows that urban–rural differences in the rate of population growth can only result when urban populations exceed their

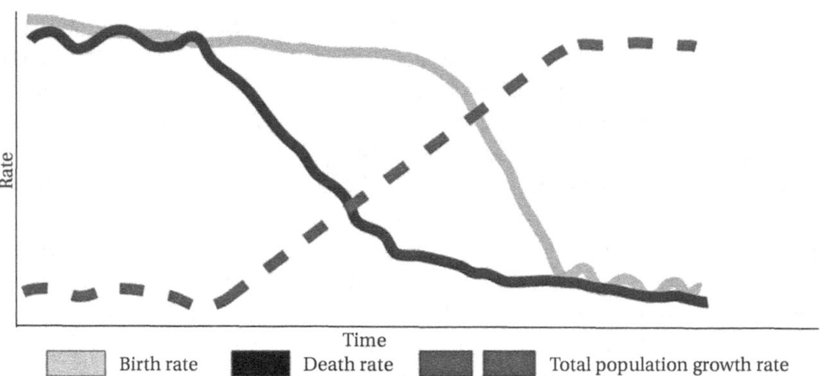

Source: Author's own

Figure 2.3 The Demographic Transition

rural counterparts in the rate of natural increase [births minus deaths] and/or in the rate of net in-migration [in-migration minus out-migration]. If the urban sector has both higher natural increase and higher in-migration, then urbanization is a certainty. However, urban excess in both components of change is not necessary for urbanization to occur. Urban areas would outpace rural areas if rural natural increase exceeded urban natural increase just as long as urban migration was sufficiently large to make up the difference.[5] The critical question, then, is what social and economic processes are associated with urban versus rural differences in natural increase and/or net in-migration? To answer this question we examine the history of European and North American urbanization during the Industrial Revolution.

Prior to the Industrial Revolution, Western European and North American population change fluctuated between periods of growth and decline. As a result, population size remained relatively small and constant over the long term. As shown in figure 2.3 mortality rates were high and uncontrolled, and birth rates were high and uncontrolled. In other words, Western Europe and North America had yet to begin the demographic transition. This changed during the late eighteenth century when a number of social changes and technological advances reduced the death rate, which in conjunction with continued high fertility, resulted in sustained natural increase in both cities and the countryside. As will be shown shortly, natural increase in rural areas led to an imbalance between population and land resources. As a consequence, surplus population migrated to cities. Natural increase in cities, in combination with net in-migration, further contributed to rapid urban population growth. Why, then, did mortality decline during the Industrial Revolution, fueling natural increase and ultimately urbanization? What factors, in addition to population pressure, resulted in rural to urban migration?

Natural Increase

At the beginning of the Industrial Revolution mortality was high in both urban and rural areas because of harvest failures and epidemics (Wrigley 1969). Cities, in particular, were very unhealthy places, and net rural to urban migration was needed to maintain population size let alone to result in urban population growth

(Langer 1963). Why did the death rate begin to decline at this time? Medical advances might seem the obvious answer. However, even though Leeuwenhoek discovered microorganisms in the seventeenth century, it was almost another one hundred years before Pasteur and Koch demonstrated the association between germs and the spread of disease. Accordingly, the explanation of lowered mortality lies elsewhere (McKeown & Brown 1968).[6]

Improved nutrition is the most important reason for lower mortality. Technical and social organizational changes broadened the food base, made it more reliable and nutritious, and more easily transferred from areas of production to areas of consumption. The introduction of the potato, which was more nutritious than the cereal crops it replaced, crop rotation, better drainage, improved livestock breeds, new types of agricultural machinery and better storage facilities all improved nutrition which in turn reduced people's susceptibility to disease and enhanced their ability to survive once infected (Drake 1969; Wrigley 1969). In addition, improved maternal nutrition increased birth weight, thereby reducing infant mortality. However, since most babies die of infectious diseases of the stomach and chest, major reductions of deaths during the first year of life had to wait for the development of medical technologies (Wrigley 1969).

Improvements in public sanitation, especially drinking water, were also effective in reducing mortality during industrialization in Western Europe and North America. While the specific mechanism of disease transmission was still unknown, scientists began to recognize the association between sickness and living conditions including water supply, housing, refuse removal, cleanliness, ventilation and nuisance control (McKeown & Brown 1968). By the second half of the nineteenth century, enhanced sanitation had proved effective against cholera and tuberculosis, and environmental health was a public policy objective in many Western European nations.

Rural to Urban Migration

While higher natural increase contributed to both urban and rural population growth during industrialization, internal migration had a distinctly urban direction. Rather than simply replacing urban deaths, rural to urban migration now became a major force in lifting the rate of urban population increase over that of its rural counterpart. Rural to urban migration resulted from rural *pushes* as well as from urban *pulls.*

Why were people pushed from the countryside into the city? First and foremost, the same agricultural revolution that contributed to reducing mortality and increasing natural increase in both rural and urban areas had the indirect effect of increasing rural unemployment and displacing rural populations. Agricultural technology increased the productivity of farming thereby reducing the need for agricultural labor. Landowners needed large tracts of land to benefit from investments in new technologies. Accordingly, they enclosed their lands and drove peasants and tenant farmers out of agriculture. With natural increase producing rural population pressure, in the absence of rural industry to absorb unemployed workers, displaced persons and their growing families had nowhere to go but to the cities.

What forces pulled rural people into cities? At the same time that technology reduced the need for agricultural labor, it was increasing the demand for workers in urban industries. Manufacturing technologies in textiles and apparel, metallurgy and machine tools among others greatly enhanced industrial output and paved the way for mass production. Moreover, the invention of the steam engine in the early 1800s had a profound effect on both the scale and location of industrial production. Steam power concentrated production in cities because steam loses its energy when transmitted away from central boilers. Accordingly, manufacturing became concentrated in large-scale (mostly urban) production sites. The steam engine also resulted in new modes of transportation such as steam ships and the railroad that made it possible for cities to import agricultural surpluses to feed the growing industrial workforce. In addition, finished products could be exported to far flung markets both at home and abroad.

Technology, while a necessary condition for urbanization was not sufficient. As Tilly (1974) has observed, machines without organization to manage the production process will not result in the rise and growth of urban society. Tilly had two master organizational innovations in mind – capitalism and the nation state. Capitalism involved the market where manufactured goods could be exchanged, the division of labor which functionally integrated the work of many specialists (Durkheim 1997), and bureaucracy where formal rules replaced informal norms as a way of regulating relationships among workers and owners, producers and consumers, and capitalists and the nation state (Weber 1978). Stable centralized states and accountable local governments contributed to urbanization by regulating situations where collective activity was required on a continuing basis. The nation state enforced trade and labor regulations, and protected foreign contact, thereby making capitalist investment less risky and more attractive. In addition, technological and organizational changes permitted cities to mobilize natural and human resources in their hinterlands for the benefit of urban-based enterprises. While the city and the countryside advanced together, the city was dominant.

Do the Same Forces Explain Urbanization in Developing Countries Today?

Many observers question why rural people move to urban areas in developing countries where unemployment is comparably high regardless of urban–rural location. In other words, they ask why people move from one area of limited employment to another area with a similar lack of opportunity? If people are simply exchanging one lagging area for another then the European and North American urbanization experience based on rural pushes and urban pulls would be seriously questioned. The situation in today's developing countries would seem to be characterized as *push without pull.*

Urbanization in today's less developed countries (LDCs) is taking place in the context of high natural increase. However, while natural increase accounts for the majority of urban population growth, rural to urban migration is still substantial. Data from the United Nations show that 54 percent of urban population growth in LDCs is attributable to natural increase while 46 percent is the result of net in-migration (McGee & Griffiths 1998).[7] Given the high pace of urbanization in today's LDCs, this means that large numbers of persons are moving to cities from the countryside (U.N. 2008). Are people irrational? Are they moving to cities only to find that they are no better off than before their moves?

Most scholars believe that rural–urban migration makes good sense in today's developing world. First, conditions of rural push are extreme. Rural fertility is significantly higher than urban fertility, thereby producing high population pressure in the absence of non-agricultural jobs (ORC Macro 2007). Second, while unemployment may be high in LDC cities, official employment statistics often hide the substantial opportunities available in the informal economy (International Labor Office 2002). In other words, when informal activity is accounted for, urban pull is generally thought to be much stronger than that measured by official statistical agencies.

Scholars have also observed that what may seem irrational from an immediate benefits perspective, might be more reasonable when viewed over the longer term (Todaro & Smith 2002). In other words, while rural to urban migrants may experience unemployment and/or an income loss immediately after they move, their income prospects are generally higher over the longer term compared with what they would have earned in their communities of origin. Finally, many scholars have shown that migration is a family and household behavior, and that while migrants themselves may not benefit economically, their children benefit from access to improved education and medical care and improved employment trajectories over their working lives. Moreover, migration helps families diversify their risks by spreading members among different urban and rural locations, which makes them less vulnerable to economic crises that might affect particular localities. Since families often pool collective resources including income, migration tends to level income variability that might occur if all of a family's workers were located in the same place. In conclusion, the European and North American explanation of urbanization featuring natural increase and rural to urban migration seems to fit the situation in today's developing countries quite well. While the specifics are certainly different, the basic argument continues to explain why urban population growth comes to exceed that of rural areas, thereby leading to highly urbanized societies.

Urbanization Can Be Reversed

Since urbanization typically accompanies the broader process of social and economic development, many scholars believe that it is a continuous, irreversible process. However, research has shown that once a society becomes highly developed and highly urbanized, the relative rate of population growth and the direction of net internal migration often reverses in favor of smaller, less dense areas. We turn now to an examination of *counter-urbanization* in the U.S. and in other highly developed nations. Counter-urbanization is typically defined as a redistribution of population down the hierarchy of urban centers so that there is a negative association between a center's initial population size and its rate of net migration (Fielding 1982).[8]

The Population Turnaround in Rural America

Rather than experiencing a continuous process of ever-increasing urbanization, the United States has had four major reversals in the direction of rural–urban migration since 1970 (Johnson & Cromartie 2006)[9]. Prior to this time, the nation's level of urbanization increased regularly with each succeeding census (see Figure 2.4). While the *pace* of urbanization had slowed by 1970, because each additional percent urban becomes increasingly difficult to obtain once a nation reaches a high *level* of urbanization, the trend was still toward increasing urban concentration. Then, in 1975, Calvin L. Beale of the U.S. Department of Agriculture published a monograph showing that for the first time in recorded history, rural areas grew faster than their urban counterparts (Beale 1975). Moreover, this growth was the result of net in-migration from urban to rural counties. The immediate response to Beale's report was skepticism and disbelief. Other demographic researchers doubted the accuracy of the population estimates, and some claimed that the rural growth was simply further suburbanization. However, Beale's contention that rural areas were now growing at a faster rate than urban areas has stood the test of time. Within a couple of years even the strongest critics agreed that the "population turnaround" was real and important (Long & Hansen 1977).

The reasons for the rural population turnaround were complex, but four interrelated factors, deconcentration of employment, modernization of rural life, population aging, and preferences for rural living were at its root. After decades of urban industrial concentration, manufacturing establishments began to locate and/or expand in rural areas searching for lower wage workers, fewer and weaker regulations, less unionization and compliant local governments that were willing to subsidize industrial re-locations. In addition, the 1970s saw rural areas gain parity with respect to electrification, all weather roads, and telephone service. These two structural transformations, jobs and community infrastructure, meant that persons who preferred rural living could now actualize their residential preferences with a minimum of economic and lifestyle sacrifice (Brown et al.1997). In addition, an increasing number of American workers were retiring earlier with more secure incomes. Some of these older persons chose to relocate in rural retirement destinations that featured outdoor amenities and other community attributes conducive to retirement living (Brown & Glasgow 2008).

As shown in Figure 2.4, the 1970s rural turnaround did not usher in a stable pattern of rural population growth and net in-migration exceeding that of urban areas. By the 1980s, the urban sector had regained its growth advantage, and the net flow of migration was from rural areas into cities once again. In fact, research shows that retirement destinations were the only type of rural community to maintain a strong record of growth and in-migration during this decade. The first half of the 1990s saw the relative rate of growth and net in-migration swing back to favor rural areas once again. Rural areas were doing a better job of retaining their population than during the 1980s, but the advantage proved to be short lived. In fact, by the end of the decade, urban areas had regained their growth and migration advantage. Research by Cromartie (2001) shows that 339 counties switched from growth during the early 1990s to decline five years later, with rural decline concentrated in Appalachia, the Great Plains and the Corn Belt.

If the direction of rural–urban population change is somewhat unpredictable, what can one say about the future of urbanization in the United States.? Do the last forty years predict that urban areas have regained their growth advantage

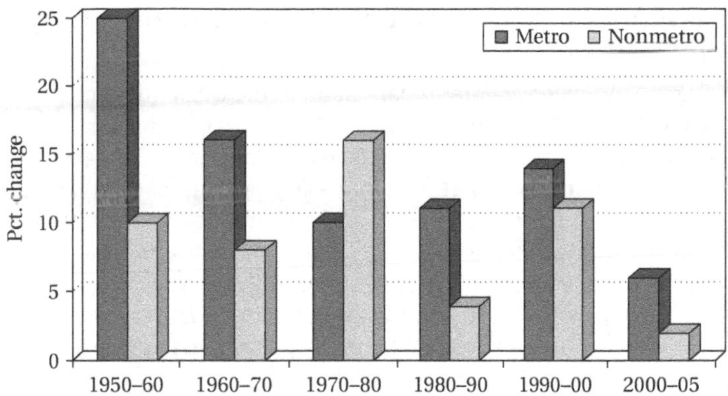

Source: Based on USDA-ERS data

Figure 2.4 Metro and Nonmetro Population Change

after a period of restructuring and that increased urbanization will be the trend of the future? Or does the past forty years suggest that urban–rural differences have converged so completely that net rural growth will be the trend? In our opinion, neither of these scenarios is convincing. Rather, while long-held preferences for rural and small town living will maintain a strong pressure for urban to rural migration, these preferences will only result in counter-urbanization when economic conditions are relatively strong in rural areas. Over the long term, we believe that the nation's degree of urbanization will most likely stall at its current level of around 80 percent. Rural gains in periods of rural prosperity will likely be counterbalanced by declines in periods when the rural economy is relatively weak. Moreover, we think that urban to rural migration will be increasingly contingent on the costs of transportation and on leveling continuing differences in access to modern infrastructure such as broadband and modern medical services. The changing directions of international migration, which until recently have been overwhelmingly toward urban destinations (Massey 2008), also suggests caution when predicting a future for urban–rural population redistribution in the U.S.

The American Counter-Urbanization Experience is not Unique

In fact, most other highly developed nations also experienced some degree or other of rural resurgence during the 1970s, and many of them reversed to urban concentration in the 1980s. Detailed studies in the United States, eight European countries and Japan reported a distinct shift away from concentration in the largest metropolitan centers towards medium sized and small settlements (Champion 1989). However, Champion has shown that between 1980 and 1990, three of the eight Western European countries and three of four Scandinavian countries resumed a pattern of population concentration in their largest areas (as was true in the U.S.). In contrast, Mediterranean Europe and the U.K. maintained a pattern of counter-urbanization (Champion 1998).

Data are only available to extend this European analysis past 1990 in the U.K. The United Kingdom was not one of the countries identified as resuming

Box 2.1 Population Redistribution in Post-Socialist Hungary

In this chapter we examined counter-urbanization in the U.S. and in other highly developed capitalist countries. The general argument was that the link between development and urbanization tends to weaken once a country reaches a high level of capitalist development. After this point, conditions in urban and rural areas converge and structural aspects favoring urban concentration are potentially leveled by telecommunications, commuting, and other technological and social changes that permit regular interaction over long distances. Accordingly, when economic conditions are favorable, some persons "vote with their feet," and move to rural areas, thereby actualizing their residential preferences. If enough persons make such moves, counter-urbanization results.

We wondered if a similar process of counter-urbanization was emerging in Eastern Europe as countries transformed from state socialist to capitalist economic systems. The connection between economic restructuring and population redistribution in Eastern Europe is established through at least four attributes characteristic of post-socialist countries: (a) labor displacement resulting from the radical downsizing of the urban-industrial complex; (b) the concentration of post-socialist economic development in selected suburban locations; (c) the persistence of social networks linking urban industrial workers with friends and family in rural villages; and (d) lower costs of living in rural areas. Research demonstrates that counter-urbanization did indeed occur in Hungary between 1994 and 2001 (Brown & Schafft 2002; Brown et al. 2005). This research shows that post-socialist counter-urbanization involves both suburban expansion and migration to rural villages that were located within 30 km of a large urban area. Migration to more remote rural villages was rare. This suggests that counter-urbanization is contingent on commuting to urban jobs, not on rural economic development. In fact, other research in post-socialist Hungary demonstrates that capitalist development is strongly biased against the most rural locations (Brown et al. 2007).

While the pattern of counter-urbanization in Western Europe and North America is more dispersed than in Hungary, the situations are quite similar. In particular, population deconcentration seems to be contingent on longer distance commuting in both contexts. For example, research in England shows that in-movers to rural areas are 1.5 times as likely to commute a long distance to work compared with longer-term rural residents. (Champion et al. 2009)

population concentration during the 1990s, so it is important to determine if counter-urbanization has persisted to the present day. Champion's most current research extends his analysis from 1993 to 2003 (Champion & Shepherd 2006). His study shows that the rural rate of population growth exceeded that of urban areas during this period (2.5 percent and 5.7 percent respectively). Moreover, his study showed that the rate of population growth was especially high in the *most rural* districts. In contrast with the U.S. and much of Northern and Western Europe, then, the U.K. has experienced continuous population deconcentration for at least forty years. Interestingly, rural districts were not only growing larger they were also aging. We will take a closer look at rural aging in the U.K. and U.S. in Chapter 6.

Conclusions

In this chapter we have discussed how urbanization is conceptualized and measured; we have examined the forces responsible for its increase in both developed and developing societies, and we have established that urbanization is not an irreversible process. Accordingly, we now know that simple statements such as "the world is now more than 50 percent urban" (U.N. 2008) mask complex differences across geographic situations, politico-economic regimes and statistical systems.

We have acknowledged a lack of agreement on what is urban and rural and how to measure it. This lack of agreement, however, should not stop us from attempting to understand why urbanization occurs and reverses; the consequences of such trends and changes for social wellbeing and environmental quality in today's world; or how public policy might help to ameliorate social and economic problems that are concentrated in central cities or lagging rural regions in developed and developing nations. In the following chapters, we will examine the structure and change of rural populations, communities, economies and environments, and we will compare these conditions and changes with the urban experience. We will use this information to determine how rural communities have persisted during recent decades, and how they have been transformed. This analysis will inform our judgments about the likely future of rural populations, communities, economies and environments. One of our guiding themes will be to understand how structural changes in economy, society and environment have affected the challenges and opportunities encountered by rural persons in their everyday lives.

Notes

1 An economy of scale means that the unit cost of producing a good or service is diminished because costs are spread across a large number of persons.

2 Most statistical agencies examine urbanization by aggregating data into metropolitan statistical areas and comparing population growth in these areas with that occurring in nonmetropolitan areas. Metropolitan statistical areas are conceptualized as regional economies based around large cities.

3 Urbanized areas often extend beyond the central county into adjacent counties. But the majority of the urbanized area is contained in the central county (or counties).

4 Note: reclassification of territory from rural to urban can also contribute to urbanization. This can occur through annexation of rural territory by an urban place or if rural places grow past urban thresholds.

5 Similarly, urban areas would outpace rural areas if rural net migration exceeded urban net migration just as long as urban natural increase was sufficiently large to make up the difference.

6 Only in the case of smallpox is there solid evidence that medical therapy prevented or cured a disease prior to the twentieth century (McKeown & Brown 1968).

7 Moreover, natural increase's contribution to LDC urbanization has increased recently reflecting continued high fertility, especially in Africa and Asia. While the total fertility rate has declined in most LDCs since the 1980s, especially in urban areas, the number of annual births is still large because of *demographic momentum*, that is, previous higher fertility rates produced an age structure that is conducive to high numbers of births.

8 Counter-urbanization does not imply that the smallest rural settlements are necessarily growing or gaining net in-migration. Rather, it implies that the association between initial size and rate of migration is inverse.

9 The rural–urban analysis in this section is based on data for metropolitan (urban) versus nonmetropolitan (rural) counties.

References

Beale, C. 1975. *The Revival of Population Growth in Nonmetropolitan America.* RES Report 605. USDA-Economic Research Service, Washington, D.C.

Bogue, D. 1949. *The Structure of the Metropolitan Community.* University of Michigan Press, Ann Arbor, MI.

Brown, D.L. Schaffer, K. 2002. Population Deconcentration in Hungary During the Post-Socialist Transformation. *Journal of Rural Studies.* 18, 233–244.

Brown, D.L. & Cromartie, J. 2003. The Nature of Rurality in Post Industrial Society, pp. 269–283. In Champion, T. & Hugo, G. (eds) *New Forms of Urbanization: Beyond the Urban–rural Dichotomy.* Ashgate, Aldershot.

Brown, D.L., Cromartie, J., & Kulcsar, L. 2004. Micropolitan Areas and the Measurement of American Urbanization. *Population Research and Policy Review,* 23, 399–418.

Brown, D.L., Fuguitt, G., Heaton, T., & Waseem, S. 1997. Continuities in Size of Place Preferences in the United States, 1972–1992. *Rural Sociology.* 62(4), 408–428.

Brown, D.L. & Glasgow. N. 2008. *Rural Retirement Migration.* Springer, Dordrecht.

Brown, D.L., Greskovits, B., & Kulcsar, L.J. 2007. Leading Sectors and Leading Regions: Economic Restructuring and Regional Inequality in Hungary Since 1990. *International Journal of Urban and Regional Research,* 31(3), 522–542.

Brown, D.L., Kulcsar, L.J., Kulcsar, L., & Obadovics, C. 2005. Post-Socialist Restructuring and Population Redistribution in Hungary. *Rural Sociology,* 70(3), 336–359.

Champion, A. (ed.) 1989. *Counter-Urbanization: The Changing Pace and Nature of Population Deconcentration.* Edward Arnold, London.

Champion, A. 1998. Population Distribution in Developed Countries: Has Counter-Urbanization Stopped?, pp. 66–83. In United Nations Expert Group. *Population Distribution and Migration.* ST/ESA/SER.R/133. U.N. Population Division, New York.

Champion, A. 2004. Lest We Re-Invent the Wheel: Lessons from Previous Experience. In Champion, A. & Hugo, G. (eds) *New Forms of Urbanization: Beyond the Urban–Rural Dichotomy.* Ashgate, Aldershot, pp. 25–42.

Champion, A. & Shepherd, J. 2006. Demographic Change in Rural England. In Lowe, P. & Speakman, L. (eds) *The Ageing Countryside.* Age Concern Books, London, pp. 29–50.

Champion, A., Coombes, M., & Brown, D.L. 2009. Migration and Longer Distance Commuting in Rural England. *Regional Studies.*

Cromartie, J. 2001. Nonmetro Out Migration Exceeds Immigration for the First Time in a Decade. *Rural America,* 16(2), 35–37.

Cromartie, J. 2006. Metro Expansion and Nonmetro Change in the South, pp. 233–254. In Kandel, W. & Brown, D.L. (eds) *Population Change and Rural Society.* Springer, Dordrecht.

Cromartie, J. & Bucholtz, S. 2008. Defining the "Rural" In Rural America. *Amber Waves,* June, 28–33.

Davis, K. 1967. The Urbanization of the Human Population, pp. 11–32. In *Cities.* Penguin Books, Harmondsworth.

Drake, M. 1969. *Population in Industrialization.* Methuen, London.

Duncan, O., Scott, W., Lieberson, S., Duncan, B., & Winsborough, H. 1960. *Metropolis and Region.* Johns Hopkins Press, Baltimore.

Durkheim, E. 1997 [1893]. *The Division of Labor in Society.* Free Press, New York.

Fielding, A. 1982. Counter-Urbanization in Western Europe. *Progress in Planning,* 17, 1–52.

Hawley, A. 1950. *Human Ecology: A Theory of Community Structure.* Ronald Press, New York.

Hines, F., Brown, D.L., & Zimmer, J. 1975. Social and Economic Characteristics of the Population in Metropolitan and Nonmetropolitan Counties, 1970. *Agricultural Economic Report* No. 272. USDA-ERS, Washington, D.C.

International Labor Office. 2002. *Women and Men in the Informal Economy: A Statistical Profile.* ILO, Employment Sector, Geneva, Switzerland.

Johnson, K. & Cromartie, J. 2006. The Rural Rebound and its Aftermath: Changing Demographic Dynamics and Regional Contrasts, pp. 25–50. In Kandel, W. & Brown, D.L. (eds) *Population Change and Rural Society.* Springer, Dordrecht.

Langer, W. 1963. Europe's Initial Population Explosion. *American Historical Review,* 69(1), 1–17.

Long, L. & Hansen, K. 1977. *Migration Trends in the United States.* U.S. Bureau of the Census. Unpublished.

McGee, T. & Griffiths, C. 1998. Global Urbanization: Towards the Twenty-First Century. In United Nations Expert Group, pp. 49–65. *Population Distribution and Migration,* ST/ESA/SER.R/133. New York: U.N. Population Division, New York.

McKenzie, R. 1933. *The Metropolitan Community.* George Bell, New York.

McKeown, T. & Brown, R. 1968. Medical Evidence Related to English Population Changes in the Eighteenth Century, pp. 16–39. In Heer, D. (ed.) *Readings on Population.* Prentice-Hall, Englewood Cliffs, N.J..

Massey, D. 2007. *World City.* Polity, Cambridge.

Massey, D. 2008. *New Faces: New Places.* Russell Sage, New York.

ORC Macro. 2007. *MEASURE DHS STAT compiler.* http://www.measuredhs.com.

Sassen, S. 2006. *Cities in the World Economy.* Pine Forge Press, Thousand Oaks, CA.

Tilly, C. 1974. *An Urban World.* Little Brown, Boston.

Tisdale, H. 1942. The Process of Urbanization. *Social Forces.* 20, 311–316.

Todaro, M. & Smith, S. 2002. *Economic Development,* 8th edn. Addison Wesley, Boston.

United States Department of Agriculture-EconomicResearch Service. 2007. *Nonmetro Population Growth Slows.* USDA, Washington, D.C. (downloaded from http://www.ers.usda.gov/Briefing/Population/Nonmetro.htm.)

United Nations Population Division. 2008. *World Urban Prospects: The 2007 Revision.* United Nations, New York. (downloaded from http://esa.un.org/unup).

Weber, M. 1978. *Economy and Society.* University of California Press, Berkeley, CA.

Wrigley, E. 1969. *Population and History.* McGraw-Hill, New York.

PART II

RURAL COMMUNITIES, INSTITUTIONS, AND ENVIRONMENTS

3 Understanding Community in Rural Society

A community is a group of people organized around certain commonly held interests and attributes that help to create a sense of shared identity. When asked to describe themselves, people typically report a set of personal attributes, but they also report their most proximate and salient social relationships including family and community. Hence, communities are an essential aspect of human life, providing critical formal and informal resources and comprising an important component of personal identity.

In this chapter we will examine a number of fundamental questions relating to community in contemporary rural society including:

- What is the nature of the social bond that produces social cohesion in community?
- What is the relationship between community and urbanization?
- How might community be understood as a sociological concept?
- How does community emerge within human populations?
- Why and how do communities change over time? Why do they persist?

Understanding Community

According to Philip Selznick (1992), community implies a web of affective relationships that are qualitatively different from those constituting other kinds of human groups. Being a part of a community implies a long-term, continuous social interaction that contributes to the formation of personal identity, and to social and economic production and reproduction. As a result, members share a sense of belonging, of "we-ness." Community also involves commitment to a shared culture, including shared values, norms and meanings. As a result, community has moral authority. Selznick's characterization of community is an ideal type, seldom realized in reality, but a useful heuristic device for social scientific analysis. Further, this approach contends that community is a *variable* aspect of collective human life (Calhoun 1980). Not all communities have the same degree of identity, moral authority and/or collective mobilization and so forth, but to be a community they must possess some degree of these attributes.

Perhaps most fundamentally, social interaction in community engages generic functions rather than special purposes. For example, while one may participate in local civic associations like a parent teacher organization or a volunteer fire department as part of one's involvement in community, the commitment to these organizations is typically more deeply embedded in a broader set of interactions within the multiple realms of community life. According to Selznick

(1992), people participate in community affairs as "whole people," not as compartmentalized role players with single purposes. Since people occupy multiple roles and memberships, their varied interests often overlap and reinforce each other. Community is not simply an aggregate of persons living together as free agents. A community is a collectivity that has identities and purposes of its own.

Community may be place-based and oriented around the identification with a particular neighborhood or area. However, social interaction does not have to occur in a geographic place to signify the presence of community. In fact, most social scientists agree that genuine community relationships can develop outside of geographic locality. Delanty (2003) promotes the idea of community in which communication is the essence and medium of belonging. In fact, given the degree of geographic and social mobility in modern society, Delanty and others believe that face to face interaction is no longer viable as the primary mode of belonging from most people.

As Urry (2000) has observed, new electronic technology can produce "community without propinquity." "Virtual communities," for instance, are characterized by a wide array of bulletin boards, blogs and wiki-based networks and facilitated by current and emerging technologies such as Facebook, Myspace, Twitter and YouTube. Moreover, the widespread adoption of broadband in American households, 64 percent in 2009, shows that a majority of Americans can participate in virtual communities if they so choose (National Telecommunications and Information Administration 2010).[1] While "virtual communities" involve a different form of social interaction than face to face communities, most scholars believe that they produce social bonds and social cohesion. However, while electronically mediated relationships produce a degree of community, they tend to be "thin communities." Castels (1996) and others contend that virtual communities do not substitute for communities of propinquity. As Wellman (2001) has shown, virtual relationships tend to supplement existing social relationships rather than supplant them.

Hence, even in the midst of the communication revolution brought about by a dizzying range of information technology that facilitates social interaction at a distance, scholars continue to appreciate the importance of geographically bounded social relationships. As Wilkinson (1991) pointed out, because people continue to live together in geographic places, place-based social relationships still play a central role in meeting people's daily needs; they continue to be adaptive mechanisms between individuals, families and larger social structures; and they are often an integral component of personal identity. Hence, in this book our principal focus is on social relationships that occur in geographic locales.

Has Urbanization Undermined Community?

As discussed in Chapter 2, the U.S. and all developed nations are highly urbanized. Many scholars have wondered whether urbanization weakens the bonds of community. This is one of the main concerns that gave rise to the new discipline of sociology during the height of the Industrial Revolution. Scholars were curious about whether the bases of social solidarity were being undermined as nations were transformed from agrarian to urban-industrial societies. If community was being eclipsed as a side effect of urbanization and industrialization, how would people solve their everyday problems; how would social life be regulated; what structures would buffer persons and families from outside forces; how would people form their personal identities?

The urbanization–community question motivated a large amount of sociological thinking during the late nineteenth and early twentieth centuries. In particular, as we mention in the introductory chapter, the work of Ferdinand Toënnies and Emile Durkheim was especially influential. Both were concerned with the maintenance of social and moral order in newly urbanizing societies. They observed that as urbanization proceeded, informal mores and folkways were replaced by more formal mechanisms of social coordination such as contracts and work rules. They worried that the displacement of traditional modes of social control would lead to social disorganization unless strong third party enforcement was employed.

Toënnies (1887) contrasted two ideal type societies: (a) gemeinschaft ("community") and gesellschaft ("society"). In the former, intimate social relationships produce coordination and social order. In a self-regulating gemeinschaft society, individuals are embedded in multiple, mutually reinforcing roles which produce a clear sense of commitments, obligations and social boundaries. In contrast, gesellschaft societies are coordinated by rational, contractual and associative bonds. Norms are related to the performance of tasks expected of the occupants of specific roles. Since people are not embedded in a comprehensive set of mutually reinforcing roles in a gesellschaft society, social order is maintained by institutional actors such as the police and the courts who are vested with third party enforcement powers.

Durkheim (1933) was also concerned with how moral and social order would be maintained during the transformation from agrarian to urban-industrial, that is, capitalist society. Similar to Toënnies, Durkheim developed ideal types to compare the bases of moral order and social solidarity in primitive and capitalist society. He observed that primitive societies were small, undifferentiated and localized, and controlled by a "repressive collective conscience." He labeled this mode of social control "mechanical solidarity," and observed that it produced clear rules, clear sanctions and a high degree of conformity.

In contrast, in advanced industrial societies, Durkheim argued that people are allocated to diverse roles by a complex division of labor. Using a natural sciences analogy, he labeled this form of interdependence "organic solidarity." Durkheim believed that while the economy would be regulated by formal norms and regulations associated with particular roles, such norms would not produce moral solidarity. He feared that people would be released from moral restraints, a situation he labeled "anomie." Accordingly, he believed that the transition of a society from "primitive" to "advanced" would bring about social isolation and disorder.

Community Lost or Community Transformed?

Toënnies' and Durkheim's writings stimulated a large amount of research on the social impacts of urbanization in developed nations including a major school of sociological analysis centered around the city of Chicago. Louis Wirth's writings were particularly influential. In "Urbanism as a Way of Life," Wirth (1938) argued that the city supplants traditional modes with a way of life that at once offers the individual a greater sense of freedom and a heightened awareness of isolation. This essay encouraged a generation of scholars to empirically examine the relationship between urbanization and social relationships. Perhaps most notable, Claude Fischer's (1984) subcultural theory of urbanism contended that big city life did not produce normlessness, social isolation, and alienation. Rather, he observed that increased population size and concentration results in a different type of social integration, one characterized by membership in social networks defined on the basis of social, racial, and ethnic attributes. Accordingly, rather than being isolated or anomic, Fischer proposed that urbanites were embedded in a diverse set of cultural experiences that effectively regulated their behavior and produced a high degree of social solidarity.

Even though research by Fischer (1982), Gans (1962), and others cast doubt on the so-called "eclipse of community," the idea has not died an easy death. Virtually every empirical investigation of the question concludes that cities have vibrant social lives. For example, Bell and Boat (1957) conducted interviews with men in a variety of San Francisco neighborhoods and showed that informal relationships are fairly frequent and likely to be personal, close, and intimate. As recently as 1991, the National Opinion Research Center examined the "eclipse of community" question and showed that the percentage of adults who spent a social evening weekly with relatives, friends, parents, siblings, neighbors and friends was virtually identical among persons living in cities, suburbs, and rural areas.

Perhaps the most compelling examination of the "eclipse of community" question was conducted by Barry Wellman (1979) in a metropolitan-wide study of social relationships in Toronto. Wellman showed that Toronto residents participated in a wide range of intimate relationships, and that these relationships were distributed throughout the metropolis rather than being concentrated in a single area of immediate residence. He concluded that social relationships, rather than being "lost," had simply been "liberated" from immediate residential contexts. Urban relationships were contingent on belonging to a "metropolitan web" of social networks rather than living in close physical proximity. In other words urbanization has not resulted in the eclipse of community, it has simply transformed the nature of relationships and the kinds of spaces where interaction occurs.

Two Sociological Approaches to Understanding Community

Sociologists broadly use two complementary approaches to examine the nature of the social bond that sustains collective engagement and facilitates the accomplishment of collective goals: (a) community as a field of social interaction, and (b) community as a social system, e.g., an integrated set of institutional domains. Each of these positions is summarized in the following section.

Community as a Field of Social Relationships

In the social field approach to community, the bounds of community are established by a web of social relationships that express mutual interests of participants in the common life of the population. From this perspective, community boundaries are flexibly created, challenged, reinforced, and reconfigured by patterns of continuous social interaction. The focus is not on the space (or place) itself, but on the social interaction that gives this space meaning. At the same time, as Wilkinson (1991) and others have argued, locales often create a powerful context for collective identity and social interaction. Given this, it's not difficult to understand how particular bureaucratically defined locales such as school districts, municipalities and even counties become proxies for community as they help to establish social boundaries (in tandem with bureaucratic boundaries!) and shared social context.

Understanding community as a social field emphasizes the multiple interactions, interrelations, and commitments that tie people together within and across social groups and that in their totality produce collective social meaning. According to Cohen (2004: 13), "consciousness of community is . . . encapsulated in perception of its boundaries, boundaries which are themselves largely constituted by people in interaction." Hence, the community field tends to be defined by the perception of symbols rather than by institutional participation, and these symbolic boundaries are continuously recreated by people through their social interaction (Gertz 1975). The community field is dynamic since the web of social relationships encapsulated within these symbolic boundaries tends to shift over time. As Luloff and Bridger (2003) argue, the interactional approach to community also provides a theoretically effective means of understanding collective action. The place-based social connections that tie people together within a particular place not only give the place-based community intrinsic value, but also provide community members with an "adaptive capacity" to "manage, utilize, and enhance the resources available to them to address local issues and problems" (Luloff & Bridger 2003: 212).

Social Networks and Social Capital

Contemporary thinking about the kinds of social relationships that constitute community has often focused on what has become identified as "social capital," or the benefits and resources emanating from or available to members within particular social networks. While emphasizing social networks and interaction, social capital approaches to community have tended to focus far more on the *instrumental* values of community. That is, instead of focusing on the symbolic value of community membership and how that symbolic value shapes the identity and actions of community members, social capital focuses more on how social networks yield particular benefits, and how those benefits may be understood as a particular kind of "capital." Because of this, critics of social capital theory have often described it as overly individualistic and economistic in nature and therefore inadequate for explaining collective action as more than simply the aggregated result of individuals "maximiz(ing) their utility by making a cost-benefit analysis of alternative courses of action" (Luloff & Bridger 2003: 207).

Nevertheless, as evidenced by its exponential increase in popularity amongst scholars in the last two decades (Schafft & Brown 2003), social capital has proven a particularly attractive concept to help explain developmental outcomes for people and communities. One of its attractions is that it is intuitively easy to grasp, its usage as a sociological concept long presaged by familiar sayings such as "it's not what you know, but who you know," or, in the case of family networks, "blood is thicker than water." In short, individuals and families are said to possess social capital to the extent that they are able to access essential information and resources by virtue of their social network connections.

Social capital has been used as a conceptual device to explain everything from the determinants of academic success to how social networks steer the migration process, and contribute to migrant adaptation (Coleman 1990; Portes 1998). This is its other appeal: if it is social capital that indeed

> determines the difference between livable, cohesive societies on the one hand, and societies torn apart by conflict, distrust and poverty on the other, then by somehow (re)investing in social capital in deficient families, communities and/or countries, one may hope to enact positive change. (Schafft & Brown 2003: 329; see also Terrion 2006; Scholten & Holzhacker 2009)

Conceptualized as an individual-level attribute, social capital possesses more immediately economistic connotations. People may decide, as rational actors, to "invest" in building social relationships if they believe that such investment will eventually pay off (e.g., through professional "networking"). However, many theorists, like Putnam (1993), Woolcock (1998) and others have proposed that social capital can also be thought of as a community or aggregate-level attribute useful for explaining why some places are more successful than others in producing a high level of material wellbeing. In its aggregate-level usage, social capital is often defined as the collective norms, trust and networks of affiliation that ease transaction costs, enhance access to information and resources, and facilitate collective action. Therefore, places with a higher density of social capital are predicted to have superior developmental outcomes and a higher quality of life (Flora & Flora 2003; Besser 2009).

Putnam (1993; 1999), for example, has argued that community-level social capital has very specific collective benefits. First, it helps to resolve social problems in circumstances where there are strong social norms of cooperation and collaboration. Business and social interactions flow more smoothly between people when mutual trust is high. A strong sense of shared identity and belonging may result in increased empathy and caring for other community members and commitment to the welfare of the community as a whole. Last, Putnam argues that strong social capital facilitates the flow of information useful for improving not only the lives of individuals, but for community wellbeing overall.

Many proponents of the utility of social capital as an aggregate-level concept contend that there are two types of social capital, bonding and bridging, which can promote development when properly balanced, but which can undermine development when one form of social capital overwhelms the other. In other words, these theorists argue that not only are there different *types* of social capital, but that different types in different combinations may yield significantly different outcomes (Woolcock 1998; Schafft & Brown 1999; Larson et al. 2004; Scholten & Holzhacker 2009). Similar to Granovetter's (1973) notion of strong and weak ties, bonding social capital involves close in-group solidarity while bridging social capital connects diverse groups both in and outside of a community (see Figure 3.1).

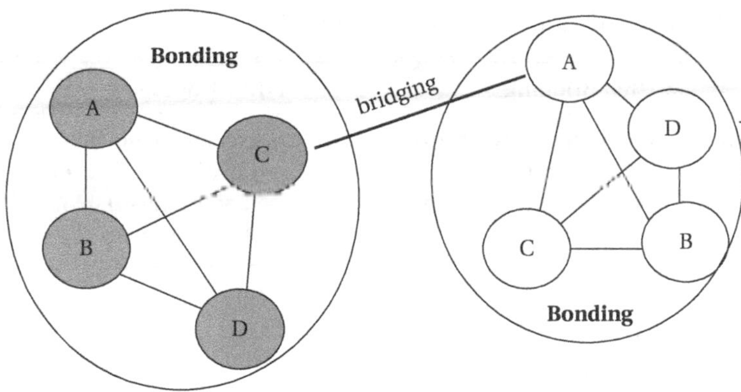

Source: Author's own

Figure 3.1 Bonding and Bridging Social Capital

Communities with a combination of high bonding and bridging social capital are theorized to be inclusive and participatory (Flora & Flora 2003) (see Table 3.1). Because they have diverse internal relationships and strong external linkages, these communities are able to mobilize both internal and external resources to accomplish locally initiated change that benefits the wider community. At the other extreme, communities lacking both bonding and bridging capital tend to be extremely individualistic, lack social cohesion, and are socially and economically isolated. As a result, they have few options, and are often caught in a vicious cycle of decline.

Communities with a high density of one form of social capital but a relative lack of the other are exposed to risks that could be minimized if their bonding and bridging relationships were in better balance. For example, resources can be trapped in particular groups and withdrawn from wider use in communities with high bonding but low bridging capital. These communities are typically characterized by contentious factions and ineffective relationships with outside organizations, communities, and businesses. In contrast, when bridging social capital is strong but internal cohesion weak, external forces can collude with local elites to undermine wider community interests. These communities are characterized by clientelism, hierarchical relationships, and extreme inequality. In these instances, change is typically motivated by outside interests for and by local elites (see e.g., Duncan 1999). To return to Wilkinson's concept of the "community field" as the social structure that reconciles partial and general goals, communities with a balance of bonding and bridging relationships can overcome specific interests and accomplish collective ends. Communities lacking social capital altogether, or having a high density of only one kind, are either apathetic or are at risk of being controlled by internal and/or external elites who may or may not have the community's best interest at heart (Narayan 1999).

Social Exclusion

Despite the meteoric popularity of social capital in the 1990s and 2000s as a sociological concept employed to explain social outcomes, the concept and its

Table 3.1 Typology of Community Social Capital

	High Bridging	Low Bridging
High Bonding	**Participatory community** • Inclusion • Diverse Horizontal ties inside • Diverse Vertical ties w/ outside • **Locally initiated change motivated by local goals**	**Factions & Conflict** • Conflict w/outside • Factionalism inside • **Resistance to change**
Low Bonding	**External control exercised via local elites** • Clientism • Most internal & external ties are vertical • **Change is motivated by outside interests for/by local elites**	**Absence of social cohesion/ community** • Apathy • Extreme individualism • **Few options and/or opportunities. "Will take anything"**

Source: Based on Flora & Flora 2003.

proponents have had to withstand multiple critiques (Fine 2001; Fulkerson & Thompson 2008; Schafft & Brown 2003). One of the more significant concerns is the extent to which social capital is able effectively to account for the role of power in how the structure of social norms and networks regulate the distribution of scarce resources.[2] Further, absent an understanding of how social networks distribute and regulate resources, understandings of community development outcomes are framed around "stocks" of social capital rather than how those stocks come to exist in the first place. Because of this, commentators such as Ben Fine (2001) have speculated that the embracing of social capital by multinational actors such as the World Bank amounts to the "rich and powerful speculating on how to improve the lot of the poor through prompting their self-help and organization without questioning the sources of their economic disadvantage" (Schafft & Brown 2003: 339).

The unequal distribution of power in communities resonates with discussions of social exclusion. In contrast with the strict materialist concept of poverty, the lack of income and other financial resources, social exclusion is

> a more comprehensive formulation which refers to the dynamic process of being shut out, fully or partially, from any of the social, economic, political or cultural systems which determine the social integration of a person in society. (Walker & Walker 1997: 8)

Hence, even though as a concept social exclusion is more far-reaching than poverty, it is a determinant of poverty. As opposed to emphasizing the more static attributes of communities (e.g., "stocks" of social capital), the concept of social exclusion emphasizes the *processes* by which the distribution of power and resources are controlled (Molnár & Schafft 2003; Commins 2004). In other words, instead of asking how much social capital a community has at a particular moment in time, the question becomes how and why over time resources have come to be distributed as they are, and what that distribution means for the welfare of the community and for the varied people within it.

People do not choose to be socially excluded. Rather, as Byrne (2005: 3) has observed, social exclusion involves "power as it is exercised by competing interests in the process of urban governance."[3] In other words, the distribution of power in a community can facilitate participation or contribute to social exclusion, lack of voice, and lack of opportunities for social participation. As Veit-Wilson (1998: 45) has commented, the social exclusion discourse emphasizes "the role of those who are doing the excluding" and how this reduces the power of the excluded.

Social exclusion is more likely to occur in some kinds of areas than in others. For example, Madanipour and his colleagues (1998) showed how exclusion structures social relations in central cities while Philip and Shucksmith (2003) examined the dynamics of unequal access in rural environments. Moreover, it is not possible to understand nature and degree of social exclusion in particular communities without examining their history and understanding how the legacy of the past affects contemporary social relationships (Schafft & Brown 2003).

Community as a Social System

In contrast to the interactional approach described above, other scholars have conceptualized community in terms of the configuration of particular institutional domains and the functions that institutions play for maintaining collective wellbeing. Roland Warren (1963) describes community as an integrated set of institutional domains that perform major functions critical for producing and reproducing organizations and structures that satisfy local society's material needs. This perspective, often referred to as *structuralist*, derives from Emile Durkheim's (1933) seminal volume, *The Division of Labor in Society*. This view is more concrete and materialistic than the social field perspective described above. It conceptualizes community as a *sustenance unit*, an institutionalized solution to the problems of everyday life such as making a living, socializing children, teaching cogitative skills and knowledge, managing public life, protecting public safety, and inculcating norms, values, and moral-ethical standards.

Community as a social system involves relatively lasting arrangements among concrete institutional entities such as education, the church, local government, the economy, and the polity. The key insight, as shown in Figure 3.2, is that community involves relationships *between* institutional spheres rather than being constituted by the particular spheres themselves. The division of labor between institutional spheres is the source of social cohesion that sustains community. This view of social solidarity is shaped by the same logic as Wilkinson's (1991) community field, the social space that resolves partial interests and general purposes.

While the social systems approach has been criticized as being static (Smith 1995), proponents argue that community change is accomplished through gradual adaptation and marginal adjustments. Accordingly, a community's institutions both fulfill essential tasks and maintain the system. This is a gradualist

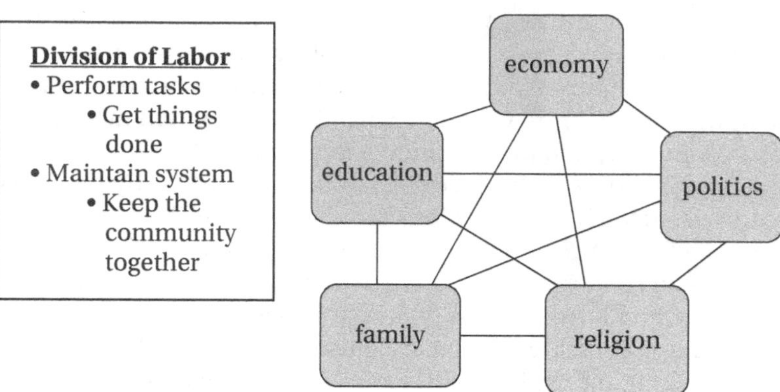

Source: Author's own

Figure 3.2 Community as a Social System

view of social change in which communities continuously adapt to internal pressures and stresses in their environments by making marginal changes in social, economic and political arrangements. The resulting dynamic equilibrium minimizes the need for fundamental systemic transformation.

Internal Structure and External Relationships

Local communities, including rural communities, were never really separate and independent societies, even though this autonomy forms part of the contemporary rural mystique. While community analysis necessarily focuses on internal organization, it also concerns relationships with the external environment. The nature of these external linkages can negatively affect community viability, especially if they involve economic and/or political inequalities. Local communities that are subordinated to outside forces can be exploited and manipulated, and their resources can be expropriated. This negative position was uncontested for many years and supported by influential studies such as Vidich and Bensman's (1958) *Small Town and Mass Society* which used a case study of a single rural community to examine how local community life and institutions were increasingly subsumed by the bureaucratic, political and economic forces of an urbanizing mass society.

In contrast, effective links to outside organizations can provide access to financial and political capital that can have beneficial development outcomes. In his classic study, *The Community in America*, Warren (1963) examined the internal (horizontal) and external (vertical) dimension of community. He observed that it is the interaction between the inside and the outside that affects community vitality and wellbeing. Strong outside forces are less able to undermine local autonomy if local institutions are effective, and if separate institutional domains are able to reconcile their narrow needs with the community's broader goals.

Empirical support for this observation was provided by Young and Lyson (1993) in a study of branch plants and social welfare in the American South. Their study showed that while poverty and infant mortality rates were higher in counties with large, non-locally owned manufacturing firms, this relationship only held when social structure, as indicated by the degree of political pluralism, was weak. In contrast, counties with both branch plants and a high degree of pluralism had lower poverty and infant mortality rates, and higher median family income.

Are the Social Field and Social System Approaches Antagonistic?

These two views of community do not necessarily contradict each other; in fact, in many respects they may be understood as complementary. As Selznick (1992) has observed, both shared consciousness (the social field approach) and structural differentiation (the social system approach) are needed to sustain interdependent activity over time and across a diverse set of issues. John Dewey's (1927) theory of the emergence of the public sphere also makes space for both an interactional and a structural component of community. Dewey contends that a social system's structures, including government, are created by interacting people who strive to solve collective problems.

Boundaries and Borders

How are community boundaries determined? Like many other aspects of community, this depends on whether one approaches the subject from a social systems or a relational perspective. From a systems perspective, the answer is deductively determined by examining the extent of institutional responsibilities and influence. These institutional boundaries are often officially determined by law or statute. Where are the city limits? How far does the school district extend? Where does a fire district's responsibility and legal liability end? Other times, institutional boundaries are determined by the market or by technology. Where do people switch from one local newspaper or radio station to another? Which cable company is the local service provider?

In contrast, the relational perspective uses an inductive approach to boundary delineation. Boundaries are defined and given meaning by patterns of symbolic and social interaction. Accordingly, rather than defining boundaries *a priori*, this approach lets the interaction speak for itself with respect to the periphery of one community and the beginning of another. For example, where does membership in one congregation transition to a different congregation? How does membership in social movements reflect issues that are grounded in one area versus another?

Similar to systems-based boundaries, relational boundaries are objectified forms of social difference that maintain a degree of closure from other communities as well as a degree of social and economic permeability. What differentiates relational boundaries from their systemic counterparts is that they are based in symbols, e.g., on conceptual distinctions, shared meanings and opposition to others. As Cohen (2004) has observed, social relations are repositories of meaning. Once symbolic boundaries are widely accepted, they can be transformed into social boundaries, thereby constraining and facilitating social interaction (Lamont & Molnár 2002).

In reality, community boundaries are produced institutionally *and* by patterns of social interaction. They are the product of symbols and of jurisdictions.

Communities involve symbolic interaction and identity formation, but they also involve institutional solutions to everyday challenges such as making a living, socializing and educating children, and obtaining essential services. In Box 3.1 we view the dynamic process of boundary production, maintenance and reproduction through the lens of the Amish, a relatively traditional population group living in the midst of contemporary American society.

Community Power

A consideration of community power provides an instructive means of suggesting the complementarity between the social field and social system approaches to community given that the distribution of power depends on social relationships as well as on positional placement in economic, social and political institutions. According to Max Weber, *power* is the ability to have one's way even in the face of opposition and resistance (Gerth & Mills 1946). Power can be exercised by force, influence, or position within social groups such as organizations or communities. Community power structure is a critical determinant of local development choices and trajectories and the extent to which the benefits of such trajectories are widely shared or concentrated in particular groups.

While the distribution of power in communities varies widely, a comparison of two ideal types: (a) pluralism and (b) power elite highlights the social bases of unequal power, and its consequences for community wellbeing. Pluralism and power elite are diametrically opposed views of community power. In the former, power is widely dispersed; in the latter power is concentrated in well established interest groups. These two models of community power are compared in Table 3.2.

In addition, the pluralism versus power elite comparison shown in Table 3.2 can be related to the typology of social capital shown previously in Table 3.1. The top right-hand box in Table 3.1 which is characterized by high bonding and high bridging capital is consistent with pluralism's dispersed power while the power elite model is consistent with the upper left-hand cell, which is characterized by high bonding but low bridging capital. Participatory change is the expected result when the two capitals are balanced and power is dispersed as in the upper right hand cell. In contrast, when power is deeply embedded in networks that are isolated from each other, factional conflict and resistance to change are expected.

Pluralism

In the pluralist model, power is dispersed among many competing groups which act to limit each other, and therefore avoid domination by a particular minority. The pluralist community is governed by shifting coalitions of many interest groups. Hence, pluralist communities do not have permanent power blocks. Each interest group can secure some but not all of its desires. Groups that lose on one issue know that they have a fair chance of winning on others. Accordingly, losing on a particular issue does not result in defection from the community. Pluralism is about negotiating alliances and compromises among competing groups. Since the capacity to acquire power is widely spread throughout the community, power is exercised somewhat independently of property, wealth, and social status.

Box 3.1 The Amish: Negotiating Community Boundaries in a Modernizing World

An Anabaptist sect, the Amish originally migrated to Southern Pennsylvania in the 1700s and 1800s from what is now Switzerland and Southern Germany. The descendants of those migrants now have communities in twenty-seven states, with populations concentrated in Indiana, Pennsylvania, Ohio, and Wisconsin (DeWalt 2001). The primary social units for Amish are the immediate family and the church district, which generally comprise twenty to twenty-five families who live within buggy-driving distance of each other. Amish society places a strong emphasis on agriculture and home-based economic livelihood activities; therefore, Amish communities continue to be located almost exclusively in rural areas where farm land is available.

One of the most distinguishing characteristics of the Amish is their maintenance of community boundaries that both symbolically and physically separate Amish from non-Amish. The Amish have considerable diversity across subgroups, and conservative Old Order Amish and more liberal Mennonite groups have quite different norms regarding the degree of acceptable integration into non-Amish society. Generally, though, maintaining the boundaries of Amish community includes living in accordance with church *ordnung*, the rules that clearly define social norms constituting community practice and distinguish Amish community members from outsiders. These rules include the wearing of traditional dress, the growth of beards by married men, and the use of horse and buggy (although when necessary Amish will frequently hire non-Amish to drive them to and from destinations further afield). There are also prohibitions on the use of electricity from utility poles, and, with some exceptions, the use of telephones and computers.

Wilkinson and others have in various ways noted how the "friction of rural space" (1991: 106) caused by dispersed population, sparse institutional and economic infrastructure, and distance from urban amenities constitutes a particular obstacle for rural communities and rural community development. Hence, for many rural residents and those engaged in rural community development, strategically developing formal and informal social ties beyond the community, and developing physical infrastructure, is a key part of rural development and the strengthening of rural community resources.

However, for the Amish, the exact *opposite* is true: Amish community has been, to a very large extent, *dependent* upon the "friction of rural space" for the maintenance of community and community boundaries. The use of horse and buggy for transportation in and of itself provides a very specific delineation of community and community boundaries since those boundaries are circumscribed by the members of the church district, all of whom must be within buggy range. Limiting the use of telephones and computers also reduces non-essential contact with the non-Amish world. The same is true for agricultural livelihood strategies that keep families home-based, and limit the contacts of young people with the outside world (Howley et al. 2008).

However, demographic and economic factors are changing the dynamics of how Amish maintain community boundaries. Because of high fertility levels, for the last number of decades, the Amish population has doubled about every twenty years

Box 3.1 (continued)

(Kraybill & Nolt 2004). The most recent figures tracking Amish population change between 1992 and 2008 indicate that the population has grown from 125,000 to 231,000, or about an 85 percent increase (Young Center for Anabaptist and Pietist Studies 2008).

As a consequence, and with farm land increasingly scarce, Amish economic activity has become less agriculturally based and increasingly reliant upon non-agricultural micro-enterprise (Smith et al. 1997; McConnell & Hurst 2006) such as light goods manufacturing, sometimes tying into the tourism trade, as around Lancaster, Pennsylvania capitalizing on "Pennsylvania Dutch Country" as a tourist destination.[4] Other Amish increasingly rely upon employment with non-Amish, such as in construction and labor. The decline of the traditional farming base and the increased exposure to non-Amish through commercial enterprises and participation in the labor market has necessarily meant the re-negotiation of community norms and boundaries, and the ways that church district *ordnung* is constructed and interpreted.

A recent *Wall Street Journal* article reported on Amish men in Indiana who were increasingly working in full-time manufacturing jobs in the recreational vehicle industry, and making significant amounts of money. Others opened their own manufacturing businesses. In response church bishops gradually weakened restrictions on the use of telephones, fax machines, and even websites. Downturns in manufacturing, however, led to layoffs that caused bank runs on an Amish lending cooperative, and enough unemployment and financial distress that some church districts decided to allow laid-off workers to seek government unemployment benefits, something that ordinarily would never have been considered within the Amish community (Belkin 2009).

Internal debates concerning the maintenance and definition of Amish community in the context of a modernizing world are nothing new. One of the first big schisms between Amish groups dates back to 1849 when factions disagreed over whether to use rubber tires on buggies. However, continued economic and demographic change within the twenty-first century will undoubtedly continue to reshape the ways in which the Amish construct their identity in negotiation with an urbanizing and globalizing world.

Pluralism is said to sustain democracy since political contestation and citizen participation are its hallmarks. Power is exercised through negotiation and voting. Each group strives to preserve its ability to affect decisions. Coalitions are formed for a limited time depending on the particular issue being decided. Since power blocks are temporary, no group is permanently frozen out. For example, environmentalists might join with local businesses to promote green development but they might oppose each other on the issue of providing tax breaks to attract a large multinational manufacturer.

Power Elite

In the power elite model, in contrast, a permanent minority controls community governance, and has coercive powers that can be used to repress and exploit the

Table 3.2 Pluralism vs. Power Elite

	Pluralism	Power Elite
How is power distributed?	**Dispersed** among competing interests	**Concentrated**
Are power blocks permanent?	**No**. Coalitions shift as issues change	**Yes**. The elite governs
How is power exercised?	**Through negotiation & voting.**	**Through "agents"** of the permanent coalition—a veneer of democracy
Is the distribution of power associated with other aspects of stratification?	**No**. Power is exercised independently of property and status	**Yes.** Class, status and power are closely related

Source: Author's own

majority. Elites move freely from one position of authority to another and enjoy common associations and background characteristics such as schooling and family ties. Power accrues from holding positions in business, government and other institutions (Mills 1956). Moreover, power, like wealth, can be accumulated and passed from generation to generation. Power conforms to other dimensions of stratification. If wealth is distributed hierarchically, so is power. In this model power is concentrated and manipulated by permanent power blocks. While power elite communities may have a veneer of democracy, elected officials are typically agents of the permanent elite. Moreover, the media is typically controlled by the elite, thereby denying a free flow of information and critical debate. As a result, communities ruled by power elite are generally unresponsive to community needs and preferences.

Empirical Evidence

Empirical evidence supports both views of community power. For example, Dahl (1961) examined key decisions on important issues such as urban renewal in New Haven, Connecticut, and concluded that the city was governed by a pluralistic system. His research showed that a wide range of groups was involved in these issues, and that there was minimal involvement of the same people across issue areas over time.

In contrast, Logan and Moloch (1987) developed an elite model to explain urban land-use changes. They contend that a permanent coalition of builders, bankers, and real estate speculators, labeled the "growth machine," promotes economic development as being in the public's interest, regardless of whether the public actually benefits or is harmed. Moreover, since the growth machine controls the media, it can neutralize oppositional messages and promote a pro-growth ideology that legitimizes the development agenda. Conflict arises because opponents of growth tend to see undeveloped land as having intrinsic "use value" while the growth machine only values land for the economic rents it generates when exchanged. When these two views come into conflict, the growth machine is able to deploy its allies in local government and the media to ensure that the pro-growth agenda prevails.

The Community Challenge: Balancing Autonomy and Collective Responsibility

Both the social systems and social field approaches engage the fundamental question of why people sacrifice some of their personal freedom in order to join communities. As we have shown in this chapter, people receive benefits from community membership. By obeying a community's norms, rules and regulations, persons gain access to institutions that help them manage the material challenges of everyday life, and they obtain a sense of belonging that gives their lives meaning and contributes to their sense of self. Moreover, being involved in communal relationships that have moral authority tempers individualism and promotes common goals. However, some scholars are concerned that personal freedom and communal commitment are out of balance in the United States, having swung too far toward the individualistic side. These scholars, known as communitarians, have established a social movement aimed at elevating community and subordinating individualism in modern American life.

Communitarianism

There is a fundamental tension between individual rights and collective commitments in community and society (Young 1995; Bauman 2001). People seek the security of community and of belonging; yet, they also long for freedom and autonomy from the collective norms and social rules that may oppress them. In recent years, many scholars have argued that the balance between rights and commitments has swung too far toward individual freedom, and away from civic responsibility. This concern, broadly labeled "communitarianism," has given rise to an active area of scholarship, and to an influential social movement (Etzioni 1995). As Delanty (2003: 75) has observed, "communitarianism has opposed moral individualism in favour of a more social conception of the person. Communitarianism has inevitably defined itself in opposition to the two main liberal political theories: the social liberalism of John Rawls and the market liberalism of neoconservatism." In other words, "While liberals see the individual as relatively autonomous, communitarians argue for the priority of the group" (Delanty 2003: 75).[5]

While the general communitarian concern is the perceived excess of individual rights over collective commitments, this logic can also lead them to worry about more specific issues such as immigration and cultural diversity. Accordingly, in the communitarian calculus, minorities and immigrants must adapt to the majority culture. This is not to say that communitarians necessarily oppose immigration or reject diversity, but they are concerned with protecting the pre-existing cultural community that may be unsettled by in-migration from abroad. In other words, immigration is acceptable as long as immigrants assimilate to the majority culture.

In addition to their concerns about an excess of individualism over collective responsibility and national fragmentation resulting from the politics of cultural identity, some communitarians perceive a decline of civic participation that they believe is undermining social cohesion. Civic communitarians such as Robert Putnam (1999) worry that persons have withdrawn from organizational and associational life and that this withdrawal diminishes social cohesion, weakens the state, and impoverishes democracy. This brand of communitarianism tends to be nostalgic for a highly romanticized (and mythologized) Tocquevillean civil society in which a rich associational life produced strong and responsive democracy. Communitarianism is a "discourse of loss." What is not clear, however, is whether the community perceived as being lost ever existed, or if the lost community actually promoted either personal freedom or collective accomplishment (Delanty 2003; Kelly 2009a, 2009b).

Communitarianism is motivated by strong moral and ideological concerns. Many social critics blame crime and other social problems on the perceived collapse of community, and they believe that the civic sphere, the so-called "third space" situated between the state and the market, has a role in regulating behavior. Amitai Etzioni (1995) is the foremost proponent of this view. He believes that the family, school, neighborhood, and voluntary associations should play a central role in regulating social behavior. As Delanty (2003: 89) observes, Etzioni's vision of community is "expressed in terms of personal proximity, locality, small groups and personal responsibility for society." Etzioni's position has been influential in American sociology and has stimulated an entire area of research on "neighborhood effects" which examines the impact of proximate social relationships on a wide range of problematic behaviors including crime, school dropout rates, drug use, and unwed teen childbearing (Sampson et al. 1999). It is hard to disagree with the goal of establishing a balance between individual rights and collective responsibilities; however, communitarian's critics believe that the movement privileges social order over personal autonomy and infringes on individual freedom. This critique is discussed in the boxed text below.

Conclusions

Strong community organization, whether viewed from a systemic or a relational perspective, is essential for personal and communal wellbeing. Weak communities can neither produce nor reproduce high levels of social welfare and quality of life. A high concentration of wealth, power, and honor undermines community responsiveness to both individual and collective needs. Moreover, communities with a high degree of social exclusion and weak, unresponsive institutions cannot reconcile partial and general needs. This inability to reconcile needs tends to undermine collective efficacy and the ability to mobilize resources, reproduces ineffective institutions, and increases community vulnerability to outside forces.

In contrast, inclusive communities with strong social relationships, responsive institutions and low degrees of inequality are more *sustainable* than other places. They are able to balance development with social needs and environmental quality, to avoid short-term solutions that compromise long-term

Box 3.2 Communitarianism's Critics

In 1990, Amitai Etzioni established a social movement named the Responsive Community to counterbalance what he perceived as a period of unduly high individualism in the United States. The Responsive Community was a social network where scholars and activists could participate in a forum to develop and promote communitarian theory, philosophy, and policies. Etzioni (1996) contended that social order and personal autonomy are not a zero sum. In fact, he believes that both enhance each other up to a point, but then turn antagonistic. In the "responsive community" envisioned by communitarians, the balance between order and autonomy is maintained in the "mutually enhancing zone." Society moves forward in a dynamic equilibrium reshaping itself in response to member needs.

Communitarianism has attracted strong critics. We are not necessarily among them, but since a movement that seeks to establish a balance between individual rights and collective responsibilities seems intuitively desirable, we feel it is important to explain the nature of criticism. Delanty (2003) has observed, communitarianism is an inherently conservative vision of community, shaped by moral sentiments and civic virtues and contingent on small face to face groups, volunteerism and patriotism. Benjamin Barber (1999) has characterized communitarianism as a form of familism, and communitarians as "clansmen." He is concerned that the strong identity politics that issue from communitarianism are incompatible with justice, equality and inclusiveness. He characterizes this as "authoritarian orderliness." Jean Cohen (1999), another vocal critic of communitarianism, contends that the strong emphasis on social order and on voluntary associations as intermediating bodies stifles political contestation and undermines democracy. She contends that communitarians such as Putnam and Etzioni fail to involve the public sphere – the political and civil space where people communicate and attempt to persuade one another via argumentation and criticism of issues of common concern.

Communitarianism has also been criticized as opposing cultural pluralism. As Delanty (2003) observes, this leads to a vision of society where cultural diversity is divisive and where community is being torn apart by cultural conflicts. Following this logic, some communitarians oppose immigration because they see it as challenging social cohesion and moral solidarity. In contrast, the view of community as a pluralistic social field articulated earlier in this chapter is not threatened by immigration and ethnic diversity because adherents to this perspective believe that solidarity is produced by overlapping memberships and by a multiplicity of identities and allegiances.

wellbeing, and plan for the future in a way that enhances individual opportunity while strengthening the public good. Moreover, they are able to include a wide variety of persons and interests in longer-term solutions, thus enhancing community stability and avoiding the dilemmas of collective action, which often lead to defection and an inability to mobilize community resources in support of collective goals. Finally, strong communities are better able to negotiate reasonable bargains with state and regional-level governments, transnational corporations and other external forces, while weaker communities are often forced to take what is offered on terms that are imposed from outside. People cannot live where they cannot make a living, and employers are hesitant to locate in communities lacking strong and responsive institutions. Hence, as will be discussed in Chapter 8, community development and economic development advance together. In fact, one might say that they are two sides of the same coin.

Notes

1 Note, even though the percentage of households with broadband access is significantly lower in rural areas, it is still widespread and growing more so.
2 It is worth noting that French sociologist Pierre Bourdieu viewed social capital precisely as a conduit of social power, and, as such, a mechanism by which individuals and elites belonging to particular social networks, consolidated power and resources. However, Bourdieu was also interested in social capital as an individual-level attribute (1985).
3 Byrne (2005) focuses on urban exclusion, but as Philip and Shucksmith (2003) showed, social exclusion also characterizes many rural areas.
4 For example, see: http://www.padutchcountry.com/.
5 One of this book's reviewers commented that "I would think that it [communitarianism] is opposed to 'egoistic individualism' and that it actually reflects Durkheim's concept of 'moral individualism,' that individualism that recognizes one's responsibilities."

References

Barber, B. 1999. Clansmen, Consumers and Citizens: Three Takes on Civil Society, pp. 9–29. In Fullinwider, R. (ed.) *Civil Society, Democracy and Civic Renewal.* Rowan & Littlefield, New York.

Bauman, Z. 2001. *Community: Seeking Safety in an Insecure World.* Polity, Cambridge.

Belkin, D. 2009. A Bank Run Teaches the "plain people" about the Risks of Modernity. *The Wall Street Journal.* 1 July, p. A1.

Bell, W. & Boat, M. 1957. Urban Neighborhoods and Informal Social Relations. *American Journal of Sociology.* 62(4), 391–398.

Besser, T. 2009. Changes in Small Town Social Capital and Civic Engagement. *Journal of Rural Studies.* 25,185–193.

Bourdieu, P. 1985. The Forms of Capital, pp. 241–258. In Richardson, J.G. (ed.) *Handbook of Theory and Research for the Sociology of Education.* Greenwood Press, New York.

Byrne, D. 2005. *Social Exclusion.* Open University Press, Buckingham.

Calhoun, C. 1980. Community: Toward a Variable Conceptualization for Comparative Research. *Social History,* 5(1), 105–129.

Castels, M. 1996. *The Information Age,* Vol. 1: *The Rise of the Network Society.* Blackwell, Oxford.

Cohen, A. 2004. *The Symbolic Construction of Community.* Routledge, London.

Cohen, J. 1999. American Civil Society Talk, pp. 55–85. In Fullinwider, R. (ed.) *Civil Society, Democracy and Civic Renewal.* NY: Rowan & Littlefield, New York.

Coleman, J. 1990. *Foundations of Social Theory.* Harvard University Press, Cambridge, MA.

Commins, P. 2004. Poverty and Social Exclusion in Rural Areas: Characteristics, Processes and Research Issues. *Sociologia Ruralis,* 44(1), 60–75.

Dahl, R. 1961. *Who Governs?* Yale University Press, New Haven, CT.

Delanty, G. 2003. *Community.* Routledge, London.

DeWalt, M.W. 2001. The Growth of Amish Schools in the United States. *Journal of Research in Rural Education.* 17(2), 122–124.

Dewey, J. 1927. *The Public and its Problems.* New York: Henry Holt.

Duncan, C.M. 1999. *Worlds Apart: Why Poverty Persists in Rural America.*Yale University Press, New Haven, CT.

Durkheim, E. 1933. *The Division of Labor in Society.* Coser, L. (trans. 1984). The Free Press, New York.

Etzioni, A. 1995. *The Spirit of Community.* Fontana Press, London.

Etzioni, A. 1996. The Responsive Community: A Communitarian Perspective. *American Sociological Review*. 61(1), 1–11.

Fine, B. 2001. *Social Capital versus Social Theory*. Routledge, London.

Fischer, C. 1982. *To Dwell Among Friends: Personal Networks in Town and City*. University of Chicago Press, Chicago.

Fischer, C. 1984. *The Urban Experience*, 2nd edn, Harcourt Brace Jovanovich, San Diego.

Flora, C. & Flora, J. 2003. Social Capital, pp. 214–227. In Brown, D. & Swanson, L. (eds) *Challenges for Rural America in the Twenty First Century*. Penn State University Press, University Park, PA.

Fulkerson, G.M. & Thompson, G.H. 2008. The Evolution of a Contested Concept: A Meta-Analysis of Social Capital Definitions and Trends (1988–2006). *Sociological Inquiry*, 78(4), 536–557.

Gans, H. 1962. *The Urban Villagers*. The Free Press, New York.

Gertz, C. 1973. *The Interpretation of Cultures*. NY, Basic Books.

Gerth, H. & Mills, C.W. 1946. *From Max Weber: Essays in Sociology*. Oxford University Press, New York.

Granovetter, M. 1973. The Strength of Weak Ties. *American Journal of Sociology*. 78(6), 1360–1380.

Howley, A., Howley, C., Burgess, L., & Pusateri, D. 2008. Social Class, Amish Culture, and an Egalitarian Ethos: Case Study from a Rural School Serving Amish Children. *Journal of Research in Rural Education*. 23(3), 1–12.

Kelly, U.A. 2009a. *Migration and Education in a Multicultural World: Culture, Loss and Identity*. Palgrave, New York.

Kelly, U.A. 2009b. Learning to Lose: Rurality, Transience and Belonging. *Journal of Research in Rural Education*. 24(11). Retrieved July 26, 2009 from http://jrre.psu.edu/articles/24-11.pdf.

Kraybill, D.B. & Nolt, S.M. 2004. *Amish Enterprise: From Plows to Profits*. Johns Hopkins Press, Baltimore, MD.

Lamont, M. & Molnár, V. 2002. The Study of Social Boundaries in the Social Sciences. *Annual Review of Sociology*, 28, 167–195.

Larson, L., Harlan, S.L., Bolin, B., Hackett, E.J., Hope, D., Kirby, A., Nelson, A., Rex, T. R., & Wolf, S. 2004. Bonding and Bridging: Understanding the Relationship Between Social Capital and Civic Action. *Journal of Planning Education and Research*, 24, 64–77.

Logan, J. & Moloch, H. 1987. *Urban Fortunes: The Political Economy of Place*. University of California Press, Berkeley and Los Angeles.

Luloff, A. E., Bridger, J.C. 2003. Community Agency and Local Development, pp. 203–213. In Brown, D.L. & Swanson, L.E. (eds) *Challenges for Rural America in the Twenty-First Century*. University Park, PA: Penn State Press.

McConnell, D.L. & Hurst, C.E. 2006. No 'Rip Van Winkles' Here: Amish Education Since Wisconsin v. Yoder. *Anthropology and Education Quarterly*, 37(3), 6–12.

Madanipour, A., Cars, G., Allen, J. (eds) *Social Exclusion in European Cities*. Jessica Kingsley, London.

Mills, C. W. 1956. *The Power Elite*. Oxford University Press, New York.

Molnár, E. & Schafft, K. 2003. Social Exclusion, Ethnic Political Mobilization and Roma Minority Self-Governance in Hungary. *East-Central Europe*, 30(1), 53–73.

Narayan, D. 1999. *Bonds and Bridges: Social Capital and Poverty*. Policy Research Working Paper 2167. Policy Research Department. World Bank, Washington, D.C.

National Opinion Research Center. 1991.

National Telecommunications and Information Administration. 2010. "Digital Nation." Washington, D.C.: U.S. Dept. of Commerce. Downloaded on May 31, 2010 at: http://www.ntia.doc.gov/reports/2010/NTIA_internet_use_report_Feb2010.pdf.

Philip, L. & Shucksmith, M. 2003. Conceptualizing Social Exclusion. *European Planning Studies*, 11, 461–480.

Portes, A. 1998. Social Capital: Its Origins and Applications in Modern Sociology. *Annual Review of Sociology*, 24, 1–24.

Putnam, R. 1993. *Making Democracy Work*. Princeton University Press, Princeton, N.J.

Putnam, R. 1999. *Bowling Alone*. Simon & Shuster, New York.

Sampson, R., Morenoff, J. & Earls, F. 1999. Beyond Social Capital: Spatial Dynamics of Collective Efficacy for Children. *American Sociological Review*, 64(5), 633–660.

Schafft, K.A. & Brown, D.L. 1999. Social Capital and Grassroots Development: The Case of Roma Self-Governance in Hungary. *Social Problems*, 47, 201–219.

Schafft, K.A. & D.L. Brown. 2003. Social Capital, Social Networks and Social Power. *Social Epistemology*, 17(4), 329–342.

Scholten, P. & Holzhacker, R. 2009. Bonding, Bridging and Ethnic Minorities in the Netherlands: Changing Discourses in a Changing Nation. *Nations and Nationalism*, 15(1), 81–100.

Selznick, P. 1992. *The Moral Commonwealth: Social Theory and the Promise of Community*. University of California Press, Berkeley.

Smith, D. 1995. The New Urban Sociology Meets the Old: Rereading Some Classical Human Ecology. *Urban Affairs Review*, 30, 432–457.

Smith, S.M., Findeis, J.L., Kraybill, D.B., & Nolt, S.M. 1997. Nonagricultural Micro-Enterprise Development among the Pennsylvania Amish: A New Phenomenon. *Journal of Rural Studies*, 13(3), 237–251.

Terrion, J.L. 2006. Building Social Capital in Vulnerable Families: Success Markers of a School-Based Intervention Program. *Youth & Society*, 38(2),155–176.

Toënnies, F. 1887. *Gemeinschaft und Gesellschaft*. reprint 2005. Wissenschaftliche Buchgesellschaft, Darmstadt.

Urry, J. 2000. *Sociology Beyond Societies: Mobilities for the Twenty-First Century*. Routledge, London.

Veit-Wilson, J. 1998. *Setting Adequacy Standards*. Policy Press, Bristol.

Vidich, A. & Bensman, J. 1958. *Small Town and Mass Society*. Princeton University Press, Princeton, N.J.

Walker, A. & Walker, C. (eds) 1997. *Britain Divided: The Growth of Social Exclusion in the 1980s and 1990s*. Child Poverty Action Group, London.

Warren, R. 1963. *The Community in America*. Rand McNally, Chicago.

Wellman, B. 1979. The Community Question: The Intimate Networks of East Yorkers. *American Journal of Sociology*, 85(5), 1201–1231.

Wellman, B. 2001. Physical Place and Cyberspace: The Rise of Networked Individualism. *International Journal of Urban and Regional Research*, 25(2), 227–252.

Wilkinson, K. 1991. *The Community in Rural America*. Greenwood Press, New York.

Wirth, L. 1938. Urbanism as a Way of Life. *American Journal of Sociology*, 44(1), 1–24.

Woolcock, M. 1998. Social Capital and Economic Development: Toward a Theoretical Synthesis and Policy Framework. *Theory and Society*, 27(1), 151–208.

Young Center for Anabaptist and Pietist Studies. 2008. *Amish Population Change Summary, 1992–2008.* http://www2.etown.edu/amishstudies/PDF/Statistics/Population_Change_Summary_1992_2008.pdf.

Young, F. & Lyson, T. 1993. Branch Plants and Poverty in the American South. *Sociological Forum*, 8(3), 433–450.

Young, I.M. 1995. The Ideal of Community and the Politics of Difference, pp. 233–257. In Weiss, P. & Friedman, M. (eds) *Feminism and Community*. Temple University Press, Philadelphia.

4 Community Institutions in Rural Society

In the early 1830s Alexis de Tocqueville, an historian and political theorist from a French aristocratic family, traveled to the United States for nine months in order to study the American penitentiary system, a trip sponsored by the French minister of the interior. Studying the penal system, however, was only a pretense for examining what really intrigued Tocqueville, the structure of democracy and self-governance in America and, in particular, how the American system of government might yield insights for the evolving French democracy. The resulting work, *Democracy in America*, has since become a classic text of historical sociology. In it, Tocqueville reflects on the possible dangers of the "tyranny of the majority" within democracies: the potential for the viewpoint of the majority to disregard the dissenting viewpoints of the minority. This was largely circumvented in the American case, argued Tocqueville, by both a pronounced associational life and a cultivated spirit of locality. "Look at the skill," Tocqueville writes,

> with which the American township has taken care, so to speak, to scatter its power in order to involve more people in public affairs. Independently of the electors called from time to time to fulfill their public duties, a great number of tasks and many different officers within the sphere of their power represent the powerful body in whose name they are acting. What a huge number of men thus find a source of profit in the local power system and become involved in it for themselves. (de Tocqueville 2003: 81)

Tocqueville's insights about the importance of local organizations and institutions for participatory democracy provide a frame for examining and appreciating the nature of rural communities in contemporary American society. This chapter examines associational life in rural communities by discussing some of the main political and civic institutions that provide access to a variety of resources and public goods, represent local interests, enhance and reproduce local identity, and create opportunities for participation in the civic sphere, focusing in particular on three critical local institutional domains – local government, education, and health care.

While organizations and institutions are important across all types of communities, large and small, urban and rural, they bear particular examination in the rural context not only because in rural areas local institutions (such as schools) play such an important role in community life, identity and civic participation, but also because of the equity challenges facing rural communities as they contend with ensuring appropriate service provision in the context of limited resources and small economies of scale.

Federalism and the Structure of Local Governance

The U.S. Constitution outlines a governmental system based around the distribution of power and governing authority across national, state and local governments. Federalism's legal basis is embedded in the reserved powers clause of the U.S. Constitution's 10th amendment. This clause states that powers not granted to the national government nor prohibited to the states are reserved to the states or the people. Hence, the logic of federalism is based around the twin goals of preserving the rights of states and the representation of territories at various levels (e.g., states, counties, and municipalities), while maintaining a strong union at the national level. Federalism thereby decentralizes power and political decision-making, particularly in areas most immediately relevant to local populations, while at the same time allowing for a federal or national-level regulation of interests held in common across all states (e.g., national defense, interstate and international commerce, and so on).

Following the logic of federalism, cities, villages, towns, school districts, and other local governments are essentially "creatures of the state." That is, they are chartered by the state's constitution with powers and duties delegated by the state. States authorize local governments so that programs and local expenditures are identified and managed locally. Much of the institutional infrastructure of local communities has therefore been created by local governments, which in turn have been chartered by state governments. In this respect, state policies and the creation of local governing structures have created the legal context for citizens to act collectively at the local level. While the proliferation in quantity and type of governmental institutions sometimes creates redundancies and confusion in terms of authority and accountability, local governments, at least in principle, enhance local autonomy and responsiveness to local conditions and needs.

While certain areas of authority are shared, such as the ability to levy and collect taxes, build and maintain roads, and provide for public safety, other areas of power fall to particular levels of government. The federal government, for example, has the exclusive power to print money, maintain an army, and to make laws to enforce the Constitution. State governments, by contrast, have exclusive powers to issue various licenses (such as marriage licenses and driver's licenses), establish local governments, regulate commerce within the state, and assume responsibility for education, health care, and social service provision.

Municipal governments are usually organized around centers of population and typically correspond to the U.S. Census Bureau "incorporated place"[1] geographies used for reporting statistics on population and housing. Municipal governments range widely in size from those in large urban centers such as New York City (with over eight million inhabitants) to small rural communities with as few as several hundred inhabitants. The sphere of responsibility for municipal governments generally includes the administration of police and fire departments, municipal courts, emergency medical services, housing, transportation, and public works.

In the United States, local governments proliferate. There are nearly 88,000 governmental units, nearly all of which are various forms of local governments, broadly distinguished by whether they are county governments, or whether they are sub-county governments. There are nearly 3,000 county governments,[2] as well as about 36,000 municipal and township governments, and nearly 49,000 special purpose local governments (U.S. Census 2002). County governments play a particular role within the federalist system because they often coordinate regional planning across lower levels of government (e.g., municipalities) as well as between local residents and state and national levels (Lobao & Kraybill 2005). Special purpose governments include school districts and "special district governments," generally governmental units established by a county-level authority to address a particular local community need or function such as fire protection, housing, resource conservation, highways, health, and hospitals.

Still another form of local governance is tribal governance. Over 560 American Indian tribes are recognized by the federal government, and over 300 of these tribes have reservations. Federal recognition acknowledges the right of these tribes to operate as sovereign nations with their own tribal governments having the authority to control tribal affairs, in effect engaging in the process of self-governance (Senese 1991; Gonzales 2003). Governance associated with reservation land may well encompass public safety provision, land-use planning and local economic development. However, these roles may not be applicable to tribal members not recognized by the federal government, nor to federally recognized tribes without designated reservation land. Regardless, tribal governance may still assume important roles in the area of education, such as the establishment and maintenance of tribal schools and colleges, as well as social service provision and the maintenance and preservation of tribal cultures and languages (Faircloth & Tippeconnic 2010). We further develop the concepts of tribal trust and tribal sovereignty in Chapter 7 where we examine the position and status of American Indians and other minorities in contemporary rural society.

Local Government Capacity and the Decentralization of Governance

The political process, at its most abstract, can be thought of as the means by which groups determine how to allocate different types of resources valued by the collective (Guthrie & Wong 2008). The federalist system, comprising different levels of representation, means that governments operating at different levels require a certain degree of capacity in order to secure sufficient resources to represent adequately and address the needs of the populations they serve. While local government capacity can be narrowly defined as the fiscal resources to provide essential services, capable governments also possess the institutional and leadership capacity to manage the public's business on a daily basis and technical and managerial skills to plan for the future. Lack of government capacity becomes a particular issue for rural and nonmetropolitan areas where lower levels of human resources (including professional management capacity), fewer financial and institutional resources, higher poverty rates, and sparser populations may very well result in disproportionately lower levels of organizational and community resources.

For example, Table 4.1 shows data from a national-level survey of county governments conducted by researchers from the Ohio State University. The

Table 4.1 County Government Capacity by Urban–Rural Location

	County Location			
	Metro	**Nonmetro Adjacent**	**Nonmetro Rural**	**All**
Number of full-time county government employees				
0–49	.9	4.0	27.0	14.8
50–99	4.0	21.4	34.5	23.5
100–249	15.9	41.1	29.8	28.9
250–499	17.8	20.9	7.3	13.2
500–999	23.1	10.3	1.3	9.1
1,000+	38.5	2.3	0.1	10.5
Professional staffing in last 5 years				
economic development professional	61.1	39.4	31.3	40.8
grant writer	50.8	29.4	27.5	34.0
land use planner	73.1	38.6	29.3	42.9
Services provided by county government				
water and sewer	46.3	23.3	18.0	26.6
child care/Head Start	35.7	20.1	14.6	21.3
drug and alcohol rehabilitation	54.4	35.5	26.7	35.9
elder care	42.8	25.6	17.2	25.8
housing assistance	47.0	22.8	17.1	26.2
% Respondents noting "very important" effect on county gov't finances due to:				
Loss of federal revenue	23.8	31.3	38.1	32.7
Loss of state revenue	37.8	44.9	48.0	44.6
Pressure from local taxpayers to reduce taxes	24.1	32.8	36.7	32.5
Declining tax base	12.2	31.0	39.6	30.4

Source: Kraybill & Lobao (2001)

researchers sub-classified counties by metropolitan status, examining the institutional characteristics of metropolitan counties, nonmetropolitan counties adjacent to metropolitan counties, and nonmetropolitan, non-adjacent counties. Not surprisingly, the size of the nonmetropolitan county governments is markedly smaller than that of the metro county governments. This, of course, reflects smaller population sizes, and more limited fiscal resources. Yet it also speaks to the smaller resource base that rural counties have at their command (Pruitt 2010). While 61 percent of metro county governments reported an economic development professional on staff, the same was true for only 31 percent of nonmetropolitan nonadjacent county governments. Only about one quarter of nonmetropolitan nonadjacent county governments had a grant writer on staff as opposed to over 50 percent of county governments in metro areas. While over 73 percent of metro area county governments reported having a full-time land-use planner on staff, this was true for only slightly more than one quarter of nonmetropolitan county governments. Similarly, nonmetropolitan county governments were markedly less likely to offer a range of services, from water and sewer to drug rehabilitation and housing assistance. Nonmetropolitan county governments were also much more likely to feel pressure on fiscal resources as a consequence of dwindling state and federal support, a shrinking local tax base and agitation from constituents to reduce local taxes. In short, as Warner argues, these conditions amplify the need for local governments "to balance civic concerns with market realities" (2009: 133).

Devolution and Privatization of Services

The decreased level of county government capacity reflects significant changes over time in the relationships between various levels of government. Between the Great Depression and the 1980s, the federal government played a large and growing role in local service provision. In contrast, since the 1980s public policies have strongly favored a decentralization of governing responsibility and public service activities from higher to lower levels of government (Lobao & Kraybill 2005).[3] Proponents argue that decentralization theoretically moves public policy and local decision-making closer to those it is intended to benefit, decreasing dependence on higher levels of government and increasing civic participation in local decision-making. In addition to fostering more effective governmental response to local needs, decentralization has also been promoted as a means of making local governments more efficient and entrepreneurial. Aside from the more instrumental purposes of a set of policy directives, decentralization is also argued to have been a consequence of slow national economic growth, globalization of economies, and reductions in federal assistance to support local economic development (Lobao & Kraybill 2005).

Decentralization has also often gone hand-in-hand with broader political reform agendas pushing for the increasing reliance upon market forces to provide public goods, such as the privatization of services that previously were publicly administrated. As Warner (2009) argues:

> Around the world the trends of decentralization and privatization reflect a market-based push to government service delivery that emphasizes efficiency over redistribution and market choice over deliberate discourse. Decentralization reflects a shift from national control and responsibility, and privatization presents a shift from government delivery to private market delivery (even if still financed by government). Both privatization and decentralization represent an ascendance of market-based approaches to governmental service delivery. (p. 133)

Critics of decentralization have argued that these shifts in governmental roles have increased the reliance upon market forces to create public goods such as trash removal, and emergency medical care, and that this shift cannot be assumed to automatically result in an equitable redistribution of resources across populations. This has particular implications for rural and nonmetropolitan areas which have more dispersed populations, often have distinct concentrations of poverty and weaker and/or less diversified economies. Indeed, economically disadvantaged rural and urban areas alike are far more likely to find themselves facing a vicious cycle of limited tax base, reduced public investment and economic decline while wealthier suburban areas are more likely to experience virtuous cycles of a larger tax base, increased investment and subsequent economic development (Warner & Pratt 2005).

Recent work by Warner and others has furthermore shown that local governments in rural areas spend nearly as much on a per capita basis as their counterparts in metro areas. However, they are able to offer a much narrower range of services. Similarly, while privatized, for-profit delivery of services peaked in 1997, it has since steadily dropped in rural areas. Warner explains this as a consequence of several factors. First, rural areas lack the structural characteristics, including larger market shares and larger, more vibrant economies, to make them competitive for private interests. Similarly, the reduced number of private service providers in rural areas results in thin competition or even an outright lack of market alternatives.

However, Warner also argues that recent data suggest *citizen interest* in service delivery has led local governments to back away from privatized service delivery or mix public and private provisions. That is, "local government managers have realized that citizens are interested in more than cost efficiency and service quality; they are interested in the ability to participate in decisions about the service delivery process" (Warner 2009: 141). It is unlikely that this signals an end to decentralization and privatization. But it does suggest the limits to these processes, the extent to which they unfold differently across urban and rural areas and, last, how they illuminate the ongoing conflicts between the goals of efficiency and equity in governance and the provision of public service.

Municipal Cooperation and Collaboration

One way to overcome the limited capacity of individual local governments is to enter into cooperative agreements with other local governments and organizations (Ayres & Silvis 2010). Inter-municipal agreements have been forged in areas of general governance such as code enforcement and judiciary and court administration, and to provide particular services such as health care, public safety and water infrastructure. While inter-local cooperation makes intuitive sense in the context of changing rural demographics and economies and in an era of declining fiscal resources, potential partners have to overcome numerous legal, political and economic constraints. Moreover, to be successful, communities have to change the normative environment which tends to favor inter-community *competition* over *cooperation.* This is especially critical in the area of economic development where individual communities typically compete with neighbors to attract new employers. This "go it alone" process often contributes to a race to the bottom where prospective employers are offered such generous incentives packages that winning communities may experience only nominal economic benefit. Hence, the irony is that beggaring one's neighbors often beggars winning communities themselves, especially if new employers only remain for a short period of time.

Table 4.2 Percent Distribution of Schools by Locale, 2003–2004

Locale	Districts	Schools	Students
City	5.9	25.7	30.4
Suburban	19.9	27.8	35.4
Town	18.3	15.2	12.9
Rural	55.9	31.3	21.3
Fringe	11.1	10.6	11.0
Distant	21.8	11.5	7.1
Remote	23.0	9.2	3.2
Total	100.0	100.0	100.0

Cities refer to urbanized areas (densely settled areas with 50,000 or more people), and inside a principal city. Suburban refers to territory outside a principal city, but inside an urbanized area. Town refers to territory inside an urban cluster (densely settled areas with a population of 2,500–49,999). Rural refers to all territory outside urbanized areas and urban clusters. Fringe refers to within 5 miles of an urbanized area or within 2.5 miles of an urban cluster. Distant refers to rural territory that is between 5 and 25 miles distant from an urbanized area or between 2.5 and 10 miles from an urban cluster. Remote refers to rural territory more than 25 miles from an urbanized area and more than 10 miles from an urban cluster. *Source:* Provasnik et al. 2007.

Education

In 2004 over 10 million students attended rural schools in the United Statess. However, while these 10 million students constitute over 21 percent of all enrolled K-12 students, rural areas contain 55 percent of school districts and 31 percent of schools. This reflects the smaller size of rural schools and school districts due to smaller and sparser rural populations. By contrast, while only about 6 percent of school districts (and 26 percent of schools) are located in cities, they are responsible for educating over 30 percent of all students (see Table 4.2). Of students attending rural schools, well over one-third go to schools with 400 or fewer students, and over 90 percent attend schools of 800 students or fewer. In contrast, nearly 50 percent of students in cities and over one-third of suburban students attend schools with enrollments of 800 or more (Provasnik et al. 2007).

School Districts as Social Spaces

While schools are critical local institutions for all communities, their roles in rural communities are especially significant. Rural schools are often the community's largest local employer. They also make local areas attractive places to live and raise families. As a consequence, the presence of a school can have direct effects on property values, and ancillary effects on local economic activity (Lyson 2002; Weiss 2004). Because of this, even though the mandate of schools revolves around the provision of education, schools in rural areas also inevitably play strong local community development roles (Schafft & Harmon 2010). These roles may or may not be embraced by educators and school administrators, especially those for whom the improvement of test scores has become a top priority. However, strong evidence suggests the many ways in which rural school and community well being are interconnected (Harmon & Schafft 2009).

More than any other local institution, schools help to establish a community's identity as well as its social boundaries. School districts reasonably approximate locality based communities "where people live and meet daily needs together through groups and institutions having distinctively local character and where locality relevant actions emerge from a variety of resident needs and interests" (Zekeri et al. 1994: 221). They can therefore be understood as meaningful community-level social spaces, helping to integrate other community institutions. Schools are public service-providing institutions mandated to provide education to all eligible local residents. All residents have some connection with the educational system, if only in the form of payment of property taxes. As such, schools and the districts that they comprise provide community members with an important shared identity and context for social interaction. Because of this, rural schools are often cited as promoting tight-knit, supportive relationships between students, teachers, and staff and community members. Rural schools have lower student-to-teacher ratios than schools elsewhere, which also promotes school attachment and positive student–teacher relationships. Rural teachers also report fewer behavioral problems among their students, and higher job satisfaction (Provasnik et al. 2007).

Academic Achievement in Comparative Perspective

This high degree of social solidarity is reflected in academic achievement outcomes. On average, rural students tend to do better across multiple indicators of academic achievement than their peers in cities, although students in suburban areas often tend, on average, to have the highest academic outcomes of all. The National Assessment of Educational Progress (NAEP) is the only nationally representative assessment of student proficiency in reading, mathematics and science, and is administered in the 4th, 8th, and 12th grades. Table 4.4 compares the percent of students scoring at proficient or above for all three subject areas and across all three tested grade levels. Rural students outperform students in cities in all grades and in all tested subject areas. As rural locales become more remote, assessments diminish, although with only one exception (12th grade mathematics) rural remote students consistently outperform students in cities, often by significant margins. Examining post-secondary school outcomes, rural students also have lower dropout rates than students in cities and towns, the lowest dropout rates occurring among suburban students.

At the post-secondary level however, young rural adults have lower educational attainment than their counterparts in other places. Proportionally fewer rural adults aged 18 to 29 are enrolled in post-secondary educational programs and similarly only 19 percent of rural adults 25 and older have bachelor's degrees, as compared with nearly 30 percent in cities and 31.5 percent in suburban areas.[4] This pattern has been long noted (see e.g., Hektner 1995; Lichter, McLaughlin, & Cornwell 1995; Howley, Harmon, & Leopold 1996; Gibbs 1998), and lower levels of higher educational attainment among rural youth have been attributed in

Box 4.1 Understanding the Diversity of Rural School Contexts

As we point out in various ways throughout this book, the category of "rural" masks an incredible amount of diversity with regard to community identity, cultural and historical legacies, economic structure, demographics, land-use patterns, and settlement structures. Rural schools, as institutions firmly embedded within the communities they serve, similarly reflect this diversity. Therefore, while it may be useful to discuss more broadly the characteristics of rural schools, it is also critical to keep in mind how these characteristics vary widely by region, by state, and by locality. This, in turn, has important implications for public policy and for how we think about rural schools and rural education.

Every two years the Rural School and Community Trust completes a report entitled *Why Rural Matters*, which examines the contexts of rural education on a state-by-state basis as a means of describing and illustrating "the complexity of rural contexts in ways that can help policy-makers better understand the challenges faced by their constituencies and formulate policies that are responsive to these challenges" (Johnson & Strange 2009: 1). A quick glance at several state-level indicators quickly illustrates this variation across a selection of states representing different areas of the country and possessing different degrees of rurality.

Across nearly every indicator the state-by-state differences are immediately apparent. And yet, even these figures obscure local and regional contexts. For example, Alaska and New Mexico both have significant minority populations, but Alaska's rural minority students are predominantly indigenous Alaska Natives, while in New Mexico rural minority students are predominantly Latino and American Indian. This, in part, accounts for the differences between the two states in the percentage of English Language Learners (ELLs).

The authors of *Why Rural Matters 2009* note that policy-makers need to understand several key realities when devising appropriate measures to address rural education needs. Poverty remains one of the most critical issues. Especially in the Southeast and Southwest, many states have both large rural populations and areas of high poverty concentrations, often in conjunction with large minority and ELL concentrations. These areas, they argue, often represent "geo-cultural regions" (such as the Upper Rio Grande Valley in the Southwest) that cross state boundaries. This, they argue, suggests that perhaps the most effective policy strategies do not involve state-level "one size fits all" approaches, but rather must be regional and cooperative in nature, and tailored to the specific economic, demographic and cultural characteristics of the region.

part to a lower valuing of college education because historically rural areas have been able to offer viable employment in resource extraction and manufacturing industries that offered competitive wages and did not require a college education. Rural economies, however, have shifted considerably in the last ten to twenty years, and a great many rural communities can no longer promise sustainable livelihoods in extractive or manufacturing industries (see Chapter 8). Because of this, while higher education for rural youth may mean upward mobility from a socioeconomic standpoint, it also likely means *outward* geographic mobility from rural home communities (Corbett 2007; Hektner 1995).

Box 4.1 (continued)

Table 4.3 Understanding the Diversity of Rural School Contexts

State	Pct Rural Schools	Pct Rural Student Poverty	Pct Rural Minority Students	Pct Rural ELL Students	Rural Instructional Expenditures Per pupil	Rural High School Graduation Rate	Pct Rural Reading Proficiency (per NCLB)	Pct Rural Math Proficiency, (per NCLB)
Maine	67.4	35.7	2.9	3.8	$6,972	81.8	54.0	45.6
Alaska	65.5	45.9	56.2	15.1	$8,619	55.9	40.0	35.3
Alabama	51.6	50.6	27.0	3.2	$4,358	62.4	38.2	42.6
West Virginia	51.4	52.6	6.5	2.1	$5,555	74.2	40.0	46.7
Kansas	50.6	33.8	10.5	5.9	$5,382	82.9	51.2	54.0
New Mexico	37.7	81.3	81.6	33.8	$5,124	58.4	53.5	47.6
Texas	29.6	45.8	41.4	19.0	$4,798	76.5	53.6	49.0
Michigan	29.4	34.2	8.0	4.9	$5,041	76.3	49.4	49.0
California	14.7	46.6	50.3	26.7	$4,828	75.7	51.6	48.8
New Jersey	9.5	15.9	16.9	8.2	$7,630	93.3	49.5	48.4

Source: Why Rural Matters 2009

Table 4.4 Academic Achievement Outcomes by Locality

	City	Sub-urban	Town	Rural: Fringe	Rural: Distant	Rural: Remote	Rural All
NAEP Reading achievement levels; % at or above proficient							
4th grade	23.6	34.4	28.1	33.5	29.6	26.9	31.1
8th grade	22.6	33.5	27.3	31.5	29.4	28.6	30.4
12th grade	29.5	37.2	33.2	34.2	31.3	34.1	33.4
NAEP Mathematics achievement levels; % at or above proficient							
4th grade	28.7	40.7	34.0	36.0	38.5	34.6	31.8
8th grade	22.9	33.4	26.4	30.7	27.3	25.7	28.9
12th grade	17.6	25.3	20.6	22.8	18.9	17.2	20.6
NAEP Science achievement levels; % at or above proficient							
4th grade	19.1	30.4	27.4	34.1	29.9	27.8	31.7
8th grade	19.5	31.2	28.0	31.6	28.2	30.2	30.2
12th grade	13.5	19.8	18.1	18.7	16.7	16.7	17.7
% aged16–24 HS dropouts, 2004	12.8	9.0	12.1	–	–	–	11.1
% adults 25 and over with less than a HS diploma	18.4	12.8	18.5	–	–	–	17.1
% aged 18–29 and enrolled in a post-secondary education program	36.6	36.6	31.8	–	–	–	27.1
% adults 25 and over with a bachelor's degree or higher	29.8	31.5	19.9	–	–	–	19.1

Cities refer to urbanized areas (densely settled areas with 50,000 or more people), and inside a principal city. Suburban refers to territory outside a principal city, but inside an urbanized area. Town refers to territory inside an urban cluster (densely settled areas with a population of 2,500–49,999). Rural refers to all territory outside urbanized areas and urban clusters. Fringe refers to within 5 miles of an urbanized area or within 2.5 miles of an urban cluster. Distant refers to rural territory that between 5 and 25 miles distant from an urbanized area or between 2.5 and 10 miles from an urban cluster. Remote refers to rural territory more than 25 miles from an urbanized area and more than 10 miles from an urban cluster. *Source:* Provasnik et al. 2007.

Challenges Facing Rural Schools

Rural Schools and "High Stakes" Accountability

While rural schools arguably possess distinct assets, they also face many challenges, most structural in nature. *No Child Left Behind* (NCLB), passed by the US Congress in 2002 as a reauthorization of the Elementary and Secondary Education Act, created sweeping new provisions regarding standards-based education reform. One of the primary assumptions of the legislation is that educational improvement can be produced by establishing set expectations for proficiency in various competency areas, regularly assessing students, and holding schools accountable for student outcomes. Federal funding for schooling, which makes up about eight percent of public school budgets, is contingent upon student assessments, with all students expected to be "proficient" by 2014. Proficiency is determined by standards created by each state and is measured by student performance on standardized tests. Until the program is reauthorized in 2014, schools are expected to meet benchmarked goals which indicate that they are making annual Adequate Yearly Progress (AYP). Schools that are not able to make AYP for two consecutive years must allow students to transfer to other, non-failing schools (although this option may not be feasible for students attending remote rural schools). In extreme cases schools may be closed, reopened as charter schools and/or face replacement of teachers and administrators.

Given that educational outcomes are heavily influenced by family and community context, and in particular socioeconomic status, many rural schools with large low-income student populations may therefore face particular challenges. Small school size may also affect assessment since changes in student scores from year to year at the aggregate level may be more sensitive to random variation in factors over which schools may have little or no control, such as changing student demographics (Goetz 2005) associated with the arrival of new student populations including English Language Learners who may disproportionately underperform in academic assessments.

Although rural schools have traditionally had strong community ties and are seen as being sensitive to local cultures and responsive to local needs, the emphasis on standardized testing may have the effect of narrowing the focus of education to satisfying testing requirements. As test scores become ever more concretized proxies for educational achievement, and accountability revolves increasingly around the state test, there is a danger that rural education will become de-linked from students' needs and desires, their families, and the communities in which they reside (Schafft 2010).

Recruiting and retaining teachers also poses particular dilemmas for rural schools. NCLB not only emphasizes the widespread use of standardized testing, but also includes provisions that all teachers be "highly qualified" requiring a bachelor's degree in all content areas taught, as well as full state certification or licensure. This becomes especially problematic in circumstances in which a teacher provides instruction in multiple subject areas, which is far more likely to happen in smaller, rural schools (Eppley 2009). Geographic and social isolation also makes recruitment of teachers challenging, and professional development opportunities may be more limited (Sipple & Brent 2008). In addition, teacher pay is also slightly lower in rural areas. In 2003–2004, the average salary for rural teachers was $43,000 while teachers in cities averaged $44,000 and those in suburban areas averaged $45,700 (Provasnik et al. 2007).

School Consolidation

School consolidation constitutes one of the longest standing debates in rural (and urban) education, pitting arguments for consolidation (based around efficiency and standardization as justification) against the preservation of distinct rural community traditions, and community autonomy over curricula (Corbett 2007; DeYoung & Howley 1992; Theobald 1997; Tyack 1972). Strange and Malhoit have argued that "there is no area of civic life where rural communities have been more routinely ridiculed for their stubborn resistance to what others assume to be progress." (2005: 2). Even in the early twentieth century school reformers such as Ellwood Cubberley argued for the wisdom of rural school consolidation (managed by educational professionals, presumably from outside the rural community), stating,

> managed as it has been by rural people, themselves largely lacking in educational insight, penurious and with no comprehensive grasp of their own problems, the rural school, except in a few places, has practically stood still [This problem] has now become too complex to be solved by local effort alone, and nothing short of a reorganization of rural education, along good educational and administrative lines, will meet the needs of the present and the future. (1922: 102–103)

In large part because of calls from educational reformers like Cubberley, between 1939 and 2005, the number of school districts in the United States declined from 117,000 to slightly over 14,000 (see Figure 4.1), resulting in a school transportation system that each school day transports 24 million students a total of 22 million miles on 450,000 buses (Strange & Malhoit 2005).

Proponents of consolidation have argued that it increases efficiency through economies of scale, allows student access to greater resources and increases student academic achievement. However, empirical research has frequently failed to support these claims (see e.g. Monk & Haller 1993; Howley 1996; Lee et al. 2000), in particular calling into question claims of fiscal efficiency and advantages in achievement outcomes (Yan 2006).

The largely rural state of West Virginia provides an example of how consolidation often has failed to meet the expectations of policy goals. Justified by the assumption that consolidation would lead to fiscal savings and more efficient use of resources, between 1990 and 2000 the state closed over 300 schools, in the process spending over $1 billion on consolidation efforts. Currently, however, on average West Virginia school districts spend greater percentages of their operating budgets on maintenance and utilities than they did before consolidation, and the number of administrators actually increased by 16 percent despite both school building closures and a decreasing statewide enrollment (Reeves 2004). This is not to suggest that school closure or consolidation is never justified. However, in the case of rural schools, the call for closure or consolidation has frequently originated from outside the community, often from the state level, and the short term – and often questionable – promises of fiscal savings and improved achievement

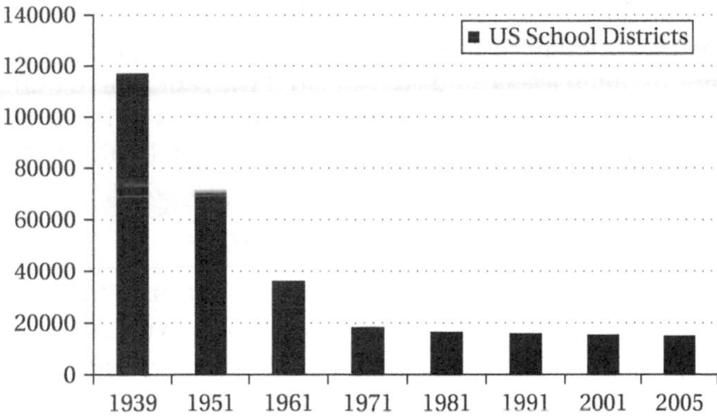

Source: Author's own. Data: National Center for Education Statistics

Figure 4.1 Decline in U.S. School Districts Due to Consolidation, 1939-2005

outcomes have overshadowed the longer-term social and economic effects on communities.

Health Care and Health-Care Institutions in Rural America

Rural America is characterized by both higher health-care needs and lower access to health-care resources than urban areas. Generally speaking, to the extent that a community is small, poor and geographically isolated, the health-care needs of its residents increase while health-care access decreases (Ziller et al. 2003, 2008; Committee on the Future of Rural Health Care 2005). Rural residents are more likely to experience chronic or life-threatening illnesses. Obesity, cardiovascular problems, high blood pressure, diabetes and cancer are all more prevalent among residents of nonmetropolitan areas (Wallace, Grindeanu, & Cirillo 2004; Committee on the Future of Rural Health Care 2005). Mental health issues are also more prevalent (Nelson 2008).

Mortality rates, when adjusted for age, provide an important means of assessing overall health of populations. In the United States, mortality rates in all areas have dropped over time, although since about 1990 age-adjusted mortality rates in nonmetropolitan areas have declined far more slowly than in metropolitan areas. In 1989, while the average annual difference between nonmetro and metro mortality rates for all causes was about six deaths per 100,000, by 2005 that difference had increased to 82 (Jones, Parker, & Ahearn 2009).

Looking at populations overall, rates of alcohol use and abuse and the use of illegal drugs are slightly higher in metropolitan than in nonmetropolitan areas. However, young people aged 12–17 in nonmetro areas have higher rates of alcohol and drug use than their urban peers (Lambert, Gale, & Hartley 2008). Since the mid-1990s, the manufacture and abuse of methamphetamine has been especially problematic in many rural areas. One of the main ingredients, anhydrous ammonia, is an agricultural fertilizer and widely available in rural areas where methamphetamine can be manufactured with reduced risk of detection. Cheap and highly addictive, methamphetamine is also a potent neurotoxin that can cause permanent brain abnormalities, dementia, and psychiatric disorders. Abuse of methamphetamine constitutes a serious public health problem in many nonmetropolitan areas, and is associated with additional numerous social problems including child abuse and neglect, criminal activity and environmental contamination at manufacture sites (Haight et al. 2005; Reding 2009).

Why do Rural Areas Lag Behind in Health Status?

Research shows that the rural–urban health gap results from differences in demographic composition, economic restructuring leaving many workers without employer supplied health insurance, and a lack of institutional capacity to provide adequate care. Glasgow, Johnson, and Morton (2004) argue that rural–urban health disparities are related to lower population densities and smaller local economies, which result in reduced market demand for safe and adequate housing, health care, and employment providing health-care benefits. Ironically, in the midst of agricultural plenty, access to healthy foods such as fresh fruits and vegetables is more limited in some rural communities because of reduced access to full service grocery stores. This lack of access is thought to contribute to nutritional deficiencies, obesity and a wide range of health problems.

Higher levels of health-care needs are also partially a factor of economic and demographic differences across the rural–urban continuum. Poverty, strongly associated with negative health outcomes, concentrates in nonmetropolitan and urban core areas (see Chapter 10). Similarly, nonmetropolitan populations are disproportionately aging populations (see Chapter 6). The percentage of population 65 years old or greater is 12 percent in metropolitan counties, but 15 percent in nonmetropolitan counties, and in approximately one quarter of nonmetropolitan counties the percentage of people 65 years old and older is at least 18 percent. This is due to the aging of rural baby boomers, outmigration of younger people from farming dependent and economically declining nonmetropolitan areas, and the growing attractiveness of many rural areas as retirement destinations (Brown & Glasgow 2008; Jones, Kandel, & Parker 2007).

Aging rural populations are heterogeneous (Glasgow 2004); retiring rural in-migrants and those aging in place each pose different health-care challenges for rural areas. Retirees moving into rural areas often have private insurance and disposable incomes and thus represent potential benefits to rural economies and health-care infrastructure. At the same time, many rural retirement destinations lack the health and human service infrastructure to meet new demands from retiring populations. Rural elders who are long-term rural residents are more likely to be poor, have lower educational attainment and be in worse health than their urban counterparts (National Advisory Committee on Rural Health and Human Services 2008).

Rural economic change has also played an indirect but important role in health-care access. Contractions in traditional rural economic mainstays such as manufacturing, farming and resource extraction industries have been accompanied by a rise in service sector employment, often low paid and with fewer benefits, including health insurance (see Chapter 8). Using 2001–02 pooled data, Ziller et al. (2008) found that almost one-third (30.3 percent) of

Box 4.2 Food Deserts: An Indicator of Rural Distress?

Areas in which people have limited access to full-scale retail grocery food stores are often referred to as *food deserts*. Nearly six percent of the U.S. population lacks the food they need or would like because of problems with grocery store access (USDA 2009). However, food access is not simply a matter of convenience, since people who have limited access to full-scale groceries may rely more on energy-dense foods purchased at convenience stores, thereby increasing their risk of obesity, malnutrition and obesity related illness (Morland, Diez Roux, & Wing 2006). Currently, over 66 percent of U.S. adults are overweight or obese (Ogden et al. 2006) and obesity attributable deaths have been estimated at 280,000 per year (Allison et al. 1999). Food deserts, as such, may be important indicators of the relative wellbeing of places and the people who live in those places.

Some of the earliest work identifying food deserts examined food access in urban areas in the United Kingdom (see e.g., Beaumont et al. 1995). This research, in part, attempted to identify relationships between social inequality and increasing spatial inequalities regarding food access, noting the extent to which low-income neighborhoods were also likely to have limited food access (Guy & David 2004).[5] More recent research has examined similar relationships in rural areas.

Morton and Blanchard (2007), for example, found that 803 U.S. counties could be considered "low access" areas because at least half of the county population lived greater than 10 miles from a large grocery store. They further found that 418 U.S. counties could be considered food deserts because *no* residents lived within ten miles of a large grocery store. These counties on average had higher proportions of people without high-school diplomas, higher poverty rates, and overall older populations.

In a similar study in Pennsylvania, Schafft, Jensen, and Hinrichs (2009) looked at the rates of childhood obesity within school districts by examining body-mass index data from middle-school students collected by the state Department of Health. They used Geographic Information Systems (GIS) techniques and zip code business pattern data to locate all grocery stores within the state having fifty or more employees. They then created ten-mile buffer zones around each point representing a large grocery store location. Zip code areas whose geographic center lay outside of the buffer zone area were labeled food desert zip codes. They then computed the percentage of the population within each school district living outside of the ten-mile buffer zones. School districts with greater than 50 percent of their population residing in food desert zip codes were labeled "food desert school districts." Figure 4.2 shows a map of Pennsylvania with the locations of all large grocery stores as well as food desert zip code and school district areas.

The researchers found that rates of obesity not only were higher in school districts with limited access to large grocery stores, but over time these rates were increasing faster than in non-food desert districts. While food desert school districts in Pennsylvania are on average poorer than non-food desert districts, the researchers found that even when statistically controlling for district socioeconomic status, the relationship between residence in a food desert and childhood obesity remained.

While these findings raise important questions about the relationship between social inequality, spatial inequality, and health outcomes for rural populations, the concept of a food desert is still contested. This is particularly the case regarding how food deserts should be most appropriately defined and measured. For example,

Box 4.2 (continued)

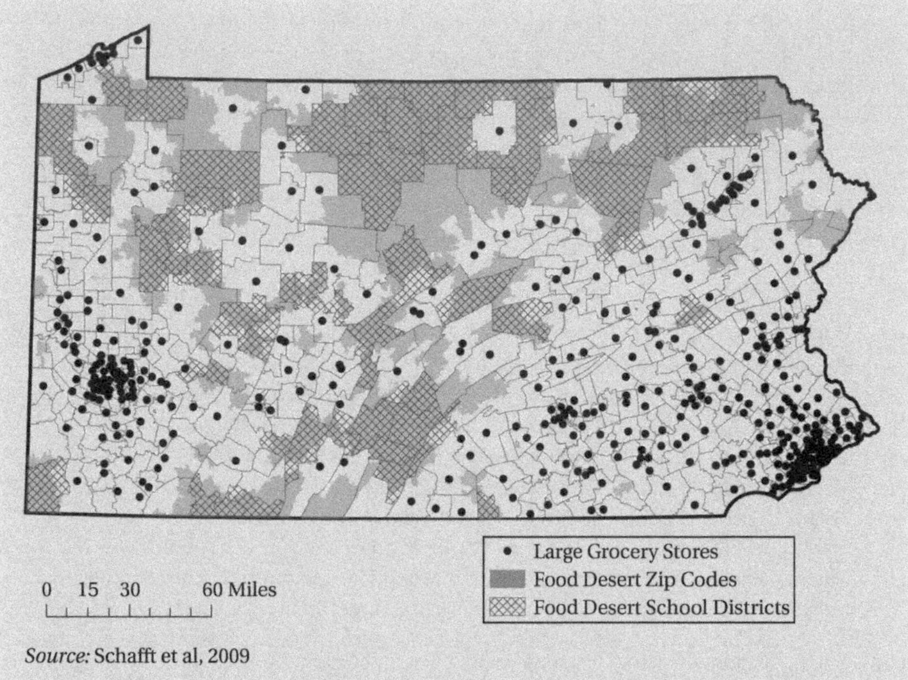

Source: Schafft et al, 2009

Figure 4.2 Pennsylvania School Districts, Grocery Stores, and Food Deserts

food deserts are often operationalized and measured quite differently depending on whether the study is based within an urban or a rural setting. Urban studies usually operationalize food desert areas using relatively short distance proximities to grocery stores (Algert, Agrawal, & Lewis 2006; Berg & Murdoch 2008) on the assumption that for city residents, walking distances are a more appropriate indication of access to full-scale groceries.

Similarly, studies irrespective of area are often unable to account for the extent to which people "trip chain" and plan their food purchases ahead of time to coincide with trips taken to places with greater grocery store access. For example, rural to urban work commuting patterns could place rural residents in regular proximity to larger grocery stores even though those stores may not be close to the rural place of residence. Last, food desert studies also often do not take into account how, when, and where people obtain food in places other than large grocery stores, such as restaurants, farmers' markets, or through gardening, hunting, and other self-provisioning activities.

All the same, there is a growing body of research that has strongly suggested that certain segments of the population – both urban and rural – have uneven access to healthful food options and that this uneven access is associated with negative health outcomes. In this respect, food deserts represent one more way of considering the structural features of communities and how varying social, economic and health resources are unevenly spread across space – and what this means for the wellbeing of rural people and communities.

non-elderly families in nonmetropolitan areas contained at least one member who lacked health insurance coverage as compared to families in metropolitan areas where only 28 percent of families contained a member with no coverage. In nonmetropolitan nonadjacent counties, 8.9 percent of families lacked health insurance entirely as compared to 6.3 percent of families in metropolitan areas. For those who lack insurance, visiting a physician's office is often cost-prohibitive. Preventive health-care is thus often sacrificed and medical care may be otherwise delayed.

In the U.S, while about 20 percent of the population lives in rural areas, only about 9 percent of physicians practice there (Agency for Healthcare Research and Quality 2008). Typically physicians in rural areas work out of clinics with small staffs of additional primary health-care providers such as nurses and physician assistants (NACRHHS 2008). Just as attracting and retaining teachers in rural areas is a problem for rural schools, rural areas are underserved by physicians for many of the same reasons. Rural areas are often isolated from the amenities of urban and large town areas, have limited health-care facilities and offer more limited educational and employment opportunities for family members. Also, as for teachers, earning potential in rural areas is often distinctly lower, a non-trivial factor given the cost of medical training.

Similar to schools, hospitals have important economic effects for rural communities, as, like schools, they represent a major source of employment, meet critical community needs, increase the attractiveness of local areas for residents and prospective employers, and support the local economy. Because of this, hospital closure can have serious adverse effects on rural economies and communities. Between 1990 and 2000, nearly 8 percent of all rural hospitals closed, mostly smaller hospitals treating relatively fewer patients. Closure was mainly a consequence of hospital relocation, consolidation or merger, with rising costs a major contributing factor in the reorganization (Department of Health and Human Services 2003; Morton 2003). Hospital closure has been mitigated to some extent by the federal Critical Access Hospital program created in 1997 to support the economic sustainability of small rural hospitals and ensure that Medicare recipients in rural areas would have access to health services. Still, research has shown that hospital closure not only results in reduced health-care access and service provision, but also has significant negative consequences for rural economies (Holmes et al. 2006).

Because of the size and social structure of many rural communities, health-care providers are often far more integrated into community life than their urban counterparts (Schmidt 2008). As Nelson states,

> Practicing medicine in a small setting generally means living and working in the same place (i.e. "being part of the community"). A dominant theme for rural health-care professionals is one of familiarity. Everyone knows one another, and certainly everyone knows the community's physician or nurse. (2008: 40)

Structural forces such as limited resources and geographic isolation, and external forces such as public and rural health policies, may shape the extent and quality of rural health care. The Committee on the Future of Rural Health Care argues that "efforts to strengthen what are often fragile delivery systems in rural areas will be more successful to the extent that they engage key stakeholders in the community (e.g., employers, schools, local government)" (2005: 51). That is:

> This community orientation, combined with the smaller scale of rural health, human services, and community systems, may afford rural communities an opportunity to demonstrate more rapidly the vision of balancing and integrating the needs of personal health care with broader communitywide initiatives that target the entire population. (2005: 55)

This orientation to health-care provision presents its own set of structural and organizational challenges. Coordinating diverse stakeholders with diverse needs and agendas is not easy or simple. And yet, it is consistent with Wilkinson's notion of "interactive community" and the harnessing of collective interests and networks of interaction for community development (see Chapter 3).

The Promise of Telemedicine for Rural Community Health-care Delivery

Telemedicine is an emergent strategy for rural health-care provision. Telemedicine refers to clinical health care conducted using information and communication technology, linking patients with doctors and specialist medical services not available locally. It also holds the promise of electronic record keeping and transfer, enabling the sharing of patient data across sites and health-care providers, thereby improving the quality and timeliness of health-care information. Telemedicine is "envisioned as a technology application [enabling] the seamless transfer of patient data across the continuum of care" (NACRHHS 2008: 46), thereby reducing costs and travel time as well as the possibility of misdiagnosis and medical error. Telemedicine can also be used for training and education purposes, using videoconferencing and webcasting to deliver workshops, lectures and demonstrations to practitioners at a distance. The range of applications varies from simple email communication to the remote monitoring and care of patients.

The U.S. Congress and the Federal Communications Commission (FCC) jointly designed the Rural Health Care Program of the Universal Service Fund in order to ensure that rural health-care providers would not have to pay higher rates than their urban counterparts for telecommunications and internet services. In 2007, the FCC dedicated $417 million to fund the Rural Health Care Pilot Program (RHCPP) as a means of creating broadband telehealth networks, thereby expanding health-care coverage and access to underserved populations. The funding will produce 69 broadband telehealth networks in forty-two states, serving hospitals, health clinics, universities, correctional facilities, and health centers.

While these developments are promising, and hospitals and health clinics are increasingly making use of information technology for telemedicine, the high costs of developing and maintaining telemedicine systems have been prohibitive for many rural health-care facilities. Staff must be recruited and trained to operate systems locally. Many remote rural areas also lack sufficient broadband infrastructure to support telemedicine systems (NACRHHS 2008), although this is increasingly less of a problem. Nonetheless, telemedicine and the use of information technology to facilitate health-care provision presents significant benefits

Box 4.3 Community Partnerships for Health Promotion

Wayne Highlands School District is located in rural Northeastern Pennsylvania. It covers over 430 square miles and its school buses, in total, travel a remarkable 1.2 million miles each year, transporting its 3300 students back and forth to school. Wayne Highlands provides a good example of collaboration across community institutions. In the mid 1990s the district teaching staff along with the school nurses argued that a more comprehensive approach to student health was needed. They felt, along with the district administration, that the best approach might be to work directly with community health and social service agencies in order to inform their efforts and attract external funding and other resources. The school district partnered with three other area school districts, local, county and state level health and social service agencies, private businesses and the Wayne Memorial Hospital to create the *Together for Health* program.

This program was created to help inform students about wellness and provide them with basic information to make good choices regarding personal health and nutrition. The program provides 7th to 11th grade students with the opportunity to assess their health status using a Personal Wellness profile, along with optional clinical lab assessments done in partnership with the hospital. While the data are primarily intended for students to increase their awareness of health and healthy living choices, the school has also used the data to revise their curriculum and the content of the student health and wellness programs to reflect student needs. Since its inception over 10,000 students have taken part in this programming and 85 percent have completed Wellness Profiles. An annual health fair hosted by the hospital puts students in contact with volunteers from over twenty organizations. The district has branched out its efforts, in collaboration with the hospital and other agencies to create a family resource center providing resources to new parents, a community dental clinic, and a Winter Walking Program, opening three of its schools during the winter months for community member exercise. Wayne Memorial Hospital, in the meantime, is actively pursuing connections with Wayne Highlands and a local community college to promote job training in the health fields as a way of "growing their own" and addressing shortages in nursing staff.

for rural areas and constitutes an additional justification for the expansion of broadband connectivity in underserved areas.

As we have shown, rural communities lag behind their urban counterparts on many measures of health status. While many of these disparities reflect demographic, economic, and socioeconomic differences that would not be directly affected by changes in health-care policies, they also reflect institutional weaknesses which could be strengthened by health-care reforms. As Rickets (1999) has observed, rural needs are not typically included on national level health-care reform agendas. He points to the importance of developing a "rural health policy network" to marshal information and construct arguments in support of a wide range of rural health issues. Such a network could be successful in raising the salience of rural health-care issues during national debates and ensuring that institutional reforms will contribute to enhancing rural health status throughout the nation.

Conclusion

Communities are comprised of the relations of affinity and identity possessed by groups of people. Moreover, as we emphasized in Chapter 3, communities can also be thought of as institutionalized solutions to the challenges of everyday life. Through their institutions, communities educate and socialize youth, protect public health and safety, provide religious affiliation and spiritual guidance, manage elections and other aspects of local governance, and plan for the future. Moreover, in certain instances such as with schools, formal community institutions can help to reproduce community identity and provide opportunities for civic engagement and participation. Local institutions also help to delineate community boundaries.

As we have shown in this chapter, it is not that rural communities lack schools, churches, town councils, hospitals, libraries, police forces, or trash removal, but rather that their capacity to produce public goods, and the choice of providers, is often limited. Moreover, rural institutions have all in various ways faced significant challenges during recent decades. For example, both schools and hospitals have faced consolidation and closure, while local governments have faced decreasing state and federal support at the very time that their responsibilities have increased as a result of devolution.

As many scholars have observed, while community can develop outside of geographic territory, people live together in geographic spaces so territory remains important (Wilkinson 1991). This territorial perspective on community focuses attention on the social interaction that gives territory social meaning, and on the institutional structures people develop to solve their daily problems. In this chapter we have focused on health, education and governance, three institutional domains that are fundamental to collective life, and life quality. We have shown that in the midst of macro-level forces and structural transformations that have undermined the autonomy of local places, local institutions continue to play critical formal roles in providing basic services and resources for populations. While imperfect and limited in many ways, local institutions are still a fundamentally important aspect of rural community life in the twenty-first century.

A critical question facing rural communities is whether "go it alone" strategies for providing services and resources continues to be reasonable or whether more places should be developing inter-municipal agreements with their neighbors. While inter-community cooperation poses a wide range of legal, economic and political challenges, many scholars, practitioners and local officials see cooperative agreements and regional approaches to development as the wave of the future (Green & Robinson 2010).

Notes

1 Incorporated places are Census designated places, such as towns, villages, and cities that have a governing structure. Unincorporated places, in contrast, are places without an immediate local government. For unincorporated places, the county government is the major "local" government.

2 County-level governments in Louisiana are referred to as "parishes" and in Alaska are referred to as "boroughs."
3 This has been the case in both U.S. and European contexts (Hopkins 2002; Warner 2003; Lowndes & Sullivan 2008). The national share of state and local expenditures was increased since 2008 perhaps indicating a reversal in devolution. However, Medicaid accounts for most of this reversal.
4 See our discussion in Chapter 10 concerning the relationship between educational attainment and diminished risks of poverty.
5 See also Smith, Butterfass, & Richards (2010) for a recent U.S.-based example of similar work.

References

Agency for Healthcare Research and Quality (AHRQ). 2008. *National Healthcare Disparities Report 2008.* U.S. Department of Health and Human Services, Rockville, MD.

Algert, S.J., Agrawal, A., & Lewis, D.S. 2006. Disparities in Access to Fresh Produce in Low Income Neighborhoods in Los Angeles. *American Journal of Preventive Medicine,* 30(5), 365–370.

Allison, D.B., Fontaine, K.R., Manson, J.E., Stevens, J., & Van Itallie, T.B. 1999. Annual Deaths Attributable to Obesity in the United States. *Journal of the American Medical Association,* 282, 1530–8.

Ayres, J.S. & Silvis, A.H. 2010. Principles of Working Together: Developing Relationships that Support Community Development Initiatives, pp. 155–168. In Robinson, J.W. Jr. & Green, G.P. (eds) *Introduction to Community Development: Theory, Practice and Service-Learning.* Sage, Los Angeles.

Beaumont, J., Lang,T., Leather, S., & Mucklow, C. 1995. *Report from the Policy Sub-Group to the Nutrition Task Force Low Income Project Team of the Department of Health.* Institute of Grocery Distribution: Radlett, Hertfordshire.

Berg, N. & Murdoch, J. 2008. Access to Grocery Stores in Dallas. *International Journal of Behavioural and Healthcare Research,* 1(1), 22–37.

Brown, D.L. & Glasgow, N. 2008. *Rural Retirement Migration.* Springer, New York.

Committee on the Future of Rural Health Care. 2005. *Quality through Collaboration: The Future of Rural Health.* The National Academies Press, Washington, D.C.

Corbett, M. 2007. *Learning to Leave: The Irony of Schooling in a Coastal Community.* Fernwood, Black Point, NS.

Cubberley, E. (1922). *Rural Life and Education: A Study of the Rural–School Problem as a Phase of the Rural–Life Problem.* Boston: Houghton Mifflin.

de Tocqueville, A. 2003. *Democracy in America and Two Essays on America.* (Bevan, G. trans.) Penguin, London.

Department of Health and Human Services (DOHHS). 2003. *Trends in Rural Hospital Closure 1990–2000.* U.S. Department of Health and Human Services, Washington D.C.

DeYoung, A.J. & Howley C.B. 1992. The Political Economy of Rural School Consolidation. *Peabody Journal of Education,* 67, 63–89.

Eppley, K. 2009. Rural Schools and the Highly Qualified Teacher Provision of *No Child Left Behind:* A Critical Policy Analysis. *Journal of Research in Rural Education,* 24(4), 1–11. Retrieved Aug. 24, 2009 from http://jrre.psu.edu/articles/24-4.pdf.

Faircloth, S.C. & Tippeconnic, J. 2010. Tribally Controlled Colleges and Universities: Global Influence and Local Design, pp 174–181. In Schafft, K.A. & Jackson, A. (eds) *Rural Education for the Twenty-First Century* Penn State University Press, . University Park, PA.

Gibbs, R.M. 1998. College Completion and Return Migration Among Rural Youth, pp. 61–80. In

Gibbs, R.M., Swaim, P.L., & Teixeira, R. (eds) *Rural Education and Training in the New Economy.* Iowa State University Press,Ames, IA.

Glasgow, N. 2004. Healthy Aging in Rural America, pp. 271–281. In Glasgow, N., Morton, L.W., & Johnson, N.E. (eds) *Critical Issues in Rural Health.* Blackwell Publishing, Ames, IA.

Glasgow, N., Johnson, N.E., & Morton, L.W. 2004. Introduction, pp. 3–14. In Glasgow, N., Morton, L.W., & Johnson, N.E. (eds) *Critical Issues in Rural Health.* Blackwell Publishing, Ames, IA.

Goetz, S. 2005. Random Variation in Student Performance by Class Size: Implications of NCLB in Rural Pennsylvania. *Journal of Research in Rural Education*, 20(13), 1–8.

Gonzales, A. 2003. American Indians: Their Contemporary Reality and Future Trajectory, pp. 43–56. In Brown, D.L. & Swanson, L.E. (eds) *Challenges for Rural America in the Twenty-First Century.* Penn State Press, University Park, PA.

Green, G.P. & Robinson Jr., J.W. 2010. Emerging Issues in Community Development, pp. 295–302. In Robinson, J.W. Jr. & Green, G.P. (eds) *Introduction to Community Development: Theory, Practice and Service-Learning.* Sage, Los Angeles.

Guthrie, J.W. & Wong, K. 2008. Education Finance from the Perspective of Politics, Political Cultures and Government, pp. 61–77. In Ladd, H.F. & Fiske, E.B. (eds) *Handbook of Research in Education Finance and Policy.* Routledge, New York.

Guy, C.M. & David, G. 2004. Measuring Physical Access to 'Healthy Foods' in Areas of Social Deprivation: A Case Study in Cardiff. *International Journal of Consumer Studies*, 28(3), 222–234.

Haight, W., Jacobsen,T., Black, J., Kingery, L., Sheridan, K., & Mulder, C. 2005. 'In These Bleak Days': Parent Methamphetamine Abuse and Child Welfare in the Rural Midwest. *Children and Youth Services Review*, 27, 949–971.

Harmon, H. & Schafft, K.A. 2009. Rural School Leadership for Collaborative Community Development. *The Rural Educator*, 30(3), 4–9.

Hawley, A. 1950. *Human Ecology.* Ronald Press, New York.

Hektner, J.M. 1995. When Moving up Implies Moving out: Rural Adolescent Conflict in the Transition to Adulthood. *Journal of Research in Rural Education*, 11(1), 3–14.

Holmes, G.M., Slifkin, R.T., Randolph, R.K., & Poley, S. 2006. The Effect of Rural Hospital Closures on Community Economic Health. *Health Research and Educational Trust*, 41(2), 567–585.

Hopkins, J. 2002. *Devolution in Context: Regional, Federal and Devolved Government in the European Union.* Cavendish, London.

Howley, C.B. 1996. Compounding Disadvantage: The Effects of School and District Size on Student Achievement in West Virginia. *Journal of Research in Rural Education*, 12, 1, 25–32.

Howley, C.B., Harmon, H.L., & Leopold, G.D. 1996. Rural Scholars or Bright Rednecks? Aspirations for a Sense of Place among Rural Youth in Appalachia. *Journal of Research in Rural Education*, 12(3), 150–160.

Johnson, J. & Strange, M. 2009. *Why Rural Matters 2009.* Rural School and Community Trust, Arlington, VA.

Jones, C.A., Kandel,W., & Parker, T. 2007. Population Dynamics are Changing the Profile of Rural America. *Amber Waves*, 5(2), 30–35.

Jones, C.A., Parker, T.S., & Ahearn, M. 2009. Taking the Pulse of Rural Health Care. *Amber Waves*, 7(3), 10–15.

Kraybill, D., & Lobao, L. 2001. County Government Survey: Changes and Challenges in the New Millenium. Rural County Governance Center Research Report No. 1. National Association of Counties, Washington, D.C.

Lambert, D. Gale, J.A., & Hartley, D. 2008. Substance Abuse by Youth and Young Adults in Rural America. *Journal of Rural Health*, 24(3), 221–228.

Lee, V.E., Smerdon B.A., Alfeld-Liro, C., & Brown S.L. 2000. Inside Large and Small High Schools: Curriculum and School Relations. *Educational Evaluation and Policy Analysis*, 22(2), 147–171.

Lichter, D.T., McLaughlin, D.K., & Cornwell, G. 1995. Migration and the Loss of Human Resources in Rural America, pp. 235–256. In Beaulieu, L.J. & Mulkey, D. (eds) *Investing in People: The Human Capital Needs of Rural America.* Westview, Boulder, CO.

Lobao, L. & Kraybill, D.S. 2005. The Emerging Roles of County Governments in Metropolitan and Nonmetropolitan Areas: Findings from a National Survey. *Economic Development Quarterly*, 19(3), 245–259.

Lowndes, V. & Sullivan, H. 2008. How Low Can you go? Rationales and Challenges for Neighborhood Governance. *Public Administration*, 86(1), 53–74.

Lyson, T.A. 2002. What does a School Mean to a Community? Assessing the Social and Economic Benefits of Schools to Rural Villages in New York. *Journal of Research in Rural Education*, 17(3), 131–137.

Monk, D.H. & Haller, E.J. 1993. *Organizational Alternatives for Small Rural Schools.* Cornell University Department of Education, Ithaca, NY.

Morland, K., Diez Roux, A.V., & Wing, S. 2006. Supermarkets, other Food Stores, and Obesity: The Atherosclerosis Risk in Communities Study. *American Journal of Preventive Medicine*, 30, 333–339.

Morton, L.W. 2003. Rural Health Policy, pp. 290–302. In Brown, D.L. & Swanson, L.E. (eds) *Challenges for Rural America in the Twenty-First Century.* Penn State Press, University Park, PA.

Morton, L.W. & Blanchard, T.C. 2007. Starved for Access: Life in Rural America's Food Deserts. *Rural Realities*, 1(4), 1–10.

National Advisory Committee on Rural Health and Human Services (NACRHHS). 2008. *The 2008 Report to the Secretary: Rural Health and Human Services Issues.* Office of Rural Health Policy, U.S. Department of Health and Human Services, Washington, D.C.

Nelson, W.A. 2008. The Challenges of Rural Health Care, pp. 34–59. In Klugman, C.M. & Dalinis, P.M. (eds) *Ethical Issues in Rural Health Care.* Johns Hopkins University Press, Baltimore, MD.

Ogden, C.L., Carroll,M.D., Curtin, L.R., McDowell, M.A., Tabak, C.J., & Flegal, K.M. 2006. Prevalence of Overweight and Obesity in the United States, 1999–2004. *Journal of the American Medical Association*, 295, 1549–55.

Provasnik, S., KewalRamani, A., McLaughlin Coleman,M., Gilbertson, L., Herring, W., & Xie, Q. 2007. *Status of Education in Rural America.* U.S. Department of Education National Center for Education Statistics, Washington D.C.

Pruitt, L.R. 2010. Spatial Inequality as Constitutional Infirmity: Equal Protection, Child Poverty and Place. *Montana Law Review*, 71(1), 1–114.

Ricketts, T. 1999. *Rural Health in the United States.* Oxford University Press, New York.

Reding, N. 2009. *Methland: The Death and Life of an American Small Town.* Bloomsbury, New York.

Reeves, C. 2004. *A Decade of Consolidation: Where are the Savings?* Challenge West Virginia, Harts, WV.

Rural School and Community Trust. 2007. *Why Rural Matters 2007: The Realities of Rural Education Growth.* Rural School and Community Trust, Washington D.C.

Schafft, K. 2010. Economics, Community, and Rural Education: Rethinking the Nature of Accountability in the Twenty-First Century, pp. 275–289. In Schafft , K.A. & A. Jackson (eds) *Rural Education for the Twenty-First Century: Identity, Place, and Community in a Globalizing World.* Penn State University Press, University Park, PA.

Schafft, K.A. & Harmon, H.L. 2010. Schools and Community Development, pp. 245–260. In Robinson, J.W. Jr., & Green G.P. (eds) *Introduction to Community Development: Theory, Practice and Service-Learning.* Sage, Los Angeles.

Schafft, K.A., Jensen, E.B., & Hinrichs, C.C. 2009. Food Deserts and Overweight Schoolchildren: Evidence from Pennsylvania. *Rural Sociology*, 74(2), 153–177.

Schmidt, E.L. 2008. Reflections on Fifty Years in Rural Health Care, pp. 99–104. In Klugman, C.M. & Dalinis, P.M. (eds) *Ethical Issues in Rural Health Care.* Johns Hopkins University Press, Baltimore, MD.

Senese, G.B. 1991. *Self-Determination and the Social Education of Native Americans.* Praeger, New York.

Sipple, J.W. & Brent, B.O. 2008. Challenges and Strategies Associated with Rural School Settings, pp. 612–630. In Ladd, H.F. & Fiske, E.B. (eds) *Handbook of Research in Education Finance and Policy.* New York, Routledge.

Smith, C., Butterfass, J., & Richards, R. 2010. Environmental Influences Food Access and Resulting Shopping and Dietary Behaviors among Homeless Minnesotans Living in Food Deserts. *Agriculture and Human Values*, 27, 141–161.

Strange, M. & Malhoit, G. 2005. Bigger isn't Always Better: Why We Should Preserve Small Rural Schools and Districts. *Leadership Insider: Practical Perspectives on School Law and Policy.* October, 2–4.

Theobald, P. 1997. *Teaching the Commons.* Westview, Boulder, CO.

Tyack, D.B. 1972. The Tribe and the Common School: Community Control in Rural Education. *American Quarterly*, 24(1), 3–19.

United States Department of Agriculture (USDA). 2009. *Access to Affordable and Nutritious Food: Measuring and Understanding Food Deserts and their Consequences.*

U.S. Department of Agriculture, Washington, D.C.

Wallace, R.B., Grindeanu, L.A., & Cirillo, D.J. 2004. Rural/Urban Contrasts in Population Morbidity Status, pp. 15–26. In Glasgow, N., Morton, L.W., & Johnson, N.E. (eds) *Critical Issues in Rural Health.* Blackwell Publishing, Ames, IA.

Warner, M. 2003. Competition, Cooperation and Local Governance, pp. 252–261. In Brown, D.L. & Swanson, L.E. (eds) *Challenges for Rural America in the Twenty-First Century.* Penn State Press, University Park, PA.

Warner, M. E. 2009. Civic Government of Market-Based Governance? The Limits of Privatization for Rural Local Governments. *Agriculture and Human Values,* 26(2–3), 133–143.

Warner, M.E. & Pratt, J.E. 2005. Spatial Diversity in Local Government Revenue Effort Under Decentralization: A Neural Network Approach. *Environment and Planning C: Government and Policy,* 23(5), 657–677.

Weiss, J.D. 2004. *Public Schools and Economic Development: What the Research Shows.* KnowledgeWorks Foundation, Cincinnatti, OH.

Wilkinson, K. (1991. *The Rural Community in America.* Greenwood Press, New York.

Yan, W. 2006. *Is Bigger Better? A Comparison of Rural School Districts.* Harrisburg, PA, Center for Rural Pennsylvania

Zekeri, A., Wilkinson, K.P., & Humphry, C.R. 1994. Past Activeness, Solidarity, and Local Development Efforts. *Rural Sociology,* 59(2), 216–235.

Ziller, E.C., Coburn, A.F., Loux, S.L., Hoffman, C., & McBride, T.D. 2003. *Health Insurance Coverage in Rural America.* The Kaiser Commission on Medicaid and the Uninsured, Washington D.C.

Ziller, E., Coburn, A.F., Anderson, N.J., & Loux, S.L. 2008. Uninsured Rural Families. *Journal of Rural Health,* 24(1), 1–11.

5 Natural Resources and Social Change

The economy of communities in rural America, as well as the social and cultural identities of rural people, are bound up in their land and landscapes. Agriculture, as we discuss in Chapter 9, is an obvious example of this intimate relationship, as is the extraction of natural resources in the form of renewable resources, like timber, and non-renewable resources, such as oil, gas and minerals. The social and economic viability of many rural communities in the Western and Midwestern United States is also fundamentally shaped by resource *scarcity* such as water access and availability (Gasteyer 2008), patterns of which are already shifting as a consequence of global climate change (Molnár 2010; Speth 2008). Natural resources within and available to rural localities across multiple geographic and socio-cultural contexts can have tremendous impacts on community structure, local economies, and the ability of communities to adapt to changing local and global conditions.

Moreover, social and economic activities in diverse rural contexts affect environmental quality, and natural resource issues often emerge in sustained debates over public versus private land use and land use change (Glenna 2010; Jackson-Smith 2003). Other communities, though they may vary widely in locality and by type of resource base, similarly struggle with the legacies of resource extraction economies, economies often controlled by outside interests, regardless of whether those communities are Appalachian coal towns or logging towns in the Pacific Northwest (Caudill 1963; Duncan 1999; Erikson 1976; Sherman 2009).

Given this variation in rural contexts, it's unsurprising that beliefs and opinions about environmental issues also vary widely. A study by the Carsey Institute found that 29 percent of rural respondents favored prioritizing job creation over natural resource conservation, while 43 percent believed conservation should be prioritized. This research also shows that community context is strongly associated with environmental beliefs and opinions on environmental issues. For example, people living in poor and declining rural communities were less likely to perceive global warming and urban sprawl as significant issues than their counterparts living in rural areas with rich natural amenities (Dillon & Henly 2008).[1]

These differences in perceptions and beliefs have powerful implications for environmental policies since rural Americans in poor and declining places "may perceive environmental initiatives as the source of, rather than a response to, the economic decline in their communities" (Dillon & Henly 2008: 5). In sum, natural resource economies affect and are affected differently by different growth regimes: e.g., by rapid growth (recreation, tourism and retirement destination areas), chronic decline (agriculturally dependent Great Plains), and boom/bust areas, such as the oil shale energy towns in the American West.

In this chapter we examine how natural resources in rural areas affect and are affected by economic activities, community structure, and community mobilization. We focus on some of rural America's traditional extractive resources such as oil and minerals, but we also examine the role of natural amenities, and how rural landscapes themselves can take on important local resource roles. We also look at new and emerging forms of resource extraction in rural areas, including those associated with "green" technology, such as wind, biofuels, and solar power. Last, we discuss what the future might hold regarding the ways in which natural resources and the environment help shape the social, political, and economic structures of rural communities.

Natural Amenities: An Engine of Growth?

Much of the iconography of rural America is associated with its landscapes and areas rich in natural amenities such as mountains, lakes, rivers and seashores, as well as cultural amenities such as picturesque villages and historical areas. These amenities make rural areas attractive as places to live and work, and create value for recreation and tourism development. In the case of retirement migration, for example, retirees who relocate to amenity-rich rural areas often bring not only financial capital but significant life experience and professional skills, and many retirees relocating to rural areas use their talents in a variety of civic endeavors (Brown & Glasgow 2008).

Tourism-based development may not be realistic for all rural areas with high levels of natural amenities, but research shows that those that have chosen to commodify their amenities in the form of recreation and tourism can expect to benefit through economic growth and population retention (Krannich & Petrzelka 2003). Moreover, amenity-related population growth can directly contribute to the level of human resources in rural areas. Revenues from parks and recreation-based amenities in rural areas fuel the construction of new housing and promote job creation in construction, services, and commercial establishments (Jones, Fly, Talley, & Cordell 2003; McGranahan 1999).

Rasker (2005) notes for example that in the West, with rural economies historically centered around resource extraction, combining wilderness preservation with economic development would seem a contradiction in terms. However, recent proposals in Idaho combine new wilderness area designations with local economic development initiatives. These proposals recognize that rural economies in the West are decreasingly able to depend upon resource extraction as an economic base, and increasingly centered around services and amenity-based development.

The economic and demographic shifts that shape this different approach to rural development in the Western United States have led some to suggest the emergence of a "New West." Winkler and colleagues note:

> The migration of new people into selective locations has contributed to a transformation of the region's small and rural places . . . Second home and condominium developments, and increasingly "trophy home" developments have become more common as both year-round and seasonal residents are drawn to the recreational and aesthetic values of the landscape and the quality-of-life attributes associated with rural settings. (Winkler et al. 2007: 479)

Amenity-based development, however, has the potential for both positive and negative consequences. For example, recreation and tourism-related job creation may be primarily in the form of lower wage service sector work, lacking employee benefits and/or viable career ladders. Moreover, recreation and tourism jobs are often seasonal, leaving some residents unemployed for part of the year.

New arrivals may also create cultural and social tensions that threaten to disrupt the community status quo (Salamon 2003). These conflicts may not necessarily seem serious to outsiders, but they can represent what for many residents are uncomfortable or undesirable changes in community. For example, recreation and retirement based in-migration may stimulate the housing sector, but may also result in the displacement of limited resource persons who were born and raised in the community (Krannich and Petrzelka 2003). Additionally, while research shows that long-term residents of high-growth amenity and outdoor recreation rural areas earn higher wages than their counterparts in other rural areas, cost of living increases in these areas tend to offset the financial benefit associated with increased earnings (Hunter et al. 2005). These changes have not affected all resource-based rural communities in the same ways, and rural sociologists continue to focus research on amenity-based natural resource areas, examining the demographic, economic and cultural shifts that are taking place there, and what these shifts imply for rural people across a wide variety of rural places (Robbins et al. 2009).

Environmental Contexts for Community Development and Conflict

The natural and cultural landscape can play a significant role in shaping community identity (Gottfried 1996), strengthening the connection people feel to the place in which they live (Brehm, Eisenhauer, & Krannich 2004; Cheng, Kruger & Daniels 2003; Tuan 1974). This, in some instances, may provide the basis for community agency and political mobilization. As we discussed in Chapter 3, the role of locality oriented social interaction is one of the principal foundations of rural community structure and change. As Wilkinson (1991) observed:

> Each actor has a real interest in the local aspects of local social life. This interest, which local residents have in common whether or not they experience it consciously, is pursued in social interaction and thus is shared. This particular shared interest that arises in social interaction – the shared interest in things local – gives the elemental bond of the interactional community. (p. 35)

These shared interests, in part shaped by unique sets of cultural, historical and environmental attributes, can be mobilized to strengthen a community's capacity and its ability to promote or constrain change. As Bridger and Alter (2008) explain, community development, from this perspective, entails more than simply the enhancement of economic activity in community, but rather the development of community by "strengthening the relationships between the economic, social, environmental, and political dimensions of local life" (p. 108) and, as a consequence, the strengthening of local problem-solving capacity.

For example, Pavey and colleagues (2007) describe participatory community development efforts in Tennessee centered on natural resource management concerns within the Emory-Obed Watershed. They worked with local residents to describe the relationship between the area's natural resources and its prospects as a place to live and work. Then they used this relationship to articulate a local "community of interest," building community capacity in the process by mobilizing the efforts of local residents. The community group began holding monthly meetings to discuss local change, ultimately developing a grant proposal focused around the development of sustainable agriculture and natural resource activities. Residents interviewed who had taken part in these efforts "indicated that they had gained new ways of perceiving their community, formed new connections to other community members and outside experts, and identified opportunities for action as the community moves forward into the future" (pp. 106–7).

These findings were similar to those by Stedman and colleagues (2009) examining the extent to which community based watershed organizations are able to foster community capacity while simultaneously addressing environmental issues. In a study of twenty-eight rural watershed organizations they found that "Effective groups are more likely to form partnerships and concentrate community involvement, allowing them to adapt and move on to address other issues. As such, they tend to build consensus rather than create conflict" (p. 196).

Participatory community development efforts, however, also entail multiple challenges. These challenges are often organizational in nature, but may easily also emanate from dilemmas connected to internal divisions, power struggles within communities, and/or historical patterns of social exclusion that can derail community level collective or participatory efforts (Prins 2005; Schafft & Greenwood 2003). This is no less true of collective efforts connected to natural resource issues, especially those that raise controversies connected to land use, the distribution of resources and/or the remediation of environmental hazards. These controversies may threaten to *divide* community interests rather than unite them and/or spur local social movements focused on particular environmental issues.

Shriver and Kennedy, for example, describe community conflict in an Oklahoma community with severe environmental contamination resulting from nearly a century of zinc and lead mining. While it might seem reasonable to assume that dangerous environmental conditions confronting an entire locality would provide a catalyst for increased community solidarity, "a common feature of contaminated communities," they write, "is the emergence of competing factions . . . in some communities citizen groups emerge to challenge the local power structure . . . while in other cases the community groups are pitted against one another" (2005: 492).[2] This is often the case because of multiple uncertainties over the severity of the environmental and health risks (since in many cases environmental contamination may be invisible to the casual observer), and the way in which environmental conflicts may pit the concerns of residents against the interests of local economic concerns such as employment and property values.

In the case described by Shriver and Kennedy, the community of Picher, Oklahoma was divided over a proposal from the Oklahoma Governor to relocate the entire community and convert the area into a wetland, after $100 million in remediation efforts had failed to significantly reduce the contamination. The proposal created bitter and unresolved dilemmas within the community between factions that were strongly in favor of a buyout and relocation, and factions that downplayed the environmental hazards, framing the possibility of relocation as a violation of personal and property rights. Ultimately, the environmental problems in Picher were concluded to be so severe that a $60 million federal buyout began in May, 2006, and by 2010 Picher had essentially become a ghost town.[3] Similar debates, however, are ongoing in Treece, Kansas, a town just across the state line from Picher, which did not receive federal buyout funding, even though it too is similarly contaminated.

Farming and Urban Development

There has been considerable concern in the United States over what is often seen as the inherent conflict between agriculture and urban development. In fact, in the late 1970s President Jimmy Carter commissioned a National Agricultural Lands Study (NALS) to examine the extent to which urban expansion was resulting in farm land conversion, thereby compromising the nation's ability to provide for its domestic food and fiber needs, and export agricultural commodities globally (Lehman 1990; USDA and President's Council on Environmental Quality 1981). While farm land preservation groups like the American Farm Land Trust framed this situation as a national environmental emergency, the NALS research staff produced convincing evidence that only a modest amount of crop and pasture land was being converted to urban and built up uses. Moreover, their research showed that the rate of growth of the number of households at the time was sufficiently low that demands for residential construction, while considerable (and especially in the peripheries of growing cities), would not compromise agricultural production capacity. Additionally, since most major land using infrastructure such as railroads, the interstate highway system and major airports were already in place, immense amounts of new land would not be required (Brown et al. 1982).[4] Subsequent research over the last twenty-five years has supported these findings and the conclusion that farm land conversion is not a major problem overall, even if it may be in particular locations. Research by the USDA's Economic Research Service shows that urban and built up uses have remained stable over recent decades, accounting for about four percent of total land use (Nickerson 2005). Cropland, pastureland and forestland have also been steady during this period accounting for approximately 23 percent, 31 percent, and 30 percent of total land use respectively (Nickerson 2005).[5]

Even though agricultural land conversion is not a major environmental problem in the aggregate, disagreements over land use can lead to conflict at the local level. The basic conflict is between persons and groups who value land for its intrinsic uses such as agriculture, open space, wildlife habitat and recreation (use value), and interests that value land for profit that can be made when it is bought and sold for development (exchange value). As Molotch and Logan (1987) observed, conflict over land use often exposes fundamental inequalities within urban society since use value advocates are often over matched by the better organized "growth machine," the coalition of builders, bankers, insurance companies, and land speculators who promote the idea that urban development serves widespread social needs. While their conclusions are still somewhat controversial, Molotch and Logan contended that the benefits of urban development mostly accrue to the growth machine, and are seldom widely distributed throughout the community. Moreover, because the growth machine often controls local government and local media, their strong influence over these community institutions often results in land use policies that do not reflect the public's will.

Resource Extraction as a Social Process

While much of rural America has been shaped by histories of resource extraction, a big part of this story is the extent to which rural environments, communities and people have been dependent upon outside economic interests that provide the capital and resources with which to extract and process natural resources such as coal, gas, timber or mineral resources (England & Brown 2003). This relative degree of control by interests internal or external to areas of pronounced natural resource extraction is variable. However, some scholars suggest that a model of *internal colonial dependency* is useful for understanding communities and regions characterized by extreme dependency and resource exploitation. Internal colonial dependency theory is closely tied to understandings of national – and global – economies having "core" areas, typically established metropolitan areas functioning as the center of political, cultural and economic power, and peripheral areas that are politically and economically subordinate.

In this model, areas peripheral to national and/or international centers of economic and political power are exploited for their natural resources with little of the generated wealth returning to promote development of the peripheral areas. In the process, raw materials are extracted by outside interests who utilize local labor for the main extractive activity. The resource (along with the wealth generated by value-added processing) is then removed from the region to the benefit of the controlling outside interest. Under these circumstances *local* political and economic control is limited. Often in its place patronage systems proliferate (Duncan 1999), economies remain undiversified and underdeveloped, poverty is widespread as, often, is environmental degradation from the resource extraction. Outside interests often frame environmental problems as an acceptable trade-off for the generation of local economic activity, and/or minerals or energy necessary for national economic growth. However, those interests do not have to live with the longer-term consequences of environmental degradation (as in the examples of Picher, Oklahoma and Treece, Kansas) or the boom-bust cycles often associated with resource extraction economies (Caudill 1963; Marshall 2002; Walls & Billings 1977; White 1998).

Boomtowns and Bust Cycles

England and Brown (2003) note that resource extraction as a social process tends to consist of three distinct developmental phases.[6] The first is a build-out phase in which the infrastructure to extract, refine and/or process the resource, such as the construction of drilling rigs, and processing facilities is developed and established. This initial phase demands considerable labor power associated with the development of the infrastructure. At this point in the process there is often a considerable influx of workers, often unattached single men, working long hours, most of whom will stay only as long as the labor is needed. Local businesses and community infrastructure including housing, restaurants, stores, and services may also undergo considerable expansion to meet the needs of newcomers.

The second phase, argue England and Brown, is operational, in which workers from the initial build-out are no longer needed. The strain on local infrastructure eases, but that may also be accompanied by declines in the demand for local goods and services. This phase continues until the resource is depleted to the extent that extraction activities are no longer economically viable. At this point the extraction activity radically contracts or shuts down. Workers lose jobs and move elsewhere. Others retire, and the community experiences sharp economic contractions as unemployment increases, incomes diminish, housing and property values drop, and services and infrastructure built for a larger population are no longer economical to operate. In places where undiversified economies are overwhelmingly dependent upon resource extraction, these development phases, if not managed properly to foster longer-term sustainable economic development, can easily result in the phenomena of boomtowns and bust cycles.

Boomtowns are places that experience rapid population growth, typically associated with mining or some other form of resource extraction.[7] In the American West, boomtowns have perhaps most often been associated with the Gold Rush in the mid nineteenth century in which thousands of small towns sprang up nearly overnight as prospectors flooded westward looking for mineral wealth. The Gold Rush transformed San Francisco from a small port town prior to 1840 into a major metropolitan area with over 150,000 people by 1870. Other Gold Rush towns, however, faded quickly once the rush was over, leaving hundreds of abandoned "ghost towns" in isolated parts of California, Nevada, Montana, Colorado, Alaska, and other places (many of which, ironically, are now tourist destinations).

Boomtowns, as an economic and sociological phenomenon, caught the attention of social scientists in the 1970s and 1980s when hundreds of small communities in the West experienced rapid growth as sudden spikes in energy prices led to the exploration and development of new energy sources. In these communities, often in isolated, rural areas with extractable resources such as coal, natural gas, uranium and/or oil shale, rural people found themselves confronted not only with significant economic opportunities, but also considerable challenges.

Early boomtown literature hypothesized a strong relationship between the influx of outsiders to a community and an increase in social problems and disruptions including public disturbances, drug and alcohol abuse and strain on local governments and social services. In one of the earliest examinations of the boomtown phenomenon, Kohrs described the social change in Gillette, a Wyoming boomtown:

> Divorce, tensions on children, emotional damage and alcoholism were the result. Children went to school in double shifts; hotels turned over linens in triple-shifts. Jails became crowded and police departments experienced frequent changes in personnel in the tradition of frontier justice. Out of frustration with the quality of

> living, it appeared that mayors shuttled in and out of office regardless of party like bobbins in a loom. (1974: 3)

More recent work has suggested that many of the negative consequences of the "boom" phase may be exaggerated (Hunter et al. 2002). In fact, much of the disruption often appears to occur prior to the arrival of the "boom," and is associated with internal divisions within the boomtown community itself as residents split into factions in the face of anticipated changes that would appear to threaten the nature of the community (Brown et al. 1989; Krannich et al. 1985). On the other hand, a significant amount of research suggests that economic impacts are not spread evenly across communities, economic sectors or local residents. As Jacquet (2009) notes, building out physical and institutional infrastructure such as housing, social and governmental services and retail during the boom phase creates long-term planning dilemmas.

> Providing the foundation for long-term economic development requires attracting companies and sectors unrelated to the energy industry, which in turn requires government investment in housing, infrastructure, and services during the boom times to make the community attractive to these companies. An ideal situation would entail the attraction of non-energy development companies precisely during the time of the energy-industry downturn, a situation that would be difficult if not impossible to engineer on a consistent basis. (Jacquet 2009: 24)

Effective community planning in the context of boomtown development scenarios, in short, poses substantial challenges when local communities lack adequate planning capacity and when development activity is centered around maximizing short-term returns on efforts rather than devising strategies that might leverage the economic "boom" as a springboard for sustainable and longer-term development.

New Forms of Resource Extraction: Generating Green and Renewable Energy

In April 2010, a deep water offshore oil rig run by British Petroleum exploded in the Gulf of Mexico, killing eleven workers and producing what has since become the largest oil spill in U.S. history. This catastrophe comes at a time in which there is increasing recognition that current global energy consumption patterns (and especially those of developed countries) are unsustainable given depleted fossil fuel resources, the increasing difficulty, costs and risks of extraction, and the threat of global climate change as a consequence of human-produced greenhouse gases. Many scientists believe that "peak oil" has already been reached – the point at which global oil production begins to inexorably decline because of deleted oil fields and the difficulty and costs of extracting oil from alternate sources such as coal and tar sands. And yet the global economy, from transportation to manufacturing to agriculture, is utterly dependent at this time on fossil fuel (Lerch 2007). Because of this, it is hardly surprising that oil exploration is taking place in increasingly risky and challenging circumstances, such as deep water drilling. It is also hardly surprising that there is rapidly increasing interest in the development of alternative and renewable energy sources, such as wind and

Box 5.1 The Case of Marcellus Shale – Implications for Rural and Regional Development?

Marcellus Shale, an enormous layer of shale rock approximately one mile beneath the earth's surface, extends from New York's Southern Tier, through the western half of Pennsylvania and into Ohio and West Virginia (see Figure 5.1). As late as 2002, the U.S. Geologic Survey estimated that the Marcellus formation contained 1.9 trillion cubic feet (TCF) of natural gas. In 2009, as a consequence of the development of new drilling and extraction technologies, that estimate rose to 2,445 TCF with potentially as much as 489 TCF estimated as recoverable (Considine et al. 2009). The significance of these estimates is profound given that in 2008 the domestic consumption of natural gas in the United States was only 23.2 TCF (U.S. Energy Information Administration 2009).

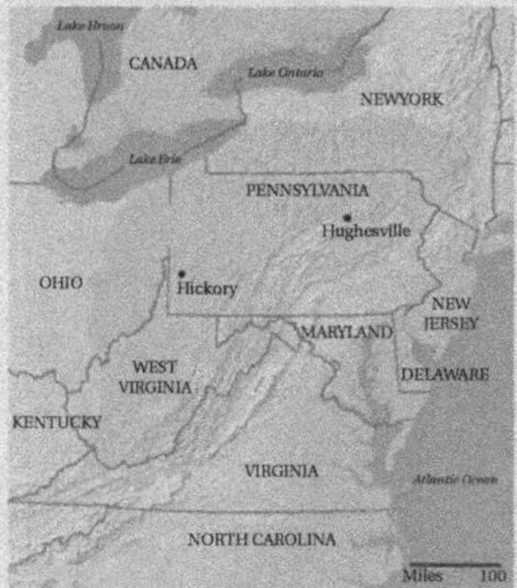

Source: Penn State Marcellus Initiative for Outreach and Research

Figure 5.1 Extent of Marcellus Shale Coverage

Small-scale drilling in Marcellus Shale has occurred for decades with rigs boring vertical wells into the shale bed that intersect with horizontal fractures in the formation where the gas is contained. In the early 2000s, however, advances in drilling technology enabled rigs to drill deep into the shale layer and then to drill horizontally along fracture lines. The gas is recovered using a technique called *hydro-fracturing* in which large quantities of water, sand, and chemicals are forced into the well, causing the shale layers to break apart along fracture lines, while sand in the fracturing fluid holds the fractures open. This enables gas, previously trapped within the shale, to flow into the well and from there to the surface. Although this type of drilling is more expensive than earlier vertical wells, it is a far more effective means of natural gas recovery (Considine et al. 2009; Jacquet 2009).

Horizontal drilling in the Marcellus region is still in its beginning stages. Even so, it is rapidly expanding. The Pennsylvania Department of Environmental Protection in 2008 issued 476 permits for drilling in the Marcellus formation and 195 wells were drilled. In 2009, however, 1,984 permits were issued and 763 wells were drilled. In Pennsylvania in 2008 alone, 14,000 new jobs were created through Marcellus development with another 15,000 new jobs created in secondary economic sectors associated with the new development and influx of workers. By 2020 Marcellus-related development could contribute $13.5 billion to the state's economy (Considine

Box 5.1 (continued)

et al. 2009). Most of the development is taking place in rural and poorer parts of the state, and many landowners have already found themselves suddenly wealthy as they sell drilling leases to gas companies for many thousands of dollars per acre in addition to percentage fees for gas recovered from the wells.

What lessons from the boomtown literature can be applied to the Marcellus region? Jacquet notes that "the boomtown experience is in many ways dependent on the ability of a community to absorb a population influx relative to a community's base population" (2009: 52). Most of the literature of the 1970s and 80s focused on Western boomtown areas characterized by small and geographically isolated towns. While much of the Marcellus region is rural and small town, populations are not as geographically dispersed as in Western states and so absorbing new populations may be more manageable. At the same time, there will undoubtedly be additional strains on local governments and services and infrastructure such as roads, bridges, sewers, and water supply.

One area of potential conflict involves the rights of individual landowners versus the broader impacts on communities and the environment. Landowners able to sell leasing rights stand to make significant amounts of money and therefore are likely to support gas development both on their own land as well as within their communities more broadly. In some places landowners have joined together to collectively bargain with gas companies for leasing rights. However, this will unquestionably produce new inequalities and it is not clear how much of the new wealth will remain within these communities. In particular, the increased demand for housing may result in price inflations that will displace lower income persons and those on fixed incomes.

Some of the greatest concerns are environmental. Each well throughout its operation requires between two and ten million gallons of water, all of which must be trucked onto the site. In total, between development of the well site, construction of the drill rig and the trucking of water onto and off the site and the final remediation of the site will range from an estimated 5,650 to 8,505 truckloads (NYSDEC 2009) contributing to noise, air pollution, and wear on local roads, many of which were not designed for heavy trucks. Drilling a mile or more beneath the ground, the Marcellus wells are far deeper than the water table, and the drill shafts are lined with concrete to prevent accidental contamination of groundwater. However, 30-70 percent of the fracturing fluid returns to the surface where it must be treated to remove salts and toxins from the fracturing compounds as well as radioactive materials also contained in the shale beds.[8] All of the used fracturing fluid must be removed from the site to water treatment facilities before it can be returned to the environment. While gas developers point out that hydro-fracturing has been used for decades and that these techniques can be used with little adverse environmental impacts, citizens and public interest groups have noted multiple environmental violations by gas developers including illegal dumping of fracturing fluid and drill slurry.[9]

For instance, residents of Dimock, Pennsylvania in 2009 introduced a lawsuit against Cabot Oil & Gas Corporation claiming that natural gas drilling has contaminated groundwater and reduced property values. A similar lawsuit was brought against another gas company in Southwestern Pennsylvania, citing changes between baseline and post-drilling residential well water quality such that post-drilling arsenic in well

Box 5.1 (continued)

water was 2,600 times above the federally acceptable level, benzene 44 times and naphthalene five times (Hurdle 2009a; 2009b).

Development in the Marcellus Shale region of Pennsylvania and New York is in its beginning stages, but it will have profound social, economic, and environmental effects on the region, especially on rural communities. In particular, state and local governments will need to take proactive steps to accommodate new populations and adequately provide services, ensure that there is sufficient oversight to minimize environmental risks, and manage the economic development so that once the natural resource is gone communities and regions are able to transition in economically sustainable ways.

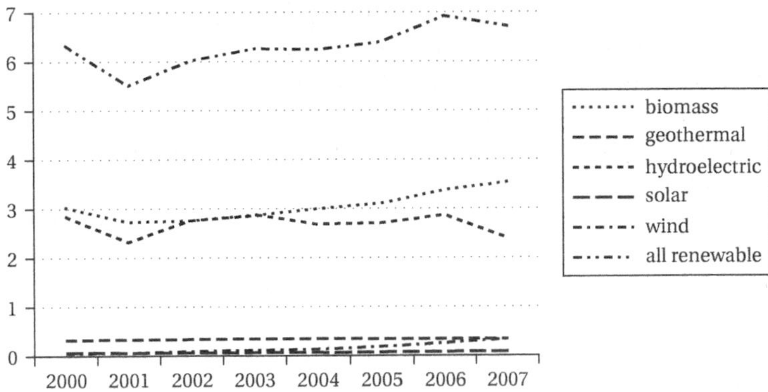

Source: Energy Information Administration, Renewable and Alternative Fuels Data

Figure 5.2 U.S. Renewable Energy Consumption, 2000–2007

solar power, geothermal energy and biomass, much of which can be produced in rural areas and therefore has direct implications for rural economy, society and environment. As of 2007 renewable energy accounted for slightly less than 7 percent of the U.S. energy consumption. This reflects a generally steady, though modest increase since the early 2000s, with most increases in the use of biomass derived energy, in particular from biofuels (see Figure 5.2).

Biofuels and Ethanol Production

Biofuels in the U.S. consist of ethanol produced from corn, although ethanol is also widely produced from sugar cane, as is the case in Brazil. As of 2007 in the U.S. there were nearly 130 ethanol facilities, producing nearly 7 billion gallons of ethanol per year, most of which is used to mix with gasoline (Carolan 2009). While biofuels have long been promoted as a means of reducing reliance on fossil fuels (Carolan 2009), and more recently as a way of reducing greenhouse gas emissions (Simon 2007), increases in biofuel production have had unintended negative consequences (Patel 2008; Richter 2010). Global surges in food prices and food insecurity occurred as agricultural production was reoriented away from food crop production and into biofuel crop production. Food prices increased 75 percent between 2005 and 2008, sparking global food riots, with wheat prices increasing 50 percent, prices for rice rising 70 percent, and a doubling in the cost of maize, signaling what some observers termed a new "post-food-surplus era" (McMichael 2009: 32). Research suggests that 60–70 percent of the price increases in corn and as much as 40 percent of price increases in soybeans can be attributed to biofuel production (Headley & Fan 2008).

Further, ethanol production, especially from corn, is not terribly efficient. Energy inputs needed to produce the ethanol comprise about 90 percent of the energy content of the final biofuel. Similarly, as Nersesian points out, not only does ethanol production affect food availability and prices, but it has "only a marginal impact on greenhouse gases since the savings in carbon emissions from corn ethanol is about equal to the carbon emissions of fossil fuels consumed in growing and processing corn and distributing ethanol" (2010: 381–2). Further, there is a mismatch between current levels of fuel consumption and the amount of corn-based ethanol that can currently be produced. Figures show that even if all domestic corn production in 2005 was devoted towards ethanol, it would still only yield enough biofuel to supply less than 15 percent of vehicle fuel use in the U.S. (Kleinschmidt 2007). For these reasons, the enthusiasm for corn-based ethanol has waned since the early 2000s and the Obama administration, while still allocating substantial support and subsidies for ethanol production, terms ethanol as a "transitional fuel" rather than the answer to eliminating fossil fuel dependence (Little 2009).

More promising forms of domestic ethanol production may ultimately involve cellulosic ethanol produced from materials such as wood processing residues, agricultural waste and special field crops such as switch grass (Solomon & Luzadis 2009). However, at this time there is insufficient technology to make large-scale production of cellulosic ethanol feasible (Nersesian 2010; Halvorsen, Barnes, & Solomon 2009). While the technological challenges are not insurmountable, Carolan (2009) points out that infrastructure build out and capital investments on the production end of ethanol have so far been oriented around corn and sugar cane.

> The process by which cellulose is converted to sugars, then to ethanol, is more complex and thus more expensive than that used to derive ethanol from corn. Any shift, therefore, away from corn-based ethanol would require a major retooling of today's ethanol plants, which will soon number in the hundreds . . . the economic reality now, for example, of owning a $100,000 combine with corn and soybean heads – and the supporting infrastructure these commodities require (e.g., storage and drying facilities) – is such that these capital investments make it very difficult for an operator to diversify or switch to raising different commodities. (2009: 98)

Because of this, Carolan (2009) argues that the current biofuel industry in the U.S. may be constrained by a "path dependency" in which previous investments and infrastructure development favor certain types of further development (in this case, in the U.S., corn-based ethanol production) and constrain others (cellulosic ethanol production).

Wind Power

Although currently the percentage of domestic power derived from wind energy is relatively low, the U.S. Department of Energy proposes using wind power to supply 20 percent of U.S. energy by 2030, and funding provided by the American Recovery and Reinvestment Act of 2009 has significantly contributed to the expansion of wind power development. In 2009 more wind power infrastructure was installed in the U.S. than in any previous year, resulting in sufficient energy generation capacity to supply power to 2.4 million homes. Wind power contributed $17 billion to the U.S. economy and employed 85,000 people in 2009 (U.S. Department of Energy 2008; 2010).

Some wind power generation is done offshore (see Box 5.2 for example), however, offshore wind farms are more expensive to construct and maintain and therefore represent a relatively small proportion of all wind power generation (Richter 2010). Instead, the majority of wind farms are on land with over half of new turbines installed in 2009 in Texas, Indiana, and Idaho (U.S. Department of Energy 2010). Figure 5.3 shows a simplified map of average wind speeds across the continental U.S. Ideal places for wind farms are those areas where there are steady winds at moderate speeds, such as in the Midwest. Both variable wind speeds and wind speeds that are too high risk damaging wind turbines (Richter 2010).

Wind farms have been identified as an additional driver of rural economic development. For example, ranchers and other landowners in areas where wind

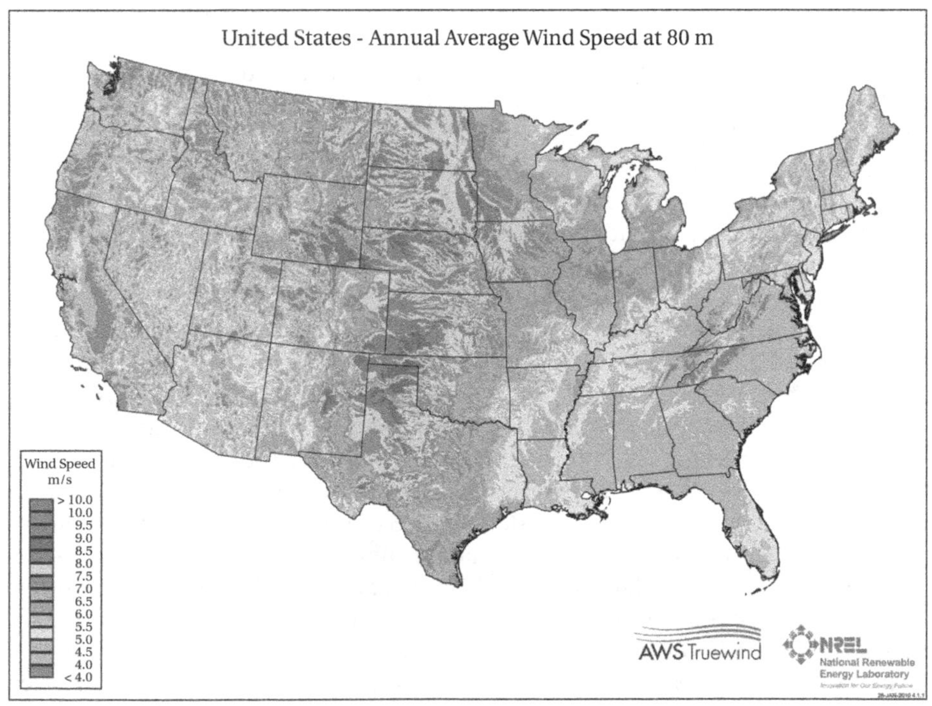

Source: http://www.windpoweringamerica.gov/pdfs/wind_maps/us_windmap_80meters.pdf

Figure 5.3 United States Wind Map

power generation is feasible can lease land for wind turbine installation for between 2–3 percent of gross revenues, with royalties of about $2,000 per year per turbine. Property tax payments from large-scale wind power projects added $4.6 million in annual tax revenue to Pecos County, Texas in 2002, $2 million in Prowers County, Colorado, and $1.2 million for a stateline project on the border of Oregon and Washington (U.S. Department of Energy 2004).

Wind energy is attractive given that the resource (wind) is free, renewable, and, once constructed and installed, turbines generate no greenhouse gases. Technological advances have increased both the efficiency and the energy generating potential of turbines. However, wind power generation comes with its own set of challenges. Wind turbines can disrupt the landscape of natural areas. Some concern has been expressed by environmentalists about the possible effects of turbines on bird and bat mortality, especially in migration throughway areas. Another challenge for large-scale development of wind energy is that many areas with the most potential for wind power generation are also far removed from population centers, and because of this any significant development would need to be accompanied by a power grid buildout in order to move energy to where it is most needed (Nersesian 2010; Richter 2010).

Solar and Geothermal Energy

Solar energy generation has many parallels to wind power, and poses similar challenges and opportunities for rural communities and environments. Its power source (the sun) is free and renewable (although like wind, as a power source it is intermittent and can only be generated during daylight hours). Like wind power too, areas where utility-scale energy generation is possible, like in the Southwest,[10] are often somewhat distant from population centers where the energy is needed. The two main types of solar energy systems are solar thermal systems which heat water to run generating turbines and/or for various industrial and commercial processes, and photovoltaic systems that convert sunlight directly into electricity (Nersesian 2010; Richter 2010). One of the main drawbacks to solar energy is its cost. At present solar photovoltaic energy costs just under $3 per kilowatt hour (kWh) and solar thermal just over $2 per kWh, as compared to wind (at under 90 cents per kWh) and coal (at less than 50 cents per kWh) (Richter 2010). This does not mean that solar power does not constitute an important alternative energy source, but that at a utility-scale level its promise at this point is limited.

Geothermal energy uses the heat contained within the earth as an energy source. Sources of geothermal energy are generally limited to areas where porous hot rock has contact with ground water. By 2005 there were nearly 500 geothermal plants in the United States, generating about nine gigawatts of electricity, or the rough equivalent of nine large coal fired or nuclear plants. The cost of geothermal energy production is competitive with other sources of energy, but large-scale production is limited, and currently most utility-scale production in the United States is located in Nevada and California. Both solar and geothermal power, however, have been promoted, on smaller scales, as alternative energy sources for farms and residences, using geothermal heat pumps and residential and small-scale solar energy systems.

Box 5.2 Green Energy: From "NIMBY" to "BANANA"

Green technology and the possibilities for clean, renewable energy like wind or solar power are attractive on a number of levels, from reducing greenhouse gases and decreasing reliance on fossil fuels, to job creation and rural economic development. Historically, energy development installations such as nuclear and coal fired electricity plants have generated the strongest "NIMBY" (Not In My Backyard) responses from local residents who see these plants as threats to health and safety. However, while green energy is seen as safer and more environmentally friendly, it too generates NIMBY responses (Wolsink 2010; van der Horst 2007).

An example of vocal and ongoing opposition to wind power has been in Massachusetts to the proposed development of a wind farm in the Nantucket Sound five miles off the coast of Cape Cod. This installation would involve the erection of 130 turbines across twenty-four square miles of water, and would supply as much as 75 percent of the energy used on Cape Cod. Members of the Wampanoag, an American Indian nation with reservation land on Martha's Vineyard, objected to the development of the wind farm because they argued the wind turbines would disrupt the tribe's traditional morning sun greeting, an important spiritual practice for tribal members. They further argued that the turbines would disturb ancestral tribal lands and burial grounds. In order to prevent the building of the wind farm, the Wampanoag pressed the National Park Service to list the Nantucket Sound on the National Registry of Historic Places. In January, 2010, the National Park Service decided in favor of the Wampanoag. This decision may further delay development of the wind farm, already in the planning stages for about nine years, although its ultimate construction seems increasingly likely given the plan's approval by U.S. Interior Secretary Ken Salazar in April, 2010. The outcome of this conflict is significant because it establishes a precedent for other bodies of water (where wind farms could be sited) to receive similar designations, disrupting or preventing other green energy projects (Ball 2009; Wirzbicki & Daley 2010).

Solar energy also generates public opposition. California has set a goal of producing 20 percent of its energy by 2020 through renewable energy sources. Although a number of large-scale solar energy projects have already been constructed in Southern California's Mohave Desert, these projects and proposals for others have met stiff opposition from lawmakers and environmental groups who argue that the solar collectors and transmission lines would damage pristine and delicate desert environments. The controversy has led one renewable energy developer to suggest that NIMBY may not be the most appropriate acronym with regard to green energy development. Rather, he contends that BANANA: *Build Absolutely Nothing Anywhere Near Anyone* (Stone 2010) is perhaps more accurate.

Alternative energy has recently been proposed as a means of supporting rural development in Indian Country. Over 14 percent of residents on Indian reservations lack access to electricity, as compared to just over two percent of the population as a whole. And yet Indian tribes own and manage nearly five percent of the total U.S. landmass, an area that contains an estimated ten percent of the country's energy resources. There are already some promising examples of alternative energy generation on reservation lands.

The Campo Kumeyaay Nation, for example, in 2005 completed a 60 megawatt, 25 turbine wind farm, with plans for a second 160 megawatt windfarm in 2010. In Arizona the Hualapai tribe has installed photovoltaic generators to power its water pipeline, and the tribe is currently pursuing plans to build a utility-scale solar energy project. Last, the Confederated Tribes of Warm Springs in Oregon uses geothermal energy for its resort and casino, saving $400,000 annually on heating costs (National Wildlife Federation 2010). As fuel prices rise, alternative energy sources, such as those described above, will likely become increasingly important in rural areas as a means of supplying energy, but also as a source of local revenue and of "green" jobs.

Conclusions

The development and extraction of natural resources in nearly every instance involves some degree of conflict over the control of resources, the rights of local communities and residents, and private interests versus public goods. Perhaps the most obvious example of this is the legacy of resource extraction in Appalachia and other areas where there have been bitter, longstanding and ongoing conflicts between outside economic interests and local communities, frequently creating or exacerbating internal divisions within communities based on race, class and/or political privilege (Caudill 1963; Duncan 1999; Erikson 1976; Richard & Brod 2004). However, conflicts can occur in multiple ways and across multiple contexts, as we have observed with regard to green technologies and the extraction of alternative energy sources in rural areas. These conflicts can concern not only local control and impacts on local economies but other issues as well, including those associated with cultural identities, the interests and values of "newcomers" versus "old-timers," economic growth versus environmental protection, the visual integrity of rural landscapes, and also conflicts at far broader scales such as, in the case of biofuels, the demand for new energy sources versus the imperative for global food security. These conflicts are not easily resolved and have not only economic and environmental dimensions, but deep moral and ethical dimensions as well.

Aside from conflict associated with natural resource development, a second major theme implicit in this chapter is uncertainty. In rural communities dependent upon the extraction of non-renewable resources such as oil and gas – and even renewable resources such as timber and fisheries (Sherman 2009; Constance & Bonnano 2009), there is uncertainty about how long the resource will be able to provide an economic base, how communities will transition socially and economically throughout the process of the resource extraction, and whether communities will be able to maintain social, economic and even environmental viability once the extractive activity is completed. There is also uncertainty regarding the effects of changing technology on exploitable resources, as we have seen in the case of natural gas bearing Marcellus shale, most of which, until a few years ago, was considered inaccessible, or in the case of deep water oil drilling which, as in the case of the oil spill in the Gulf of Mexico, has made the access to new energy reserves possible, but at a profoundly high social and environmental price.

Perhaps the greatest uncertainty of the twenty-first century is connected to the inevitable changes occurring as a consequence of global climate change, coupled with the rising demand for increasingly scarce energy sources (Dunlap 2010; McKibben 2010; Molnár 2010; Speth 2008). Global climate change will have dramatic effects on food security and natural resource demands as temperature and seasonal rainfall patterns shift and terrestrial and aquatic ecosystems change. Many other sectors will be affected as well, almost certainly in ways we are still unable to fully comprehend. Both nationally and internationally the effects of climate change will not be evenly spread, and already vulnerable populations will be disproportionately at risk of experiencing the effects of adverse climatic events, as well as threats to livelihood and food security (Nagel, Dietz, & Broadbent 2009). These changes will likely reshape debates around natural resources as well as the role of extractive activities in rural areas.

Rural sociologists and other rural scholars will need to pay close attention to these changes, engaging with scholars across the social and physical sciences as well as with policy-makers and rural people and communities (Dunlap 2010). This work will be critical as a means of documenting what these changes mean for rural people, communities, landscapes and ecosystems. But more importantly, it will play a key role in the extent to which we can identify both the vulnerabilities and resiliencies of rural areas, and, to the extent possible, minimize the risks associated with climate and community change, and identify opportunities, such as the development of alternative energy sources, that can help not only rural but *global* societies adapt to the profound social and environmental shifts to come.

Notes

1 The study also notes that environmental attitudes are strongly associated with religious belief and denominational affiliation, and that combinations of residence and religious belief are especially powerful in predicting environmental opinions. In particular, the study notes that born-again Christians in economically declining rural communities are least likely to perceive environmental threat (Dillon & Henly 2008).

2 For a further illuminating example from an international perspective, see Gille's (2000) fascinating case study of community conflict generated by the proposed siting of a hazardous waste incinerator in a rural Hungarian community.

3 In January, 2010, The History Channel broadcast an episode of its show, *Life Without People*, focused on Picher to document the deterioration of physical infrastructure once communities are no longer inhabited and maintained.

4 This study and many others, however, have found that farm land conversion can be a problem in particular places, especially those with particular climactic or soil characteristics.

5 These figures are for the lower 48 states. They are 19%, 26%, and 29% for all states.

6 This can be considered especially the case for non-renewable resource extraction, although even renewable resources development, such as wind and solar power, can have distinct "build out" phases.

7 Many small towns in the South and Midwest have also experienced population "booms" associated with the establishment of meat-processing plants attracting immigrant labor, a phenomenon we discuss in greater detail in Chapter 7.

8 Chemicals used in the fracturing fluid are proprietary secrets and not made publicly available. Therefore it is difficult to assess the extent of the toxicity of the fracturing fluid chemicals.

9 See, for example, www.shaleshock.org or www.nofrackingway.com.

10 Eight of the thirteen largest solar thermal power plants in the world are located in rural areas in the American Southwest, five of them in the Mohave Desert in Southern California (Nersesian 2010).

References

Ball, J. 2009. Renewable Energy, Meet the new NIMBYs. Sept. 4. *Wall Street Journal.* Accessed Jan. 15, 2010 at: http://online.wsj.com.

Brehm, J.M., Eisenhauer, B. W., & Krannich, R. S. 2004. Dimensions of Community Attachment and their Relationship to Wellbeing in the Amenity-Rich Rural West. *Rural Sociology,* 69(3), 405–429.

Bridger, J. C. & Alter, T. R. 2008. An Interactional Approach to Place-Based Rural Development. *Community Development,* 39(1), 99–111.

Brown, R. B., Dorius, S. F., & Krannich, R. S. 2005. The Boom-Bust Recovery Cycle: Dynamics of Change in Community Satisfaction and Social Integration in Delta, Utah. *Rural Sociology,* 70(1), 28–49.

Brown, D. L. & N. Glasgow. 2008. *Rural Retirement Migration.* Dordrecht, Springer.

Brown, D. L., Brewer, M., Boxley, R., & Beale, C. 1982. "Assessing Prospects for the Adequacy of Agricultural Land in the United States." *International Regional Science Review,* 7(3), 257–284.

Brown, R. B., Geersten, H. R., & Krannich, R. S. 1989. Community Satisfaction and Social Integration in A Boomtown: A Longitudinal Analysis. *Rural Sociology,* 54(4), 568–586.

Carolan, M. S. 2009) A Sociological Look at Biofuels: Ethanol in the Early Decades of the Twentieth Century and Lessons for Today. *Rural Sociology,* 74(1), 86–112.

Caudill, H. M. 1963. *Night comes to the Cumberlands: A Biography of a Depressed Area.* Boston, Little, Brown & Company.

Cheng, A. S., Kruger, L. E., & Daniels, S. F. 2003. Place as an Integrating Concept in Natural Resource Politics: Propositions for a Social Science Research Agenda. *Society and Natural Resources,* 16, 87–104.

Considine, T., Watson, R., Entler, R., & Sparks, J. 2009. An Emerging Giant: Prospects and Economic Impacts of the Marcellus Natural Gas Play. July 24. The Pennsylvania State University , College of Earth and Mineral Sciences. University Park, PA. (report).

Constance, D. & Bonnano, A. 2009. Contested Terrain of the Global Fisheries: "Dolphin-Safe" Tuna, The Panama Declaration, and the Marine Stewardship Council. *Rural Sociology,* 64(4), 597–623.

Dillon, M. & Henly, M. 2008. *Religion, Politics, and the Environment in Rural America.* Carsey Institute Issue Brief No. 3, Fall. Durham, NC, The Carsey Institute.

Duncan, C. M. 1999. *Worlds Apart: Why Poverty Persists in Rural America.* New Haven, Yale University Press.

Dunlap, R. E. 2010. Climate Change and Rural Sociology: Broadening the Research Agenda. *Rural Sociology,* 75(1), 17–27.

England, L. & Brown, R. 2003. Community and Resource Extraction in Rural America, pp. 317–328. In Brown, D.L. & Swanson, L.E. (eds) *Challenges for Rural America in the Twenty-First Century.* University Park, PA, Penn State Press.

Erikson, K.T. 1976. *Everything in its Path: Destruction of Community in the Buffalo Creek Flood.* New York, Simon & Schuster.

Gille, Z. 2000. Cognitive Cartography in a European Wasteland: Multinational Capital and Greens Vie for Village Allegiance, pp. 240–267. In Burowoy, M., Blum, J.A., George, S., Gille, Z., Gowan, T., Haney, L., Klawiter, M., Lopez, S.H., Rian, S.Ó., & Thayer. M. (eds). *Global Ethnography.* Berkeley, University of California Press.

Glenna, L.L. 2010. Value-Laden Technocratic Management and Environmental Conflicts: The Case of the New York City Watershed Controversy. *Science, Technology, & Human Values,* 35(1), 81–112.

Gottfried, H. 1996. "Corridors of Value: Rural Land and Rural Life." *Rural Development Perspectives,* 12(1), 13–18.

Halvorsen, K. E., Barnes, J. R., & Solomon, B. D. 2009) Upper Midwestern USA Ethanol Potential from Cellulosic Materials. *Society and Natural Resources,* 22, 931–938.

Headley, D. & Fan, S. 2008. Anatomy of a Crisis: The Causes and Consequences of Surging Food Prices. *Agricultural Economics,* 39, 375–391.

Hunter, L. M., Krannich, R. S., & Smith, M. D. 2002. Rural Migration, Rapid Growth, and Fear of Crime. *Rural Sociology,* 76(1), 71–89.

Hunter, L. M., Boardman, J. D., & Saint Onge, J. M. 2005. The Association Between Natural Amenities, Rural Population Growth, and Long-Term Residents' Wellbeing. *Rural Sociology*, 70(4), 452–469.

Hurdle, J. 2009a. Pennsylvania Lawsuit Says Drilling Polluted Water. Nov. 9. *Reuters*. Accessed January 20, 2010 at: http://www.reuters.com/article/idUSTRE5A80PP20091109.

Hurdle, J. 2009b. Pennsylvania Residents Sue over Gas Drilling. *Reuters*. Accessed January 20, 2010 at: http://www.reuters.com/article/idUSTRE5AJ2NB20091120.

Jackson-Smith, D. B. 2003. Transforming Rural America: The Challenges of Land Use Change in the Twenty-First Century, pp. 305–316. In Brown, D.L. & Swanson, L.E. (eds), *Challenges for Rural America in the Twenty-First Century*. University Park, PA, Penn State Press.

Jacquet, J. 2009. *Energy Boomtowns and Natural Gas: Implications for Marcellus Shale Local Governments and Rural Communities*. NERCRD Rural Development Paper No. 43. January. University Park, PA, The Northeast Regional Center for Rural Development.

Jones, J. E., Fly, J. M., Talley, J., & Cordell, H. K. 2003. Green Migration into Rural America: The New Frontier of Environmentalism? *Society and Natural Resources*, 16, 221–238.

Kohrs, E. V. 1974. *Social Consequences of Boom Town Growth in Wyoming*. Paper presented at the Rocky Mountain American Association of the Advancement of Science Meeting, April 24–26. Laramie, Wyoming.

Kleinschmidt, J. 2007. *Biofueling Rural Development: Making the Case for Linking Biofuel Production to Rural Revitalization*. Carsey Institute Policy Brief No. 5 (Winter). Durham, NH, Carsey Institute.

Krannich, R. S., Greider, T., & Little, R. L. 1985. Rapid Growth and Fear of Crime: A Four-Community Comparison. *Rural Sociology*, 67(1), 71–89.

Krannich, R.S. & Petrzelka, P. 2003. Tourism and Natural Amenity Development: Real Opportunities?, pp. 190–199. In Brown, D.L., & Swanson, L.E. (eds), *Challenges for Rural America in the Twenty-First Century*. University Park, PA, Penn State Press.

Lehman, T. 1990. The Politics of the 1981 National Agricultural Lands Study. *Environmental History Review*, 14(1/2), 129–149.

Lerch, D. 2007. *Post Carbon Cities: Planning for Energy and Climate Uncertainty*. Post Carbon Press, Sebastpol, CA.

Little, A. 2009. *Power Trip: From Oil Wells to Solar Cells – Our Ride to the Renewable Future*. New York, Harper.

McGranahan, D. A. 1999. *Natural Amenities Drive Rural Population Change*. Food and Rural Economics Division, Economic Research Service, U.S. Department of Agriculture, Washington, D.C.

McKibben, B. 2010. *Earth: Making a Living on a Tough New Planet*. New York, Times Books.

McMichael, P. 2009. The World Food Crisis in Historical Perspective. *Monthly Review*, 61(3), 32–47.

Marshall, S. 2002. *"Lord, We're Just Trying to Save Your Water": Environmental Activism and Dissent in the Appalachian South*. Gainesville, University Press of Florida.

Molnár, J. 2010. Climate Change and Societal Response: Livelihoods, Communities, and the Environment. *Rural Sociology*, 75(1), 1–16.

Molotch, H. & Logan, J. 1987. *Urban Fortunes: The Political Economy of Place*. Berkeley and Los Angeles, University of California Press.

Nagel, J., Dietz, T., & Broadbent, J. 2009) *Workshop on Sociological Perspectives on Global Climate Change, May 30–31, 2008*. (conference proceedings). Washington, D.C., National Science Foundation.

Nersesian, R. 2010. *Energy for the 21st Century: A Comprehensive Guide to Conventional and Alternative Sources* (2nd edn.). M.E. Sharpe, Armonk, NY.

New York State Department of Environmental Conservation (NYSDEC). 2009. *Draft Supplemental Generic Environmental Impact Statement on the Oil, Gas and Solution Mining Regulatory Program: Well Permit Issuance for Horizontal Drilling and High-Volume Hydraulic Fracturing to Develop the Marcellus Shale and Other Low-Permeability Gas Reservoirs*. September. Albany, NYSDEC.

Nickerson, C. 2005. "Land Use and Land Management: Major Uses of Land." *Briefing Room*. USDA-ERS. Accessed at: http://www.ers.usda.gov/Briefing/LandUse/majorlandusechapter.htm.

Patel, R. 2008. *Stuffed and Starved: The Hidden Battle for the World Food System.* Brooklyn, Melville House.

Pavey, J. L., Muth, A. B. Ostermeier, D., & Steiner David, M. L. E. 2007. Building Capacity for Local Governance: An Application of Interactional Theory to Developing a Community of Interest. *Rural Sociology,* 72(1), 90–110.

Prins, E. 2005. The Challenges of Fostering Community Participation: A Case Study of a Community-Based Organization in Rural California. *Community Development,* 36(2), 15–34.

Rasker, R. 2005. Wilderness for its Own Sake or as Economic Asset? *Journal of Land, Resources, and Environmental Law,* 25(1), 15–20.

Richard, R. T. & Brod, R. L. 2004) Community Support for a Gold Cyanide Process Mine: Resident and Leader Differences in Rural Montana. *Rural Sociology,* 69(4), 552–575.

Richter, B. 2010. *Beyond Smoke and Mirrors: Climate Change and Energy in the 21st Century.* New York, Cambridge University Press.

Robbins, P., Meehan, K., Gosnell, H., & Gilbertz, S.J. 2009. Writing the New West: A Critical Review. *Rural Sociology,* 74(3), 356–382.

Salamon, S. 2003. *Newcomers to Old Towns: Suburbanization of the Heartland.* Chicago, University of Chicago Press.

Schafft, K. A. & Greenwood, D. J. 2003. The Promises and Dilemmas of Participation: Action Research, Search Conference Methodology and Community Development. *Journal of the Community Development Society,* 34(1), 18–35.

Sherman, J. 2009. *Those Who Work, Those Who Don't: Poverty, Morality, and Family in Rural America.* Minneapolis, University of Minnesota Press.

Shriver, T. E., & Kennedy, D. K. 2005. Contested Environmental Hazards and Community Conflict over Relocation. *Rural Sociology,* 70(4), 491–513.

Simon, C. 2007. *Alternative Energy: Political, Economic and Social Feasibility.* Rowman & Littlefield Publishers, Lanham, MD.

Solomon, B. D. & Luzadis, V. A. (eds) 2009. *Renewable Energy from Forest Resources in the United States.* New York, Routledge.

Speth, J. G. 2008. *The Bridge at the End of the World: Capitalism, The Environment and Crossing From Crisis to Sustainability.* New Haven, CT, Yale University Press.

Stedman, R., Lee, B., Brasier, K., Weigle, J. L., & Higdon, F. 2009. Cleaning up Water? Or Building Rural Community? Community Watershed Organizations in Pennsylvania. *Rural Sociology,* 74(2), 178–200.

Stone, D. 2010. Not in Anyone's Backyard. *Newsweek Web Exclusive.* Accessed: http://www.newsweek.com/id/230681/page/1.

Tuan, Y. F. 1974. *Topophilia: A Study of Environmental Perception, Attitudes and Values.* Englewood Cliffs, N.J., Prentice-Hall.

U.S. Department of Energy 2004) *Wind Energy for Rural Economic Development.* U.S. Department of Energy, Washington, D.C.

U.S. Department of Energy 2008) *Wind Energy by 2030: Increasing Wind Energy's Contribution to the U.S. Electrical Supply.* U.S. Department of Energy, Washington, D.C.

U.S. Department of Energy 2010. *Wind Energy Today 2010.* U.S. Department of Energy, Washington, D.C.

USDA and President's Council on Environmental Quality. 1981. *Final Report: National Agricultural Lands Study.* Washington, D.C., USDA and CEQ.

U.S. Energy Information Administration. 2009. *Natural Gas Year-in-Review 2008.* Washington D.C., U.S. Department of Energy.

Van der Horst, D. 2007. NIMBY or not? Exploring the Relevance of Location and the Politics of Voiced Opinions in Renewable Energy Siting Controversies. *Energy Policy,* 35(5), 2705–2714.

Walls, D. & Billings, D. 1977. The Sociology of Southern Appalachia. *Appalachian Journal,* 5, 131–144.

White, S. E. 1998. Migration Trends in the Kansas Ogallala Region and the Internal Colonial Dependency Model. *Rural Sociology,* 63(2), 253–271.

Winkler, R., Field, D. R., Luloff, A. E., Krannich, R. S., & Williams, T. 2007. Social Landscapes of the Inter-Mountain West: A Comparison of "Old West" and "New West" Communities. *Rural Sociology,* 72(3), 478–501.

Wilkinson, K. P. 1991. *The Community in Rural America.* Middleton, WI, Social Ecology Press.
Wirzbicki, A. & Daley, B. 2010. Decision on Cape Wind Project Expected Soon. Jan. 14. *Boston Globe.* Accessed Jan. 15 at: http://www.boston.com.
Wolsink, M. 2010. Near-Shore Wind Power – Protected Seascapes, Environmentalists' Attitudes, and the Technocratic Planning Perspective. *Land Use Policy,* 27(2), 195–203.

PART III

RURAL POPULATIONS

6 Youth, Aging, and the Life Course

The age composition of rural communities has a profound impact on health care, educational programs and infrastructure, housing, cultural and recreational amenities, transportation, the justice system, and many other aspects of community life. As Fuguitt and his colleagues (1989) noted in their seminal study of rural population dynamics:

> The age–sex composition of a population shapes community needs and demands for goods, services, and economic opportunities as well as patterns of consumption, life style and social relationships . . . The age–sex composition of a population imposes requirements and limitations on each of its institutions. (p. 105)

Moreover, since age composition is dynamic, *changes* in a community's age profile bring both challenges and opportunities to small towns and rural areas (Jones et al. 2007).

In this chapter we use both micro and macro perspectives to study the determinants and consequences of aging in rural contexts. We focus on two broad age groups of particular importance to rural community life – youth and young adults and older persons. At the micro-level, with respect to individual aging, we use the *life course perspective* as an integrating framework to examine challenges facing youth, young adults, and elders in contemporary rural society. At the macro level we analyze the dynamics of population aging, and explore challenges rural communities frequently encounter, including the loss of youth and young adults due to rural out-migration, the in-migration of older residents, and/or aging-in-place.

Individual Aging versus Population Aging

Social scientists differentiate between *individual aging* and *population aging.* Individual aging refers to the progression of persons through the life course. Individual aging is a bio-social process that is reflected in changes in the age-graded social roles people occupy as they grow older. In contrast, population aging refers to changes in a population's age structure that result from the redistribution of persons among age groups. When the share of older persons increases, populations are said to be aging. Conversely, when younger persons become relatively more numerous, populations are said to be growing younger. Population aging is a universal process in today's world. In the United States and other highly developed nations, rural aging is typically more extreme than urban aging.

In other words, while population aging has wide ranging implications for community wellbeing, aging can also be viewed as a process of individual and/ or household development. As we discuss in this chapter, aspects of human behavior such as migration, school enrollment, health and illnesses, employment, criminality, and many other roles, statuses, and behaviors are more likely to occur at certain ages than at others. When these behaviors occur early in one's life, they have a cumulative impact in later life

Individual Aging in Rural Communities

The Life Course Perspective as an Integrating Framework

Individual aging is not a random process. Rather, persons progress through their lives in an organized manner. In the past, this progression was referred to as the *life cycle,* and it was thought that persons transitioned from earlier to later statuses in a linear and irreversible fashion directly associated with advancing biological age. However, social scientists are now more likely to examine an individual's aging experience from the standpoint of the *life course* rather than the life cycle. The life course perspective emphasizes aging as not only a *biological* process, but a social and psychological process as well that is embedded within sets of shared norms about the various roles and experiences typically associated with different chronological ages.

Certain statuses typically follow others. For example, retirement generally follows career. However, the progression is not necessarily linear nor is it irreversible. As Phyllis Moen (2000) has observed, people do not necessarily age in lock step from one status and its associated social roles to another. Many people are "off time." That is, they move back and forth between statuses in variable ways. Retirement obviously follows work, but some people re-enter the labor market after retiring. Work typically follows education, but many people re-enroll in school after beginning their careers and some even do so after retirement. Starting a family often follows both completing school and beginning one's career, but many women have their first child before either of these events. In other words, while biological aging may be a linear process of increasing age, the life course is not necessarily locked in place in concert with advancing biological age. In this respect the life course perspective acknowledges the multiple ways in which social context – and the ways in which individual decision-making is embedded within that social context – affects how people live and experience their lives from birth to death.

The other important insight from the life course perspective is that wellbeing in later life is contingent on earlier experiences, behaviors and decisions. In other words, we "collect baggage" as we progress through the life course, and this baggage can either improve our situation or detract from it. Moreover, these advantages and disadvantages tend to cumulate as we age. For example, school dropouts earn less throughout their lives because fewer years of schooling places them at a comparative disadvantage as soon as they enter the labor force and at each stage in their subsequent careers. In other words, starting at a lower level places one on a different career trajectory, and this disadvantage persists as people grow older and advance through their working lives.

The cumulative effects of early experiences and decisions while affecting economic wellbeing in later life can have impacts beyond economic security.

For example, serving time in prison during one's late teens or early adulthood represents a significant constraint upon future life chances. Convicted felons have lifelong difficulty obtaining well paying work, securing marital partners, voting, and participating in civil society (Pettit and Western 2004; Western 2006). Divorcing is another decision that has both financial and social implications in later life. For example, divorced parents who become estranged from their children are often denied informal care giving later in life. This is important because research shows that assistance from adult children can help older persons maintain independent living and other aspects of social and economic wellbeing (Pillemer et al. 2000).

Challenges Facing Rural Youth and Young Adults

Educational Attainment

For some time now rural schools, at least at the secondary level, have compared favorably with or have outperformed their urban counterparts in the areas of achievement and graduation rates. A recent report released by the U.S. Department of Education examined the percentages of 4th and 8th grade students scoring at a proficient or higher level on reading, math, and science examinations, and found that rural students consistently outperformed students in cities, although students in suburban schools scored highest in reading and math. Rural secondary students also compared favorably in terms of dropout rates and graduation rates. In 2004 in rural areas, 11 percent of residents aged 16–24 had dropped out of high school as compared with 13 percent in the cities and 9 percent in suburban areas. Similarly, the average freshman graduation rate in 2002–2003 was 75 percent in rural areas and only 65 percent in cities (although 79 percent in suburban areas) (Provasnik et al. 2007).

Gibbs (1998) used data from the National Longitudinal Survey of Youth (NLSY) to compare academic attainment rates for adults at age twenty-five who reported residence in either urban or rural places at age fourteen. Eighty-six percent of adults growing up in urban areas graduated from high school, as did fully 85 percent of those who grew up in rural areas. However, Gibbs also found that although graduation rates in rural and urban schools were comparable, 65 percent of urban high school graduates went on to attend college, while this was true for only 56 percent of students who had attended rural schools at age 14. Of the rural students who went on to college, only 70 percent returned to live in rural areas. Hence, while high school graduation rates were virtually the same across urban and rural places, fewer rural graduates went on to enroll in college. Of those who did go on to higher education, nearly one-third did not end up returning to rural America. These patterns appear largely to have continued to the present time (National Education Association, 2001; Provasnik et al. 2007 USDA-Economic Research Service 2003).

Post-Secondary Educational Attainment in Rural Areas

Adults living in rural areas, however, on average have lower levels of educational attainment than their urban counterparts. According to the 2000 U.S. Census, 23 percent of rural persons aged twenty-five and older had not completed high school. While this is a marked improvement over 1990 (31 percent), it is still significantly higher than the corresponding figure for metropolitan adults (19 percent). Similarly, in 2004, only 13 percent of rural adults had bachelor's degrees, as compared with 17 percent nationwide (Provasnik et al. 2007). These differences are significant given that data show the value of education to the economic status of individuals steadily increasing over time. While in 1979, a male with a bachelor's degree could expect to make 51 percent more in lifetime earnings than a peer with only a high school diploma, by 2004 that difference had jumped to 96 percent. Between 1984 and 2000, about two-thirds of job growth in the United States was accounted for by positions requiring a bachelor's degree or more, while economic opportunities considerably decreased for those with high school diplomas or less (Glasmeier & Salant 2006; Kirsch et al. 2007; Webster & Alemayehu 2006).

These figures may exaggerate the urban–rural education gap since they include older cohorts of rural Americans who went to school when achievement and attainment gaps were markedly much more pronounced. Perhaps more significantly, these figures also do not take into account how migration and migration selectivity affect the composition of rural populations – specifically the historical patterns of outmigration of adults with higher educational levels than either the remaining "base" population or the population of in-movers to rural areas (Fulton, Fuguitt, and Gibson 1997).

Because of this, human capital deficits remain a feature of rural areas and constrain opportunities for rural workers to obtain stable, well paying jobs and achieve basic economic security.[1] Additionally, human capital and educational attainment are not evenly spread across rural populations. Racial minorities and persons living in the rural South are far more likely to enter the labor force with serious educational deficiencies, deficiencies that are strongly associated with the chances of being poor (USDA-Economic Research Service 2003). Of course, causation runs in both directions; persons with low education are more likely to be poor and poor people are less likely to stay in school. There are many reasons for this, but one that is often overlooked, student transiency, has a particularly strong negative impact on educational attainment among the rural poor. Student transiency is the result of frequent short distance residential dislocations. While residential mobility is often associated with the search for enhanced opportunity, the opposite seems to be the case for many poor rural families. Evictions, relationship instability, domestic violence, loss of jobs, and other family emergencies often result in residential dislocation and changing schools (Schafft 2005, 2006). The social, residential, and academic disruption that results is both a factor of economic insecurity and a major contributing factor to academic underachievement. This may be especially the case in rural areas because the likelihood is increased that changing schools also means changing school districts where curricula may be different and in which record transfer delays slow service provision to underperforming students.

Criminal Behavior and Substance Abuse

Criminal behavior is concentrated in adolescence and early adulthood (Steffensmeier et al. 1989). Once persons advance into their mid thirties, they tend to become integrated within a web of roles and commitments, and consequently to be much less likely to engage in criminal behavior. If youth offenders are caught, prosecuted and convicted, serving time can have wide ranging adverse affects during later life. As Western (2006: 6) has observed, "While the life course is integrative, incarceration is dis-integrative . . ." Popular associations with rural community life include strong images of public safety, informal social control, and low risk of crime, but the truth does not conform to the *rural mystique.* In fact, rural youth are almost as likely as urban youth to participate in criminal behavior.

Crime rates have been on the decline in the United States in both rural and urban areas, but falling crime rates benefited urban and suburban locations more than rural locales. While it is true that rural crime rates are still lower than urban rates, they have declined much less rapidly during recent years compared with their urban counterparts (Duhart 2000; Rennison 2001). In addition, the latest data from the U.S. Bureau of Justice Statistics show that in the midst of the overall decline, the risk of violent crime and adolescent violence has risen in rural areas (Spano & Nagy 2005). Consequently, criminologists have focused increasing attention on rural crime, especially that committed by young men (Osgood & Chambers 2000). Incarcerated rural youth face a steep challenge. Most jails, and the rural communities in which they are located, are ill-equipped in both funding and human resources to address the multiple social and educational needs of the incarcerated, 60 percent of whom lack a high school diploma or GED, and 95 percent of whom will eventually return to life outside the prison walls (Solomon et al. 2008).

It is unsurprising that there is a strong link between substance abuse and criminal behavior, and this association is especially strong in rural areas. Over one-third of rural violent crimes involved the use of alcohol, a figure far in excess of that in urban and suburban communities (Duhart 2000). Rural–urban differences in the prevalence of drug and alcohol use among youth[2] are relatively small, but rural youth report more problems from their use of alcohol than is true of urban youth (Edwards 1995). For example, almost 40 percent of rural 12th graders reported using alcohol while "driving around" compared with about one quarter of urban high school seniors. And, as indicated earlier, rural offenders are more likely to report using alcohol while committing a violent crime (Duhart 2000). Rural youth are also more likely to abuse methamphetamine and oxycontin (Hartley 2007). This is especially true in the smallest rural communities, those with the least resources to prevent or treat problems (Hartley 2007).

Challenges Facing Older Rural Adults

Maintaining Supportive Social Networks

As Krout (1988) has observed, residence in rural settings can affect the status and experiences of older persons. However, consistent with our earlier discussion of

Box 6.1 Drug Abuse in Rural America: Methamphetamine Addiction

We met Deborah (not her real name) during a 2007 study of persistence within family literacy programs among low-income adults in Pennsylvania. At the time we spoke with Deborah, she was a 31 year old mother of 4 and currently enrolled in an adult education family literacy program in rural Pennsylvania, and attempting to complete a Graduate Equivalency Diploma (GED) program, the equivalent of a high school degree. She had only completed 8th grade, in part because of the frequent residential moves made by her family when she was growing up. This led to multiple school changes and eventually to her "not caring" about schooling, and ultimately to her dropping out.

When we spoke, she was trying to straighten her life out after completing a several-month-long jail term for burglary, connected to her introduction to and abuse of methamphetamine. She was working hard to stay drug free and provide a stable environment for her children, as well as meet her educational and career goals, but she described facing numerous obstacles.

> I went for my GED like four separate times. I never went for the test, but I went to the classes. I haven't went for my GED in the last five years. It was more or less I was leaving the children's dad and I had my own apartment. So I was working, plus the two kids and it was just a little too much at the time . . . I think a lot of [the teachers] have been through it. Yeah, there's not like one of them who hasn't really been through maybe what one of us has been through. Maybe it's dealing with drugs or dealing with a family that moves around a lot or self-esteem issues, bad relationships, just not, not being involved with their schooling because their parents weren't involved with their schooling.

> I got caught up in drugs real quick. Got in trouble immediately. It was meth. Yeah, I was high on meth and like six of us decided to go out and do this burglary, you know. And really it's just meth, they say, meth equal sorcery. It's a funny drug. It is. It's just really, you turn instantly bad. You really do. It's not like cocaine or I guess heroin. I've never done heroin, but it's like, it's a very mind-controlling drug. Being on it, I lost everything. All my memories, my children, you know, baby books and I almost lost my life and my children you know. And I'm very angry at that thought – very angry, you know. So I got to stay away from it. It's really very hard.

the life course, biography and history also affect older persons' current wellbeing. Since people often spend much of their lives in a number of different communities, senior citizens' income, health and other trajectories are affected by their experiences in previous social and economic environments as well as by opportunities present in their current residential context (Glasgow and Brown 1998).

One challenge facing older persons, regardless of where they live, is to maintain supportive networks of social relationships. This can be difficult because even though people maintain some social roles throughout their lives, they leave others behind as they advance in age. For example, retiring from a long time career can sever important social ties as can moving from one's lifelong home to a retirement community. Research shows that older persons who maintain social roles and are embedded in strong social networks tend to be healthier, to live longer, and benefit in various other ways (Moen et al. 1992; Young and Glasgow 1998). While "social integration," can be defined in various ways, Pillemer and his colleagues (2000) contend that social integration is the degree to which people are embedded in meaningful social roles and relationships, the most proximate of which are family, friendships and affiliations with community organizations. Accordingly, social integration involves both formal and informal social participation, e.g., organizational memberships and/or community volunteering as well as participation in family and friends networks. Informal social relationships provide social support and buffer older persons from outside forces while formal involvements provide bridging ties to a variety of social venues where resources and information related to health, social opportunities, household maintenance, financial management, and other day-to-day needs can be obtained (see Chapter 3 for a discussion of bonding and bridging relationships).

Maintaining social relationships in rural communities can be strongly affected by population dynamics. As will be shown later in this chapter, many rural communities have experienced chronic out-migration of young adults thereby severing social ties between parents and children. In addition, since rural populations are older than their urban counterparts, the chances in rural areas that friends and colleagues will die or move to be closer to their adult children also puts long standing relationships at risk. On a more positive note, many rural communities are destinations for migrants in their early to mid sixties who are seeking amenity rich environments to live in during retirement.

While *retirement in-migration* brings income, wealth, and experience to destination communities, it also places older in-migrants at the risk of being socially isolated. Recent research has demonstrated that this concern appears to be misplaced. In fact, older in-migrants to rural retirement communities in the U.S. were shown to be almost as socially involved as similar aged persons who had lived in these communities for twenty or more years (Brown and Glasgow 2008). Older in-migrants established rich networks of formal and informal ties quickly after their arrival. Moreover, the study showed that while older persons were moving to rural communities for amenity reasons, over one-third had at least one adult child living within a half hour of their homes. In other words, they were simultaneously satisfying amenity and family reunification motives. This could have important implications for in-migrants wellbeing over time as they age-in-place in retirement destination communities.

Health Status and Access to Health Care

Discussions of aging typically raise concerns about health, illness, and access to medical care, and this is certainly true with respect to aging in rural areas. Although chronic disability among older persons has declined since 1980 in both urban and rural America, older persons are still more likely than younger persons to suffer from a number of chronic health conditions (Federal Interagency Forum on Aging Related Statistics 2004). Moreover, the risk of chronic disease is not equally spread across the country. Research shows that persons living in the most rural communities have higher age-adjusted rates of heart disease, cancer, and other chronic conditions compared with similar aged persons who live in more urban environments (Johnson 2004).[3] In other words, regardless of whether currently living in a rural community is a cause of poorer health, older rural persons have higher chronic disease rates thereby requiring access to relatively high levels of health and other kinds of support services. This can be a challenge for rural elders, especially those who live in isolated, low density and/or sparsely populated areas.

Krout (1998) has observed that older rural persons depend on a continuum of care to maintain their health, wellbeing and residential independence. However, there is a disconnect between older rural person's greater needs and the supply of services available in their immediate communities. This rural service disadvantage results from urban biases in government programs, higher per capita costs of service delivery due to small population size and low population density, inadequate transportation and a shortage of trained practitioners willing to locate in rural communities (Krout 1994; Coward et al.1994). The continuum of care ranges from community- and home-based services that help relatively healthy and well-off elders live independently, to residential providers of health and social services, such as nursing homes, assisted living, and continuing care retirement communities. Accordingly, some services are available through formal institutional domains such as local government, the public and private health-care system, and private sector businesses that operate residential retirement facilities, as well as through a wide variety of non-governmental, not for profit community-based organizations. Some of these organizations focus on specific needs such as health care, nutrition or transportation while others emphasize a wider range of supports including transportation, housing, nutrition, legal, adult day care, information, and referrals, etc. Some older rural people lack access to essential services because such services are not available locally; others cannot utilize local services because of financial, transportation, or other barriers; and some needy persons simply refuse to utilize available services because they oppose public intervention in their lives. Regardless of the reasons, older persons are often at a disadvantage when dealing with this complex and diverse situation. Area Agencies on Aging (AAA) can play an important role in helping rural elders make sense out of the complicated system (Krout 1998). AAAs are essentially *aging services networks* that is, systems of service planning, development, coordination, funding, and delivery that enhance service availability and build bridges between older persons and the services they need.

Population Aging in Rural Communities

Why Populations in Developed Nations are Growing Older[4]

The changing distribution of persons among a population's age groups is affected by changes in fertility, mortality, and migration. In the United States, the share of persons age 65 and older increased from 9 percent in 1960 to 13 percent in 2010.

Hence, as shown in figure 6.1, the pace of aging over the past 50 years has been steady but not precipitous. While declines in mortality at older ages and increased longevity might seem to be the obvious reason for population aging, sustained low fertility since the post-Second World War baby boom has actually been more responsible for increasing the proportion of older persons.[5] It should be noted, however, that future increases in population aging in the U.S. will undoubtedly be more closely associated with further declines in mortality at older ages. This is because in a low mortality rate society like the U.S., the majority of all deaths occur after age 65. As Weeks (2008: 342) has observed, "At a life expectancy of 65 with replacement level fertility, the average age is 38; the average age rises to 41 as life expectancy increases to 80. The percentage of persons aged 65 and older increases from 15 percent to 24 percent . . ."

Age-selective migration also has a direct effect on age structure by adding or subtracting persons from specific age groups. In addition, migration can indirectly affect age structure, and this impact can be experienced over a long time horizon. For example, long-term out-migration of persons in their child-bearing years not only subtracts young persons from a population, but diminishes the population's reproductive potential, thereby resulting in fewer children and further aging.

Rural Aging

In the United States and in most other developed nations, aging is somewhat more advanced in rural than in urban areas (15 percent and 12 percent respectively).[6] About 7.5 million rural persons were age 65+ in 2004, an increase of 2.3 percent since 2000.[7] This increase is partly a result of pre-retirement age persons who survive to age 65, thereby being defined as elderly. The number of persons surviving into older age will be an even stronger component of rural aging in the near future as the large post-Second World War baby boom cohorts reach age sixty-five (Plane 1992). Migration, the other main reason for rural aging, has also had a big impact (Fuguitt and Beale 1993). As discussed earlier in this section, migration can have both direct and indirect impacts on age composition. With respect to rural aging in the United States, two different migration dynamics are at work: (a) long-term out-migration of young adults and their children (and their reproductive potential), and (b) in-migration of retirement and pre-retirement age adults (Brown and Glasgow 2008; Jones et al. 2007). Both of these migration streams contribute to aging the rural population, and help to explain why rural areas are older than their urban counterparts.

Fertility's decreasing role in rural population growth, and in determining rural age composition, is attributable both to declines in the size of the reproductive age population and to significant declines in fertility rates among women of reproductive age.[8] Between 1930 and 1970, the rural population grew modestly, and this growth was almost entirely due to natural increase (the excess of births over deaths). Since 1970 (as shown in Chapter 2), natural increase has played an increasingly small role in rural population growth, and the lack of natural increase has contributed to the advancing age of the rural population.

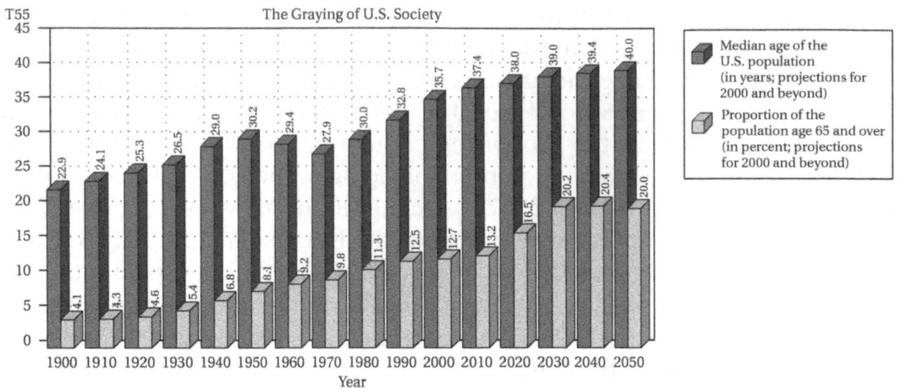

Source: Macionis, *Society: The Basics,* Figure 3.4 "The Graying of the U.S. Society" p. 78, © 2006 Prentice-Hall, Inc. Reproduced by permission of Pearson Education, Inc.

Figure 6.1 The Greying of the U.S. Population

Three Community-Level Challenges of Rural Population Aging

Youth Out-Migration and Brain Drain

Geographic mobility is most likely when people are going through life-course transitions such as completing school, getting married, beginning a career, and buying a house, and these transitions are concentrated in the early adult years. Accordingly, young adults have higher than average rates of geographic mobility. Regardless of rural–urban location, therefore, the volume of both in- and out-migration is high during the young adult years. What differentiates urban and rural areas, however, is whether in-migration is sufficient to result in an overall gain. Rural areas experienced net out-migration of young adults in each decade between 1950 and 2000, and this net loss was greatest during decades when the rural population declined overall (the 1950s, 1960s and 1980s). Net out-migration at younger ages diminished, but was still negative, during the rural population turnaround decades of the 1970s and 1990s (Johnson and Cromartie 2006).

Given the elevated mobility of youth, from a community's standpoint, it's important to attract enough in-movers to replace the outflow. In other words, the balance between gain and loss is more important than the loss itself. *Brain drain,* the popular label for this phenomenon conjures up images of young persons fleeing lagging areas, transferring their education, experience, and reproductive potential elsewhere. But brain drain is more correctly conceptualized as the inability to replace out-migrants, not out-migration in and of itself. Hence, a main challenge facing many rural communities is insufficient in-migration of young adults, rather than higher than average out-migration (Dietz 2007). Seeing one's children move away is a painful experience, and communities rightly try to entice them to stay. However, since most current policies focus more strongly on population retention than on population attraction, a more balanced approach of attraction and retention would be more likely to alleviate rural brain drain (Grassmueck et al. 2008).

In addition to the number of persons moving in and out of rural communities, the selectivity of migration is even more important for maintaining community vitality. Migration selectivity refers to the probability that certain kinds of people are not only more likely to move, but to move in and out of certain kinds of places. Research shows, for example, that rural net out-migration at young adult ages was highly selective of the better educated individuals during 1989–2004 (Domina 2006). As the author comments, "... highly educated nonmetropolitan youth are leading contemporary nonmetropolitan out-migration" (p. 373). Rural communities are therefore faced with a substantial challenge when overall migration loss occurs simultaneously with a net loss of the best prepared youth.

Retirement In-Migration

While young people are much more likely to move than older people, almost ten percent of Americans age 60+ migrated between 1995 and 2000, with a disproportionate share moving to rural communities. Moreover, older in-migration to rural areas tends to be concentrated in particular amenity rich destinations, places where the in-migrants had prior experience as visitors or workers, and/or places where older in-migrants already had social connections prior to their moves. In the year 2000, 274 U.S. rural counties (about 12 percent of the total) had a high enough rate of older in-migration (15 percent or higher at ages 60+) to be designated by the U.S. Department of Agriculture as *rural retirement destinations* (RRD). The geographic location of RRDs is shown in Box 6.2.

Being a retirement destination poses both opportunities and challenges for rural communities, and for migrants themselves. As indicated in our discussion of individual aging, moving at a relatively advanced age puts persons at risk of becoming socially isolated. Even though research shows that this concern tends to be exaggerated (Brown and Glasgow 2008), older in-movers have to establish new social relationships and/or reinvigorate existing ones in their new communities. They do this by volunteering, participating in local politics, and/or joining and often leading arts and cultural organizations. Moreover, about one-third of older in-movers have an adult child living within one half hour of their new home, hence day-to-day interaction with children and grandchildren becomes possible (Brown and Glasgow 2008).

From a community's perspective, older in-migrants have been characterized as "Grey Gold." They are wealthier, healthier, and more highly educated than similar aged persons who have lived in retirement destination areas for a longer time. Numerous studies show that retirement migration provides substantial economic benefits for destination communities (Stallman et al. 1999). In fact, a number of states have explicit policies aimed at attracting older persons to rural communities as an economic development strategy (Reeder 1998). In addition to strictly economic benefits, older in-migrants volunteer in a wide variety of local organizations, often providing technical and professional expertise that would be costly and/or difficult to obtain in a rural place. They provide financial support to arts and cultural organizations, and they become leaders in these and other community organizations. Older in-migrants also tend to become politically active in their new communities. They participate in campaigns, run for office, and help to mobilize the local population in favor of, or in opposition to, proposals for new community initiatives.

Box 6.2 Two Faces of Rural Aging: Retirement Destinations and Locations of Natural Population Decrease

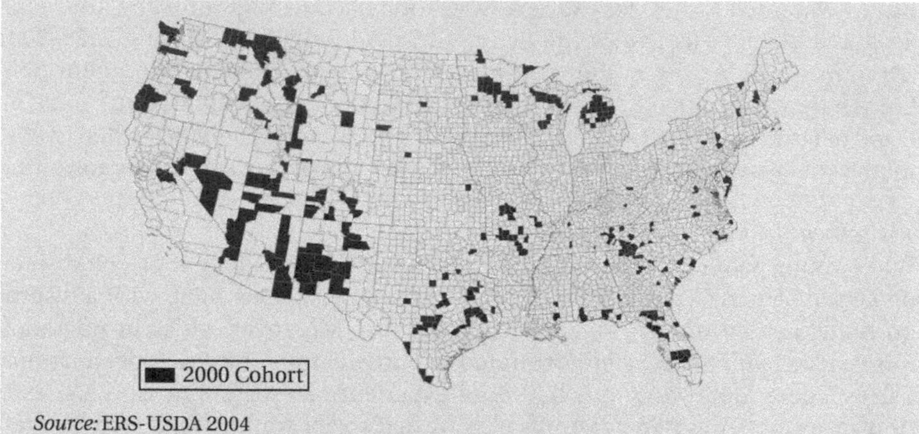

Source: ERS-USDA 2004

Figure 6.2 Rural Retirement Destination Counties, 2000

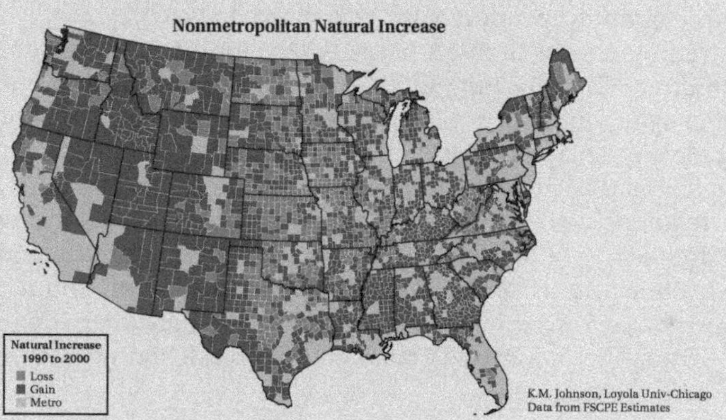

Figure 6.3 Natural Decrease Counties

RRDs are concentrated in the South and Southwest, but as can be seen in Figure 6.2, they are also located in the upper Midwest, the Northern Rockies and Pacific Northwest and in scattered parts of the Northeast. Natural decrease counties, in contrast, are highly concentrated in the nation's agricultural heartland in the Great Plains and Corn Belt with a secondary concentration in Appalachia. About four out of ten RRDs are also natural decrease counties. These 141 counties are located in the upper Great Lakes and in the Southwest. Compared with the majority of natural decrease counties, these areas have higher rates of population growth and in-migration. RRDs with natural decrease are slightly older than other RRDs, but the difference is not great.

While these benefits are clearly acknowledged by longer-term residents, interviews with community leaders in RRDs indicated concerns that older in-migrants might displace longer-term community interests (Brown and Glasgow 2008). For example, rising real estate prices can reduce the supply of affordable housing. Volunteering reduces public sector costs, but it may also diminish the demand for paid professional workers, thereby reducing a community's ability to retain and attract young professionals. Older in-migrants who take positions of cultural leadership are sometimes insensitive to traditional ways of doing things and may impose their tastes and preferences on the community. And, older in-migrants who are elected to public office often do so by competing with a place's more established leadership. In other words, attracting older in-migrants has both opportunities and costs, and communities would be wise to consider strategically how older in-migration might integrate into a broader vision of rural community development and revitalization.

Natural Decrease

Persistent out-migration of younger persons has both immediate and longer-term impacts on a population's age structure. Younger persons are immediately subtracted from a population, and children that they might have had during their reproductive years are not added to the youngest age groups. If net out- migration at younger ages continues for several decades, it culminates in population structures with relatively few adults of childbearing age, few children, and many more older adults. Even if the young couples who remain in such areas have children at relatively high rates, they cannot produce enough babies to offset deaths at the older ages. The overall result is natural decrease, an excess of deaths over births. In the absence of net in-migration, natural decrease leads to stagnant population change or long-term decline (Johnson 1993; Johnson and Cromartie 2006).

Natural decrease is heavily concentrated in rural regions. The incidence of natural decrease is especially high in sparsely settled areas remote from large cities where dependence on agriculture remains relatively high. As can be seen in Figure 6.3, natural decrease is particularly prevalent in the Great Plains, the Corn Belt, and Appalachia. Over 800 rural counties (about 41 percent of the total) had more deaths than births between 2000 and 2005. This is an increase from 670 between 1990 and 2000, and about 600 during the 1980s (Cromartie and Kandel 2007; Johnson and Cromartie 2006). Natural decrease areas are not necessarily poor. In fact, they compare quite favorably with other rural areas, including rural retirement destinations, the county type generally thought to be most prosperous (Brown and Glasgow 2008). Their biggest challenge, however, is to be able to respond to the high demand for aging-related services and especially health care. This is compounded by the fact that natural decrease areas tend to be small, sparsely populated and isolated from urban access, all attributes that make service provision both difficult and expensive.

Conclusions

In this chapter we have explored the implications of individual and population aging in rural environments. We showed that people encounter both opportunities and challenges as they advance through the life course and decisions made early in life affect one's wellbeing later on. Dropping out of school, being a single parent, abusing alcohol or drugs, working at a dead-end job with no benefits, adversely affect one's social and economic security as a young adult, and this adverse effect cumulates in later life. In contrast, graduating from college, postponing childbearing, staying out of legal trouble, and working at a job with career mobility and benefits all enhance one's wellbeing throughout the life course.

That said, individual-level decisions are not made in a vacuum. Rather, the life circumstances that one is born into and encounters in one's community pose sets of opportunities and constraints that make certain outcomes far more likely than others. In other words, individual decision-making is embedded within an array of social, cultural, and economic contexts. While dropping out of school, for example, can be argued on some level to be the consequence of an individual's "choice," on the other hand the risk of a young person dropping out of school will be significantly increased if that person's youth experience is marked by social and academic disruption, a dysfunctional home life and/or a community in which formal education is seen as contradictory and/or irrelevant to local norms and values or the most direct route to abandoning, likely for good, one's home and family.

While it is unclear whether living in a rural environment in and of itself, affects one's wellbeing at various stages in the life course, it is undeniable that rural economies contain fewer and less diverse opportunities, and that rural communities provide a more constrained range of institutional and organizational supports for families and individuals. Accordingly, living in a rural community can amplify the risks and benefits that accompany various life stages.

In response to this social and economic deficit in rural communities, high school and college graduates often move away because local economies offer few opportunities adequately matched to their educational accomplishments. In contrast, retirees and pre-retirees are drawn to rural communities by amenities or long-standing family and friendship ties. This seems to be a "win-win" situation for in-migrants and communities alike as long as in-migrants are relatively young and healthy. It can become problematic, however, if older in-migrants age-in place in destination communities only to find that health care, transportation, and other essential services are unavailable.

Our discussion of population aging emphasized that age-selective migration now has the biggest impact on increasing the average age of the rural population. In the context of universally low fertility, youth out-migration and retirement age in-migration both produce older rural populations by adding and subtracting persons from particular age groups and indirectly by reducing the ratio of births to deaths. Increased longevity also contributes to rural aging, since mortality is now concentrated at older and older ages. Similar to our discussion of individual aging, population aging results in both challenges and opportunities for rural communities. Many young adults leave, taking their education and training with them, while older in-migrants bring rural communities a lifetime of experience, skills, technical knowhow, and a wide variety of social and economic resources.

Rural areas will not reverse the trend toward increased aging. In fact, it is estimated that 20 percent of the U.S. population will be sixty-five and older by 2050 when the average age of the U.S. population reaches forty years (see figure 6.1). Successful adaptation to an older society should maximize the opportunities while minimizing the costs associated with aging. At the individual level, enhancing the fit between a person's needs and abilities and the environment he/she lives in will contribute to successful aging (Riley and Riley 1994; Carp 1988). Similarly, from a community standpoint, local vitality can be affected by the number, characteristics and wellbeing of older persons, their demand for goods and services, their civic engagement and social participation (LeMesurier 2006). Communities should promote an inclusive environment that encourages high levels of social participation among residents of all ages. While individual and community implications of aging are analytically separate, they are mutually intertwined in reality. In other words, promoting successful aging benefits older people and their communities (Brown & Glasgow 2008).

Notes

1 There is also evidence that under certain contexts rural students lag behind suburban and central city students in high stakes testing. A study conducted in Illinois showed that except for schools located in Chicago, rural schools had the highest chances of being placed on the "academic warning list" In accordance with guidelines under "No Child Left Behind" (Beck 2005).

2 This study focused on substance abuse among 12th graders.

3 Wallace and Wallace (1998) reported only modest differences in health status between rural and urban older persons, but their study compared the entire metropolitan and nonmetropolitan sectors. Johnson (2004), in contrast, disaggregated the nonmetropolitan sector and showed that age adjusted measures of health status varied markedly from the most urban to least urban counties.

4 Population aging is a world-wide phenomenon, even in sub-Saharan Africa. For example, the UN predicts that over 5% of Sub-Saharan Africa's population will be age 65+ by 2050 compared with 3% in 2000 (United Nations Population Division, 2003).

5 The *total fertility rate* in the U.S. declined from 3.5 births per woman during her childbearing years in 1960 to 2.1 births per woman in 2008.

6 Rural populations are aging more rapidly than urban populations in virtually all more developed nations (Brown 2009).

7 Age 65+ is the conventional dividing line between the elderly and younger age groups in the U.S. However, this is an entirely arbitrary definition. As some commentators have observed, "60 is the new 40" (Bogert 2010).

8 Urban and rural total fertility rates in the U.S. are now approximately equal at 2.1 children per woman during her childbearing years.

References

Beck, F. 2005. How Do Rural Schools Fare Under a High Stakes Testing Regime? pp. 64–70. In Beaulieu, L. & Gibbs R. (eds) *The Role of Education: Promoting the Economic and Social Vitality of Rural America.* Starkville, Southern Rural Development Center.

Bogert, R. 2010. "Is 60 the new 40?" Los Angeles Times, Jan 7 downloaded on November 9, 2010 at http://www.latimes.com/sns-health-60-new-40,0,1525238,story.

Brown, D.L. 2009. "Rethinking the OECD's New Rural Demography" presented to the OECD Rural Policy Conference. Québec, Canada, October 9.

Brown, D.L. & Glasgow, N. 2008. *Rural Retirement Migration.* Dordrecht, Springer.

Carp, F. 1988. Significance of Mobility for the Well-Being of the Elderly, pp. 1–20. In Transportation

Research Board. *Transportation in an Aging Society: Improving Mobility and Safety for Older Persons.* Washington, D.C., National Research Council.

Coward, R., Bull, C., Kukulka, G., & Galliher, J. 1994. *Health Services for Rural Elders.* New York, Springer.

Cromartie, J. & Kandel, W. 2007. Deaths Exceed Births in Over 800 Nonmetro Counties. *Briefing Room: Population and Migration: Trend 4—Natural Decrease on the Rise.* Washington, D.C., USDA-Economic Research Service. accessed from: http://www.ers.usda.gov/Briefing/Population/Natural.htm.

Dietz, R. 2007. A Brain Drain or an Insufficient Brain Gain? *Upstate New York At-A-Glance,* 2(August). Buffalo, Federal Reserve Bank.

Domina, T. 2006. What Clean Break? Education and Nonmetropolitan Migration Patterns, 1989–2004. *Rural Sociology.* 71(3), 373–398.

Duhart, D. 2000. Urban, Suburban and Rural Victimization, 1993–98. Bureau of Justice Statistics Special Report. Washington, D.C., U.S. Department of Justice, Office of Justice Programs, Bureau of Justice Statistics.

Edwards, R. 1995. Alcohol, Tobacco, and Other Drug Use by Youth in Rural Communities. Washington, D.C., North Central Regional Educational Laboratory. Accessed from: http://www.ncrel.org/sdrs/areas/issues/envrnmnt/drugfree/v1edward.htm.

Federal Interagency Forum on Aging Related Statistics. 2004. *Older Americans 2004: Key indicators of Well-Being.* Washington, D.C., U.S. Government Printing Office.

Fuguitt, G. & Beale, C. 1993. The Changing Concentration of the Older Nonmetropolitan Population , 1960–1990. *Journal of Gerontology: Social Sciences,* 48(6), S278-S288.

Fuguitt, G., Brown, D.L., & Beale, C. 1989. *Rural and Small Town America.* New York, Russell Sage Foundation.

Fulton, J.A., Fuguitt, G.V., & Gibson, R.M. 1997. Recent Changes in Metropolitan–Nonmetropolitan Migration Streams. *Rural Sociology,* 62(3), 363–384.

Glasgow, N. & Brown, D.L. 1998. Older, Rural and Poor, pp. 187–207. In Coward, R. & J. Krout (eds) *Aging in Rural Settings.* New York, Springer.

Gibbs, R.M. (1998). College Completion and Return Migration Among Rural Youth, pp. 61–80. In Gibbs, R.M., Swaim, P.L., & Teixeira, R. (eds) *Rural Education and Training in the New Economy.* Ames, Iowa State University Press.

Glasmeier, A., & Salant, P. 2006 . *Low-Skill Workers in Rural America Face Permanent Job Loss.* Carsey Institute Policy Brief No. 2. Durham, NH, Carsey Institute.

Grassmueck, G., Goetz, S., Shields, M. 2008. Youth Out-Migration from Pennsylvania: The Role of Government Fragmentation versus the Beaten Path. *Regional Analysis and Policy,* 38(1), 77–88.

Hartley, D. 2007. Substance Abuse Among Rural Youth: A Little Meth and a Lot of Booze. *Research and Policy Brief*. Portland, Maine Rural Health Research Center.

Johnson, K. 1993. When Deaths Exceed Births: Natural Decrease in the United States. *International Regional Science Review,* 15 (2), 179–198.

Johnson, K. & Cromartie, J. 2006. The Rural Rebound and its Aftermath: Changing Demographic Dynamics and Regional Contrasts, pp. 25–49. In Kandel, W. & Brown, D.L. (eds) *Population Change and Rural Society.* Dordrecht, Springer.

Johnson, N. 2004. Spatial Patterns of Rural Mortality, pp. 37–45. In Glasgow, N., Morton, L., & Johnson, N. (eds) *Critical Issues in Rural Health.* Ames, Blackwell.

Jones, C., Kandel, W., & Parker, T. 2007. Population Dynamics Are Changing the Profile of Rural Areas. *Amber Waves,* 5(2), 1–7.

Kirsch, I., Braun, H., Yamamoto, K., & Sum, A. (2007). *America's Perfect Storm: Three Forces Changing our Nation's Future.* Princeton, N.J., Educational Testing Service.

Krout, J. 1998. Services and Service Delivery in Rural Environments, pp. 247–266. In Coward, R. & Krout, J. (eds) *Aging in Rural Settings.* New York, Springer.

Krout, J. 1994. *Providing Community-based Services to the Rural Elderly.* Thousand Oaks, CA, Sage.

Krout, J. 1988. The Elderly in Rural Environments. *Journal of Rural Studies,* 4(1), 104–114.

Le Mesurier, N. 2006. The Contributions of Older People to Rural Community and Citizenship, pp. 133–146. In Lowe, P. & Speakman, L. (eds) *The Ageing Countryside: The Growing Older Population of Rural England.* London, Age Concern England.

Moen, P., Fields, V., & Quick, H. 2000. A Life-Course Approach to Retirement and Social Integration, pp. 75–107. In Pillemer, K., Moen, P., Wethington, E., & Glasgow, N. (eds) *Social Integration in the Second Half of Life*. Baltimore, Johns Hopkins Press.

Moen, P., Dempster-McClain, D., & Williams, R. 1992. Successful Aging: A Life Course Perspective on Women's Roles and Health. *American Journal of Sociology*, 97(6), 1612–1638.

National Education Association. 2001. Making Low Performing Schools a Priority: An Association Resource Guide. Washington, D.C., National Education Association.

Osgood, W. & Chambers, J. 2000. Social Disorganization Outside the Metropolis: An Analysis of Rural Youth Violence. *Criminology*, 38(1), 81–115.

Pettit, B. & Western, B. 2004. Mass Imprisonment and the Life Course: Race and Class Inequality in U.S Incarceration. *American Sociological Review*, 69(4), 526–546.

Pillemer, K., Moen, P., Wethington, E., & Glasgow, N. (eds). 2000. *Social Integration in the Second Half of Life*. Baltimore, Johns Hopkins Press.

Plane, D. 1992. Age Composition Change and the Dynamics of Interregional Migration in the U.S. *Annals of the Association of American Geographers*. 82(1), 187–199.

Provasnik, S., KewalRamani, A., McLaughlin Coleman, M., Gilbertson, L., Herring, W., & Xie, Q. 2007. *Status of Education in Rural America*. (July) Washington D.C., National Center for Education Statistics.

Reeder, R. 1998. Retiree Attraction Policies for Rural America. *Agriculture Information Bulletin* No. 741. Washington, D.C., USDA-Economic Research Service.

Rennison, C. 2001. *Criminal Victimization 2000: Changes 1999–2000 with Trends 1993–2000*. Washington, D.C., U.S. Government Printing Office.

Riley, M. & Riley, J. 1994. Structural Lag: Past and Future, pp. 15–36. In Riley, M., Kahn, R., & Foner, A. (eds) *Age and Structural Lag*. New York, John Wiley & Sons.

Schafft, K. 2005. Bouncing Between Disadvantaged Rural School Districts: The Hidden and Disturbing Problem of Student Transiency, pp. 28–35. In Beaulieu, L. & Gibbs, R. (eds) *The Role of Education: Promoting the Economic and Social Vitality of Rural America*. Starkville, Southern Rural Development Center.

Schafft, K. 2006. Poverty, Residential Mobility, and Student Transiency within a Rural New York School District. *Rural Sociology*, 71(2), 212–231.

Solomon, A.L., Osborne, J.W.L., LoBuglio, S.F., Mellow, J., & Mukamal, D.A. 2008, *Life After Lock-Up*. Washington, D.C., The Urban Institute.

Spano, R. & Nagy, S. 2005. Social Guardianship and Social Isolation: An Application and Extension of Lifestyle/Routine Activities Theory to Rural Adolescents. *Rural Sociology*, 70(3), 414–437.

Stallman, J., Deller, S., & Shields, M. 1999. The Economic and Fiscal Impact of Aging Retirees on a Small Rural Region. *The Gerontologist*. 39(5), 599–610.

Steffensmeier, D., Allan, E., Harer, M., & Streifel, C. 1989. Age and the Distribution of Crime. *American Journal of Sociology*, 94(4), 803–831.

United Nations Population Division. 2003. *World Population Prospects: The 2002 Revision*. New York, United Nations.

USDA-Economic Research Service. 2003. Rural Education at a Glance. *Rural Development Research Report* No. 98. Washington, D.C., USDA-ERS.

Wallace, R. & Wallace, R. 1998. Rural–Urban Contrasts in Elder Health Status: Methodologic Issues and Findings, pp. 67–83. In Coward, R. & J. Krout (eds) *Aging in Rural Settings*. New York, Springer.

Webster, B. H., & Alemayehu, B. (2006). *Income, Earnings, and Poverty Data from the 2005 American Community Survey*, U.S. Census American Community Survey Reports. Washington, D.C., U.S. Census Bureau.

Weeks, J. 2008. *Population: An Introduction to Concepts and Issues*. New York, Wadsworth.

Western, B. 2006. *Punishment and Inequality in America*. New York, Russell Sage Foundation.

Young, F. & Glasgow, N. 1998. Voluntary Social Participation and Health. *Research on Aging*, 20(3), 339–362.

7 Racial and Ethnic Minorities in Rural Areas

Rural areas have often been thought of as less racially and ethnically diverse than urban areas. Michael Woods argues that in places like the United States, the United Kingdom, and Australia, rural landscapes have been socially constructed as iconic of national identity. This has had the effect of "positioning rural space as a repository of historic national values (that) explicitly or implicitly identified the rural with a homogeneous ethnic group" (2005: 282), constructing rural areas as a "White" space and in many instances reinforcing the social exclusion of racial and ethnic minorities in those areas (Groenke & Nespor 2010; Holloway 2007; Panelli et al. 2009). Woods further argues that imaginations of rurality as a "White" space have been reinforced by the historical role of *urban* areas as destinations for (often *non*-White) immigrants, and hence as racially and ethnically diverse places, as contrasted with rural areas.

In fact, in the United States nonmetropolitan areas *are*, on the whole, less ethnically diverse than metropolitan areas. At the same time, rural America is often far more racially and ethnically diverse than popular imagination would presume. The minority experience has deep roots in rural America, from the largely rural "Black Belt" of the Southeast, to the Latino border areas of the Southwest, to the rural American Indian reservation lands. Additionally, recent data suggest that many rural areas are now becoming more diverse, and some significantly so.

In this chapter we take a close look at the historical roots and contemporary realities of the experiences of racial and ethnic minorities in America. We begin by discussing the concepts of race and ethnicity, and how they have both been used as social – and *sociological* – constructs. We then look at the socio-demographic characteristics of rural minority populations, focusing in particular on three principal minority populations in the United States: African Americans, American Indians, and Latinos. We conclude by discussing more recent trends of immigration, settlement, and resettlement that are changing the social and demographic makeup of many rural areas.

Thinking about Race and Ethnicity

Race refers to the way in which different human populations have been identified and categorized on the basis of particular physical attributes, such as skin color. As a concept, ethnicity is often conventionally used more or less interchangeably with race, although it more specifically refers to particular geographic origins, cultural beliefs, practices, and/or behaviors that are associated with a distinct racial group or groups. While in the past race was often understood as or assumed to be biologically or genetically based, suggesting relatively coherent bio-physical distinctions between human groups, the consensus now among social and biological scientists is that race is meaningless as a scientific classification given the mobility and genetic sharing of human populations[1] and the lack of any plausible justification for making racial distinctions on the basis of physical or biological characteristics (Schwartz 2001).

Although race is invalid as a means of biological categorization, it is a powerful *social construct.*[2] In other words, characteristics associated with racial difference, such as skin color, have no intrinsic meaning from the standpoint of classifying populations, but they can be important markers of social difference if society *defines* them as meaningful. For example, race (and by extension the presumed "superiority" of some groups over others) has historically been used to establish social hierarchies and, by extension, to legitimate the domination and subjugation of one group or groups by another. It was used in part to justify the slave trade in the Americas, and later the persecution and oppression of American Indians, African Americans and other racial and ethnic groups in the United States (Berry, Grossman, & Pawiki 2007; Churchill 1999; Hochschild 1999; Jaspin 2007; Loewen 2005; Schultz 2005).

This phenomenon, of course, is not limited to the American experience. Race provided an ideological basis for colonialization in the global South. During the Second World War, Adolf Hitler's Third Reich provided significant resources and status to Nazi anthropologists in order not only to legitimize the concept of a pure German "race," but to use racial pseudoscience in the service of state sanctioned "racial hygiene," including population selection, relocation, and ultimately the extermination of millions of Jews, Gypsies, homosexuals and others who violated the Reich's notion of racial purity (Schafft 2002; 2004). More recently, racial and ethnic identity has provided the basis for genocide in places such as Rwanda and the former Yugoslavia (Hinton 2002), and it continues to be at the root of serious conflict in many other places around the world.

The American Anthropological Association's *Statement on Race* asserts:

> Race thus evolved as a world view, a body of prejudgments that distorts our ideas about human differences and group behavior. Racial beliefs constitute myths about the diversity in the human species and about the abilities and behavior of people homogenized into "racial" categories. The myths fused behavior and physical features together in the public mind, impeding our comprehension of both biological variations and cultural behavior, implying that both are genetically determined. Racial myths bear no relationship to the reality of human capabilities or behavior. (AAA, 1998, ¶8)

In other words, even if the scientific consensus asserts that race is meaningless as a bio-physical means of distinguishing between human groups, as *social* constructs both race and ethnicity have powerful meanings. As Apple (2009: 651–652) explains, race:

> is an historically produced and mediated social construct filled with and generated out of structures and identities of exclusion and inclusion (pointing) to the social processes and institutions by which and through which certain groups have consistently been denied person rights, whereas other groups are seen as fully the norm by which all other groups are to be measured.

The ways in which people identify themselves, are identified by others, and the social, political, economic, and *spatial* implications of that identification have significant effects on the distribution of resources and the life chances that are available to people. Moreover, as we will see later in this chapter, one's race or ethnicity has direct implications for educational outcomes, socioeconomic status, and, often, residence. Because of this, even though race and ethnicity are socially constructed categories, population data on race and ethnicity (such as gathered by the U.S. Census Bureau) has tremendous importance for public policy formation and also for better understanding of longer-term social and demographic trends, including patterns of inequality and life chances.[3]

Race and Rurality

In the United States, most recent census data show that nationwide about 74 percent of the population identifies as White. In nonmetropolitan areas, however, that percentage climbs to nearly 85 percent. Similarly, while nationwide the Black or African American population comprises about 12 percent of the total population, that percentage drops to less than 8.5 percent in nonmetropolitan areas. Persons of Asian descent make up about 4.4 percent of the total population, but they comprise less than one percent of the nonmetropolitan population. Of minority populations, only American Indians and Alaska Natives are more likely to reside in nonmetropolitan areas than metropolitan areas: 1.9 percent versus 0.8 percent, largely due to the majority of reservation and tribal lands that are located in nonmetropolitan areas. Persons identifying as Latino make up about 15 percent of the total population, but only about 6.6 percent of the nonmetro population (see Figure 7.1). Based on nationwide figures then, nonmetropolitan areas can be considered markedly less racially and ethnically diverse than metro areas.

These statistics, however, hide several critical factors important for understanding the nature of racial and ethnic diversity within rural areas, and by extension the intersection between rurality and the minority experience. The data in Figure 7.2 show the changes in total nonmetropolitan population between 1990 and 2008 for African Americans, American Indians, Asians, and Latinos. During this

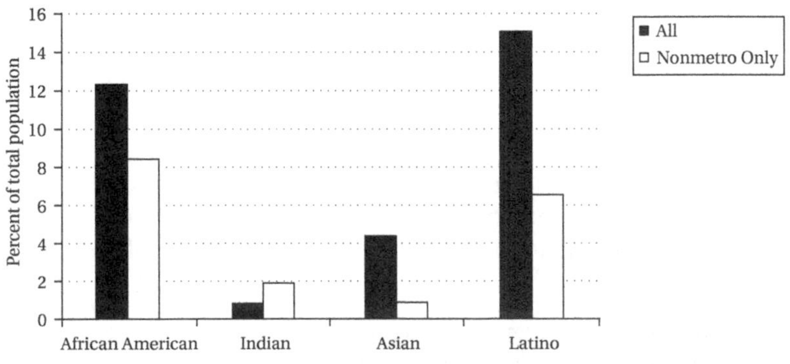

Source: Author's own. Data from 2000 census.

Figure 7.1 Racial Composition in the United States, and Nonmetropolitan Areas Only, 2000

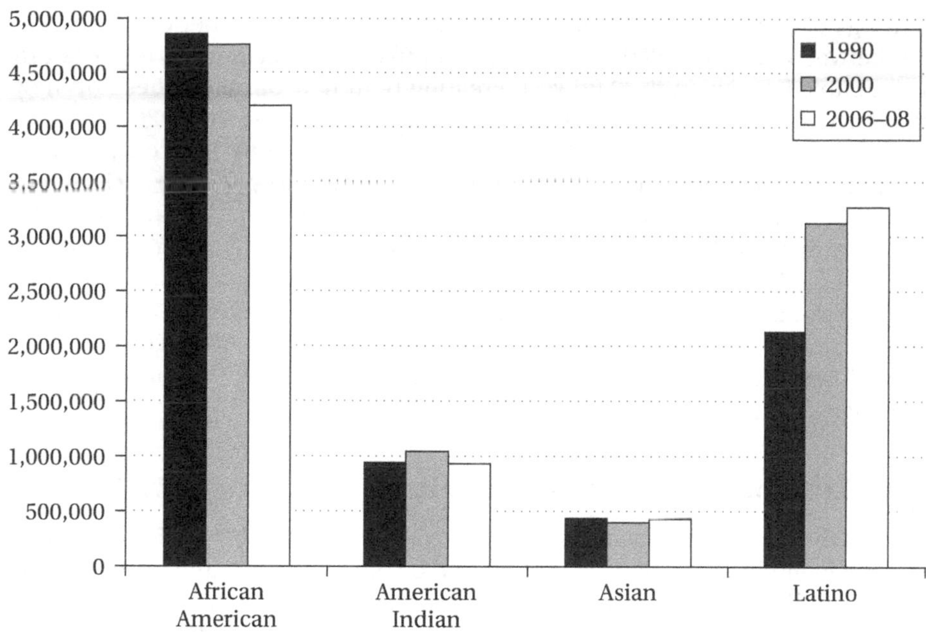

Source: 2006-08 American Community Survey 3-Year Estimates, Table C02003, B03001; Census 2000 SF1 Table P3, P4; 1990 CP-1-1 Census of Population General Population Characteristics.

Figure 7.2 Number of Nonmetropolitan Residents, 1990—2008, by Racial and Ethnic Group

time period the drop in the total numbers of rural African Americans is clear. The same trends however are not nearly as evident for American Indians and Asians, while for Latinos the period between 1990 and 2008 is marked by steady *increases* in the total number living in nonmetropolitan areas.

Nationwide data can also hide significant *regional* variations in ethnic and racial concentration. For instance, nearly 90 percent of African Americans living in nonmetropolitan areas live in the Southern region of the United States. This compares with slightly more than 6 percent in the Midwest and less than 2 percent in the West.[4] Out of all African Americans living in nonmetropolitan areas, nearly 70 percent live in only 5 states: South Carolina, Georgia, Alabama, Mississippi, and Louisiana. This concentration reflects the legacy of America's slave past,[5] with critically important implications for contemporary race relations in the Deep South (Harris and Worthen 2003). Similarly, rural Latino populations have historically clustered in the Southwest with nearly 70 percent living in eight states: Texas, New Mexico, California, Arizona, Colorado, Washington, Florida, and Kansas (Probst et al. 2002). Rural American Indian populations are likewise concentrated in the West and Southwest (Gonzales 2003). Only rural Asian populations, which constitute a very small percentage of the nonmetropolitan population, are geographically dispersed.

Additionally, while ethnically and racially diverse immigrant populations have historically tended to settle in urban areas, in the last fifteen to twenty years two new immigration trends have emerged with increasing numbers of immigrants settling in "non-traditional" migration destinations in rural America. For example, between 1990 and 2000 alone, Latino populations tripled in size in the South and doubled in size in the Midwest, creating both new opportunities and new challenges for rural receiving communities (Marrow 2008; Salamon 2003).

Last, conventional racial and ethnic categories frequently ignore significant diversity *within* minority populations. Few people, for instance, can easily name twenty or even ten American Indian tribes. Yet most American Indians primarily self-identify with their tribal affiliation, and there are 562 federally recognized tribes in the United States, representing different languages, cultures, customs, geographies and histories. Similarly, the term "Latino," a category of ethnicity, refers to persons originating from Latin America or Spain, regardless of race. "Asian" may likewise refer to persons from a wide range of national backgrounds, languages, cultures (see Box 7.1).

Race, Ethnicity, and Life Chances in Rural Areas

Despite the many complicated issues connected to race and ethnic identity, how one self identifies and how one is identified by others has real and lasting implications for life chances. Table 7.1 shows economic and educational attainment data for different racial and ethnic minority groups, differentiated by residence within metropolitan and nonmetropolitan areas. As we discuss in greater detail in Chapter 10, social and spatial inequality are closely associated. Poverty concentrates in central cities, but also in nonmetropolitan areas. Poverty rates are also generally higher among minority populations and are similarly highest in nonmetropolitan areas. That is, for most minority groups, minority status and nonmetropolitan residence represents a "double jeopardy," dramatically increasing the risk of experiencing poverty.

In nearly every instance, nonmetropolitan poverty rates are higher for all racial and ethnic groups and age categories.[6] While Whites and Asians are roughly comparable in terms of poverty rates, falling somewhat under the average for total population in each residential category, Black, American Indian and Latino populations show markedly higher poverty rates than Whites and Asians, and this is especially true in nonmetropolitan areas and among persons under 18 years of age. For example, nearly 46 percent of African American children in nonmetropolitan areas live in poverty. This contrasts starkly with the poverty rate of nonmetropolitan White children, at 18 percent, or the poverty rate of White children in metropolitan areas, at 14 percent. Similarly, nonmetropolitan Blacks, American Indian and Latino elders experience between two and three times the poverty rate for nonmetropolitan seniors as a whole. In addition, median income levels are lower in nonmetropolitan areas across all ethnic groups.

These disparities are explained in part by differences in educational attainment, which has a significant positive effect on overall earning potential, and a significant negative effect on the likelihood of experiencing poverty. As discussed in Chapter 4, educational attainment rates overall are markedly lower in nonmetropolitan areas. While nearly 30 percent of metropolitan residents have a bachelor's degree or higher, the same is true of only about 17 percent of nonmetropolitan residents. Only Asians among rural minority groups stand out for their

Box 7.1 Defining and Enumerating Race and Ethnicity

The United States Census Bureau collects information on race and Hispanic origin for every individual living in the United States. The federal government considers race and Hispanic origin to be two separate categories since race refers to one of five racial categories established by the U.S. Office of Managements and Budget (White, Black, or African American, American Indian and Alaska Native, Asian, and Native Hawaiian and Other Pacific Islander), whereas Hispanic refers to persons of Spanish or Latino background, regardless of race. In 2000 the U.S. Census Bureau provided a new option for racial identification, enabling people to identify themselves as belonging to two or more racial groups. At that time 2.4 percent of the population identified themselves as belonging to two or more races. Because of this change in enumeration and classification, Census data from the 2000 and later may not be entirely comparable with data collected earlier. The complete definitions for racial categories appear below (Grieco & Cassidy 2001: 2).

"White" refers to people having origins in any of the original people of Europe, the Middle East, or North Africa. It includes people who indicated their race or races as "White" or wrote in entries such as Irish, German, Italian, Lebanese, Near Easterner, Arab, or Polish.

"Black or African American" refers to people having origins in any of the Black racial groups of Africa. It includes people who indicated their race or races as "Black, African A., or Negro," or wrote in entries such as African American, Afro American, Nigerian, or Haitian.

"American Indian and Alaska Native" refers to people having origins in any of the original peoples of North and South America (including Central America), and who maintain tribal affiliation or community attachment. It includes people who indicated their race or races by marking this category or writing in their principal or enrolled tribe, such as Rosebud Sioux, Chippewa, or Navajo.

"Asian" refers to people having origins in any of the original peoples of the Far East, Southeast Asia, or the Indian subcontinent. It includes people who indicated their race or races as "Asian Indian," "Chinese," "Filipino," Korean," "Japanese," Vietnamese," or "Other Asian," or wrote in entries such as Burmese, Hmong, Pakistani, or Thai.

"Native Hawaiian and Other Pacific Islander" refers to people having origins in any of the original peoples of Hawaii, Guam, Samoa, or other Pacific Islands. It includes people who indicated their race or races as "Native Hawaiian," "Guamanian or Chamorro," "Samoan," or "Other Pacific Islander," or wrote in entries such as Tahitian, Mariana Islander, or Chuukese.

high educational attainment and low poverty. In fact, the rate of nonmetropolitan Asians with a bachelor's degree or more exceeds that of all metropolitan residents as a whole. Hence, educational attainment would appear to be a significant factor in life chances and economic status across ethnic groups with rural minorities having lower education and hence lower income and higher poverty rates. This, however, only tells a part of the story when considering historical patterns of discrimination and social exclusion experienced by most minority groups, and especially in rural areas. In the sections to follow, we look in depth at three different racial and ethnic minority groups, African Americans, American Indians, and

Table 7.1 Economic and Educational Attainment Status of U.S. Racial and Ethnic Groups by Metropolitan Status, 2006–2008*

	Metro						Nonmetro					
	All	**White**	**Black**	**Indian**	**Asian**	**Latino**	**All**	**White**	**Black**	**Indian**	**Asian**	**Latino**
Economic Status												
Poverty Rate												
total	13.15	10.50	24.66	25.31	10.62	21.23	16.09	13.71	34.02	31.13	13.00	26.61
under 18	18.19	13.61	34.50	32.78	11.50	27.96	22.24	18.25	45.66	38.32	14.15	33.21
65+	9.81	8.32	20.85	19.54	12.04	19.29	11.82	10.45	30.81	24.30	9.02	24.36
Median Income	54,756	59,027	36,700	41,400	69,783	42,319	41,053	42,986	23,799	30,812	52,068	33,500
Educational Attainment												
less than HS	14.91	12.29	18.60	23.10	14.50	39.05	18.26	16.44	30.53	25.64	16.81	45.32
HS Grad	13.33	28.05	32.54	30.24	16.73	27.29	18.59	37.57	38.76	36.41	24.28	28.65
Some College	27.60	28.21	30.49	31.83	18.89	20.68	27.28	27.88	22.32	28.86	23.33	18.37
Bachelor's +	29.50	31.46	18.37	14.83	49.88	12.98	17.13	18.11	8.40	9.09	35.59	7.65

Source: American Community Survey (3 year estimates).
* Percent unless otherwise indicated.

Latinos, tracing their historical presence in rural America, their current status as well as future prospects.

African Americans in Rural Areas

The status of African Americans in the United States is indelibly marked by the legacies of slavery and racism. This is particularly true of African Americans living in nonmetropolitan areas who are, as we previously note, overwhelmingly concentrated in the South. Over half of the 500 counties identified by the USDA as "persistent poverty counties" are also located in the South, and as Harris and Worthen (2003) point out, most of these counties comprise the "Black Belt," a stretch of counties extending from Texas to Virginia and containing nearly 80 percent of the nonmetropolitan Black population. The Black Belt thus represents a stark illustration of the intersection between race, place and poverty.

African peoples were first brought to colonial America in the early 1600s, primarily as indentured servants. The race-based system of slavery took full form in the 1700s as hundreds of thousands of African men, women, and children were kidnapped and/or sold to slave traders, and forcibly taken across the Atlantic to provide labor for the colonies, mainly in the Caribbean and the agricultural South. By 1860 there were 3.5 million slaves in the slave-holding states.

The post Civil War period in the early second half of the nineteenth century held some promise for newly freed Blacks with new federal protections and rising numbers of African American land holders, politicians, elected officials, educators, and entrepreneurs However, this promise proved to be short lived. The Compromise of 1877 led to the removal of federal troops who had been posted in Southern states and whose presence had helped to protect many of the basic civil rights extended to newly freed African Americans. The withdrawal of troops was followed by the implementation of grandfather clauses (stipulating that only persons whose grandfather had voted could themselves vote), poll taxes and reading comprehension requirements that strengthened the social and political exclusion of African Americans in the South. Jim Crow laws stipulating "separate but equal" status for African Americans provided a legal context for the already comprehensive social, political and economic exclusion experienced by African Americans. "What remained and dominated in the wake of the post-Reconstruction compromise," write Harris and Worthen (2003), "were well-entrenched norms and patterns of social and political interaction between Whites and Blacks that were deeply rooted in the dynamics of the plantation/slave economy" (p. 35).

As Wilson argues, "power relations within production made possible a rigid racial division of labor that restricted the vast majority of Southern Blacks to a few manufacturing operations, and these were primarily unskilled position" (2007: 76). Rural African Americans working in agriculture were largely dependent upon sharecropping, tenant-share arrangements in which housing, food, farm supplies, and often portions of land to till were provided to tenant workers. Through this arrangement the landlord was able effectively to purchase and therefore control the labor power of the sharecropper. Sharecropping was a form of "debt bondage" that tied rural Blacks to the land thereby assuring White landowners an adequate supply of cheap labor. As Austin explains:

> At the end of the year, the landowners 'settled crops' with their sharecroppers by giving them money and/or a share of the crops. Sometimes, the owners had to lend money to the sharecroppers on the next year's crops if a family of sharecroppers failed to make any money on the crop. In other words, the family often worked for an entire year, received nothing at settlement, and had to borrow money from the landowner. (2006: 30–1)

Despite the predominance of sharecropping and systematic economic disenfranchisement, there were over 900,000 farms owned by African Americans in 1920, most of which were dependent on Whites for year-to-year operating capital. Shortly after that time, however, the number of African American farms began to diminish. Floods and, in particular, the decimation of cotton crops by boll weevils[7] severely depressed the South's agricultural economy. Federal assistance was directed to Southern farmers, but local government control of assistance often meant that White elites were able to direct the funds and resources as they saw fit, further disadvantaging African American farmers (Austin 2006). Moreover, since government assistance enhanced White farmers' access to labor saving equipment that was only efficient when used on larger acreages, White landowners became hesitant to lend Blacks money to operate their farms as sharecroppers, or to rent Blacks land so they could work as tenant farmers. Accordingly, the tenant and share cropping systems that had tied Blacks to the rural South began to crumble, displacing large Black populations.

During the first half of the twentieth century agriculture became increasingly mechanized thereby displacing more and more labor. As immigration was stifled by restrictive legislation, and as manufacturing and industrialization further expanded in the Northern states, increasing numbers of African Americans left the South in search of greater economic opportunities and, in particular, more tolerant racial climates in what has been called the "Great Migration" (Wilkerson 2010). The Great Migration began around 1910–1920 when over 500,000 Blacks left the South, more than had left in the preceding five decades! Between 1870 and 1940 the South experienced a net outmigration of two million African Americans, with an additional 3.1 million between 1940 and 1960, and another 1.4 million in the 1960s. While much of the migration stream was directed towards industrializing areas around Detroit, Chicago, Cleveland, Cincinnati, Baltimore, Philadelphia, and New York City, others moved West, principally to urban centers in California. As a consequence, while in 1890 about 90 percent of the African American population resided in the South, only 50 percent lived there by 2000 (Frey 2004; Wilson 2007).

However, a reversal in migration flows occurred beginning in the 1970s when for the first time in the century, the South experienced a net in-migration of African Americans that continued into the 1990s and beyond. While the South experienced a net migration loss of 216,000 African Americans between 1965 and 1970, ten years later the South experienced a net migration *gain* of 195,000, and between 1995 and 2000, 348,000 African Americans (Wilson 2007). While much of this movement was to urban areas in the South (Lichter et al. 2007), in the 1990s it still accounted for a growth of the South's rural African American population by nearly 10 percent (Falk, Hunt, & Hunt, 2004).

This return migration was driven by declining economic opportunities in the

Northern cities as well as increasing incidence of urban crime and violence. It was also driven by historical and family connections in the South that many African American families had maintained (Stack 1996). As Falk and his colleagues explain:

> In contrast to the increasingly grim sense of life in the Northern inner cities, the South – somewhat ironically given its racial legacy – began to emerge as a region that offered a more promising economic future and a chance to connect (or reconnect) with historically significant African-American places and institutions. (2004: 492)

Does Black return migration signal a resurgence of the rural Black population in the region? In and of itself, it most likely does not, especially since most return migration is not directed towards rural areas. That said, a distinguishing characteristic of Black migrants to the South is that in-migrants tend to have higher educational attainment and are more likely to be in the labor force than their counterparts in the origin areas *and* the regions to which they are moving (Falk et al. 2004).[8] Stack (1996) has written convincingly of how return migrant have used their human capital to assume leadership roles in receiving communities. However, it is still unclear as to what the ultimate effects will be for rural community development within the Southern Black Belt and the implications for political, economic and social change in African American communities.

American Indians in Rural Areas

The American Indian[9] population represents an extraordinarily diverse set of ethnic and tribal groups with 310 federal Indian reservations located over thirty-three states (Gonzales 2003). The history of the American Indians since the arrival of Europeans has been one of tremendous hardship and suffering, and yet at the same time, characterized by a remarkable resiliency. Despite colonization of their land, persecution, displacement, disease, famine, and at the hands of the U.S. government serious and sustained attempts at cultural assimilation, American Indians have managed to maintain their culture, identity, and language, often despite great odds.

As a population, American Indians have also experienced significant growth. In 1900 the population was estimated at 237,000, mostly confined to rural reservations, while one hundred years later, the population had grown to 2.5 million. Much of the American Indian population increase in recent decades is due to more individuals identifying as American Indians, with as much as three-fifths of the increase in population between 1970 and 1980 due to changes in self-identification (Berry, Grossman, & Pawiki 2007; Gonzales 2003). Berry and colleagues contend that such identity-switching occurred because "some of the stigma of being identified as Native American was reduced by indigenous political mobilization of the 1960s and 1970s . . . along with other ethnic pride movements. This change affected people of mixed racial and ethnic ancestry who previously might have refused to identify their Native American background because of stigma as well as individuals with trace Native American background who wanted to affirm their support for marginalized groups or a romanticized ethnic identity" (2007: 60–61). Because of the history of treaties between Indian tribes and the U.S. government and the specific benefits and rights granted by those treaties, ethnic identification for American Indians has real and tangible implications that may go far beyond how one personally decides to self-identify.

While the U.S. Census determines American Indian identity through self-identification, each tribal government has its own methods for determining tribal affiliation, often on the basis of "blood quantum" (the percentage of one's background that is exclusively of American Indian descent). This has led to conflict in certain instances where some tribal members dispute the authenticity of other person's claims to membership. The "Cherokee Freedman" case is a recent example. It is little known that some Cherokees owned slaves and fought on the Confederate side during the Civil War. In 1866, the Cherokees signed a treaty guaranteeing newly freed Cherokee slaves citizenship in the tribe. Over time some "freedmen" were struck from the tribal rolls because they lacked Cherokee blood. However, in 2006 the Cherokee tribal court forced the tribe to recognize freedmen as official members, and 1,500 signed membership cards at that time (Lee-St. John 2007).

Among all minority groups in the United States, America Indians are unique in the federal recognition of the sovereign status of Indian tribes. As we discuss in Chapter 4, the federal government legally recognizes more than 560 American Indian tribes, granting tribal governments the authority to control tribal affairs including education, public safety, land use planning, and economic development. Sovereign nation status originally stemmed from colonial-era treaty-making with native peoples. This precedent established, the United States continued to consider recognized Indian tribes as sovereign nations, albeit as "domestic dependent nations" for which the federal government has the obligation, through a trust relationship, to "protect and preserve the interests of Indian tribes and their members" (Gonzales 2003: 45).

A major part of this trust relationship involves tribal reservation lands that are managed by the federal government in trust for tribal members. About four-fifths of Indian reservation land is Indian owned and held in trust by the federal government. This means that the land is fully under tribal authority and not subject to state laws, but that there are federal limitations placed on land use. Federal Indian reservation lands comprise nearly 55 million acres, or about two percent of the landmass in the Unites States. Reservations, most of which are located in isolated and arid parts of the U.S.,[10] and range in size from only a few acres to, in the case of the Navajo reservation, about 16 million acres (or about the size of West Virginia). Not all tribes have reservations, and some tribes have more than one reservation (Berry, Grossman, & Pawiki, 2007; Gonzales, 2003). Rather than representing land provided to tribes by the government, the lands instead reflect treaty arrangements whereby in the process of ceding originally occupied land, the government "reserved" or set aside lands that may or may not have comprised ancestral tribal homeland.

During the 1950s and 1960s the federal government, in part as a means of undermining the political and economic power of some tribes, developed policies encouraging tribal members to move from reservations to urban areas. This was done through financial incentives and promises of employment and housing opportunities, coupled with cuts in federal aid to rural reservations. In total

Box 7.2 Minority Self Governance: A Comparative Example

Tribal governance is one example of a legal provision granting an ethnic minority group quasi-independent governing status. While tribal governments have limited powers, they have nonetheless been a critical part of the ways in which American Indians have maintained cultural identity and some degree of political autonomy. Another example is the minority self-government system in Hungary.

In 1993, emerging out of several decades of state socialism along with the other East Block countries in the region, and at a time of intense ethnic conflict to the South in the former Yugoslavia, Hungary enacted Act 77 on the Rights of National and Ethnic Minorities. This legislation created the legal context for the establishment of minority self governments at both national and local (municipal) levels. The stated intent of the Act was to preserve and maintain "cultural autonomy" for Hungary's minority groups.

Similar to tribal governments, the role of minority self governments is to help ensure the wellbeing of their minority constituency, broadly through cultural independence, but the law also states that local minority self governments can establish educational institutions and foundations, become involved in the production of local printed or electronic media, establish and run enterprises, engage in economic development activities. Unlike tribal governments, the role of minority self governments at both local and national levels in terms of legislation and policy-making, is primarily consultative and minority self governments act as advocates for their minority constituencies within the broader political process. At the local level, minority self-government representatives have the right to attend all municipal government meetings, and though they lack voting rights, they have some limited veto power over local decision-making that concerns minority cultural, educational and language issues.

In the mid 1990s the first elections for minority self governments were held. At that time 817 local minority self governments were formed, mostly in smaller villages and towns, representing twelve separate minority groups. A second round of elections was held in 1998 and this time minority self governments were established in 1,363 municipalities (approximately one self government for every three municipalities), representing thirteen minority groups.

While Hungary's minority self-government system was unique, it has also been criticized on a number of levels. First, with the exception of Roma/Gypsies, relatively small minority populations live within Hungary's borders. On the other hand, there are large populations of ethnic Hungarians who live just outside Hungary's boundaries in Romania, Slovakia, Serbia, and elsewhere. Some have argued that the legislation served principally as a strategic means of pressuring neighboring states to pass similar legislation (to the benefit of ethnic Hungarians), while at the same time demonstrating "progressive" minority policies to the West and possibly speeding accession to the European Union.

Second, the only minority group of any significant size are Roma/Gypsies who comprise about eight percent of Hungary's total population and are distinct among minority groups given their very poor social, economic and political status. The minorities law seemed to offer new possibilities for Roma/Gypsy participation in the political sphere. But many argued that the law gave few meaningful political powers to minority groups, fewer resources. Further, the law provided municipal governments

Box 7.2 (continued)

with an excuse to pass responsibilities for attending to Roma/Gypsy community and social needs to minority governments, even though those minority governments in most cases hardly had the resources or political power to address meaningfully serious problems of housing, poverty, discrimination, racial violence, unemployment and other troubles affecting Roma/Gypsy communities. That is, although the minority self governments were conceived as primarily means of promoting and strengthening *cultural* identity, the main problems affecting Roma/Gypsies were more properly social and structural in nature.

Perhaps most damning though was the fact that even though the minority governments were established for the purpose of promoting "cultural autonomy," elections for minority self governments were held at the same time as municipal elections and there was no procedure put in place to prevent non-minorities from voting in minority self-government elections or even from running for office as minority candidates, since according to the Hungarian constitution, minority group status is entirely self-identified. This made it easily possible to subvert the election process.

For example in the village of Jászladány the established Roma minority self-government developed an acrimonious relationship with the mayor and the rest of the municipal government. After several years of conflict, at the next election cycle the wife of the mayor (an ethnic Hungarian like her husband) ran for office as a Roma self-government candidate, winning the election in 2002 through the votes from ethnic Hungarians in the village. This effectively ended the challenges to the municipal government's authority by the Roma minority self government.

Not all experiences have been this conflictual, but the example points to the limits and contradictions of Hungary's minority self-government system and how the authority of these self-governing bodies can quickly become nullified if they begin to pose too many challenges to the social and political status quo (Kovats 1999, Molnár & Schafft 2003; Schafft & Brown 2000).

between 1952 and 1972, about 100,000 American Indians moved from rural reservations to urban areas in large part through the Bureau of Indian Affairs Direct Employment Program. Ironically, this helped develop a stronger pan-Indian identity, influenced by the civil rights movements in the 1960s as well as groups like the Black Panthers that similarly functioned to consolidate ethnically based cultural and political power. Currently just under one-third of American Indians live on reservations or tribal lands. Many others live in urban areas, particularly in the West, such as the Los Angeles, Phoenix, and Tucson metropolitan areas.

Reservation land that is not trust land may be owned by non-Indians. This, argues Gonzales (2003), dates back to the General Allotment Act of 1887 (also known as the Dawes Act) which made possible the conversion of collectively owned tribal land into individual parcels with deeds held by tribal members, or instead deeded to White settlers and/or sold to private interests. One consequence of this was the fragmentation of reservation land not held in trust, creating sometimes Byzantine bureaucratic and administrative dilemmas since the federal government also manages land and mineral rights leasing on reservation lands with revenues paid back to the tribe. Many observers consider the sale of non-trust land to non-Indians as another example of the federal government's attempts to assimilate American Indians by reducing their degree of residential segregation.

In December, 2009, in what represented one of the largest class action lawsuits ever brought against the federal government, a preliminary agreement was reached to compensate tribal members for federal mismanagement of funds derived from leasing reservation lands. The settlement calls for $1.4 billion in compensation to tribal members with an additional $2 billion set aside to buy up fractional interests in reservation land, returning it to reservation land held in trust. Fragmentation of reservation land into fractional interests had over time made much of this land unusable and created untenable logistical dilemmas for both the Department of the Interior and landowners, such as the example of a single forty-acre piece of land, valued at $20,000, which has 439 owners, most of whom receive less than $1 per year, but yet which costs the federal government $40,000 to administer the trusts (Savage 2009). This will not resolve the problem of fragmented reservation lands because many may not be willing to sell their parcels, but it represents an important legal decision in favor of American Indian tribes and the possibility of reversing land tenure practices that have had cumulatively negative consequences for tribal members and tribal sovereignty.

Indian Gaming and Economic Development

Long marked by poverty and unemployment, in the 1970s tribes began to initiate gambling enterprises on reservation lands. Though there was initial resistance at the state level, in 1987 the Supreme Court decided that gambling could be offered without restrictions on reservations in states where gambling was already permitted. There are now over three hundred casinos and other gaming facilities on reservations in twenty-nine states, with gambling revenues increasing from $212 million in 1989 to nearly $13 billion in 2001. In 1988 the U.S. Congress passed the Indian Gaming Regulatory Act (IGRA) which directed that the revenues generated from gaming were to be used exclusively for tribal governments, the welfare of tribes and tribal members, economic development, and local governments.

Casino revenues in many cases have had dramatic effects on the wellbeing of American Indian communities and economic development. In 2001, 300,000 jobs were associated with tribal casinos, three-quarters going to non-Indians. Casinos have also had a significant effect on reducing unemployment on reservations and removal of people from welfare (Gonzales 2003). Although the economic impacts of Indian gaming have been dramatic, there is also ambivalence about whether gambling is consistent with Indian culture and values. Much, though not all, of this ambivalence often comes from outside the American Indian community:

> Gaming as a form of economic development fuels critiques because too many Americans indigenous "tradition" represents the opposite of casinos, which embody capitalism, nonproductive market exchange, and money itself. Conservative critics of tribal sovereignty as "special rights" argue that tribes' embrace of casino capitalism indicates that they are no longer "really" Indians and thus do not deserve special legal status. (Cattelino 2004: 84).
>
> Some commentators have argued though that far from betraying a commonly held cultural ethos gaming has been a means of establishing unprecedented

economic development, renewed engagement with tribal life, and, in the process, new political power (Rosenthal 2004). Even with this new revenue stream, however, American Indians remain one of the nation's most impoverished populations. While gaming represents a new and significant means of increasing social and economic wellbeing for tribal members, it is far from representing a more comprehensive economic development strategy.

American Indians and the Tribal College Movement[11]

Beginning in the 1960s American Indians initiated an important new effort aimed at self-determination, education, and community development. The Tribal College Movement was an attempt to reverse decades of educational disenfranchisement and increase post-secondary educational opportunities for American Indians by establishing institutions of higher education, tribally controlled and structured to account for the social, cultural, and political realities encountered by contemporary American Indians. As Faircloth and Tippeconnic note:

> Tribal communities recognized the importance of education in maintaining their cultural and linguistic capital and in gaining access to economic capital; however, many of them felt that existing mainstream institutions of higher education were inaccessible or didn't work in concert with their traditions and values. (2010: 178)

The first tribal college, Navajo Community College (later changed to Diné College) was founded in 1968 on the Navajo reservation in Arizona. This was shortly followed by the founding of the Oglala Lakota College established in 1971 on the Pine Ridge reservation in South Dakota. There are now about forty tribal colleges and universities across the United States and Canada, with additional colleges proposed. As of 2005, tribal colleges and universities in the United States enrolled about 17,000 degree-seeking students (about 80 percent of whom were American Indians), and an approximately equal number of non degree-seeking students.

While as institutions of higher education the most immediate role is educational, tribal colleges also help to meet the needs of tribal communities in the areas of economic development, community health and cultural preservation. Tribal colleges in the United States have also recently begun developing global ties to other indigenous institutions through collaborations and exchanges with institutions in Canada, New Zealand, and Central America, fostering "reciprocal relationships, both locally and globally, that provide much needed educational services for indigenous people and communities" (Faircloth and Tippeconnic 2010: 180). As such they represent unprecedented educational opportunities for tribal and indigenous peoples to attain post-secondary education and training attuned to the social, cultural, and political realities of students' home communities while at the same time developing global connections with indigenous communities elsewhere.

Latinos in Rural Areas and the Changing Patterns of Immigration

As of 2000, rural Latinos were largely concentrated in the South and Southwest (Kandel and Parrado 2006). This reflected historical settlement patterns including the fact that most of this territory was annexed to the United States in 1848 as a result of the Mexican–American war. Many scholars see this as a war of conquest that was motivated by the ideology of "manifest destiny." One of its unintended consequences was the marooning of a sizable Mexican population in what then became American territory. In addition, and perhaps more importantly, established Latino settlements in the rural Southwest reflect the settling out of Mexican farm workers who were actively recruited to the U.S. throughout the twentieth century, and increasingly since the introduction of the Bracero Program during the Second World War in which replacing domestic labor shortages in agriculture with Mexican workers was seen as an integral part of the nation's war effort. The program was continued until 1964, with over 4.5 million work contracts signed by temporary Mexican farm workers coming to the United States for agricultural employment (Mize 2006).

While the Bracero program was terminated in 1964, it contributed to the establishment of durable migration networks linking the United States and Mexico (Chavez 2009). Hence, Mexican migration to the U.S. did not cease with the project's termination, in fact, it has accelerated in recent years, reflecting dramatic differences in economic wellbeing in the U.S and Mexico, and explicit recruitment practices on the part of particular industries such as food processing, meat packing, and construction.

Patterns of Latino Migration

Immigrant settlement is never evenly distributed within destination countries. Rather, immigrants have historically made strong use of formal and informal social networks to secure housing and employment, and reduce the costs and risks of migrating. Because of this, migrant destinations have historically mostly been centered around larger "gateway" urban areas (Lichter & Johnson 2006), very often places with existing ethnic enclaves of other migrants and clusters of businesses and economic activities associated with particular ethnic minorities (Massey 1985; Portes 1995).

Portes, describing urban ethnic enclaves, writes:

> First, their emergence is signaled by the transformation of certain urban areas, which acquire a "foreign" look that is complete with commercial signs in the immigrants' language and a physical layout of business that accords with the group's cultural practices. Second . . . enclaves are economically diversified. In addition to trade, they commonly encompass industrial production and specialized services both for the ethnic and external markets. Third, at some point in their development, enclaves become "institutionally complete," allowing newcomers to lead their lives entirely within the confines of the ethnic community. (Portes 1995: 27–28)

As Pfeffer and Parra point out then, "ethnic enclaves represent contexts with concentrated social resources" (2009: 241) that facilitate social integration into new places, provide employment opportunities and reduce the multiple tangible and intangible costs of migration.

While previously key migration destinations in the United States were principally in urban centers in the Northeast and Southwest, such as New York City and Los Angeles, during the 1990s demographers began to detect marked shifts in the patterns of immigrant settlement. In particular, they noted movement to "non-traditional" migration locations, often in rural areas as well as places that had not previously attracted many migrants (Barcus 2006; Kandel & Parrado 2006; Kandel & Cromartie 2004). The patterns of nonmetropolitan immigration in many cases have been so pronounced that, as Katherine Donato and colleagues observe, they have "offset native population decline in some nonmetropolitan areas and fueled growth in others" (2008: 76) such that the percentage of foreign born persons living in nonmetropolitan areas jumped from 1.9 percent in 1990 to 3.2 percent in 2000.

Massey and Capoferro (2008) note that these trends have been especially pronounced among Mexican migrants, who historically concentrated in places like Texas, California, and Arizona.[12] As late as the period between 1985 and 1990, 63 percent of Mexican migrants went to California and an additional 20 percent went to either Texas or Illinois. However, ten years later only 28 percent of Mexican migrants went to California. The migration flows to Illinois and Texas remained relatively stable, although many other states began to attract Mexican migrants as well, including states that had not previously experienced much in-migration, such as Georgia, North Carolina, Ohio, and Tennessee.

Massey and his colleagues argue that several factors account for the redistribution of Mexican migrants to non-traditional destinations. The first was the Immigration Reform and Control Act (IRCA) in 1986, which imposed new sanctions on employers who hired undocumented workers, increased resources to border patrols and provided amnesty for undocumented agricultural workers and other undocumented workers who had continuous residence in the United States from early 1982 until 1986. The IRCA had the effect of providing over three million people with residence documents, which attracted additional undocumented workers to California, in the process flooding local labor markets. Newly documented workers were also suddenly able to move around with less fear of problems with immigration officials.

This was followed in the mid 1990s by Governor Pete Wilson's campaign for re-election in which he ran on a strong anti-immigration platform, one of the centerpieces of which was Proposition 187 that attempted to prohibit undocumented workers from accessing a range of public services including public school enrollment and other social services. While most of the provisions were never implemented because they were found to be unconstitutional, Proposition 187 nonetheless had the effect of making California a far less hospitable environment for Mexican migrants.

Around the same time as Proposition 187, the Immigration and Naturalization service implemented new border patrol strategies that involved "selective hardening" of parts of the border between the United States and Mexico, principally border areas that had previously been very porous and the sites of much illegal movement back and forth. In San Diego, California, an 8-foot tall steel fence was erected for fourteen miles and this was coupled with high-intensity floodlights and border patrols every few hundred yards. Similarly in El Paso, Texas the Border Patrol instituted an aggressive crackdown on illegal border crossings, significantly reducing the volume of illegal crossings.

Massey and Carafello argue that while these border crackdowns in areas that had traditionally been primary crossing points for Mexican migrants had the effect of reducing illegal crossings at these places, they did not reduce illegal immigration overall, but instead *deflected* undocumented migrants to crossings in other more sparsely populated and patrolled parts of the U.S.–Mexico border. Simultaneously, the increased costs and risks associated with illegal border crossings provided incentives for undocumented workers, once in the United States, to stay rather than travel back and forth between Mexico and the United States. Moreover, militarization of the border and increasing propensity to move permanently meant that new waves of immigrants became more likely to move as entire families rather than as individual workers. This, in turn, had the effect of increasing the rate of net population growth among undocumented migrants. Similar shifts in migration patterns were seen for other migrants from Central America, although historically these migrants had tended to have greater geographic dispersion anyway and so the shifts were not as pronounced.

While these explanations are compelling, they primarily account for "push" factors that make particular migration destinations less appealing (such as anti-immigrant legislation in California), but they do not provide insights into characteristics that make new migration destinations attractive for migrants ("pull" factors), and in particular, migration destinations in "non-traditional" nonmetropolitan areas that have little or no experience with minority and/or immigrant populations.

Donato et al. (2008) examine patterns of migration into nonmetropolitan "offset" counties, those counties that between 1990 and 2000 would have experienced net population decline were it not for the in-movement of foreign born persons. They find that immigrants in these offset counties are disproportionately recently arrived Mexicans, employed in low-skill and low-wage employment including construction, agricultural production, rug manufacture and leather tanning, and, in particular, animal slaughtering and processing.

Restructuring of the Meat-Processing Industry and the Effects on Migration

Changes in the labor needs for the meat-processing industry, and the location of meat-processing facilities in rural areas are the result of structural shifts within the meat-processing industry as a whole. Through the 1970s most meat processing was done in larger urban areas, notably Chicago, Kansas City and other Midwestern metropolises where livestock were transported by rail to slaughterhouses. From the late 1970s onward however, along with fewer and larger farms, the meat-processing industry also consolidated with fewer but larger plants. Meat-processing plants also began to relocate to rural areas where costs were lower. Processing meat nearer to where animals were grown reduced transportation costs of live animals. Cost of land was cheaper on which plants could be built, and there were often fewer environmental restrictions. There were also lower labor costs in part because of the reduced union presence in rural areas. Additionally, many rural communities facing economic troubles were only too happy to bring in new business and jobs. Automation and technological advances also meant that plants had less need for skilled work (Martin 2009).

At first many meat-processing plants in rural areas were not able to find sufficient labor, and so a critical task was labor recruitment (McConnell & Miraftab 2009). Mexican and Asian workers quickly filled this labor vacuum. The IRCA legalized several million Mexican workers in 1986, many of these who previously had been employed in seasonal agricultural work. These workers quickly discovered that they could secure year-round work in the meat-processing plants. The plants, in turn, began to recruit further through ethnic networks in part because of the need for a constant labor supply since meat processing, which is particularly dangerous and difficult work, is also associated with very high worker turnover. In effect, this labor recruiting process turns globalization on its head. Instead of off-shoring domestic employment to low labor cost locations in Asia and elsewhere, meat processers brought low cost labor to the U.S.

Gouveia and Stull (1997) document the changing economic and demographic structure of Lexington, Nebraska which has experienced large influxes of Latino workers attracted by the local siting of a multinational meat-packing firm. The community, experiencing years of economic decline and outmigration following the farm crisis of the 1980s (see Chapter 9), did its best to attract new industry using a number of tax abatements and other local incentives. Their efforts succeeded in attracting a large beef-packing plant to the town. After the plant opened, it quickly became apparent that local labor was insufficient to maintain production. Accordingly, Latino migrants were quickly recruited to supply a ready pool of cheap labor for the low-wage work being offered. While the local job base was significantly expanded, the pay was only slightly higher than the minimum wage, and the municipality's infrastructure and social support systems were severely strained by the sudden in-migration of limited resource workers, most of whom did not speak English.

Some observers have noted the parallels between rural communities where new meat-packing plants have been established and other "boomtowns" associated with natural resource extraction (Broadway & Stull 2006). In these places sudden increases in population, even though associated with economic activity, were also often thought locally to be connected to social problems such as increased crime rates, drug and alcohol abuse, and other social ills (see chapter 5). Broadway (2007), for example, in a comparative study of two meat-packing communities, Brooks, Alberta, and Garden City, Kansas, described how the siting of large meat-packing plants resulted in influxes of immigrant labor, followed by housing shortages and increased demand for social services. Both places also experienced significant increases in jobs, though these were low-paying jobs, and average income in both places fell.

As Martin (2009) points out though, many small towns face either accepting the challenges of new immigrants or risk further depopulation. In eleven Great Plains states, those counties lacking any town larger than 2,500 people lost over one-third of their residents over the course of the past fifty years. In many small and rural communities then, the influx of immigrants may signal a new lease on life to economically declining places where populations have been steadily shrinking and aging. While there is often concern among long-term residents that sudden arrivals of newcomers (especially those who also happen to be racial and/or ethnic minorities) may be accompanied by increases in crime, drug use, and other social problems, more recent work focused on migration "boomtowns" suggests that these concerns may not be warranted. Crowley and Lichter (2009) using a variety of secondary sources find that large in-migrations of Latino immigrants have had few negative economic impacts on destination communities, and they find no evidence that such influxes are associated with rising crime rates.[13] Similarly, other studies point to new patterns of social, residential and economic integration of new minorities in rural and small towns (Pfeffer & Parra 2009; Salamon 2003), even those that bear historical legacies of racial exclusion (McConnel & Miraftab 2009).

This does not signal the end of racism and nativism within rural communities. More likely, most migrant boomtowns are "sites of both conflict and accommodation" (McConnell & Miraftab 2009: 617) as long-term residents weigh new changes in local culture and community against the very real threat of economic demise, and as newcomers socially and economically integrate into new communities and develop new ties to place.

Conclusions

Rural America as a whole is and has tended to be far less racially and ethnically diverse than America's urban areas. Yet as we have shown in this chapter, not only do racial and ethnic minorities have long histories in rural America, but there are also areas where there have historically been and continue to be large minority concentrations. Additionally, there are new and dramatic changes that have recently been taking place across many rural and small towns as new minority populations move in. In the case of Latino populations, much of this movement has its roots in macro-scale structural changes in rural economies and especially in the structure of the meat-processing industry. Changes in immigration and border regulations have also had important effects on the patterns of immigration and changes in rural ethnic diversity. But changes in rural diversity are not entirely due to changes in Mexican migration and settlement patterns alone, but to in-migration of other immigrants as well and to changes migration patterns of native born populations, including African Americans.

Many areas of rural America have tragic histories of racial conflict and exclusion, legacies that continue to exist in the form of de facto racial segregation, and a range of social and economic disparities. And yet there are reasons to be hopeful as we consider the potential implications of African American return migration to the South, the development, advancement, and global spread of indigenous institutions of higher education, and the ways in which many rural communities are embracing the social, economic, and cultural benefits of diverse newcomers. It will remain an important task of sociologists, demographers, economists, educational researchers, and others to continue to gauge the multiple effects and outcomes of these new patterns of ethnic and demographic change and in doing so better understand the ways in which communities can best respond to these changes, maximizing the welfare of newcomers, rural minority populations, and of rural America more broadly.

Notes

1 Studies of human genetics have suggested that about 94% of physical variation is contained *within* conventionally understood "racial groups and only about 6% of the variation is accounted for by cross-group differences" (AAA 1998).

2 It is well worth noting that bio-physical constructs are *themselves* socially constructed (and often, according to many commentators, quite arbitrarily). And yet, when socially legitimized as agreed-upon categories, they assume an artificial "naturalness." However, they are not "natural." Rather they are the socially constructed categories people create and use to talk about nature (Sismondo 2010).

3 See Chapter 10 for a discussion of the relationship between minority status and risk of poverty.

4 Figures calculated from U.S. Census 2006–2008 American Community Survey 3-Year Estimates.

5 In 1860, over 40% of the people in each of these states were slaves, with South Carolina having a 57% slave population.

6 Only nonmetropolitan Asians 65 years and older, as a group, have lower poverty rates than their metropolitan counterparts.

7 Boll weevils were the subject of the songs of many rural musicians from that time. One song, "*Mississippi Boweavil Blues*" recorded in the 1920s by Charlie Patton, an African American musician from the Mississippi Delta region, includes the lyrics, "*Boll weevil told the farmer, I ain't gonna treat you fair. Take all the blossoms and leave you an empty square.*" Mike Rugel, an historian and musicologist with the Delta Blues Museum in Clarksdale, Mississippi, has noted that poor Southern Blacks may have had a strong identification with the boll weevil, a disdained and seemingly insignificant insect that nonetheless had the capacity to single-handedly cripple and subvert the South's agricultural ruling class. For more information, see Rugel's *Uncensored History of the Blues* podcast at http://uncensoredhistoryoftheblues.purplebeech.com/.

8 This is contrary to the expectations of conventional migration theory in which movers migrate to areas of greater economic opportunity than origin areas and in which stable residents at the places of destination (not new in-migrants) have the higher economic status. Falk et al. note that this may suggest "the dominance of pull (over push) factors that positively select these recent migrants to the South" (2004: 501).

9 We follow Gonzales (2003) and use the term "American Indian" to refer to those persons living within the United States who are descendants of the original North American aboriginal populations. This terminology is consistent with the term used by most to self-identify, and it is consistent with terminology used in federal legal statutes. Furthermore, it avoids the potential confusion of the frequently used term "Native American," which implies that somehow others born in the U.S. are not "native."

10 For example, nearly 30% of Arizona is Indian reservation.

11 This section draws heavily from Faircloth and Tippeconnic (2010).

12 Prior to the Great Depression in the 1930s, 86% of Mexican immigrants went to Texas, California, and Arizona. After the Second World War, California attracted the most Mexican immigrants, and by 1970 California was home to over 50% of Mexican immigrants and Texas to 27% (Massey & Capoferro 2008).

13 They do, however, suggest that such influxes are likely to put significant strains on schools and health-care providers, and they further suggest that social problems could rise dramatically if the industries attracting immigrants (e.g., often meat-processing plants) were to close and/or relocate (Crowley & Lichter 2009; cf. Broadway & Stull 2006)

References

Anthropological Anthropological Association (AAA). 1998. Anthropological Association statement on "race." May 17. Accessed November 15, 2009 at: www.aaanet.org/stmts/racepp.htm.

Apple, M.W. 2009. Is Racism in Education an Accident? *Educational Policy*, 23(4), 651–659.

Austin, S.D.W. 2006. *The Transformation of Plantation Politics: Black Politics, Concentrated Poverty and Social Capital in the Mississippi Delta.* Albany, NY State University of New York Press.

Barcus, H.R. 2006. New Destinations for Hispanic Migrants: An Analysis of Rural Kentucky, pp. 89–109. In Smith, H.A. & Furuseth, O.J. (eds) *Latinos in the New South.* Burlington, VT, Ashgate.

Berry, K.A., Grossman, Z., & Pawiki, L.H. 2007. Native Americans, pp. 51–70. In Miyares, I.M. & Airriess C.A. (eds) *Contemporary Ethnic Geographies in America.* Lanham, MD, Rowman & Littlefield.

Broadway, M. 2007. Meatpacking and the Transformation of Rural Communities: A Comparison of Brooks, Alberta and Garden City, Kansas. *Rural Sociology*, 72(4), 560–582.

Broadway, M. & Stull, D.D. 2006. Meat Processing and Garden City, KS: Boom and Bust. *Journal of Rural Studies*, 22, 55–66.

Cattelino, J.R. 2004. Casino Roots: The Cultural Production of Twentieth-Century Seminole Economic Development, pp. 66–90. In Hosmar, B., O'Neill, C. & Fixico, D. (eds) *Native Pathways: American Indian Culture and Economic Development in the Twentieth Century.* Boulder, University Press of Colorado.

Chavez, S. 2009. The Sonoran Desert's Domestic Bracero Programme: Institutional Actors and the Creation of Labour Migration Streams. *International Migration*, 48, 1–32.

Churchill, W. 1999. The Tragedy and the Travesty: The Subversion of Indigenous Sovereignty in North America, pp. 17–71. In Johnson, T.R. (ed.) *Contemporary Native American Political Issues.* Walnut Creek, CA, Altamira Press.

Crowley, M. & Lichter, D.T. 2009. Social Disorganization in New Latino Destinations? *Rural Sociology*, 74(4), 573–604.

Donato, K.M., Tolbert, C., Nucci, A., & Kawano, Y. 2008. Changing Faces, Changing Places: The Emergence of New Nonmetropolitan Immigrant Gateways, pp. 75–98. In Massey, D.S. (ed.) *New Faces in New Places: The Changing Geography of American Immigration.* New York, Russell Sage.

Faircloth, S. & Tippeconnic, J. 2010. Tribally Controlled Colleges and Universities: Global Influence and Local Design, pp. 175–190. In Schafft, K.A., & Jackson, A. (eds). *Rural Education for the Twenty-First Century: Identity, Place, and Community in a Globalizing World.* University Park, PA, Penn State University Press.

Falk, W.W., Hunt, L.L., & Hunt, M.O. 2004. Return Migrations of African Americans to the South: Reclaiming a Land of Promise, Going Home, or Both? *Rural Sociology*, 29(4), 490–509.

Frey, W.H. 2004. *The New Great Migration: Black Americans' Return to the South, 1965–2000.* The Living Cities Census Series. Washington D.C., The Brookings Institution.

Gonzales, A. 2003. American Indians: Their Contemporary Reality and Future Trajectory, pp. 43–56. In Brown, D.L. & Swanson, L.E. (eds) *Challenges for Rural America in the Twenty-First Century.* University Park, PA, Penn State University Press.

Gouveia, L., & Stull, D.D. 1997. Latino Immigrants, Meatpacking, and Rural Communities: A Case Study of Lexington, Nebraska. JSRI Research Report no. 26. Lansing, Julian Samora Research Institute, Michigan State University.

Grieco, E.M. & Cassidy, R.C. 2001. *Overview of Race and Hispanic Origin.* Census 2000 Brief C2KBR/01-1. Washington, D.C., U.S. Census Bureau.

Groenke, S. & Nespor, J. 2010. "The Drama of their Daily Lives": Racist Language and Struggles Over the Local in a Rural High School, pp. 49–71. In Schafft, K.A. & Jackson, A. (eds), *Rural Education for the Twenty-First Century: Identity, Place, and Community in a Globalizing World.* University Park, PA, Penn State University Press.

Harris, R.P. & Worthen, D. 2003. African Americans in Rural America, pp. 32–42. In Brown, D.L. & L.E. Swanson, L.E. (eds) *Challenges for Rural America in the Twenty-First Century.* University Park, PA, Penn State University Press.

Hochschild, A. 1999. *King Leopold's Ghost.* New York, Mariner.

Holloway, S.L. 2007. Burning Issues: Whiteness, Rurality and the Politics of Difference. *Geoforum*, 38, 7–20.

Immigration Reform and Control Act, 8 USC note 1101.1986.

Jaspin, E. 2007. *Buried in Bitter Waters: The Hidden History of Racial Cleansing In America.* New York, Basic Books.

Kandel, W. & Cromartie, J. 2004. *New Patterns of Hispanic Settlement in Rural America.* USDA Rural Development Research Report No. 99. Washington D.C., USDA.

Kandel, W. & Parrrado, E. 2006. Rural Hispanic Population Growth: Public Policy Impacts in Nonmetro Counties, pp. 155–176. In Kandel, W. & Brown, D.L. (eds) *Population Change and Rural Society.* Dordrecht, Springer.

Kovats, M. 1999. Minority Rights and Roma Politics in Hungary, pp. 145–156. In Cordell, K. (ed.) *Ethnicity and Democratization in the New Europe.* London, Routledge.

Lee-St. John, J. 2007. The Cherokee Nation's New Battle. *Time.* June 27. Accessed December 29, 2009 at: http://www.time.com/time/nation/article/0,8599,1635873,00.html.

Lichter, D.T. & Johnson, K.M. 2006. Emerging Rural Settlement Patterns and the Geographic Redistribution of America's New Immigrants. *Rural Sociology,* 71(1), 109–131.

Lichter, D.T., Parisi, D., Grice, S. & Taquino, M. 2007. National Estimates of Racial Segregation in Rural and Small Town America. *Demography.* 44(3), 563–583.

Loewen, J.W. 2005. *Sundown Towns: A Hidden Dimension of American Racism.* New York, The New Press.

McConnell, E.D., & Miraftab, F. 2009. Sundown Town to Little Mexico: Old-timers and Newcomers in an American Small Town. *Rural Sociology,* 74(4), 605–629.

Marrow, H.B. 2008. Hispanic Immigration, Black Population Size, and Intergroup Relations in the Rural and Small-Town South, pp. 211–248. In Massey, D.S. (ed.) *New Faces in New Places: The Changing Geography of American Immigration.* New York, Russell Sage.

Martin, P. 2009. *Importing Poverty?: Immigration and the Changing Face of Rural America.* New Haven, Yale University Press.

Massey, D.S. 1985. Ethnic Residential Segregation: A Theoretical Synthesis and Empirical Review. *Sociology and Social Research,* 69(2), 315–350.

Massey, D.S. & Capoferro, C. 2008. The Geographic Diversification of American Immigration, pp. 25–50. In Massey, D.S. (ed.) *New Faces in New Places: The Changing Geography of American Immigration.* New York, Russell Sage.

Mize, R. 2006. Mexican Contract Workers and the U.S. Capitalist Agricultural Labor Process: The Formative Era, 1942–1964. *Rural Sociology,* 71(1), 85–108.

Molnár, E. & Schafft, K. A. 2003. Social Exclusion, Ethnic Political Mobilization, and Roma Minority Self Governance in Hungary. *East Central Europe/L'Europe Du Centre Est,* 30(1), 53–74.

Panelli, R., Hubbard, P., Coombes, B., & Suchet-Pearson, S. 2009. De-Centring White Ruralities: Ethnic Diversity, Racialisation and Indigenous Countrysides. *Journal of Rural Studies,* 25(4), 35–364.

Pfeffer, M.J. & Parra, P.A. 2009. Strong Ties, Weak Ties, and Human Capital: Latino Immigrant Employment Outside the Enclave. *Rural Sociology,* 74(2), 241–269.

Portes, A. 1995. Economic Sociology and the Sociology of Immigration: A Conceptual Overview, pp. 1–41. In Portes, A. (ed.) *The Economic Sociology of Immigration: Essays on Networks, Ethnicity and Entrepreneurship.* New York, Russell Sage.

Probst, J.C., Samuels, M.E., Jespersen, K.P., Willert, K., Swann, R.S., & McDuffie, J.A. 2002. *Minorities in Rural America: An Overview of Population Characteristics.* Columbia, SC, South Carolina Rural Health Research Center.

Rosenthal, N.G. 2004. The Dawn of a New Day? Notes on Indian Gaming in Southern California, pp. 91–111. In *Native Pathways: American Indian Culture and Economic Development in the Twentieth Century.* Boulder, University Press of Colorado.

Salamon, S. 2003. *Newcomers to Old Towns: Suburbanization of the Heartland.* Chicago, University of Chicago Press.

Savage, C. 2009. U.S. will Settle Indian Lawsuit for $3.4 Billion, p. A4, Dec. 8. *New York Times.*

Schafft, G.E. 2002. Scientific Racism in the Service of the Reich: German Anthropologists in the Nazi Era, pp. 117–134. In Hinton, A.L. (ed.) *Annihilating Difference: The Anthropology of Genocide.* Berkeley, University of California Press.

Schafft, G.E. 2004. *From Racism to Genocide: Anthropology in the Third Reich.* Urbana, University of Illinois Press.

Schafft, K.A. & Brown, D.L. 2000. Social Capital and Grassroots Development: The Case of Roma Self-Governance in Hungary. *Social Problems,* 47(2), 201–219.

Schultz, M. 2005. *The Rural Face of White Supremacy.* Urbana, University of Illinois Press.

Schwartz, R.S. 2001. Racial Profiling in Medical Research. *New England Journal of Medicine*, 344(18), 1392–1394.

Sismondo, S. 2010. *An Introduction to Science and Technology Studies.* West Sussex, Blackwell Publishing.

Stack, C. 1996. *Call to Home: African Americans Reclaim the Rural South.* New York, Basic Books.

Wilkerson, I. 2010. *The Warmth of Other Suns: The Epic Story of America's Great Migration.* New York, Random House.

Wilson, B.M. 2007. The Historical Spaces of African Americans, pp. 71–92. In Miyares, I.M. & Airriess, C.A. (eds) *Contemporary Ethnic Geographies in America.* Lanham, MD, Rowman & Littlefield.

Woods, M. 2005. *Rural Geography.* London, Sage.

PART IV

RURAL ECONOMY AND SOCIOECONOMIC WELLBEING

8 Making a Living in Rural Communities

How do rural people make a living in the twenty-first century? How has this changed over time? Does it differ between different parts of a highly developed country like the U.S.? Do rural economies differ from their urban counterparts? How does economic structure and transformation affect a rural person's economic security, their chances for social mobility and family wellbeing? In order to investigate these complex questions, we organize this chapter around four major questions:

- What opportunity structure is provided by rural economies; how has this changed over time; and how does this compare with the structure and restructuring of urban economies?
- What attributes do rural workers bring to the labor market, and how does this match available opportunities?
- How is labor utilized in rural economies, and how does this compare with labor utilization in urban economies?
- How are rural economies linked to the global economy, and what are the implications of these local–global linkages for the economic wellbeing of rural people and communities?

The Structure and Restructuring of Rural Opportunities

Local economies, whether urban or rural, are organized by the dynamic interaction between the employers and workers. Social scientists refer to these fundamental components of local economic organization as the demand and supply sides of the local economy. Since we discussed rural education and its impact on labor supply in Chapter 4, our treatment of labor supply will be rather brief in the present chapter. Rather, our focus in this chapter is mainly on labor demand, e.g., on the kinds of economic establishments that employ rural workers and provide them with opportunities for economic security and advancement.

Local economies can be described in terms of their size, their mix of economic activities, and their linkages to other local, regional, national, and global economies. Size can be measured by examining the number of economic establishments in a local economy, the number of workers these establishments employ and/or by the quantity of goods and services produced. Rural economies are typically smaller than their urban counterparts in all of these ways. Small size, in and of itself, is neither a constraint nor a facilitator of economic growth and prosperity. However, when small economies lack diversification, as is often true of rural economies, economic security can diminish. Compared with larger economies containing a wide range of employers, undiversified smaller economies are more vulnerable to economic downturns because a particular sector's lagging fortunes can have wide-ranging adverse impacts across the community.

Industrial and Occupational Structure

Local economies can be characterized by the commodities, goods and/or services produced by establishments and/or by the nature and composition of job responsibilities held by employees. Social scientists call this first dimension "industry," and the second "occupation." While industrial composition involves dozens of separate categories, analysts typically aggregate these into five main sectors: (a) extractive, including agriculture, forestry, fishing, and mining, (b) manufacturing, including both durable and non-durable products, (c) private and consumer services, (d) producer services, and (e) government. Even though each of these sectors is very diverse, examining their relative growth and decline over time provides a basic picture of how local economies are being restructured, and how patterns of restructuring differ between geographic areas. This is important because gaining or losing employment in particular industrial sectors also means that the occupational composition of employment is probably changing in ways that may affect the quality of economic opportunities available to local workers.

The industrial and occupational composition of employment in local economies has dramatic implications for job quality, security, and advancement.[1] Some jobs are highly replacable meaning that they tend to have lower wage rates, higher turnover, fewer benefits, and few or no career ladders and opportunities for advancement. In contrast, other jobs require scarce skills, extensive training, are hard to replace and consequently offer better wages, benefits, security, and mobility prospects. In addition, occupations have different entry requirements that may or may not match prospective workers' education, experience, and training. As we will discuss later in this chapter, a mismatch between workers' skills and job requirements in the local economy is likely to result in a low level of labor utilization as indicated by both unemployment and underemployment.

As shown in Figure 8.1, the majority of rural workers are employed in the three service categories, but only nine percent have jobs in the well-paying producer service sector.[2] Over 40 percent of rural workers hold jobs in personal and consumer services which tend to be less well paid, less secure over time and lacking in advancement opportunities. About one in five rural workers is employed in manufacturing and in government while less than 5 percent work in extractive pursuits. Clearly, today's rural economy differs greatly from the past, and from the often romanticized vision of rural areas as being dominated by agriculture. As these data show, it is a mistake to conflate rural and agricultural in today's society. These data also show that while services dominate both urban and rural economies, urban economies have a much greater representation of the better-paid producer services than is true in rural areas, and a substantially lower dependence on both manufacturing and government. As will be shown shortly, the concentration of producer services in urban economies is one reason why urban incomes exceed those of their rural counterparts. In addition, this is one

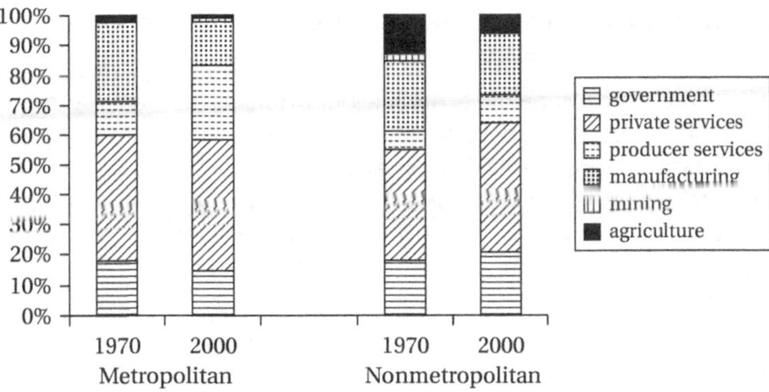

Source: Bureau of Economic Analysis

Figure 8.1 Industrial Restructuring, 1970–2000

of the reasons for "rural brain drain," e.g., the net out-migration of well-prepared young adults after they complete their education (see chapter 6).

Industrial Restructuring

The data in Figure 8.1 can also be used to compare the industrial restructuring of rural and urban economies over the last generation.[3] These data show that the basic pattern of change – decreased dependence on manufacturing and increased dependence on services, characterized both urban and rural economies. However, these data also show that the decline in manufacturing was much more rapid in urban than in rural areas (from 27 percent to 15 percent and 24 percent to 21 percent respectively). Accordingly, manufacturing remains a more important component of rural employment than is true in urban areas. These data also show that while both urban and rural economies became more dependent on services between 1970 and 2000, this transformation was much more likely to involve producer services in urban economies and low-wage, low-skill personal and consumer services in rural economies. In fact, the percentage of urban employment accounted for by producer services more than doubled during this time, from 11 percent to 25 percent while the share of rural employment represented by producer services only increased from 6 percent to 9 percent. Finally the data show a dramatic decline in extractive employment in rural areas, from almost 15 percent of all jobs in 1970 to about 5 percent in 2000. Urban employment in extractive industries also declined, but was almost nonexistent in 1970 to begin with. However, as will be discussed in Chapter 9, "farming in the city's shadow" has become an important trend in most metropolitan areas today. While not involving a large number of jobs, many persons would argue that urban farming has gained importance for social, environmental, and health reasons.

What are the implications of the changes in industrial structure shown in Figure 8.1? Is this evidence that rural areas are becoming the residual claimant for low quality, low-wage jobs? Perhaps, but not necessarily because job quality is affected both by industrial changes, changes in what is produced and by

Box 8.1 Commuting: The Separation of Work and Home

The data in Figure 8.1 describe the economic opportunities that are present in urban and rural locations, but do not necessarily describe the kinds of jobs held by people who live in urban and rural places. This is because a significant proportion of workers who live in rural areas work in urban areas. Data from the U.S. Bureau of the Census shows that relatively long-distance job commuting has increased dramatically during recent decades. In 1970, one out of five rural workers held a job in a different county from where they lived. By 2000, this figure had increased to 27 percent (Brown 2008). In 2008, data from the Cornell National Social Survey showed that about 42 percent of rural workers traveled at least twenty miles to work. While many people seem to think that rural workers travel longer distances to work because they live in more dispersed settlements, in truth there is very little rural–urban difference in trip length or time. The average trip length is about seventeen miles and the average distance is a little over half an hour. In fact, urban workers have somewhat longer commutes; for example, a higher proportion of rural workers travel less than half an hour and less than twenty miles to work (Brown. Schafft, & Champion 2009).

Rural commuting is of interest in the U.K. as well as in the U.S. Research by Champion and his colleagues (2009) found that rural workers had longer commutes than their urban counterparts, but this was mainly among rural workers who lived close by large metropolitan centers. Of greater interest, this study examined the commuting behavior of persons who had recently moved from urban to rural areas. The research showed that rural in-movers are about 1.6 times more likely than non-movers to have a relatively long commute. Persons who moved 30 to 99 km were especially likely to commute long distances. It seems likely that many of these persons have retained their urban job and simply moved their residence for either economic or quality of life reasons. In contrast, persons who moved into rural areas from cities located 100 km or more distant were more likely to move both work and residence, and to work closer to their new homes.

occupational changes, e.g., changes in how goods and services are produced. Income data from the U.S. Bureau of Economic Analysis seem to support the conclusion that industrial restructuring has diminished the quality of rural jobs. As shown in Figure 8.2, the rural–urban gap in non-farm wages increased from about $8,000 in 1990 to $15,000 in 2002. Additional evidence for the adverse impact of industrial restructuring appears to be added by Gibbs, Kusmin, and Cromartie (2005). Their research shows that low-skill jobs have been, and continue to be, more highly concentrated in rural than in urban economies (42.2 percent and 34 percent respectively in 2000). However, Gibbs and his colleagues also showed that the while the rural share of low-skill jobs exceeds the urban share, it has declined since 1990, and this decline was more related to occupational upgrading than to industrial restructuring. In particular, they showed that occupational *upgrading* in rural manufacturing was the most important reason why the share of low-skill jobs shrank in rural areas during the 1990s. Accordingly, the persistence of rural manufacturing actually enhanced rural opportunities during the 1990s because the quality of manufacturing occupations improved during this time. This is not to imply that attracting and retaining producer services wouldn't

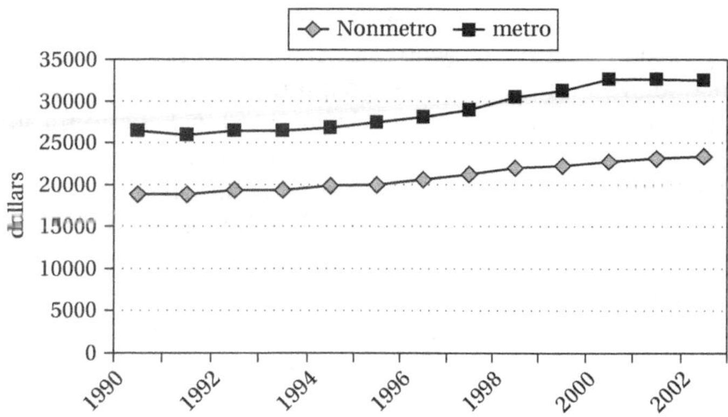

Source: Bureau of Economic Analysis

Figure 8.2 The Rural–Urban Gap in Non-Farm Wages, 1990–2002

benefit rural workers. It definitely would, but the positive impact of retaining and enhancing manufacturing employment should not be discounted.

Services: A Closer Look

Since over three-quarters of rural jobs are now in services, a closer look at this sector is in order. Most people know that the U.S. economy is a service economy, but not everyone is aware that this has been true for quite a while. In fact, as early as 1950 almost four of ten U.S. jobs were in the service sectors. The turn toward services has not always been seen as positive since service jobs have typically been considered to be low-wage, low-skill positions with little opportunity for career growth. Moreover, from a local economic development perspective, services were seen as inferior choices since their primary function was to circulate income rather than to attract it from outside of the community, thereby contributing to economic growth. Of course, not all services were seen as inferior choices. Professional services such as doctors, engineers, lawyers, and accountants have always earned high incomes and enjoyed high status, but these jobs are relatively scarce and concentrated in large metropolitan areas (Brown 1974).

The service sector underwent a radical restructuring in the late 1970s and early 1980s with the rapid increase of *producer services.* Put simply, producer services provide assistance to other businesses. The sub-sector generally includes finance, insurance, real estate, business services, legal services, insurance, management consulting, accounting, architecture, engineering, computer programming, and software and data processing (Porterfield and Sizer 1994).

Initially, social scientists thought that the boom in producer services simply reflected outsourcing by manufacturing firms that saw this as a way to enhance their productivity. However, it is now clear that the explosion of producer services reflects fundamental changes in production practices facilitated by information technology. Integrated systems of production can now be coordinated through the use of ever more specialized producer services. Accordingly, wherever goods or services are produced, producer services are needed to coordinate production.

Since producers pay a premium for this highly specialized assistance, money flows from production sites to locations where producer services concentrate. Services, once seen as simply circulating capital internally, are now seen as basic economic activities that earn income and promote local economic growth.

For rural economies, however, the challenge is whether producer services can be successfully nurtured and supported in small, relatively homogeneous economies that often lack workers with specialized technical skills and access to high speed internet (Smith 1993). At the present time, producer services are highly concentrated in urban areas, and became more so during the 1990s. What factors will enhance the abilities of rural areas to share in the growth of this economic engine? Glasmeier and Holland (1995) have observed that building a rural export economy based on services is contingent on having a conscious development policy that includes skills upgrading for the existing workforce, technical assistance, capital subsidies, and improved telecommunications. While the nation lacks an explicit rural policy focused on enhancing producer services, at least one previous constraint to service-based rural development, the availability of broadband internet service, has diminished significantly in recent years. As Stenberg and Low (2009) showed, the rural–urban "digital divide" is much narrower than in 2000, although rural residents and businesses are still less likely to have access to high speed internet than their urban counterparts.

Recreation and tourism form another type of export-based service that might contribute to rural economic growth. As Reeder and Brown (2005) showed, rural communities with attractive natural amenities often employ various strategies to promote tourism, recreation, and retirement living. Jobs that are usually associated with recreation development, such as those in hotels and restaurants, are assumed to be low paying with few fringe benefits. Some related service jobs, such as those in retail businesses, may also pay low wages. Hence, many critics discount recreation and tourism as a viable rural development option. However, low-wage workers in recreation areas may have access to more opportunities to work part-time and seasonal jobs to supplement their incomes, and some service and construction jobs associated with recreation development pay quite well. In addition, Reeder and Brown (2005) found that when earnings from all employment are measured, total earnings per resident were substantially higher ($2,000 more per worker) in counties with high dependence on recreation than in other rural counties. In other words, contrary to conventional wisdom, recreation development seems to have increased residents' earnings and may be an attractive development option for rural communities, especially those that lack well-prepared workforces.

The Rural Labor Force

Matching Demand and Supply of Labor

As indicated in the previous section, the demand for rural labor is changing along with the industrial and occupational transformation of rural economies. Traditional rural industries such as farming, mining and other extractive sectors are diminishing, and the share of jobs in manufacturing is also on the decline. While manufacturing declined less rapidly in rural than in urban areas, and

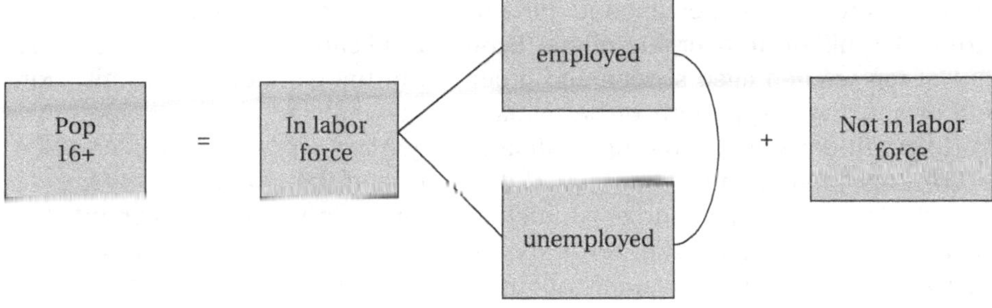

Source: Author's own

Figure 8.3 The Labor Utilization Framework

experienced occupational upgrading that enhanced wages, this sector which traditionally provided well paying jobs for workers lacking post-high school education is struggling to hold its own in the midst of stiff international competition.

As a result of these changes, fully three-quarters of today's rural jobs are in the services sectors. While many service jobs are insecure, poorly remunerated, and require little advanced education or on the job experience, better paying more secure producer services jobs typically require post-high school education and frequently a college degree. Accordingly, tomorrow's rural economy will require a well-prepared workforce with specialized technical training and well-developed workplace skills.

The Utilization of Rural Labor

The Labor Utilization Framework

Labor utilization refers to the extent to which a local economy is able to utilize the services of labor-force age persons who reside in the local area. The basic labor utilization framework (see Figure 8.3) first divides working-age persons into those who are available to work and those who are not in the workforce. Secondly, those in the workforce are subdivided into employed persons – those with jobs – including self-employed persons, and unemployed persons – those who lack jobs but who are seeking work.[4] Labor is more fully utilized when most working age persons are in the workforce and have full-time jobs.

Being out of the workforce can be a voluntary choice such as the choice to be a full-time college student or a stay-at-home parent, or it can result from circumstances beyond a person's control such as having a work-limiting disability. In addition, some persons drop out of the workforce after long periods of unsuccessful and discouraging job search.

Trends in Labor Force Participation

While more than three-quarters of men have been in the labor force throughout the last half century, less than one-third of women participated prior to 1960. Between 1940 and 1980, the labor force participation rate of women increased from 28 percent to 48 percent and the number of women in the workforce grew from 14.2 million to over 40 million (Brown & O'Leary 1979). Today, about six out of ten women aged sixteen and older are in the workforce. Perhaps more important, the age pattern of participation has changed and participation is fairly continuous across the life course even for women with young children. Accordingly, having pre-school age children, one of the major reasons for voluntarily leaving the workforce, is much less constraining of employment than was true even one generation ago. Labor force participation is virtually identical between rural and urban women, about 60 percent in both cases (Rogers 1997). This is considerably different from earlier times when urban women, especially African Americans, were considerably more likely to be in the workforce.

The vast majority of persons in the workforce are employed, with the remainder out of work but actively looking for a job. Even during recessions, about nine out of ten workers are employed (including self-employment). Unemployment rates track swings in the business cycle going up in bad times and receding during recoveries and good times. Rural unemployment rates were typically lower than urban rates during the 1970s and 1980s, but urban and rural unemployment rates have been almost identical since 1990 (Kusmin & Parker 2006).

Under-employment

However, being in or out of the workforce and being employed or unemployed does not fully account for labor utilization. Two other issues, under-employment and participation in informal activities, must be accounted for. Under-employed persons desire full-time jobs but can only find part-time, seasonal or temporary employment, and many who work full time make very low incomes. In fact, many under-employed persons earn less than the official poverty threshold, and are characterized as *working poor*. Jensen and his colleagues (1999) showed that rural workers were more likely to be under-employed than their urban counterparts. Moreover, even after accounting for differences in race, gender, marital status, and industry of employment, rural workers were more likely to slip into under-employment and less likely to slip out. In other words, rural persons *get less protection* than persons who live elsewhere (and especially in suburbs) from education, being married, being White, being male, and other factors shown to reduce the risk of being underemployed. This is a serious rural disadvantage, and will be an important part of our explanation in Chapter 10 of why some rural people are more likely to be poor than others.

Informal Economic Activities

While most rural economic activity takes place in formal labor markets, many rural families develop subsistence strategies that combine wage and salary employment and/or self employment, investments and resources obtained from the state's social welfare system with informal economic activities (Jensen, Cornwell, & Findeis 1995; Brown & Kulcsar 2001). Informal, or non-market, activities include self provisioning (gardening, fishing, gathering fruits and vegetables) and inter-household exchanges of a wide range of goods and services such as food stuffs, repair services, and/or household maintenance. Informal activities have both an economic and a social logic (see Box 8.2). Households participate to generate cash and/or to reduce the need for cash, but they also participate to build and maintain reciprocal community relationships (Hinrichs 1998). Research in the U.S. and Europe shows that resources obtained through informal economic activities tend to supplement those earned through formal activities rather than to replace them. Accordingly (and somewhat ironically), informal economic activities are more prevalent among better off households with more social connections because these are the households that both have the goods and/or services readily able to exchange and have access to the social connections that make such an exchange more likely (Brown and Kulcsar 2001).

Local–Global Linkages

Globalization

Even though rural areas tend to be geographically separate from the rest of society, they are not truly isolated from the nation's social and economic mainstream, nor have they ever been. Early in the nation's history rural communities developed a comprehensive way of life. As Hobbs (1995: 374) observed, "spatial isolation resulted in social isolation and a buffer against significant intrusion from the dominant society and culture." However, even during this early era rural communities and economies were affected by regional, national and international forces such as treaties and tariffs, the urban demand for rural commodities fueled by industrialization and state and national level politics. For example the Embargo Act of 1807 passed during Jefferson's presidency showed that the federal government could intervene with great force at the local level by controlling trade. The Act was extremely unpopular because it significantly reduced access to foreign markets for agricultural and other rural commodities. As a result, the Congress repealed the Act in 1809 just three days before Jefferson left office (Malone 1974).

Over time rural areas have become increasingly incorporated into the nation's social, political, and economic fabric. As discussed in Chapter 1, rural separateness and independence remain parts of the *rural mystique,* but advances in transportation, communication, and information technologies reduced the "costs of distance." Increased local dependence on external investment, and the greater influence of state and national policies have largely, if not completely, supplanted local institutions, thereby forging greater interdependence between rural and urban areas.

The advent of globalization has further eroded the friction of distance that had previously afforded rural economies some measure of protection from national and international forces. Some observers feel that globalization has undermined and weakened local community and economy while others believe that participation in the global economy provides new opportunities for economic vitality.

Globalization entails a fundamental transformation of the world's economy from an international federation of independent nation states to an emerging vision of the world as a globally organized and managed free trade, free enterprise economy pursued by largely unaccountable political and economic elites (Daley 2001).[6] Globalization is a form of political–economic restructuring in which supranational organizations and institutions gain significant power over nationally

Box 8.2 Informal Income and Household Exchange as a Rural Livelihood Strategy

Some scholars argue that rural residents may be especially well positioned to use informal livelihood strategies to supplement their income and improve household wellbeing. Informal livelihood strategies refer to exchanges of cash, goods and/or services that occur outside of the regulation of the state and that are done specifically to supplement a household's livelihood by either generating cash or reducing the need for cash, and/or maintain the social relationships that comprise one's social capital (Pahl & Wallace 1985; Brown & Kulcsar 2001; Slack 2007).

Informal economic activity and household exchange may be especially important for rural people for several reasons. First, relative access to land and natural resources means that rural people often have a greater opportunity to self-provision. This includes growing food in gardens, raising poultry or livestock for home consumption, hunting, fishing, and so forth. Further, because rural areas also often have fewer available services, many rural residents develop multiple skill sets to fill the vacuum, from hair cutting to auto repair. Tight community and kinship networks in rural areas may be an additional factor facilitating household exchange and informal economic activity.

Slack's (2007) study of informal work in rural Pennsylvania found that about 46 percent of surveyed households engaged in informal work, including activities such as household repair, personal services, landscaping, car repair, and selling items at flea markets and yard sales. The two most frequently cited reasons for doing this work revolved around social relationships and economic livelihood. About 78 percent of respondents reported that "help[ing] out friends and neighbors was an important motivation," while about 69 percent reported that "making ends meet" was a significant motivation for engaging in informal work. Further (and perhaps not surprisingly), economic motivations were reported more frequently among less well-off respondents.

Brown and Kulcsar (2001) found that informal exchange and economic activity was used extensively to supplement household livelihood in post-socialist rural Hungary. Based on survey data collected in a set of smaller villages, the research indicated that most households self-provisioned, and over half of all surveyed households exchanged goods and/or services with other households. However, while the researchers concluded that informal exchange was a significant means of supplementing the household economy, maintaining local social relations and building community solidarity, in Hungary this activity was *most* common among relatively better-off households.[5] In other words, informal exchange appeared to be a less viable household strategy among the poorest households. This is likely to be the case because these are the households that have the least to exchange with others, may be less well connected within local social networks, and, therefore, are more limited in their abilities to participate in informal exchange. While for many rural residents informal economic activity may represent an important livelihood strategy (an importance that appears to generally increase as income levels go down), for the most disadvantaged, the relative inability to participate in informal economic activity represents one more dimension of deprivation.

based entities. Many observers fear that national economies are being undermined by globalization and that national boundaries are losing their economic significance. Moreover, if national economies are being undermined by globalization, then local economic autonomy is also vulnerable. Globalization results from three institutional transformations: (a) the deregulation of international capital, (b) the ascendancy of transnational corporations, and (c) the increasing power of international organizations, all of which is aided and abetted by instantaneous real time transactions that are made possible by information technology.

Deregulated Capital

Deregulation followed a quarter century during which capital was regulated by Bretton Woods institutions that were developed to stabilize the world's chaotic post-Second World War economy. Bretton Woods capital regulation featured a gold-dollar standard by which all currencies were fixed to a gold value through the American dollar. This changed in 1971 in the midst of a deep recession, when President Nixon declared that the dollar would no longer be convertible into gold.[7] Since that time the relative values of nations' respective currencies have floated based on the relative strength of national economies. As McMichael (1996: 115) has observed, "the shift from fixed to floating currency exchanges ushered in an era of uncontrolled — and heightened — capital mobility . . . Financial markets, rather than trade, began to determine currency values." McMichael further observed that since the circulation of money altered profitability by changing currency values, transnational corporations (TNC) minimized risks by decentralizing their operations throughout the world. The deregulation of capital permitted transnational corporations to seek lowest cost wherever it was located, and to move their operations there. Hence, "by its effect on the transnational companies, the financial revolution accelerated the formation of a global production system" (McMichael 1996: 117).

Transnational Corporations

While transnational corporations have been dominant forces in international trade for centuries, their mode of operation has changed during globalization in ways that affect both national and local economies. Most importantly, the deregulated capital has altered the calculus TNCs use to determine where to locate their operations. By seeking the lowest costs for labor, materials and other inputs, TNCs have become increasingly disembedded from particular nations. In fact, one might easily consider TNCs as "stateless." TNCs are accountable to stock holders and board members who live throughout the world, not to the nations they operate in. Host nations, let alone host communities, have little leverage over location and re-location decisions. TNCs have no sentimentality for specific locations, urban or rural. Capital is shifted from one location to another to maximize profitability, hence encouraging international investors to keep their money in the firm.

In other words, TNCs implement international capital's investment strategy. Corporations that were previously located in particular nations now have branches all over the world. By diversifying their production locations, TNCs have access to local labor and consumer markets, and the flexibility to move resources across national borders quickly in response to changing financial and labor conditions.

Global Institutions

Global institutions are the third component of globalization's infrastructure. The International Monetary Fund, the World Bank, and the World Trade Organization were created as part of the post-war Bretton Woods system to provide financial stability, promote economic growth, and nurture development and poverty reduction in poorer regions. The International Monetary Fund was created to promote global economic stability, prevent global depression, and manage global economic crises. The World Bank was designed to alleviate poverty in less-developed countries, and the World Trade Organization was intended to establish trade rules. These are worthy goals, but many critics believe that these institutions have become handmaidens of the wealthy economies and financial elites during today's deregulated financial environment. Many informed observers including Nobel Prize winner Joseph Stiglitz, the World Bank's former chief economist, believe that all three institutions are failing to accomplish their social and economic goals. Stiglitz (2002) is not opposed to globalization per se, but rather to its non-democratic mode of governance. He contends that global institutions are shaped by the ideology of those to whom they are accountable, for example, international capital and 6–7 dominant capitalist nations. This ideology involves a simple belief in the free market combined with an antagonistic view of governments' role in making society operate harmoniously. Stiglitz believes that global institutions must become more open, transparent, democratic, and accountable to those whom they affect.

Local Opportunities and Challenges Presented by Globalization

Opportunities

While many observers believe that globalization diminishes local autonomy by making economies more vulnerable to outside control and influence, others promote a more balanced view acknowledging its positive impact on access to global resources and opportunities. Stiglitz (2002) notes that globalization has opened up international trade helping many countries grow more rapidly than would otherwise been possible, and it has reduced isolation and increased access to knowledge. The irony is that while "new foreign firms may hurt protected state-owned enterprises they can also lead to the introduction of new technologies, access to new markets, and the creation of new industries" (Stiglitz 2002: 5). In wealthier countries such as the U.S., proponents argue that globalization increases access to capital necessary for local development in lagging regions, produces jobs and reduces prices of consumer goods (see Box 8.3). Other scholars have shown that the impacts of globalization can differ across particular industries. For example, Kenny (2004) has shown that computer production tends to benefit from globalization while clothing manufacture suffers from diseconomies of scale.

Box 8.3 Is Walmart Good for Rural Communities?

Walmart is one of the world's most highly globalized firms. It operates 4,750 retail outlets, a quarter of which are located outside of the U.S.; it sources its products from around the world, and its investors and board members are highly international. Walmart creates both costs and benefits in communities where it operates retail stores. Its adverse impact on small, locally owned retail stores is well documented (Irwin and Clark 2006; Stone 1995). In contrast, research shows that Walmart generates large savings for shoppers. Hausman and Leibtag (2005) estimated that savings in food expenditures resulting from entry and expansion of Walmart are equal to almost 25 percent of a household's total food expenditures. Savings for non-food items are evidently similarly large. It is also argued that Walmart enhances consumer choice and convenience.

More controversial is its impact on employment. Depending on the methodology used, some studies show that the entry of Walmart into a community either creates new jobs (Basker 2005) or reduces retail employment (Neumark et al. 2006). Arguing that Walmart displaces retail labor, Goetz and Swaminathan (2006: 211) demonstrated that "counties with more additions of stores during 1987-1998 experienced greater increases (or smaller decreases) in family poverty rates during the 1990s economic boom period." While the jury is still out on Walmart's employment and income impacts, there is good cause to be cautious before welcoming in the retail giant.

Walmart's adverse impact on employment outside of retail is much clearer. Gary Gereffi (2005:1) and other scholars have shown that Walmart and other big box retailers have become "the most powerful companies in the global economy because they have the ability to shape global supply chains, global sourcing networks, and make decisions about where products are made." Walmart is such a dominant customer for many U.S. based manufacturers that it can now dictate the wholesale prices it will pay for goods. If these prices are below the cost of production, Walmart forces companies to produce goods at a lower price. The main way that this is done is by transferring production overseas where labor is cheaper, regulations are lax, and environmental safeguards are lower. Gereffi (2002) calls this new system a buyer-led commodity chain, and he claims that it reflects a fundamental shift of power in the world's economic system from producers to big box retailers. As Schumpeter (1975) observed, capitalism is constantly being re-invented through processes of *creative destruction*. According to Gereffi and others, we are now in the midst of an era of creative destruction in which retailers have destroyed producers' power to determine the terms of trade. International retailers like Walmart now determine prices and locations of production. From the standpoint of rural economies, this is one of the major reasons manufacturing employment has declined in recent years and so many displaced workers have lost jobs in this sector.

Challenges

Critics point out that globalization has not made life better for the world's poor people; in fact research shows that while between country inequality has declined somewhat since 2000, income inequality within countries has grown larger during the global era (Firebaugh 2003; World Bank 2009). Breecher and

Costello (1994) have characterized globalization as "global pillage" as opposed to "global village." They contend that globalization leads to a "race to the bottom" as wages, working conditions, and environmental protection fall to the level of the most desperate people, nations, and even regions within nations. As a result, they contend that globalization exacerbates polarization between haves and have nots both internationally and within countries. It is important to remember that globalization is about politics as much as about economics, hence, many critics contend that globalization leads to a loss of national sovereignty and local autonomy as international capital and transnational corporations undermine democratically elected governments' abilities to make development decisions (Stiglitz 2002; McMichael 1996; Breecher and Costello 1994). How does globalization affect *rural* economic security in a country like the United States?

International Competition and Job Displacement

To enhance their international competitiveness, manufacturing firms are shedding jobs through automation and by off-shoring to cheaper labor markets. Displacement reflects changes in the makeup of the economy, not fluctuations in the business cycle. Hence, displacement tends to involve permanent job loss rather than short-term unemployment. While automation and off-shoring benefit firms, it undermines the economic security of workers and local communities.

Research by Glasmeier and Salant (2006) shows that rural economies are especially vulnerable to job displacement.[8] As demonstrated earlier in this chapter, while the share of rural jobs that are low skill has declined, it still far exceeds the share of urban jobs that are low skill, and these are precisely the kinds of jobs that are the most vulnerable to international competition. Glasmeier and Salant (2006) showed that between 1997 and 2003, rural economies lost over 1.5 million jobs. Displacement was most likely among workers lacking education and those in non-durable manufacturing such as textiles and apparel, shoes, wood products and food processing, traditional rural mainstays. In fact, nearly half of all rural jobs lost to displacement were in manufacturing even though this sector only comprises about 20 percent of rural jobs. As a result, displacement has reduced access to relatively well paying jobs for rural persons lacking post-high school education, and it calls the future of many rural economies into question. Many rural communities will have to develop other types of employment or face long-term unemployment and economic decline.

Conclusions

In this chapter we have examined the restructuring of rural economic life during the last four decades, and we paint a somewhat pessimistic picture of future economic prospects. Traditional rural jobs in extractive and manufacturing sectors are declining; job growth in well-paying producer services is sluggish at best; wage rates, even within the same industries, pay less well than in urban labor markets; rural workers are less well prepared to obtain jobs in well-paying sectors; and rural economies are especially vulnerable to global competition, a trend that seems unlikely to change in the near future. We have indicated that economic restructuring involves more than an alteration in the kinds of goods and services produced in rural economies, or the kinds of occupational roles occupied by rural workers. Rather, economic restructuring involves a change in the nature of social relationships linking workers and employers as well as a transformation of the global organization of economic activity that adversely affects opportunity structures, incomes and economic security at the local level in rural economies (Falk & Lobao 2003).

But, it would be a mistake to accept this dreary picture as the only imaginable future for rural workers, and the families that depend on them for economic support. Moreover, since rural economies are so diverse the overall picture does not describe future prospects in many localities. At the overall level, rural economic prosperity will be affected positively or negatively by a number of forces, many of which are external to particular communities. Technology, and especially information technology, may make rural communities more competitive as locations for knowledge-based, well paying economic activities. As we discussed with respect to telemedicine (see Chapter 4), the economic costs of rural isolation can be minimized by the use of information technology and by organizational structures designed to take advantage of such technology. For example, access to broadband could reduce many of the disincentives that constrain producer services from locating in rural areas.

Rising gasoline prices, on the other hand, could adversely affect rural workers access to job opportunities. As we discussed in Box 8.1, many workers, both rural and urban, travel long distances to work. Accordingly, in the absence of more fuel-efficient vehicles, many long-distance rural commuters will be forced to spend an increasing share of their disposable income on the journey to work.

Many rural communities are benefiting from amenity-based development. The future contribution of amenities to rural development depends on the future course of income growth in the United States, with slower growth indicating lower spending on travel, recreation and tourism. As has been shown during the current recession, discretionary spending on leisure activities tends to shrink during times of economic decline (Murray 2010). Moreover, many amenity-rich communities are benefiting from retirement in-migration. As discussed in Chapter 6, retirement migration is often considered "gray gold" and is actively pursued by rural communities. Whether rural areas will continue to attract retirees is not a certainty, but rather contingent on the age at which persons retire, which has increased recently (Gendell 2008), and the rate and rural–urban direction of geographic mobility among baby boomers who are now reaching retirement age.

Finally, the future course of rural economic development is contingent on policy choices made at the state and national levels. Some of these choices will contribute to rural development while others will enhance resource mobility thereby typically disadvantaging rural economies. Of course, domestic policy choices are embedded in a global context, and their impacts at the local level are affected by international agreements, the operations of transnational corporations and by trade rules established by global organizations such as the World Trade Organization. These rural economic policy choices will be discussed in greater detail in Chapter 11.

Notes

1 These comments refer to the average firm in the various industrial categories. In reality, firms in the same industrial category can have markedly different occupational compositions. For example, mining companies are typically managed from urban headquarters while rural mining is typically comprised of miners and other production employees.
2 While the data in Figure 8.1 are aggregated into metropolitan and nonmetropolitan areas, we will use the terms urban (metropolitan) and rural (nonmetropolitan) for ease of discussion. Employment is by place of work not place of residence.
3 A "generation" is the average age at which women give birth to their first child. This figure is now 25.1 years in the U.S.
4 Self-employed persons account for about 9–10% of the employed population in both urban and rural areas.
5 This is also true in the U.S. where research has shown that informal economic activity cuts across all income levels (Jensen et al. 1995; Ratner 2000).
6 Some scholars have observed that globalization involves *re-regulation* rather than *deregulation* to favor a particular set of economic interests over another. They contend that this re-regulation is a form of privatization that results in a mass transfer of public wealth to the private sector (Bonnano & Antonio 2003; Sommers & Block 2005).
7 The 1971 recession featured both stagnant economic growth and inflation (*stagflation*). Nixon withdrew from the gold–dollar convertibility system because many nations horded inflated dollars to a point where they dwarfed U.S. gold reserves. They would be a huge liability for the U.S. Treasury if cashed in for gold.
8 Displacement is defined as losing a job held for at least three years because a company moves, a plant closes, work slacks off, or a job is eliminated.

References

Basker, E. 2005. Job Creation or Destruction? The Market Effects of Walmart Expansion. *Review of Economics and Statistics*, 87(1), 174–183.

Bonnano, A. & Antonio, R. 2003. Democracy in an Age of Globalization, pp. 43–66. In Bell, M., Hendricks, F., & Bacal, A. (eds) *Walking Toward Justice: Democratization in Rural Life*. Bristol, U.K., Elsevier.

Breecher, J. & Costello, T. 1994. *Global Village or Global Pillage: Economic Restructuring from the Bottom Up*. Cambridge, MA, Southend Press.

Brown, D. L. 1974. The Redistribution of Physicians and Dentists in Incorporated Places of the Upper Midwest, 1950–70. *Rural Sociology*, 29(2), 205–223.

Brown, D.L. 2008. The Future of Rural America Through a Social-Demographic Lens. pp. 229–247. In Wu, J., Barkley, P., & Weber, B. (eds) *Frontiers in Resource and Rural Economics*. Washington, D.C., RFF Press.

Brown, D.L. & Kulcsar, L. 2001. Household Economic Behavior in Post-Socialist Hungary. *Rural Sociology*, 66(2), 157–180.

Brown, D.L. & O'Leary, J. 1979. Labor Force Activity of Women in Metropolitan and Nonmetropolitan America. *Rural Development Research Report*, 15, Washington, D.C.: Economics, Statistics, and Cooperative Service, USDA.

Brown, D.L., Schafft, K., & Champion, T. 2009. Longer Distance Commuting and Social Participation. Paper presented to the Rural Sociological Society, Madison. July.

Brown, D.L., Bolender, B., Kulcsar. L. C, Glasgow, N. &, Sanders, S. 2011. Inter-County Variability of Net Migration at Older Ages as a Path Dependent Process. *Rural Sociology* 76(1).

Champion, T., M. Coombes, M., & Brown, D.L. 2009f. Migration and Longer Distance Commuting in Rural England. *Regional Studies*. 43(10), 1245–1260.

Daley, H. 2001. Globalization and Its Discontents. *Philosophy and Public Policy Quarterly*, 21 (2/3), 17–21.

Falk, W. & Lobao. L. 2003. Who Benefits from Economic Restructuring? Lessons from the Past, Challenges for the Future, pp. 152–165. In Brown, D.L. & Swanson, L. (eds)

Challenges for Rural America in the 21st Century. University Park, Penn State University Press.

Firebaugh, G. 2003. *The New Geography of Income Inequality.* Cambridge, Harvard University Press.

Gendell, M. 2008. Older Workers: Increasing Their Labor Force Participation and Hours of Work. *Monthly Labor Review.* January, 41–54.

Gereffi, G. 2002. Capitalism, Development and Commodity Chains, pp. 84–103. In Corbridge, S. (ed.) *Development.* London, Routledge.

Gereffi, G. 2005. Is Walmart Good for America? Frontline Interview. Available at http://www.pbs.org/wgbh/pages/frontline/shows/walmart/interview/gereffi.html. (Accessed on 2/26/2005).

Gibbs, L. 2003. Rural Education at a Glance. *Rural Development Research Report* No. 93. Washington, D.C., USDA-ERS.

Gibbs, R., Kusmin, L., & Cromartie, J. 2005. Low-Skill Employment and the Changing Economy of Rural America. *Economic Research Report* No. 10. Washington, D.C., USDA-ERS.

Glasmeier, A. & Holland, M. 1995. *From Combines to Computers: Rural Services and Development in the Age of Information Technology.* Albany, SUNY Press.

Glasmeier, A. & Salant, P. 2006. Low Skill Workers in Rural America Face Permanent Job Loss. *Policy Brief* No. 2. Durham, NH, Carsey Institute.

Goetz, S. & Swaminathan, H. 2006. WalMart and County-Wide Poverty. *Social Science Quarterly,* 87(2), 211–226.

Hausman, J. & Leibtag, E. 2005. Consumer Benefits from Increased Competition in Shopping Outlets: the Effect of Walmart. NBER Working paper No. 11809.

Hinrichs, C. 1998. Sideline and Lifeline: The Cultural Economy of Maple Syrup Production. *Rural Sociology,* 63(4), 507–532.

Hobbs, D. 1995. Social Organization in the Countryside, pp. 369–396. In Castle, E. (ed.) *The Changing American Countryside: Rural People and Places.* Lawrence, University Press of Kansas.

Irwin, E. & Clark, J. 2006. Wall Street versus Main Street: What are the Benefits and Costs of WalMart to Local Communities? *Choices* 21(2). Accessed from http://www.choicesmagazine.org/2006-2/grabbag/2006-2-14.htm (Accessed June 25, 2009).

Jensen, L., Cornwell, G., & Findeis, J. 1995. Informal Work in Nonmetropolitan Pennsylvania. *Rural Sociology.* 60(1), 91–107.

Jensen, L., Findeis J., Hsu, W., & Schacter, J. 1999. Slipping Into and Out of Underemployment: Another Disadvantage for Nonmetropolitan Workers. *Rural Sociology,* 64(3), 417–438.

Kenney, M. 2004. Introduction, pp. 1–21. In Kenney, M. & Florida, R. (eds) *Locating Global Advantage: Industry Dynamics in the International Economy.* Palo Alto, CA, Stanford University Press.

Kusmin, L. & Parker, T. 2006. Rural Employment at a Glance. *Economic Information Bulletin* No. 21. Washington, D.C., USDA-ERS.

McMichael, P. 1996. *Development and Social Change.* Thousand Oaks California, Pine Forge Press.

Malone, D. 1974. *Jefferson the President: The Second Term, 1805–1809.* Boston, Little Brown.

Murray, S. 2010. Tourism Spending Recovers, but Remains Below Pre-Recession Levels. *Wall Street Jounal.* January, 7, 2010. (Accessed January 7, 2010 at: http://blogs.wsj.com/economics/2009/12/15/tourism-spending-recovers-but-remains-below-pre-recession-levels/).

Neumark, D., Zhang, J., & Ciccarella, S. 2006. The Effect of Walmart on Local Labor Markets. Paper presented at the Allied Social Sciences Association, Bosaton MA. Available on-line: http://econ.ucsd.edu/seminars/0506seminars/Neumark_SP06.pdf (Accessed June 25, 2009).

Pahl, R.E. & Wallace, C. (1985) Household Work Strategies In Economic Recession, pp. 189–227. In Redclift, N. & Mingione, E. (eds) *Beyond Employment: Household, Gender, and Subsistence.* Basil Blackwell, Oxford.

Porterfield, S. & Sizer, M. 1994. Producer Services Growing Quickly in Rural Areas, But Still Concentrated in Urban Areas. *Rural Development Perspectives,* 10(1), 2–8.

Ratner, S. 2000. The Informal Economy in Rural Community Economic Development. TVA Rural Studies Program Contractor paper 00-03. Lexington, KY, TVA. Dounloaded on May 30, 2010 at: http://www.uky.edu/Ag/AgEcon/pubs/tva/staff/Ratner00-03.pdf.

Reeder, R. & Brown, D. 2005. Recreation, Tourism, and Rural Well-Being. *Economic Research Report* No.7, Washington, D.C., USDA- ERS.

Rogers, C. 1997. *Changes in the Social and Economic Status of Women, by Metro-Nonmetro Residence. AIB* 732, Washington, D.C., USDA-ERS.

Schumpeter, J. 1975. *Capitalism, Socialism and Democracy.* New York, Harper [orig. pub. 1942].

Slack, T. 2007. The Contours and Correlates of Informal Work in Rural Pennsylvania. *Rural Sociology,* 72(1), 69–89.

Smith, S. 1993. Service Industries in the Rural Economy: The Role and Potential Contributions, pp. 105–126. In Barkley, D. (ed.) *Economic Adaptation: Alternatives for Nonmetropolitan Areas.* Boulder, Westview Press.

Somers, M. & Block, F. 2005. From Poverty to Perversity: Ideas, Markets and Institutions over 200 Years of Welfare Debate. *American Sociological Review,* 70(2), 260–287.

Stenberg, P. & Low, S. 2009. Rural Broadband at a Glance. *Economic Information Bulletin* No. 47. Washington, D.C., USDA-ERS.

Stiglitz, J. 2002. *Globalization and its Discontents.* New York, Norton.

Stone, K. 1995. *Competing With the Retail Giants: How to Survive in the New Retail Space.* New York, Wiley.

World Bank. 2009. *World Development Report.* Washington, D.C., World Bank.

9 Farms, Farmers, and Farming in Contemporary Rural Society

Popular images of rural society contain strong connections with agriculture and the nation's agrarian past. As discussed in Chapter 8, however, fewer than seven percent of *rural* workers are now employed directly in agriculture,[1] and it is a mistake to conflate rural economy with farming (Vias & Nelson 2006). In spite of the historical declines in the importance of agriculture as a source of employment, agriculture remains a fundamental aspect of rural society that is critical to the nation's food security and overall wellbeing. Moreover, farms, farmers, and farming have considerable symbolic importance as aspects of national identity. And, since the nation's two million farms occupy almost one billion acres, or over 40 percent of the nation's land mass, farming has a significant impact on land use and the environment (USDA-ERS 2009a). In this chapter we analyze long-term trends in the structure of agriculture, examine family farmers' livelihood strategies, and discuss the social and economic environment affecting farms, farmers, and farming. We close with a discussion of the *food system* emphasizing that farming is only one aspect of a much more comprehensive set of social, economic and biophysical relationships that extend from the resource base to production activities to the marketing of food and fiber and finally to household consumption.

The Structure of Agriculture

An Overview of Agricultural Development in the United States

During colonial times, most settlers could be characterized as "hunter-farmers" (Cochrane 1993). Moreover, as Cochrane observed, food production methods transferred from Europe were not generally appropriate for use in the North American environment, hence, a new food production system had to be developed that was more appropriate to the colonial context. It is important to note that agricultural methods borrowed from American Indians were critical to the development of colonial agriculture and the survival of colonists themselves. By the time of the American Revolution, nearly 175 years after the settling of the Jamestown colony, American farmers were finally able to produce a surplus over subsistence.

While Adams, Hamilton and others among the nation's founding fathers emphasized urban and industrial expansion following the European model, Washington, Jefferson, Madison, and other highly influential leaders of the time promoted an agrarian vision of development based on the notion of independent yeoman farmers. The following quotation from Jefferson (1785) is emblematic of the prevailing Enlightenment view of agriculture's role in development during the nation's formative decades.

> Cultivators of the earth are the most valuable citizens. They are the most vigorous, the most independent, the most virtuous, and they are tied to their country and wedded to its liberty and interests by the most lasting bonds.

This view of agriculture as the engine of national development requiring more and more land to accommodate its growth potential figured greatly in Jefferson's promotion of territorial expansion into Florida, along the Gulf Coast in what is now Alabama and Mississippi as well as his purchase of the Louisiana territory. It must be acknowledged that this expansion often displaced American Indians who had resided on these lands for hundreds or even thousands of years. Hence, even though Westward expansion nearly halted during the revolutionary period, the new nation's interior was almost entirely settled during the nineteenth century. The resulting availability of new cultivatable land contributed to the development of an extensive farming system in which efficiency was relatively low (Cochrane 1993).

New *mechanical* technology increased worker productivity during the nineteenth century, but it also displaced many workers. Moreover, while agriculture had become more extensive, total agricultural output per acre did not increase much during this time because so much new land was being added to the resource base. This changed during the twentieth century with the closing of the frontier (Turner 1921). By the 1930s, in the context of a stable land base, mechanical, biological, and chemical advances began to transform agriculture from an extensive to an intensive industry with productivity increases of over 25 percent per decade (Cochrane 1993). It should also be noted that this transformation to an intensive production system was promoted by the government's New Deal programs, instituted to assist farmers during the Great Depression. In particular, these programs provided affordable credit for the purchase of equipment, chemicals, and other productivity enhancing inputs. By the end of the twentieth century, some observers believed that productivity increases in agriculture had reached their limits (Urban 1991), but Cochrane and others contend that scientific and organizational advances will continue to push farm productivity even higher.

The continuing application of new technologies to agriculture has transformed the farming sector from one dominated by independent yeoman farm entrepreneurs to a highly industrialized and concentrated sector of economy and society (Swanson 1988). Moreover, beginning around 1970, U.S. agriculture became increasingly integrated into the global economy, and global trade has favored larger producers over their small and medium-sized counterparts. As a result, the concentrating and industrializing impacts of technological change have been exacerbated by the emergence of globalization, and the tremendous increase in international agricultural trade. As Vias and Nelson (2006) have observed, the U.S. agricultural trade balance was essentially zero prior to the 1970s, but since then the increasing trend toward export-led agriculture has produced significant positive trade balances. In fact, agriculture is one of the few sectors of the U.S. economy to show a consistent positive trade balance during the last 40 years. Even during the 2008–2009 recession farm exports exceeded imports although both exports and imports fell dramatically compared with pre-recession years (USDA-ERS 2009b).[2]

Globalization and American Agriculture

Globalization and technological change have fundamentally transformed U.S. agriculture. As Lobao and Meyer (2001: 104) observed, the great agricultural transition of the twentieth century involved "the abandonment of farming as a household livelihood strategy." McMichael (2003: 302) places this observation in a political-economic context by commenting that the recent history of U.S. agriculture entails "the disappearing family farmer in a globalizing market incorporating lower-cost producers." While globalization may have benefited large-scale producers, it has not been kind to small and medium-sized farmers who cannot match the low costs of production afforded by the huge economies of scale enjoyed by their industrial-scale counterparts. Moreover, globalization is not simply a matter of markets favoring larger more efficient producers. McMichael (2003) and others have shown that trade liberalization subsidizes and depresses commodity prices in the U.S. thereby protecting agri-business. It bears remembering that the market is a *social and political construction*, not a natural phenomenon, and the market rules regulating international agricultural trade intentionally favor corporate actors over smaller enterprises. As a result, even though the volume of agricultural production has grown over time, the concentration of production into fewer and larger units continues unabated.

Frederick Buttel (2003) comments that a neoliberal form of globalization has fundamentally and irreversibly resulted in an ever more concentrated agriculture sector during the twenty-first century. By globalization, Buttel (2003: 180) means "an agricultural system featuring long-distance food supply chains that are managed by trans-national corporate agribusiness to optimize supply from farm inputs and farm-level production through processing, marketing, and consumption." The neoliberal aspect of globalization involves a transformed policy environment where national interests are subordinated to global profitmaking imperatives. Global neoliberalism in agriculture involves a substitution of globally harmonized standards in place of national farm and trade policies in such areas as tariff and non-tariff trade barriers and regulatory standards. As a result, trade rules are made by global elites rather than elected officials who, at least theoretically, are responsive to local and regional interests. Hence, neoliberal globalization involves a set of pro-corporate policies implemented by the World Trade Organization, the North American Free Trade Agreement (NAFTA) and other multilateral trade agreements to synchronize global markets in most farm commodities thereby creating profitable opportunities for private firms to invest their ever more mobile capital. As McMichael (2003: 377) has observed, while globalization is premised on the myth of the free market, in fact, "the rules governing agricultural trade promote exchanges within and among corporations that systematically disadvantage the majority of farmers."

Fewer and Larger Farms

Between 1850 and 1920, the number of U.S. farms grew from about 1.5 million to nearly 6.5 million. Since then, however, the number of farms has declined during each succeeding decade with the decline accelerating markedly since the Second

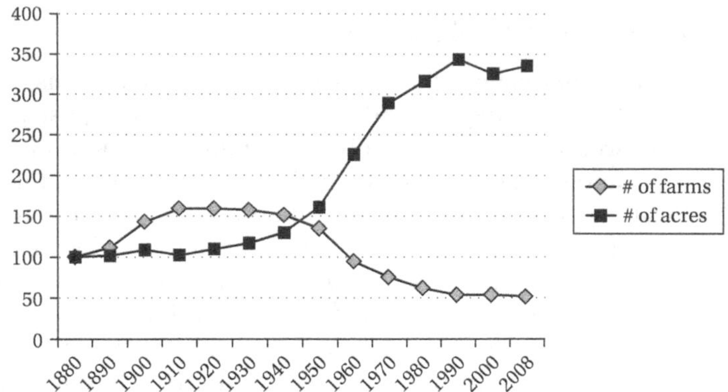

Source: Author's own, data from ICPSR, various dates.

Figure 9.1 Number of Farms versus Farm Size, Pct. Change, 1880-2008

World War. The number of U.S. farms declined by 12 percent during the 1950s, by over 30 percent during the 1960s and by over a quarter during the 1970s (van Es et al. 1988). Although the number of farms has steadily declined since the early twentieth century, the size of farms has increased. Figure 9.1 shows the percentage change in both the number of farms and in farm size from 1880 to 2008. In 1880 there were just over 4 million farms with an average size of about 136 acres. By 2008 the number of farms had dropped to less than 2.1 million (a decrease of nearly 50 percent), but the average farm size had increased over 300 percent to 335 acres.

This dramatic decline in the number of farms was largely a result of labor displacing mechanization, the demise of the tenant and share cropping systems in the South, and New Deal era farm policies that focused assistance on cash grains, cotton and several other commodities that were amenable to industrial scale production (Cochrane 1993). A prime example of the result of this trend is the development of confined animal feeding operations (see Box 9.1). Since 1980 the number of farms has stabilized at around 2.2 million, but largely as a result of technological changes and globalization, production has become increasingly concentrated in a relatively small number of very large units. In contrast, the vast majority of today's farms are not truly commercial ventures, and fail to generate sufficient income to support the farm household fully.

The Farm Crisis of the Early 1980s

As discussed above, forces outside of agriculture such as technological innovation, national policy and the trend toward globalization, affect the organization of agriculture, and the farm sector's financial wellbeing (Kenney et al. 1989). A number of these forces coalesced in the late 1970s and early 1980s to produce a "farm crisis" of epic proportions that adversely affected thousands of farm families, farm businesses, and the rural communities where they were located. From 1982 to 1986, the percentage of farms going out of business nearly tripled and the bankruptcy rate more than quadrupled (Leistritz and Murdock 1988).

Why did so many farm families lose their businesses during the 1980s? Were

Box 9.1 CAFOs

As agricultural has industrialized, practices associated with raising livestock have also fundamentally changed. The industrialization of agriculture has been driven by pressures to increase outputs while reducing costs through economies of scale. So called "factory farming" refers to raising livestock in high-density confinement as a means of increasing efficiency of production costs as well as labor and land use. Concentrated animal feeding operations, or CAFOs, are operations that may involve thousands of larger animals, such as cattle, or even tens of thousands of smaller animals, such as chickens. The increasing prevalence of CAFOs is reflected in the intensification of farming practices. For example, the state of Iowa produces one quarter of the nation's pork. Between 1980 and 2000 the number of hog farms declined from 64,000 to 10,500, while the average number of hogs raised per farm rose from 250 to 1,430 (Thorne 2007).

While in the past farms often raised crops and livestock producing at least some portion of crops for livestock feed and then using the manure as fertilizer, CAFOs necessitate the purchase of animal feed and result in the concentration of manure. Despite the efficiency of CAFOS, they have attracted strong criticism on a number of fronts. These include environmental problems associated with the concentration of manure and the subsequent pollution of soil and water, as well as air from wind-borne particles. Odors originating from CAFOs can also have strong negative effects on local housing values for those who live downwind (Isakson & Ecker 2008). The intensity of the confinement also necessitates the heavy use of antibiotics which also may contaminate groundwater and give rise to antibiotic-resistant pathogens (Gurian-Sherman 2008). Finally, many animal rights activists have argued that CAFOs are a cruel and inhumane means of raising livestock. For all these reasons some argue that while CAFOs may reflect *economically* rational practices on the part of livestock producers, they also illustrate the ecological irrationality of industrial agricultural practices by turning livestock production from an essentially balanced and sustainable activity to one that results in locally unwanted land uses and ecological imbalance.

Stronger public policies may be able to reduce some of the more negative effects of CAFOs, such as stricter monitoring of CAFO-related pollution, and enforcement of pollution regulations. While in the past, legislation like the Farm Bill has subsidized the production of grain crops that have in turn been used as inexpensive feed for livestock, public policy can instead promote smaller and pasture-based livestock operations. Glenna and Mitev (2009) provide a case example of a cooperatively owned CAFO in Bulgaria that adapted environmentally friendly practices in large part due to compliance with strict environmental regulations associated with accession to the European Union. This was coupled with the desire to increase local employment for cooperative members and make use of the manure as fertilizer in an area that has experienced marked soil depletion. In this case, the imposition of new international regulations prevented the cooperative from dumping manure from the CAFO into the Danube River. This, coupled with the fact that labor-intensive practices would provide more work for cooperative members, and that more ecologically sustainable manure disposal practices could benefit local farmers, created a local logic favorable to alternative practices.

they poor quality farmers, profligate spenders, or careless borrowers? Clearly, some farmers were to blame for their own problems, but most scholars believe that the roots of the crisis were structural rather than reflecting failure at the farm level. From the 1960s onward, U.S. farmers were encouraged to produce commodities for export as a way to overcome overproduction and low farm incomes (de Janvry and LeVeen 1986). The drive to remain competitive in world markets required an expansion of production, and hence the need for borrowed capital. As Garkovich and her colleagues (1995) have pointed out:

> During the '70s and '80s government officials, lenders and all the pundits told farmers that the solution to their problems was to get bigger. Foreign markets for American agricultural products seemed unlimited, and farmers were told that it was their patriotic duty to make "agripower and the agridollar" a part of American foreign policies. Bigger was better, and bigger was the solution to both farmers' problems and America's growing trade deficit. (136–137)

For a while, this seemed to be good advice. Farm income hit record highs from 1972 through 1974 reflecting increasing global food demand. Grain prices and land values climbed thereby permitting farmers to borrow more money to expand their acreage. However, the storm clouds began to gather late in the decade as real farm income declined and poverty among farm families increased sharply (de Janvry et al. 1987; Kenney et al. 1989). It turns out that bigger wasn't necessarily better for many U.S. farmers during the 1980s. Increased borrowing meant that many farmers were increasingly vulnerable to higher interest rates, and increased dependence on manufactured inputs such as chemicals and equipment made farmers more vulnerable to swings in commodity prices. As Lobao (1990: 45) has observed:

> By the 1980s, the conditions that fostered agricultural expansion reversed. U.S. farmers were faced with recession, a rise in the value of the dollar, declining world demand for U.S. products, and low commodity prices. Meanwhile, the cost of producing farm commodities and interest rates rose. As returns to farm land diminished, land values declined . . .

As the value of farm assets declined, an increasing number of farmers were unable to meet their debt obligations. The result was an increase in farm bankruptcies and liquidations (Leistritz and Murdock 1988). Farmers were affected throughout the country, but the deleterious effects concentrated in the nation's agriculturally dependent heartland.

A farm crisis of these proportions had not been seen since the Great Depression, and it had tremendous human costs. Many areas reported dramatic increases in family violence, divorce and alcohol abuse (McBride 1986). The crisis had a ripple effect, negatively affecting the manufacture and sale of farm equipment and other inputs. Rural banks failed, as did main-street businesses. In 1985, the Minnesota Department of Agriculture estimated that every farm foreclosure was matched by the loss of three non-farm jobs (Kabat 1985).

The farm crisis stimulated a wave of farm activism. To begin with, many direct protests were staged to hinder the auctioning of foreclosed farms. However, large-scale collective action also developed. In 1986, a "National Save the Family Farm Coalition" was established and called for higher commodity prices, production controls, immediate debt relief, a moratorium on farm foreclosures, and

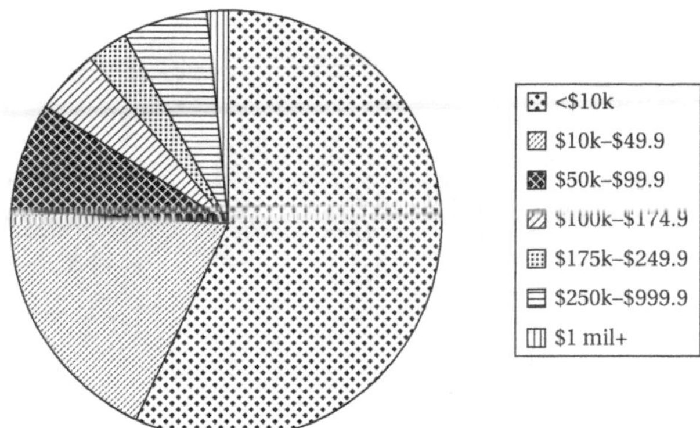

Source: Hoppe, R., P. Korb, E. O'Donoghue, and D. Banker. 2007. Structure and finances of U.S. farms: family farm report, 2007 ed. U.S. Dep. Agric., Economic Research Service, EIB No. 24.

Figure 9.2 Farms by Value of Production

emergency assistance to rural families (Aucoin 1986). Many other organizations were established during the 1980s including the North American Farm Alliance, a coalition of grass roots groups based in Ames, Iowa. In 1986, the United Farmer and Rancher Congress was organized with funding from country singer Willie Nelson's first two *Farm Aid* concerts. The Congress brought together 1,500 delegates from 38 states to develop strategies for direct action in support of farmers and agriculture.

Contemporary Structure: Concentration and Diversity

Browne et al. (1992) have observed, there is no such thing as an "average farm." They point out that farms vary in terms of scale, regional location, use of inputs, and characteristics of the operator. This diversity can be seen in Figure 9.2. The vast majority of U.S. farms are small even though agricultural production has become concentrated in a relatively small number of mega-farms. The U.S. Department of Agriculture has developed a classification of farms that differentiates family from non-family farms and then compares family farms by their scale of operation. Family farms, 98 percent of the total, are managed by family members and organized as sole proprietorships, partnerships, or family corporations. Non-family farms are organized as non-family corporations or cooperatives and farms with hired managers (USDA 2007).

The USDA family farm classification shows the high degree of concentration in U.S. agriculture. While nine out of ten American farms have gross sales of less than 250,000 per year, these small units only account for 25 percent of the nation's total farm production (as measured by gross sales). In contrast, large-scale enterprises, those with over $250,000 gross sales, account for only 7.5 percent of farms, but 60 percent of production. Non-family farms, 2 percent of all units, account for 15 percent of food and fiber sales.

The data in Figure 9.2 portray considerable diversity within the small farm category itself. Only about one-third of small farms can be characterized as viable

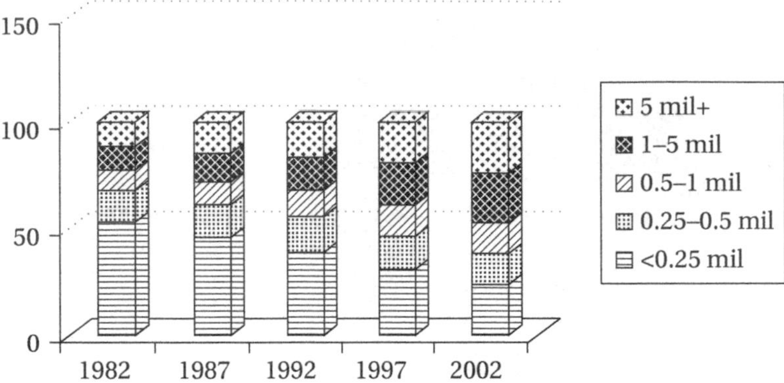

Source: Hoppe et al. 2008.

Figure 9.3 Million Dollar Farms

businesses that provide a family's primary livelihood. These units have gross sales of at least $100,000 and include an operator who reports that farming is her/his major occupation. The remainder of small farms are either limited-resource endeavors, retirement, or life-style residences. Residential units comprise almost 40 percent of U.S. farms, but only account for 5 percent of farm production (USDA-ERS 2007). On the other extreme, the three percent of U.S. farms with sales of $500,000 or more account for almost one half of all sales. Moreover, as shown in Figure 9.3, there has been significant concentration of sales even within the largest category of farms, those with $1 million or more sales. These data show that in 1982, "million dollar farms" accounted for 22 percent of sales by all *large* farms. By 2002, these same size units accounted for almost half of all sales by farms with at least a quarter million dollars in sales (Hoppe et al. 2008).[3]

The Regional Distribution of Agriculture

While fewer than seven percent of *rural* workers are now directly employed in agriculture, dependence on the sector is considerably higher in certain regions. The USDA-ERS (2005) has identified counties with much higher than average income or employment dependence on agriculture. Their data show that 440 of the nation's 3,100 counties derive at least 15 percent of earnings or employment from farming. This is a far cry from 1960 when agriculture was a dominant source of employment and income in the vast majority of the nation's nonmetropolitan counties (USDA-ERS 1997). Agriculture-dependent counties are overwhelmingly located in the Great Plains, the Western Corn Belt, or in the Pacific Northwest (see Figure 9.4).[4] While 92 percent of these counties are nonmetropolitan, it is important to note that over thirty are metropolitan counties.

Farming in the City's Shadows

Many people believe that agriculture is an exclusively rural activity, and that urban activities are incompatible with a viable farming sector (Jackson-Smith &

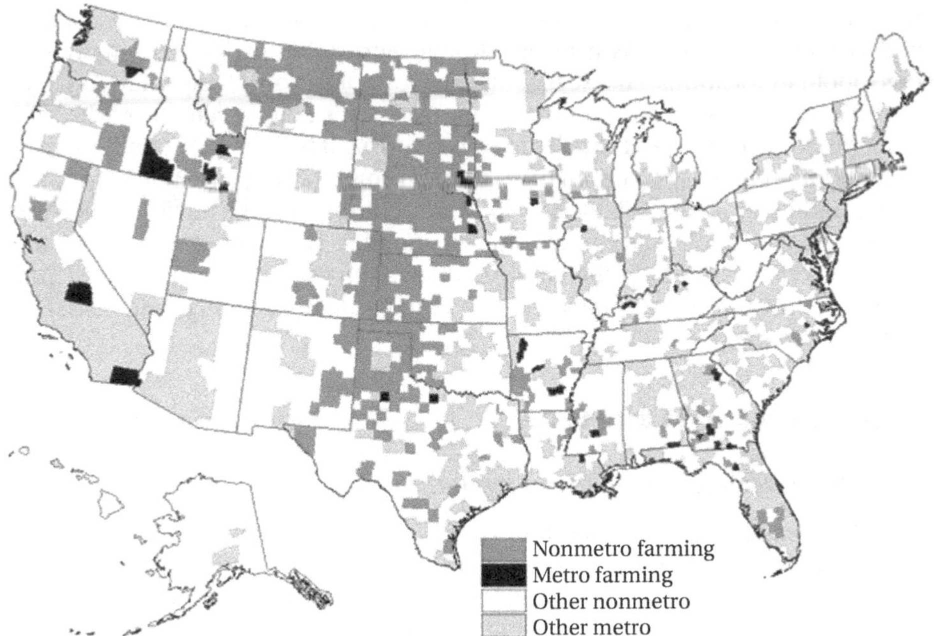

Farming-dependent counties – either an annual average of 15 percent or more total county earning derived from farming during 1998–2000 or 15 percent or more of employed residents working in farm occupations in 2000.

Source: ERS, USDA

Figure 9.4 Map of Farm Dependent Counties, 1998 –2000

Sharp 2008). While most farming at least as measured by volume of production, does occur in rural areas, a significant share of the nation's food and fiber is produced in or near to metropolitan areas (Heimlich & Anderson 2001). According to the 2002 Census of Agriculture, 41 percent of U.S. farms, and about 24 percent of farm land are located in metropolitan counties, while 34 percent of total sales of farm products originated on metropolitan farms (Bills et al. 2005). In 2002, the majority of specialty crop sales were made by metro farms including 66 percent of vegetables, 83 percent of fruit, 75 percent of greenhouse and nursery. Metro farms are also an important aspect of animal agriculture accounting for 49 percent of milk and dairy and 72 percent of equine sales. In addition, two-thirds of direct sales to consumers, and half of organic production sales originated on metropolitan farms.

While "farming in the city's shadow" can bring farmers and city dwellers into conflict, highly urbanized environments support agriculture in a number of important ways. Most importantly, metropolitan farms have direct access to a large consumer base, many of whom prefer local products. For example, over 45 percent of respondents to a 2008 statewide survey in New York State, including 41 percent of respondents from New York City and its suburbs, indicated that they would "go out of their way" to obtain locally produced food (CaRDI 2008). Metropolitan location provides opportunities for direct marketing through farmers' markets, restaurant and gourmet grocery outlets, road side stands, and U-pick operations. As a result, the per acre value of farm production in metropolitan locations far exceeds that in rural locations. This relatively high return provides a measure of protection from real estate speculators who wish to commodify the value of rural land by converting it to urban and built up uses. In addition, proximity to urban centers may provide a large pool of seasonal or part-time labor that is available at peak periods during the production cycle. Also, since most metropolitan farms are small to medium sized, off-farm employment may be a critical aspect of the household livelihood strategy, and cities include a large supply of opportunities for such employment (Heimlich and Anderson 2001).

Family Farms and Farm Families

Long-term Decline of the Farm Population

The U.S. Census first identified the rural farm population in 1920. At that time 31 million people, 30 percent of the U.S. population and 61 percent of the rural population, resided on farms.[5] Since then, the consistent trend for the farm population has been decline. The number of farm residents dropped from 31 million in 1920 to 2.1 million in 2007 (U.S. Census of Agriculture 2009), or from 30 percent to less than one percent of the nation's population. In addition, the farm population now constitutes less than five percent of the rural population. Hence, it is a mistake to equate farm population with rural population, since the majority of rural people do not live on farms.

Who are Today's Farmers?

Data are not available with which to describe today's farm resident population (Ahern 2009). Rather, the USDA collects data on farm proprietors in its Agriculture Resource and Management Survey (ARMS).[6] These data show that the principal farm operator is generally an older White male. The median age of the farm operator population is over 57 years compared with about 35 years for the nation as a whole (USDA-ERS 2009c). The average age of operators has been greater than 50 since at least the 1974. In addition, almost one-third of farm operators are 65 or older compared with 12.8 percent of the total population. One reason for the advanced age of farmers is that farmers tend to live on their farms even after they discontinue active farm work. In fact, more than 20 percent of farmers report being retired. However, the major reason for the older average age of farmers is the lack of generational replacement by younger operators. In fact, in 2008, only 17 percent of operators had ten years or less of experience. The lack of inter-generational replacement is one of the most daunting challenges facing U.S. agriculture today. Moreover, as Salamon (1992) has shown, the farm transfer process differs greatly among farm families and cultural schemes determine the generational and gender hierarchy of succession. The father–son dyad shapes succession among "yeomen" while "entrepreneurs" tend to de-emphasize what they regard as a child's premature claims.

Farm youth, even those whose parents have made clear plans for intergenerational succession, are often hesitant to take over the farm because income prospects from farming are meager compared with other opportunities. This is especially true of young adults with college education. In addition, the capital requirements needed to purchase an existing farm, or establish one's own operation, are extremely high, especially in comparison with the comparable risks and benefits associated with other investments. Complicating the farm succession issue is the fact that many farmers fail, or refuse, to make legally binding provisions for transferring their farms to their children or other family members. Accordingly, adult farm children often have to work into their forties or fifties before legal provision is made for taking over the farm. Only the most dedicated are willing to pay this price.

The vast majority of U.S. farms are operated by men. Data from the ARMS show that 89 percent of farm operators were men in 2008. However, this represents a notable decrease over the last quarter century when fully 95 percent of farm operators were men. In part, this increase in female farmers reflects women's greater longevity since women often take over the farm after the death of a spouse, especially if no adult child is willing or able to assume this role. Nearly 34 percent of female farmers were 65 or older in 2007 compared with less than 30 percent for male farm operators.

Almost 96 percent of farms are also operated by White persons. The 2007 Census of Agriculture reported that 96 percent of principal farm operators were White (U.S. Bureau of the Census 2009). Blacks or African Americans were 1.4 percent of all principal operators. American Indians or Alaska natives (1.6 percent), Asians (0.5 percent), native Hawaiian or other Pacific Islanders (0.1 percent), and those reporting more than one race (0.6 percent) made up the remainder. Most Hispanic operators (93 percent) reported their race as White. According to the Census of Agriculture, about 56,000 farm operators are Spanish Heritage, Latino, or Hispanic which would make them the largest minority population among farm operators. The low representation of minorities among farmers reflects a history of exclusion and discrimination, especially with respect to Blacks.[7]

Farmers are relatively well educated. About one-quarter have graduated from college, which is similar to the level of higher education of the total rural population. This comparability in educational attainment among farm operators is relatively new given the fact that only four percent had graduated from college in 1964 and two-thirds had not completed high school (USDA-ERS 2009c). Education is increasingly important for farm operators because farming is an increasingly information intensive and science-based activity. In addition, the operator and other farm family members need a solid education to succeed in the off-farm labor market which is now so important to their overall economic security.

Farm Labor

While 70 percent of all farm work is done by paid and unpaid family members, about one million persons perform hired farm work today. This is a dramatic decline from 1.9 million as recently as 1960 (USDA-ERS 2008). Hired farm workers make up less than 1 percent of all U.S. wage and salary workers, but they make a major contribution to agriculture by providing labor during critical production periods. In the popular imagination, hired farm workers are often portrayed as migrants who follow the grain crop from Texas to Canada or from the Great Lakes to New Jersey to harvest fruits and vegetables. However, almost two-thirds of today's farm workers live in settled communities.[8] This is increasingly true since the mid-1990s when the United States began to enforce its border with Mexico more vigorously. Hired farm workers tend to be young men with low formal education. While they are much more likely to be foreign born than all workers (42 percent versus 16 percent), the majority were born in the United States. Even though farm workers provide an essential input to one of the nation's most critical industries, they are economically vulnerable and impoverished. Hired farm work has an unemployment rate far in excess of the national average (8.5 percent versus 4.5 percent prior to the recession in 2006), and at $6.75 per hour in 2006, the median wage for non-supervisory hired farm labor was among the lowest paid for an unskilled occupation in the United States.

How Do Farm Families Make a Living?

Investigating how farm families make a living may seem an odd thing to do given the fact that farmers operate farm businesses, hence, it would seem likely that farm families make a living from their farms. However, as we will show, relatively few of today's farm families are able to survive on farm income alone. In 1995, Garkovich and her colleagues described the nature of family farming at the end of the twentieth century. Through the words of family farmers in Kentucky, they showed that while nostalgic and highly romanticized images of self reliant, independent, resourceful family farms persist, the reality of this rich tradition has changed dramatically. Nowhere can this change be seen more clearly than in the livelihood strategies farm families use to get by in contemporary America.

Data from USDA-ERS (2009c) clearly show that the typical farm livelihood strategy involves a bundle of income from farm and off-farm sources earned by various family members. Moreover, these data show that off-farm income is not merely a supplement to farm income but the key to remaining on the farm. Looking at the 97 percent of farms classified as "family farms" by USDA, almost one-half of farm operators consider off-farm work to be their principal occupation while three-quarters of farm spouses who are in the labor force consider off-farm work to be their main job. This allocation of farm household labor is mirrored in statistics on the sources of farm family income. According to the USDA's Agriculture Resource Management Survey (USDA-ERS 2007), family farms derive 59 percent of total income from off-farm earnings, 22 percent from interest, benefits, and other unearned sources, and only 17 percent from farming. Moreover, dependence on off-farm sources is especially high among families who operate small and medium-sized farms. Even among medium sales farms where the operator considers farming the principal occupation, farming only accounts for 48 percent of total family income. On limited resource farms, those with gross sales of less than $100,000, farm income is actually negative. In fact, only the largest family farms depend on agriculture for a majority of their income.

Farm Family Relationships and Gendered Division of Labor

While today's farm families are extremely diverse (USDA 2007), Garkovich and her colleagues (1995) have provided a view of family life that illuminates the nature of social relationships on small to medium-sized farms, those which account for the numerical majority of today's farm operations. Analysis of data from in-depth interviews with farmers and farm spouses in Kentucky identified both assets and costs of family life on small to medium-sized farms. This research shows that because these units are too small to hire labor, farm wives (and children) are an integral part of the farm's labor force. While wives are more likely to play subsidiary production roles such as feeding livestock, tending calves, running errands, moving equipment, etc., they also tend to keep the books, pay the bills, and have an overall knowledge of the farm's business side. This span of wives' knowledge and responsibilities, however, does not necessarily translate into egalitarian decision-making. Surveys of farm couples show that while some couples share in decision-making, husbands often have the final say regardless of the wife's responsibility for the businesses' financial management. In these situations, Garkovich and her colleagues (1995: 31) observed, that "farm women share the farm work but not the farm decisions, although they end up sharing the consequences."

Farm wives typically work the "double shift." Regardless of how fairly farm work and financial management are shared, farm wives retain primary responsibility for housework, child rearing, and household maintenance. Moreover, given the growing dependence on off-farm income among today's small and medium-sized farms, it is not surprising that a large and growing share of farm wives hold off-farm jobs. Research by the Bureau of Labor Statistics (Ilg 1995) showed that the percentage of farm wives employed off the farm increased from 59 percent in 1976 to over 70 percent in 1993. While this percentage differs by farm type, it is even high on dairy farms where the farm itself has extremely high labor needs. For example, Alberts et al. (1997) found that more than half of dairy farm wives in Minnesota held an off-farm job. Wives' off-farm employment is often satisfying, but also produces stressful role conflicts. Research by Godwin (1988) showed that a high proportion of employed farm wives wanted to increase their time in meal preparation, house and yard care, field work, caring for livestock, and running farm errands.

The Food System

As we indicated at the beginning of this chapter, only about seven percent of rural workers currently depend on agriculture for employment, but this does not mean that farms, farmers and farming are unimportant. To appreciate agriculture's place in society fully it is necessary to view farming as a constituent part of a broader *food system.*[9] The food system is a complex set of social, economic, and biophysical relationships that includes the growing, processing, and distribution of food as well as the social aspects of food consumption and relevant government policies that regulate food production, distribution, and marketing (Gillespie and Gillespie 2000). Hence, rather than being restricted to a rural land use, agriculture influences and is influenced by a broad range of social, economic, and natural processes. For example, the biophysical base of agriculture includes land, water, solar energy, and germplasm. Moreover, as Gillespie and Gillespie (2000) have observed, production, distribution, marketing, preparation and consumption of food are all influenced by culture (beliefs, knowledge, skills, values, norms) and formal and informal social relationships especially those that regulate major institutional domains such as economy, family, science, and religion. Some aspects of the food system such as research, industrial processes, marketing, and trade are conducted in the commercial sphere while others such as gardening, food preparation and consumption are primarily home-based. Finally, like any system the food system has to dispose of waste and by-products and deal with other environmental externalities.

Viewing agriculture from the food systems perspective enables one to examine farming's role in national and global economies as we have done earlier in this chapter, but it also illuminates agriculture's contributions to a wide range of social, environmental and biological issues ranging from human health, to conservation, to international relations, to community development. For example, consider food's contribution to health concerns such as the "obesity epidemic," declared in 2001 by then U.S. Surgeon General David Satcher.[10] Satcher noted that in the past twenty years the number of overweight children had doubled and the number of overweight adolescents had tripled, with 300,000 deaths per year attributable to obesity-related illness (USDHHS 2001). Accordingly, beginning in the 2006–2007 academic year, schools receiving federal lunch program assistance (which in practice means virtually all public schools) are mandated to develop wellness policies that promote nutrition, physical activity, and obesity prevention (Hinrichs and Schafft 2008). Similarly, public concern about food-borne pathogens has escalated recently with the increasing number of nationwide food poisoning outbreaks associated with a broad range of raw and processed foods such as spinach and hamburger. For example, in 2009, 550 people in 43 states were infected with salmonella as a result of eating tainted peanut butter (Ianelli 2009). These health-related examples demonstrate the merit of framing agricultural issues with a food systems approach that appreciates interrelationships between social, economic, and biophysical processes.

While locally owned farms produce sustenance for local populations, considering farming from a food systems perspective enables one to appreciate the industry's social and civic contributions to local community life. As Hinrichs (2008: 591) has observed, a local food system involves "the networks of social and economic relationships that link food producers and food consumers within a common geographic region." Direct marketing of raw farm products is local agriculture's hallmark. For example, the USDA estimates that farmers' markets have increased from 2,410 in 1996 to 4,385 in 2006 (Hinrichs et al. 2004). Similarly, since their introduction in 1985, almost 1,700 community supported agriculture organizations (CSA) were operating in 2004 (Schnell 2007). In a CSA, members pay an annual fee to a local farmer in exchange for a share of the harvest. This provides the farmer with capital; shares his risk with the consumer; and provides families with access to fresh, locally grown produce. Research shows that farmers markets and CSAs tend to be located in the urban–rural periphery where access to larger urban markets is easier. As discussed earlier, farming in the city's shadow accounts for an increasingly large share of the production of fruits, vegetables, nursery crops, and dairy products. Ironically, many rural communities lack similar access to local produce through farmers' markets and CSAs.

Community food systems also include small locally owned brewers, bakers, wineries, and specialty food manufacturers. Moreover, in some instances, local food systems supply schools and colleges, prisons, hospitals, and other institutions through a process known as "wholesale-direct" (see Box 9.2). In addition, community food systems often include gardening, hunting and gathering activities that are consumed locally and/or traded among households in the informal market (Jensen, Cornwall &, Findeis 1995; Brown & Kulcsar 2001).

Interest in local food systems focuses attention on the interrelationship between sustainable agriculture, community food security, and community development. This perspective on community agriculture is a backlash against what many perceive as excessive industrialization and concentration of farming and the lack of responsiveness to consumers and communities on the part of trans-national agrifood corporations (Bonanno & Constance, 2003). Since local food systems are rooted in particular places, many scholars believe that they provide economically viable solutions for small to medium sized farmers and consumers, are more likely to use ecologically sound production and distribution practices,[12] and to enhance civic engagement and local democracy (Hinrichs 2008; Feenstra 1997). This populist sentiment motivated Tolbert and his colleagues (2002) to examine how local capitalism, including local agriculture, might affect civic engagement, local democracy and community wellbeing.

Tolbert et al. argued that family farms and other local businesses are more deeply rooted in locality, and that family farmers and other local business owners are more likely to be engaged in civic affairs, to trust their neighbors and to be able to engage in cooperative civic activities. As a result, communities with a higher share of family farms and locally owned businesses are more able to solve problems collectively and therefore to have higher social welfare. Empirical analysis tended to support this contention by showing that small towns with higher than average measures of local capitalism had lower poverty rates, higher population retention and lower rates of unemployment.

Extending this argument, the relocalization of food systems is part of what Lyson has called *civic agriculture,* a local embedding of agricultural and food production practices as a means of identifying practices that are economically, environmentally and socially sustainable (Lyson et al. 2001). Lyson argues that civic agriculture represents a "locally organized system of agriculture and food production characterized by networks of producers who are bound together by place . . . Taken together, the enterprises that make up and support civic agriculture can be seen as part of a community's problem-solving capacity. The locally based organizational, associational, and institutional component of the agricultural and food system is the heart of civic agriculture" (2005: 92).

Lyson's perspective is inspired by two New Deal era studies of the impacts of economic concentration on community viability. In one study, Walter Goldschmidt (1978) investigated the social impacts of agribusiness on community structure in California, and found that farm consolidation had adverse consequences for

Box 9.2 Farm to School Programs and Connecting Schools with Local Agriculture

Farm to school programs are school-based efforts to increase the supply of fresh fruits and vegetables served within school cafeterias, and may also involve educational initiatives focused around health, nutrition and food. In practice, farm to school efforts assume a wide range of forms, including direct school purchases of produce from local farmers, farm tours, classroom projects on food and nutrition, or so-called "edible schoolyards," school gardens that teach students about health nutrition and how food is produced. Farm to school programs represent a relatively recent yet growing part of the "alternative agrifood" movement, a broad-based, loosely coordinated set of efforts to remake the agrifood system in ways that promote environmental sustainability, economic viability, community food security, and social justice (Allen 2004; Kloppenburg, Wubben, & Grunes 2008), often through the promotion of local, organic, and smaller-scale agricultural production.

While even ten years ago, farm to school programs were rarely recognized, a convergence of trends facing schools, communities and consumers have created conditions favorable for the spread of farm to school initiatives (Bagdonis, Hinrichs, & Schafft 2009. Perhaps most salient is the widespread recognition of the significant public health consequences of obesity-related illness among children. Accordingly, because children spend so much time in schools, school practices have been seen as one of the key areas of potential interventions aimed at reducing obesity and obesity-related illness (Nestle 2003; Vallianatos, Gottlieb, & Haase 2004).

Various legislative and public policy initiatives such as the Fresh Fruit and Vegetable Pilot program help subsidize school purchases of fresh fruits and vegetables to serve to students, and amendments to the National School Lunch Act make it possible for schools to serve local, perishable foods without advertising for bids. New organizations like the National Farm to School Network (www.farmtoschool.org) and the Community Food Security Coalition (www.foodsecurity.org) offer numerous farm to school resource materials online. Various farm-to-school "how-to" guidebooks are also now available[11], providing guidance to schools and communities.

The notion of a "how-to" guidebook suggests that there is in fact a relatively coherent set of practices that can be considered "farm to school" and that there is a particular "how-to" way to initiate these efforts. However, recent work by Hinrichs, Schafft and colleagues has strongly suggested the ways in which these initiatives not only vary significantly from site to site, but are also deeply shaped by available human, institutional and fiscal resources, organizational and logistical constraints, and most significantly the local issues that give farm to school its salience: in short, the social logic of local communities (Bagdonis, Hinrichs, & Schafft 2009; Hinrichs & Schafft 2008).

For example, urban districts where obesity and nutrition are primary concerns and where food services are large and automated and lack the flexibility to process easily various types of fresh produce (Kloppenburg, Wubben, & Grunes 2008), may be more likely to turn to "edible schoolyards" integrating school gardens into science and/or health curricula, and providing students with opportunities to taste and prepare fresh produce. In rural schools, while health, nutrition, and obesity prevention may also be a concern, farm to school may also be a way of preserving area farm land, supporting

Box 9.2 (continued)

local farmers (who also may well have children or grandchildren in the school system), and enhancing the local economy. In this respect, farm to school initiatives geared towards student health are often also directly bound up in a desire to support the health of local economics and the health of the social and physical environments in which these initiatives are based. (Schafft, Hinrichs, & Bloom 2010)

social inequality, civic engagement and other measures of quality of life. In the other, Mills and Ulmer (1970) found similar adverse community impacts resulting from the concentration of industrial production. Accordingly, Lyson's main point was that local capitalism, including that represented by local agriculture, can have beneficial impacts on various domains of life quality. Or as Leland Glenna (2010) has observed "Having banks that are too big to fail is not good for our society. Having farms that are too big not to destroy the natural environment and too big not to destroy rural communities is not good either." The last two decades or so have seen increasing popular concern over the social, environmental, and health effects of the way in which conventional agriculture and food systems operate. Stories in the media and popular press have raised new concerns about food safety, obesity, and the questions about food origins and their social, environmental, and economic impacts. As a consequence there is strong and growing interest in organic and sustainable agriculture, farmers' markets, and support for "local" foods. This interest, not only among consumers, but farmers, activists, environmentalists, academics, and policy-makers, has taken on all the characteristics of a broad based social movement, a sustained and organized collective effort to bring about social change. This can be seen in the numerous state and regional level organizations supporting and promoting alternatives to the conventional food system (Allen 2004).

However, as other commentators have pointed out, this movement is not without contradictions (such as the co-optation of organic food production by industrial agriculture) and doesn't necessarily result in more equitable labor practices or increased food security (Guthman 2004). Regardless, it suggests the ways in which the structure of conventional, industrial agriculture is being challenged and how the trends towards agricultural concentration and industrialization are not inevitable.

Conclusions

In this chapter we have shown that the farming sector has gone through a series of transformations during the last 200 years, and that farming is no longer a viable livelihood strategy for large numbers of rural Americans (Lobao & Meyer 2001). While Lobao and Meyer are undoubtedly correct in an overall, macro-structural sense, we would also observe that in the midst of this dramatic restructuring of the agricultural sector, many farm families are bundling various forms of "alternative agriculture" with off-farm work thereby producing viable livelihood strategies, and retaining land in production and small- to medium-sized family farms in business. Except for the fact that this strategy involves farming it is not so different from that employed by many American families today who piece together a livelihood from multiple jobs and the efforts of multiple members.

Taken to its extreme, however, restructuring of the farm sector has been hypothesized to lead the disappearance of American agriculture. For example, agricultural economist Stephen Blank (1998)[13] predicted that agriculture will disappear as a way of life, and as a rural land use within two generations. When Blank's book, *The End of Agriculture in the American Portfolio,* was published in the 1990s it was vigorously attacked as an extreme perspective. Yet, as Buttel (2003) has commented, Blank correctly showed that the early twenty-first century is a critical time for agriculture given the confluence of several critical trends and processes that affect the sector's future profitability, structure, and spatial location.[14] Accordingly, while Blank's "end of American agriculture" claim is unlikely to come true, it is undeniably true that agriculture is embedded in a dynamic world, and that macro social and economic changes and technological and organizational transformations will significantly affect almost every aspect of agriculture and the food system. Some of these impacts may undermine nutrition, food safety, community solidarity, and global security; others may bring benefit to families and communities throughout the world.

Even though agriculture no longer provides a major share of rural employment and earnings in most regions, farms, farmers, and farming continue to play important roles in contemporary rural (and urban) society. We have emphasized that farming cannot be separated from a broader *food system* that is characterized by complex interrelationships between social, political-economic, environmental, and biophysical processes. As a result, changes in agricultural production, transport, and marketing influence are influenced by a complex array of local and non-local forces. Since farming and agriculture cannot be isolated from society, the relationships between food and health, the environment, local democracy, and international politics have become increasingly apparent in the twenty-first century, and increasingly important for human welfare. This will, arguably, only become more pronounced as we proceed into the twenty-first century and contend with increasing global climate change and shortages of fossil fuels that will certainly alter, perhaps radically, the ways in which agriculture is practiced.

Moreover, since agriculture is deeply embedded in a neoliberal global system, the sector's future is not entirely in our own hands. Many people feel that the global agricultural system is unresponsive to consumer and community needs, which raises additional concerns about food quality and safety, food security, environmental conservation, and rural community viability. As we will discuss in Chapter 11, domestic development policy is strongly influenced by global economic concerns. In particular, rural policies, including agricultural policies, are shaped by a choice between efficiency where resource mobility trumps claims for local development, and equity where local economy and society are accorded a high priority. This policy choice will have a profound effect on the nature of American agriculture in the future, and agriculture's impact on social and economic wellbeing, health, and environmental quality.

Notes

1 While only 6.5% of nonmetropolitan workers work directly in agriculture, the number of nonmetropolitan jobs tied to agriculture through upstream and downstream linkages approaches 20%.
2 It is not clear that a positive trade balance in agriculture benefits the nation's overall trade balance. The United States imports higher value crude oil to provide the fuel and other inputs to produce lower value agricultural exports. Accordingly, a high volume of farm exports may actually reduce the nation's overall trade balance.
3 Sales are expressed in constant 2002 dollars. However, the constantly changing statistical definition of "farm" makes comparative analysis across time problematic.
4 The regional distribution of farm operators is somewhat different from the distribution of farm dependent counties. About 37% of farm operators live in the South and 42% live in the Midwest (USDA-ERS 2009c).
5 From 1920 through 1950 the determination of what is a farm depended largely on the census enumerator's judgment. In 1960, the Census Bureau instituted a more concrete definition: (a) rural territory of at least ten acres from which sales of farm products of at least $50 were made, or (b) or on land of less than ten acres from which sales of farm products of $250 or more were made. In 1980, the Census Bureau adopted a more restrictive definition. The farm population was redefined to include persons living on places of one acre or more from which at least $1000 gross sales of agricultural products were made (Fuguitt et al. 1989).
6 USDA differentiates among principal and other operators (USDA-ERS 2009c). The data in this section are for principal operators.
7 Because tens of thousands of African American farmers were unable to have their claims resolved in the previous *Pigford Case*, a class action discrimination suit between the U.S. Department of Agriculture and Black farmers in which the plaintiffs accused the USDA of discrimination on the basis of race, stating that they were turned down for USDA farm loans and/or were forced to wait longer for loan approval than other, nonminority farmers. Congress established a new remedial process for relief under the Food, Conservation, and Energy Act of 2008 ("2008 Farm Bill"). This case, the *Consolidated Black Farmers' Discrimination Litigation*, consists of discrimination claims by African American farmers authorized by Section 14012 of the 2008 Farm Bill.
8 They are most likely to work in the Southwest, South, and Midwest regions.
9 It is also important to acknowledge that agriculture produces fiber, such as cotton and flax, in addition to food. Moreover, corn, switch grass, and other farm products are becoming important feedstocks for energy production.
10 These concerns have only been amplified by popular press books such as Eric Schlosser's *Fast Food Nation* (2001), Michael Pollan's *Omnivore's Dilemma* (2006), and Raj Patel's *Stuffed and Starved* (2008), as well as similarly themed films like *Super Size Me*, *King Corn*, and more recently, *Food, Inc.*
11 See e.g., Hinrichs, Schafft, Bloom, & McHenry-Sorber 2008; Joshi, Kalb, & Beery 2006; Kalb, Markley, & Tedeschi 2004; USDA 2005.
12 Evidence that local food systems are more environmentally sustainable is mixed at best (Hinrichs 2008)
13 Note: In addition to his faculty appointment in agricultural economics, Blank served as Assistant Vice Provost at the University of California-Davis at the time his book was published. Davis is one of the nation's flagship land grant agricultural colleges.
14 These forces include: declining commodity prices and a profit squeeze on producers despite subsidies, global control of decision-making in the sector, rising costs of production because of urban pressure on land prices, and technological change that facilitates very large units and/or reduced labor demands (Buttel 2003).

References

Ahern, M. 2009. Personal communication.

Alberts, J., Kjome, D., Scheffert, P., Schwateau, C., & Wright, J. 1997. Parlor Profiles: Dairy Families Talk About Their Lives. Extension Bulletin 06658. St. Paul: University of Minnesota Extension. Retrieved December 2, 2009 from: http://www.extension.umn.edu/distribution/livestocksystems/components/6658-10.html.

Allen, P. 2004. *Together at the Table: Sustainability and Sustenance in the American Agrifood System.* University Park, PA, The Pennsylvania State University Press.

Aucoin, J. 1986. Missouri Farmers on the Front Lines, *The Progressive*, July: 33.

Bagdonis, J.M., Hinrichs, C.C., & Schafft, K.A. 2009. The Emergence and Framing of Farm-to-School Initiatives: Civic Engagement, Health and Local Agriculture. *Agriculture and Human Values*, 26(2–3),107–119.

Bills, N., Uva, W., & Cheng, M. 2005. Policy Brief: Population Settlement and Specialty Crop Production in the Northeastern U.S. California Institute for the Study of Specialty Crops, San Luis Obispo.

Blank, S. 1998. *The End of Agriculture in the American Portfolio.* Westport, Conn., Quorum Books.

Bonanno, A. & Constance, D. 2003. The Global/Local Interface, pp. 241–251. In Brown, D.L. & Swanson, L. (eds) *Challenges for Rural America in the 21st Century.* University Park, Penn State University Press.

Brown, D.L. & Kulcsar, L. 2001. Household Economic Behavior in Post-Socialist Rural Hungary. *Rural Sociology*, 66(2), 157–180.

Browne, W., Skees, J., Swanson, L., Thompson, P., & Unnevehr, L. 1992. *Sacred Cows and Hot Pototoes: Agrarian Myths in Agricultural Policy.* Boulder, Westview.

Buttel, F. 2003. Continuities and Disjunctures in the Transformation of the U.S. Agro-Food System, pp. 177–199. In Brown, D.L., & L. Swanson, L. (eds) *Challenges for Rural America in the 21st Century.* University Park, Penn State University Press.

CaRDI. 2008. Data from the 2008 Empire State Poll. Ithaca, Cornell University.

Cochrane, W. 1993. *The Development of American Agriculture.* Minneapolis, University of Minnesota Press.

de Janvry, A. & LeVeen, P. 1986. Historical Forces That Have Shaped World Agriculture: A Structural Perspective, pp. 83–104. In Dahlberg, K. (ed.) *New Directions for Agriculture and Agricultural Research: Neglected Dimensions and Emerging Alternatives.* Totowa, N.J., Rowman & Allanheld.

de Janvry, A., Runsten, D. & Sadoulet, E. 1987. Toward a Rural Development Program for the United States: A Proposal, pp. 55–93. In Summers, G., Bryden, J., Deavers, K., Newby, H., & Sechler, S. (eds) *Agriculture and Beyond: Rural Economic Development.* Madison, University of Wisconsin, College of Agriculture and Life Sciences.

Feenstra, G. 1997. Local Food Systems and Sustainable Communities. *American Journal of Alternative Agriculture.* 12(1), 28–36.

Fuguitt, G.V., Brown, D.L., & Beale, C. 1989.The Population Associated with Farming, pp. 303–335. In Fuguitt, G.V., Brown, D.L., & Beale, C. *Rural and Small Town America.* New York, Russell Sage Foundation.

Garkovich, L., Bokemeier, J., & Foote, B. 1995. *Harvest of Hope: Family Farming/Farming Families.* Lexington, University of Kentucky Press.

Gillespie, G. & Gillespie, A. 2000. Community Food Systems: Toward a Common Language for Building Productive Partnerships. Ithaca, NY, Cornell University, Division of Nutritional Sciences. Retrieved December 4, 2009 from: http://www.foodroutes.org/doclib/28/foodsys-temdefs.pdf.

Glenna, L.L. 2010. Personal communication.

Glenna, L.L. & Mitev, G.V. 2009. Global Neo-Liberalisim, Global Ecological Modernization, and a Swine Cafo in Rural Bulgaria. *Journal of Rural Studies*, 25, 289–298.

Godwin, D. 1988. Farm Wives' Preferences, Time Allocation, and Off-Farm Employment Status. *Family and Consumer Sciences Research Journal*, 17, No. 1, 110–124.

Goldschmidt, W. 1978 [1946] *As You Sow: Three Studies of the Social Consequences of Agribusiness.* Montclair, N.J., Allenhand-Osmun.

Gurian-Sherman, D. (2008). *Cafos Uncovered: The Untold Costs of Confined Animal Feeding Operations.* Cambridge, MASL, Union of Concerned Scientists.

Guthman, J.(2004). *Agrarian Dreams: The Paradox of Organic Farming in California.* Berkeley, University of California Press.

Heimlich, R. & Anderson,W. 2001. Development at the Urban Fringe and Beyond: Impacts on Agriculture and Rural Land. *Agriculture Economic Report* No. 803. Washington, D.C., USDA-ERS.

Hinrichs, C. 2008. Local Food Systems, pp. 591–595. In Goreham, G. (ed.) *Encyclopedia of Rural America.* Millerton, NY, Greyhouse Publishing.

Hinrichs, C. & Schafft, K. 2008. *Farm to School Programs in Pennsylvania.* Harrisburg, PA, The Center for Rural Pennsylvania.

Hinrichs, C., Gillespie, G., & Feenstra, G. 2004. Social Learning and Innovation at Retail Farmers' Markets. *Rural Sociology.* 69(1), 31–58.

Hinrichs, C., Schafft, K., Bloom, D., & McHenry-Sorber, E. (2008). *Growing the Links Between Farms and Schools: A How-to Guidebook for Pennsylvania Schools and Communities.* Harrisburg, PA, Center for Rural Pennsylvania.

Hobbs, D. 1995. Social Organization in the Countryside, pp. 369–396. In Castle, E. (ed.) *The Changing American Countryside: Rural People and Places.* Lawrence, University Press of Kansas.

Hoppe, R., Korb, P. & Banker, D. 2008. Million Dollar Farms in The New Century. Economic Information Bulletin No. 42. Washington, D.C., USDA-ERS.

Hoppe, R., Kolb, P., O'Donoghue, E., and Banker, D. 2007. Structures and Finance of U.S. Farming: Family Farm Report. *Economic Information Bulletin,* No. 24. Washington, D.C. USDA-ERS.

Ianelli, V. 2009. Salmonella Outbreaks. *About.com: Pediatrics.* Retrieved December 5, 2009 from: http://pediatrics.about.com/od/salmonella/a/109_salm_outbrk.htm.

ICPSR. Various dates. Number of Farms. Accessed at: http://coweeta.ecology.UGA.edu/trends/datadictionary/numberfarms.html.

Ilg, R. 1995. The Changing Face of Farm Employment. *Monthly Labor Review,* April, 3–12.

Isakson, H.R. &Ecker, M.D. 2008. An Analysis of the Impact of Swine Cafos on the Value of Nearby Houses. *Agricultural Economics,* 39, 365–372.

Jackson-Smith, D. and Sharp, J. 2008. Farming in the Urban Shadow: Supporting Agriculture at the Rural-Urban Interface. *Rural Realities,* 2(4),1–12.

Jefferson, T. 1785. August 23 Letter to John Jay.

Jensen, L., Cornwall, G., & Findeis, J. 1995. Informal Work in Nonmetropolitan Pennsylvania. *Rural Sociology,* 60(1), 91–107.

Joshi, A., Kalb, M., & Beery, M. 2006. *Going Local: Paths to Success for Farm to School Programs.* Los Angeles, National Farm to School Program.

Kabat, P. 1985. The Farmer in the Cell. *The Progressive.* 49, 50.

Kalb, M., Markley, K., & Tedeschi, S. 2004. *Linking Farms with Schools: A Guide to Understanding Farm-to-School Programs for Schools, Farmers and Organizers.* Los Angeles, LA, Community Food Security Coalition.

Kenney, M. , Lobao, L., Curry, J., & Goe, R. 1989. Midwestern Agriculture in U.S. Fordism: From the New Deal to Economic Restructuring. *Sociologia Ruralis,* 29 (2), 130–148.

Kloppenburg, J., Wubben, D., & Grunes, M. 2008. Linking the Land and the Lunchroom: Lessons from the Wisconsin Homegrown Lunch Project. *Journal of Hunger & Environmental Nutrition,* 3(4), 440–455.

Leistritz, L. & Murdock, S. 1988. Financial Characteristics of Farms and of Farm Financial Markets and Policies in the United states, pp. 13–28. In Murdock, S. & Leistritz, L. (eds) *The Farm Financial Crisis: Socioeconomic Dimensions and Implications for Producers and Rural Areas.* Boulder, Westview.

Lobao, L. 1990. *Locality and Inequality: Farm and Industry Structure and Socioeconomic Conditions.* Albany, SUNY Press.

Lobao, L. & Meyer, K. 2001. The Great Agricultural Transition: Crisis, Change and Social Consequences of Twentieth Century U.S. Farming. *Annual Review of Sociology*, 27, 103–124.

Lyson, T. 2005. Civic Agriculture and Community Problem Solving. *Culture and Agriculture*, 27 (2), 92–98.

Lyson, T., Torres, B., & Welsh, R. 2001. Scale of Agricultural Production, Civic Engagement and Community Welfare. *Social Forces*. 80(1), 311–327.

McBride, R. 1986. Broken Heartland: Farm Crisis in the Midwest. *The Nation*. 242,132–133.

McMichael, P. 2003. The Impact of Global Economic Practices on American Farming, pp. 375–384. In Brown, D.L. & Swanson, L. (eds) *Challenges for Rural America in the 21st Century*. University Park, Penn State University Press.

Mills, C.W. & Ulmer, M. 1970 [1946] Small Business and Civic Welfare, pp. 124–154. In Aiken, M. & Mott, P. (eds) *The Structure of Community Power*. New York, Random House.

Nestle, M. 2003. *Food Politics: How the Food Industry Influences Nutrition and Health*. Berkeley, University of California Press.

Patel, R. 2008.*Stuffed and Starved*. Melville House, New York.

Pollan, M. 2006. *The Omnivore's Dilemma: A Natural History of Four Meals*. New York, Penguin.

Salamon, S. 1992. *Prairie Patrimony: Family, Framing and Community in the Midwest*. Chapel Hill, University of North Carolina Press.

Schafft, K. A., Hinrichs, C., & Bloom, D. 2010.Pennsylvania Farm-to-School Programs and the Articulation of Local Context. *Journal of Hunger and Environmental Nutrition*, 5(1), 23–40.

Schlosser, E. 2001. *Fast Food Nation*. New York, Houghton Mifflin.

Schnell, S. 2007. Food With a Farmer's Face: Community Supported Agriculture in the United States. *The Geographical Review*. 97,550–564.

Swanson, L. (ed.) 1988. *Agriculture and Community Change in the U.S.* Boulder, Westview.

Thorne, P.S. 2007. Environmental Health Impacts of Concentrated Animal Feeding Operations: Anticipating Hazards – Searching for Solutions. *Environmental Health Perspectives*, 115(2), 296–297.

Tolbert, C.,Irwin, M., Lyson, T., & Nucci, A. 2002. Civic Community in Small-Town America: How Civic Welfare is Influenced by Local Capitalism and Civic Engagement. *Rural Sociology*. 67(1), 90–113.

Turner, Frederick Jackson. 1921. *The Frontier in American History*. New York, Holt.

U.S. Census Bureau. 2009. 2007 U.S. Census of Agriculture. Volume 1: U.S. Summary and State Reports. Retrieved November 25, 2009 from http://www.agcensus.usda.gov/Publications/2007/Full_Report/CenV1US1.txt.

Urban, T. 1991. Agricultural Industrialization: It's Inevitable. *Choices*. 4, 4–6.

USDA, Food and Nutrition Service. 2005. *Eat Smart—Farm Fresh! A Guide to Buying and Serving Locally Grown Produce in School Meals*. Washington D.C., USDA-FNS.

USDA-ERS. 1997. Understanding Rural America: County Types. *Agriculture Information Bulletin* No. 710. Retrieved December 3, 2009 from: http://www.ers.usda.gov/publications/aib710/aib710g.htm.

USDA-ERS. 2005. Measuring Rurality: 2004 County Typology Codes. *Briefing Rooms*. Retrieved November 25, 2009 from: *http://www.ers.usda.gov/Briefing/Rurality/Typology/*.

USDA-ERS. 2007. America's Diverse Family Farms. *Economic Information Bulletin* No. 26. Washington, D.C.

USDA-ERS. 2008. Rural Labor and Education: Farm Labor. *Briefing Rooms*. Retrieved December 2, 2009 from: http://www.ers.usda.gov/Briefing/LaborAndEducation/FarmLabor.htm.

USDA-ERS. 2009a. State Fact Sheet: United States. Retrieved November 21, 2009 from http://www.ers.usda.gov/StateFacts/US.htm.

USDA-ERS. 2009b. Foreign Agricultural Trade of the United States (FATUS): Monthly Summary. Retrieved November 22, 2009 from http://www.ers.usda.gov/Data/FATUS/monthlysummary.htm.

USDA-ERS. 2009c. Farm Household Economics and Wellbeing: Beginning Farmers, Demographics and Labor Allocations. *Briefing Room*. Retrieved November 25, 2009 from http://www.ers.usda.gov/Briefing/wellbeing/.

USDHHS. 2001. *The Surgeon General's Call to Action to Prevent and Decrease Overweight and*

Obesity. Rockville, MD, U.S. Department of Health and Human Services, Public Health Service, Office of the Surgeon General.

Vallianatos, M., Gottlieb, R., & Haase, M.A. 2004. Farm-to-School: Strategies for Urban Health, Combating Sprawl, and Establishing a Community Food Systems Approach. *Journal of Planning Education and Research*. 23, 414–423.

van Es, J., Chicoine, D., & M. Flotow, M. 1988. Agricultural Technologies, Farm Structure and Rural Communities in the Corn Belt: Policies and Implications for 2000, pp. 130–180. In Swanson, L. (ed.) *Agriculture and Community Change in the U.S.* Boulder, Westview.

Vias, A. & Nelson, P. 2006. Changing Livelihoods in Rural America, pp. 75–102. In Kandel, W. & Brown, D.L. (eds) *Population Change and Rural Society*. Dordrecht, Springer.

10 Poverty Across Rural People and Places

Poverty refers to conditions in which a person, family, or household lacks sufficient resources with which to access basic sustenance. While poverty is often measured against a statistical threshold, it is essentially a normative rather than statistical concept. People and families are considered to be poor if they fall below a set level of material resources including food, shelter, and/or other necessities. Areas are considered to be poor when their material level of living persistently falls below a national norm. The analysis of rural poverty involves two separate but interrelated questions: (a) Why are some people and families more likely to be poor than others? and (b) Why are people in some kinds of places more likely to be poor than others? As we discuss in this chapter, however, the greatest disadvantage comes when persons with characteristics predisposing them to be poor live in places also experiencing economic stagnation. In other words, rural poverty is especially persistent and intractable when the people left behind live in places that have been left behind.

Poverty is frequently assumed to be a primarily *economic* phenomenon, the consequence of inadequate income relative to need. This is true on one level, but in reality poverty is a far more complex phenomenon that contains multiple political, social, structural, and spatial dimensions. That is, poverty is a factor of limited income, but is also fundamentally connected to limited access to social resources like health-care, education, housing, and political power. Of course, income helps to shape the level of access most people have to these resources. Yet, an adequate understanding of poverty, as we will argue, cannot be reduced simply to income, even though this is the means by which it is most frequently measured.

This distinction between a strictly income-based concept of poverty and a broader concept of *social exclusion* highlights a major difference in the way American social scientists and policymakers consider poverty compared with their counterparts in Europe. Instead of examining (typically only or predominantly economic) *attributes* of individuals and households, social exclusion focuses on the *processes* of change that result in individuals' or groups' exclusion from various social domains, with consequent reductions in life-chances and social and economic opportunities, as well as civic engagement and democratic participation (Byrne 1999; Philip & Shucksmith 2003; Moffatt & Glasgow 2009). As Walker and Walker explain, social exclusion refers to the

> dynamic process of being shut out, fully or partially, from any of the social, economic, political or cultural systems which determine the social integration of a person in society. Social exclusion may, therefore, be seen as a denial (or the non-realization) of the civil, political and social rights of citizenship. (1997: 8)

As such, an attention to social exclusion is historicized, attuned to the multidimensional nature of inequality and disadvantage (and the relations between these different dimensions), and attempts to highlight the logic of local social, political and institutional contexts that shape and reproduce inequality (Molnár & Schafft 2003).

This same logic is embedded in the difference between *absolute* and *relative* poverty. Most research and policy analysis in the United States is based on an absolute measure of poverty, for example, by determining how many people and/or families fall below an absolute threshold of material wellbeing. However, in many parts of Europe, researchers and policy-makers are more likely to be concerned with inequality, e.g., how individuals or families compare with a nation's distribution of income and/or other types of valued resources. The important distinction is that a society with extreme income inequality can still be considered unjust, even when most persons have adequate food, shelter and other material necessities. Accordingly, policy responses to relative poverty typically involve redistributing income so as to reduce the gap between the top and bottom of society rather than simply moving the least well-off persons and families above some empirically determined threshold of minimum need (Galston 2008). Because this chapter focuses primarily on the United States, we will rely on absolute measures of poverty, but we also recognize different interpretations of rural poverty that might also be made using alternative conceptual approaches.

Who Is Poor in the United States?

Measuring Poverty

In order to measure the depth and distribution of poverty, governmental agencies and other bureaucratic institutions have established guidelines that can be used to identify who is and who is not in poverty. In the United States income thresholds are used as the official federal measure for poverty. This particular measure dates back to 1963 when President Lyndon B. Johnson established a poverty line of $3,000 for a typical U.S. family, based upon recommendations from the President's Council of Economic Advisors (CEA) and research conducted by Molly Orshansky (1965) for the Social Security Administration. These recommendations were based, first, around the assumption that low-income families typically spent about two-thirds of their income on non-food items, and second, the minimum estimated cost at the time for three adequate meals for a family of four at $2.74 per day. The current poverty threshold maintains this logic, but adjusts for family size and age of householder, and is updated annually by the Census Bureau to account for inflation and the rising costs of goods and services (see Table 10.1). In 2008 the poverty line for a family of four with a non-elderly householder was set at $21,200 annual income, or about $1,767 per month. Assuming, as the original measure does, an even three way split between housing costs, food, and non-food items, this leaves about $589 per month to pay for housing costs including rent or mortgage and utilities. Similarly, this leaves a food budget of about $147 per week. Assuming three meals a day for four persons, this factors to about $1.75 budgeted per person, per meal. The remaining $598 is

Table 10.1 Poverty Guidelines, 1980–2009

Persons	1980	1990	2000	2009
1	3,790	6,280	8,350	10,956
2	5,010	8,420	11,250	13,991
3	6,230	10,560	14,150	17,098
4	7,450	12,700	17,050	21,954
5	8,670	14,840	19,950	25,991
6	9,890	16,980	22,850	29,405
7	11,110	18,120	25,750	33,372
8	12,330	21,260	28,650	37,252
Each add'l adult	1,220	2,140	2,900	3,600

Source: U.S. Bureau of Census, 2009.

then allocated towards all remaining costs for the month, including (though not limited to) clothing, transportation, child care, fuel for heating and transportation, health care, and all other non-food related costs.[1]

Clearly, for those with incomes at or near the poverty line, there is little economic cushion. Unanticipated costs or domestic problems can quickly force people to make difficult decisions. As a housing authority staff person working to secure low-cost apartments for low-income families explained:

> I think what happens is the affordability. Look at the cost of rental units and the income. Calculate the budget of a single mom working at minimum wage and check the cost of housing. And if you look at that closely, it's not hard to figure out that this person is headed for financial disaster unless something happens. It's impossible to make those numbers work. The wages available and the housing costs are not compatible. You end up compromising at this point. There are people who are making choices between buying food and buying medicine. Those are hard choices. There are no other resources to offset [this situation] that they are aware of, so we see a lot of those folks in crisis because of expenses that have become uncontrollable. (Schafft 2005: 9)

Poverty Risks Vary According to Where One Lives

In the United States poverty has typically been associated with core metropolitan areas and "urban blight" (Hoppe 1993). This is unsurprising since urban core areas are where poverty is most concentrated and most visible, However, as shown by President Johnson's Commission on Rural Poverty, Michael Harrington's epic book, *The Other America,* and decades of academic research, poverty is at least as much – if not in some ways *more* – a rural problem than an urban problem (Harrington 1962; President's National Advisory Commission on Rural Poverty 1968; Jensen & McLaughlin 1993; Rural Sociological Society 1993; Brown & Hirschl 1995). Adams and Duncan (1992), for instance, have found that the rural poor were more likely to be persistently poor, with incomes below 125 percent of the official poverty line, for at least eight of their ten study years (1976–85); while research by the USDA's ERS shows that more than nine out of ten persistently

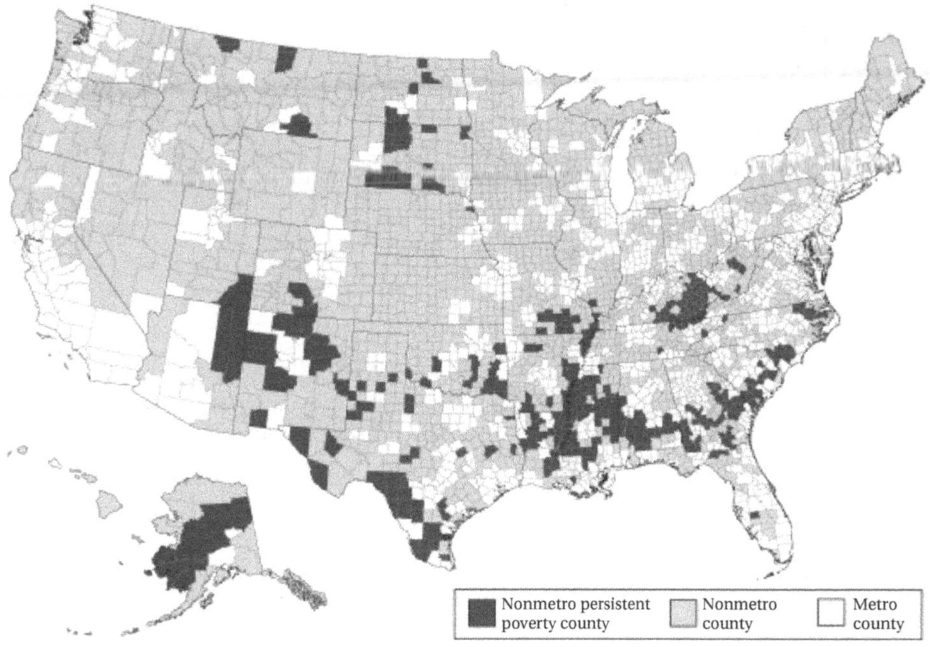

Source: USDA-ERS.

Figure 10.1 Persistent Poverty Counties, 1999

poor counties in the U.S. are rural (Jollife 2004). As shown in Figure 10.1, persistently poor rural counties are not randomly distributed throughout rural America. Rather they concentrate in less-developed regions including the Rio Grande Valley, Appalachia, and the Mississippi Delta (Jollife 2004).

Figure 10.2 shows U.S. poverty rates from 1959 to 2006. Several things are worth noting. To begin, nonmetropolitan poverty rates, and in fact poverty rates across all places, markedly declined between the late 1950s and the early 1970s. Nonetheless, poverty remains a prominent feature of the social landscape since more than one in ten persons, regardless of where they live, are still poor in the U.S. Since the early 1970s to the present, poverty rates in metro areas have hovered between 10 percent and 14 percent while in nonmetropolitan areas, rates have ranged between about 13 percent and 18 percent. Moreover, these rates are much higher for certain subpopulations, with women, minorities, children, and disabled persons especially prone to poverty across both metropolitan and nonmetropolitan areas.

This leads us to the second point: nonmetropolitan poverty rates have been consistently higher than metropolitan poverty rates throughout the last thirty years (Albrecht et al. 2000; Jensen, McLaughlin, & Slack 2003). In fact, until 1973, nonmetropolitan poverty rates were even higher than central city poverty rates.[2] Since the early 1970s poverty rates overall have increased and decreased along with periods of economic expansion and contraction, but the *gap* between nonmetropolitan and metropolitan poverty rates has remained stable at between three and five percentage points (Jensen & Jensen 2008). Given that poverty is typically associated with urban settings, at least in the popular imagination, this

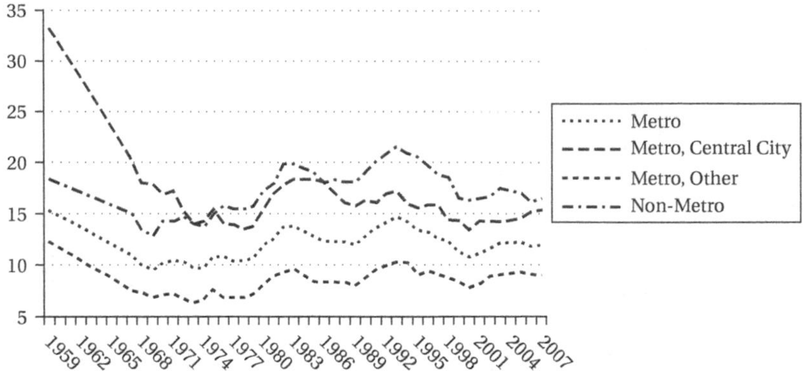

Source: Data are from U.S. Bureau of the Census, Current Population Survey, Annual Social and Economic Supplements. Data for the years 1960–66, 1984 and 2004 are interpolated.

Figure 10.2 Poverty Rates Across Metro and Nonmetro Areas

suggests that rural poverty as a social issue is frequently under-recognized. It is therefore worth paying close attention to how the particular characteristics of different places – spatial, social, political and economic – may in turn differentially shape the causes and consequences of poverty.

Poverty Affects Some Groups More Than Others

Table 10.2 shows 2007 data from the U.S. Census' American Community Survey, and examines the incidences of poverty nationwide and across metropolitan–nonmetropolitan residential areas by race/ethnicity, gender, and age. Nationwide, the poverty rate was about 13 percent, though rates vary considerably across the urban hierarchy. These data show that central cities and nonmetropolitan areas share the unenviable distinction of being the nation's poorest types of places. The highest rates, at over 17 percent, are found in the metropolitan city center areas with nonmetropolitan areas following closely behind.

The data in this table also illustrate the ways in which poverty differentially occurs across racial and ethnic groups. As we discuss in Chapter 7, poverty disproportionately affects particular minority groups, notably African Americans, Hispanics and American Indians. Nationally, poverty rates are twice as high for Hispanics as for Whites, and two and a half times as high for African Americans and American Indians. For those last two groups nationwide, one in every four persons in 2007 lived at or below the poverty line. However, racial and ethnic groups are at considerably higher risk of being poor in certain residence categories than in others. In fact, when broken down by race/ethnicity, nonmetropolitan areas consistently show the highest poverty rates. For example, 35 percent of African Americans living in nonmetropolitan areas are poor, a jump of over eleven percentage points compared with the same demographic's poverty rate in metropolitan areas. American Indian populations show similar residential differences.

Poverty also shows strong differences in incidence along gendered lines (Hays 2003). Nationwide, females are more likely to be poor than males across all

Table 10.2 Poverty Incidence by Selected Demographic Characteristics and Residential Location, 2007

	Residential Category				
	Nation-wide	**Nonmetro-politan**	**Micropolitan**	**Metropolitan**	**Center City**
% in Poverty, Total	12.95	16.59	15.38	12.39	17.23
% in Poverty by Race/Ethnicity					
White	10.23	14.11	13.06	9.49	12.99
Black	24.68	35.06	33.39	23.58	28.09
Hispanic	20.73	26.90	25.70	20.34	23.38
American Indian	25.29	34.55	26.16	21.61	23.82
Asian	10.59	17.51	12.73	10.48	13.31
% in Poverty by Sex and Age					
Female					
All	14.35	18.57	17.11	13.70	18.86
18 or younger	18.23	23.50	21.45	17.50	24.92
19–64	13.52	17.56	16.62	12.87	17.69
65 and older	11.44	15.85	12.94	10.78	13.61
Male					
All	11.51	14.54	13.57	11.03	15.52
18 or younger	17.82	22.79	20.93	17.12	24.39
19–64	9.70	12.47	11.85	9.25	12.98
65 and older	6.99	9.44	7.61	6.64	8.96

Source: U.S. American Community Survey, 2009.

geographies and across all ages, with disparities especially pronounced among the oldest population group – about 11.5 percent of women aged 65 and older are at or below the poverty line, as compared with about 7 percent of men in the same age cohort. While young persons in general are at relatively high risk of poverty (Pruitt 2010), irrespective of gender – about 18 percent of both boys and girls under age eighteen live at or below the poverty line – adult males are the least prone to poverty, regardless of where they live. Further, the economic status of both women and children is strongly correlated with the type of family in which they live.

For example, risk of poverty is dramatically higher in families headed by single women (Lichter & Jensen 2002). Snyder and McLaughlin (2004) report that in 2000 in both nonmetropolitan and central city areas about 9 percent of married couple households had incomes at or below the poverty level compared with about 40 percent of female-headed households living in such places. Recent

Table 10.3 Poverty by Educational Attainment and Residential Location, 2007

	Residential Category				
	Nation-wide	**Nonmetro-politan**	**Micropolitan**	**Metropolitan**	**Center City**
Educational Attainment (%)					
Less than High School	15.09	18.86	16.84	14.58	17.39
High School	30.00	39.48	36.71	28.44	26.41
Some College	27.08	26.28	27.40	27.10	25.64
Bachelor's Degree or more	27.84	15.38	19.05	29.88	30.55
% in Poverty by Education					
Less than High School	23.26	27.71	25.52	22.49	26.79
High School	11.31	12.96	11.92	11.04	15.23
Some College	7.59	9.47	8.85	7.29	10.12
Bachelor's Degree or more	3.50	4.00	3.92	3.44	4.70

Source: U.S.American Community Survey, 2007.

studies suggest that while in the past nonmetropolitan children were less likely to live in single-parent families, thereby receiving some protection from poverty, that pattern has reversed and single parentage is now more typical of children in nonmetropolitan areas (O'Hare & Churilla 2008). Recent data from the American Community Survey indicate that the poverty rate for children under eighteen during 2005 to 2007 was highest in the smallest counties, perhaps reflecting the high incidence of single parenthood in rural areas (Mather 2008). Interestingly, for male-headed single parent households, poverty rates were about 14 percent in central city areas and 23 percent in nonmetropolitan areas – still high (and especially in nonmetropolitan areas), but markedly lower than for female-headed single-parent households.

Educational attainment, in addition to race, is one of the strongest predictors of poverty. The data in Table 10.3 show educational attainment rates for populations across the urban hierarchy, as well as poverty rates by geography, cross-classified by educational attainment. These data show that education dramatically reduces the risk of poverty. While nearly one in four Americans with less than a high-school diploma live at or below the poverty line, the same is true for only about 3.5 percent of those with a bachelor's degree or more. This relationship exists in all residence categories, but the effect is magnified in nonmetropolitan areas because of the relatively lower levels of educational attainment within nonmetro areas.

As shown in the lower part of Table 10.3, about 19 percent of people in nonmetropolitan areas lack a high-school diploma compared with about 15 percent in metropolitan areas. Moreover, metropolitan areas have nearly twice the percentage of people with bachelor's degrees or more. In other words, human capital in the form of education is a significant hedge against the risk of poverty, but it is far more prevalent in metropolitan than in nonmetropolitan areas. Furthermore the economic returns to education vary across the urban hierarchy. Holding education levels constant, poverty rates are *higher* in nonmetropolitan and city center areas than in metropolitan areas as a whole.

Poverty risks are also lower among employed persons compared with persons who are unemployed or out of the workforce. However, research shows that rural workers, even those with full-time jobs, are less able to translate their work effort into economic security. In other words, rural persons are more likely to be characterized as the working poor. This is because rural workers are more likely to be *underemployed*, with low-skill–low-wage jobs, dead end jobs lacking career ladders, benefits, and other protections, or to have involuntarily part-time or seasonal work schedules (Jensen et al.1999).

Poverty Rates versus the Composition of Poverty

In examining the question of who is poor, a conceptual distinction must be made between the *poverty rate* and the *composition* of poverty. While the poverty rate refers to the likelihood that individuals within particular subpopulations will be poor, the composition of poverty refers to the shares of a population's poverty accounted for by various subgroups. Put more plainly, certain segments of larger populations are much more likely to be poor, e.g., to be at higher risk of being poor, but they don't necessarily comprise a large share of a population's poor members. Disabled persons, for example, typically have high poverty rates, but since they usually make up a small percentage of most populations, their share of an area's poor residents is small.

This distinction has important implications for targeting poverty assistance because some groups at high risk of being poor may be numerically small, and hence less visible to anti-poverty programs. In fact, this is one reason why rural poverty is not generally recognized as a major target of the nation's overall anti-poverty policy. As demonstrated earlier in this chapter, nonmetropolitan persons are nearly as likely to be poor as central city residents, but since only one in five Americans lives in a nonmetropolitan area, such places only constitute a small share of the nation's poor persons. This diminishes rural poverty's salience on the national anti-poverty agenda.

Problems with the Poverty Line

Persistence and Depth of Poverty

While very few would deny the perniciousness of poverty as indicated by the poverty line, this measurement has been the subject of several pointed criticisms. Firstly, even though the poverty threshold is based on empirical data, many critics contend that it is arbitrary. They observe that persons whose incomes are close to the threshold are at constant risk of falling into poverty (or conversely for those just below the line of escaping from poverty). For this reason many analysts identify what is termed *near poverty*, persons and families whose incomes fall in a zone between 100 percent and 125 percent of the poverty line. These persons are recognized as being at high risk of becoming poor and consequently they are eligible for a number of social programs.

In addition, research shows that poverty is often intermittent, with people moving into and out of the statistical category with some frequency. Most spells of poverty, in fact, are relatively short lived and reflect adverse life experiences such as losing one's job, becoming divorced, or contracting an acute illness or short-term disability (Rank 2005). In contrast, researchers also identify "deep poverty"– persons and families whose income is less than 50 percent of the official poverty line. Deep poverty tends to be chronic and persisting, but only a small proportion of the nation's poor population is chronically poor. About 12 percent of persons who are poor at any time have been poor for five or more years, and another 13 percent have been poor for three or four years. Ironically, while rural poor people are more likely to be employed, they are also more likely to be poor for long spells of time given the low-wage, part-time nature of much rural employment.

Measurement Errors

Perhaps the foremost criticism of the poverty threshold method of measuring poverty is that it does not take into account in-kind income. In-kind income includes support deriving from food stamps, Medicare, Medicaid, and housing subsidies, all of which can substantially increase a household's actual income and/or reduce its need for cash. The counter argument, however, is that the receipt of some types of in-kind income, such as Medicare, merely reflect higher health-care needs within some households than in others, and do not represent an increased standard in living. Similarly, others have noted that the poverty line cannot take into account underreporting of income that is earned outside of the formal economy (see the discussion of informal income and household exchange in Chapter 8). Such "under the table," "off the books" or undocumented income has been shown to be a significant contributor to rural livelihoods both in the U.S. and internationally (Fitchen 1981; Jensen, Cornwell, & Findeis 1995; Feldman & Ferretti 1998; Brown & Kulcsar 2001; Schiller 2001; Tickamyer & Wood 2003).

Another criticism of the federal poverty line is that it is used across geographies where costs of living may widely vary. The poverty line is a constant measure, regardless of where one lives, be it New York City or Oklahoma City, Vail, Colorado, or the Mississippi Delta. There are often clear differences in the material conditions of rural-versus-urban living that can have a direct impact on the type and quantity of resources required by residents in these areas. Because of this, the costs of those resources may vary significantly, calling into question the applicability of one threshold level across multiple contexts (Nord 2000).

In particular, it is often assumed that for a variety of reasons costs for certain goods and services may be lower in rural areas and therefore the poverty line may overestimate rural poverty levels relative to urban levels. For example, Joliffe (2006), found that rural housing costs were only about 80 percent as high as urban housing costs. Hence, adjusting for such differences between metropolitan and nonmetropolitan places showed that metropolitan poverty rates were in fact higher than nonmetropolitan rates. This suggests that rural poverty may be overestimated as compared to urban poverty, but it fails to recognize that housing, while important, is not the only good or service people need on a day-to-day basis. For example, other research has indicated that food prices are higher in rural than urban areas, in part because of the greater prevalence of smaller food stores in rural areas, reduced competition, and higher shipment costs (Kaufman & Lut 1997).

In March, 2010, the U.S. Census Bureau announced that it was developing a Supplemental Poverty Measure (SPM) that will incorporate not only income measures, but also tax payments and work expenses to estimate family resources. The Census Bureau does not intend to replace the existing poverty line measure, but rather to use the SPM as an additional means of gauging economic need across national and regional areas and across populations. As such, it represents the latest effort by the U.S. federal government to refine how poverty is measured and assessed.

In sum, the criteria for determining who is and is not poor is a subject of

Box 10.1 Transportation as an Urban–Rural Cost of Living Difference

Transportation can represent a significant cost of living differential between urban and rural places. Because of the greater spatial dispersion of rural workers and employers, rural workers travel 38 percent more miles per person than their urban counterparts. Lower income rural residents travel furthest, logging 59 percent more miles than their urban peers (Pucher & Renne 2004). Accordingly, longer distances translate into higher costs for vehicle maintenance (Zimmerman et al. 2008), and for fuel.

In 2008, fuel prices became increasingly volatile, reaching unprecedented highs during the summer months. For many this had the effect of transforming what were previously affordable commutes into significant and frequently unmanageable cuts into household budgets, especially for those who, like most rural residents, have little or no access to public transportation. A *New York Times* article from June of that year described the effects of higher fuel prices on lower income rural Americans. Josephine Cage, a worker in at a fish-processing plant in Mississippi with a thirty-mile commute, found that increases in gas prices resulted in her spending $200 per month in gasoline, or nearly 20 percent of her pay. "I make it by the grace of God," she said, and described how she managed by buying a few dollars of fuel at a time. "I can't afford to fill it up. Whatever money I have I put it in." At the same plant, ten workers, on hearing that job cuts were imminent, volunteered to quit and take buy-outs because they could no longer afford the travel costs (Krauss 2008).

Under these circumstances rural workers priced out of local housing markets, and therefore facing lengthy commutes, may necessarily find themselves in circumstances where going to work becomes economically irrational (Krauss 2008). This has serious consequences for patterns of concentrated rural poverty because eligibility for the nation's major anti-poverty program, Temporary Assistance for Needy Families (TANF), is contingent on work effort. Moreover, since TANF has strict time limits, many poor people will eventually run out of eligibility and become more dependent on work, regardless of whether the costs of working, such as increased fuel prices, overwhelm its financial returns.

continuing debate, and no completely acceptable solutions have been reached to determine how to adjust the poverty threshold to take into account cost of living and other differences across geographic areas (Citro & Michael 1995; General Accounting Office 1995; Nord 2000; Zimmerman, Ham, & Frank 2008). Regardless of how imperfect the measures may be, measures such as the poverty line have very real implications for public policy and economically distressed people. These measures are used to determine need, how social policy is constructed and who is eligible for anti-poverty program resources. Hence, this is an instance where the hackneyed phrase, "more research is needed" is clearly merited.

Poverty as a Multidimensional Concept

While indices like the poverty threshold have obvious utility for governmental and other bureaucratic agencies to assess basic social conditions, establish guidelines for who should and should not receive social services, and so forth, poverty is inherently multidimensional. The lived experience of poverty often entails a lack of access to health care, child care, and social services, diminished educational and employment opportunities, limited political power, and exposure to living environments that may be physically unsafe and/or environmentally hazardous. Consider the following profiles of some poor adults interviewed over the course of several years in rural Pennsylvania and New York.

Sharon Wright

Sharon Wright[3] is 44 and lives with her teenage son, boyfriend, and her boyfriend's toddler-aged son in a low-income apartment complex in a town of 7,000 in Northern Pennsylvania. Their only income comes from welfare and child support, and amounts to about $1,000 per month. She also receives housing assistance, offsetting the cost of the rent. Her town, like others in the area, shows pronounced signs of economic decline, with empty storefronts, housing, and buildings in poor condition, and several large, empty buildings in the center of town and on the outskirts where manufacturing firms once employed hundreds of local people. These firms closed ten to fifteen years earlier in part due to overseas competition. There are some nearby outdoor recreational areas and some limited service employment to be found, but most locals consider seven or eight dollars an hour a good wage.

The area where Sharon lives is strikingly decrepit with a mixture of trailers and cinder-block buildings that resemble old army barracks. The neighborhood was described by another area resident as the town's "rural ghetto." The apartment likewise shows signs of age and has chronic problems with cockroach infestations. Earlier in the winter the heater had broken down, and she and her boyfriend and her boyfriend's 21-month-old son spent several days heating the apartment by the oven before the heater was fixed. The apartment is better than the last one in which she lived.

> There was mildew and we just wondered why we were sick all the time . . . water leaked in and had the floors all wet and there was one gas heater on the wall and that was it. It heated the whole apartment, and the hot water tank we basically had to share with the neighbors.

Health problems as a teenager led to a hospital stay and school absences. This coupled with an unstable home life eventually proved too much to cope with leading her to drop out of school in the middle of the tenth grade. An early marriage (producing three children) fell apart after a string of domestic abuse finally led Sharon to place a restraining order on her ex-husband. She said,

> You know, looking back when I was younger I did not care about school. And you know now I wish I could finish school and get the jobs I wanted. Because a lot of people tell you 'oh, do you have a GED?' No. 'Well I am sorry but I cannot take you.' Yes. So I mean I do not have a problem getting a job. I would like to climb the ladder. I do not want to stay down on the bottom of the ladder.

Sharon is not currently working, though she is looking for work. Her work history is spotty, in part due to her lack of educational qualifications and in part due to chronic domestic problems. She is currently attempting to get a GED through an adult education program, but has had difficulties, again because of health problems that have interfered with her academic progress. Regardless, she has doubts that people with a GED or diploma are much better off than those without, and her experience is that local employers are tending to hire younger people than her anyway.

John and Doris Clark

John Clark is sixty years old, and his wife, Doris, is fifty-eight. Neither has a high-school diploma. They live in a rural area in New York State's Southern tier with their granddaughter, Megan, over whom they gained legal custody after a judge ruled that Megan's mother was unfit to parent because of drug abuse problems. The Clarks had recently moved from their home of nearly twenty-three years after a foreclosure by the bank due to mortgage non-payment.

John had experienced a work-related injury, and the claim was contested by his employer because of the employer's contention that the injury actually originated from previous employment. "I just got approved for social security," John explained.

> I've got my social security disability. But if that would have kicked in earlier, we wouldn't be here. When you get off work and the doctors say you're totally disabled, you have to go in front of a social security doctor, and it can get denied. The truth is, it took two years to go through the court . . . it's a back injury plus there's other complications too. I got high blood pressure and so I was at risk for back surgery. I got three herniated disks. So that's the way it goes. It's affected everything.

While the claim was tied up in court, John and Doris were without income and were unable to pay the mortgage. "The bottom line," John explained, "was I took my retirement in one lump sum because I had to have a place to live." John and Doris, with Megan, moved into their son's trailer after John was forced to withdraw his retirement funds.

> So that's really terrible what's happened because we lost our home. It makes you pretty sick, but there's nothing you can do about it. We only owed 10 more years on it. I had to refinance it after 20 years. It made me furious. And then to end up losing it anyway.

Ann Lewis

Ann Lewis is fifty years old and in recovery from a recent heart attack. She lives with her adult daughter and her daughter's four children, the oldest of whom, Megan, fifteen, she has legal custody over because of earlier drug abuse problems experienced by Megan's mother. Ann completed her GED and even enrolled in some college courses for a few semesters before having to quit because her job at the time, at Walmart, demanded flexible hours on her part, which she didn't have because of her course schedule. She was most recently employed at a grocery but lost her job after her heart attack when she needed time off from work. This forced her to move into her daughter's two-bedroom trailer.

> I am at my daughter's temporarily, believe me, and I stress the word temporarily. I mean, I'm more stressed now. Watching three kids all the time, and these kids are wild. I mean ASAP [as soon as possible]. Any kind of money to get an apartment and I am gone (Schafft 2006: 225).

Her doctors have told her she isn't supposed to go back to work, but she doesn't know how else she will support herself and Megan. She was also diagnosed with diabetes one year earlier, but she had difficulties keeping health insurance because she was making too much income at the time of the diagnosis. She had stopped taking her medications because of the expense and suspects there may have been a relationship between her heart attack and going off the medications. Economic and social instability have led to residential instability as well. Over the past five years, Ann and her granddaughter have moved twelve times, living in thirteen different residences. Megan has changed schools as frequently, all as a result of household moves. She used to aspire to be a veterinarian, but has had some negative experiences at the schools she has attended, and now she wants to drop out once she turns sixteen.

Poverty as a Continuum of Insecurity

While the descriptions above provide only the briefest of glimpses into the lived experience of poverty, they nonetheless help to illustrate the multidimensional nature of poverty. Each of the people described here, at the time they were interviewed, had incomes below the poverty line. However, it's not just limited income that describes their experiences, but limited access to a range of resources, including: safe and secure housing, educational opportunities, health care, and at times the social supports that can provide a critical hedge against deprivation. Poverty, therefore, entails a continuum of insecurity that is not only economic, but extends into a range of other dimensions of wellbeing.

Why Are Some Persons and Families More Likely To Be Poor Than Others?

As we have shown, certain characteristics or attributes like race, gender, education and family structure increase the risk of poverty. While this tells who is most likely to be poor, it doesn't tell us *why* they are poor. Explanations of poverty fall broadly into individual-level and structural-level explanations. In each case the

Box 10.2 Residential Mobility and Education

Human capital theory tends to interpret residential change as the consequence of decision-making performed by rational "free agents" maximizing returns on their investments of time, energy and resources. Put more simply, from this perspective a move is an investment of time, energy and resources. However, it is an investment with an anticipated payoff. For example, people move in order to take advantage of opportunities: a more desirable home or neighborhood, a better school system, or a new job. Such moves are seen as voluntary, premeditated and opportunity-related.

Research from the early 1990s, however, has documented high-frequency and often short distance residential movement of poor families within and across poor communities in rural areas that would seem to violate these assumptions. Janet Fitchen's work (1992; 1994; 1995) was instrumental in showing how this movement of poor families was very frequently the consequence of housing problems and unforeseen social and economic crises, and therefore was neither particularly voluntary, pre-meditated or opportunity-related in the way that residential moves are typically perceived (cf., Foulkes & Newbold 2005, 2008).

Schafft (2006) conducted a study of poverty-related residential mobility and its association with high rates of turnover within the public-school system after discovering that annual turnover rates of 20 percent or more were common in disadvantaged rural New York school districts. Collecting historical data from twenty-two household heads and parents of K-12 students who were income-eligible for the federal free lunch program and who had transferred into their school mid-year, a combined total of fully 109 residential moves were made in the five years preceding the interviews (with some families moving ten or more times over the preceding five years) while the children within these families made a combined total of 166 school changes, 92 percent of which were the direct result of residential change. Most of the moves were short distance. Of the 109 moves, 91 were made within-state. The average distance moved (excluding interstate movement) was about twenty miles and twenty-eight were made within the same municipality.

According to human capital perspectives, most residential movement would be accounted for by "pulls" to opportunity at the destination. This research classified all residential moves according to whether they were primarily motivated by "pulls" or, rather, by "pushes" at the place of origin. Fully 78 percent of moves were the result of "pushes," the majority of which were housing-related including evictions and threats of evictions, overcrowding, unsafe conditions and expense. Other pushes included social factors such as domestic violence, conflicts with neighbors and the ending of romantic relationships. Notably, of the "pulls" employment opportunities accounted for only three of the 109 moves. Most pulls involved either better housing opportunities or the pull of family networks.

This movement obviously puts children at extreme educational disadvantage when considering the disrupted educational experience moving between schools, coupled with what are often home environments that are equally unstable (Killeen & Schafft 2008). Further, while pronounced student transiency is associated with household economic disadvantage and occurs in both rural and urban environments, students are more likely to cross school district boundaries in rural settings, which involves changes of curricula and greater logistical issues associated with records transfer, a particular problem if the child receives special educational services. Smaller school districts given

Box 10.2 (continued)

the smaller economies of scale, are less likely to have resources at their disposal to address the wide range of student needs that accompany transient students. Last, given the high stakes testing environment associated with the No Child Left Behind Act, transient, low performing students may be, rightly or wrongly, seen as liabilities to schools struggling to increase test scores and work within tight budgets (Schafft, Killeen, & Morrissey, 2010).

locus of causation is different. Individual-level explanations tend to hold individuals, at least to some degree, responsible for their economic circumstances, and look to the ways in which particular behaviors and individual attributes perpetuate cycles of poverty. These explanations resonate with certain commonly held American values based around the virtues of self-reliance, persistence, entrepreneurship and meritocracy. That is, in a "land of opportunity," anyone can be successful with hard work and persistence. Conversely, those who aren't successful must not be trying hard enough.

Structural explanations, on the other hand, tend to identify institutional and political factors as contributing to the risk that certain people or groups are more likely to be poor. These factors include job scarcity, the match between job requirements and workers' skill sets, inadequate social safety nets, discrimination and poor schools, among others. Rank (2005), for example, has advocated a "structural vulnerability" explanation of poverty. His argument asserts that poverty is analogous to a game of musical chairs in which there are too few well-paying jobs that will adequately support the number of families in need of jobs. Simultaneously, social policies don't provide the support services needed by poor families lacking access to well-paid employment, such as child care, health care, transportation, and housing. Those most likely to be on the losing end of this game of "musical chairs" are those with the human capital attributes that put them at the greatest disadvantage for competing in the labor market – those who are under-educated, minorities, single parents, and so on.

The Structural Explanation in More Detail

The structural perspective contends that poverty results when workers are mismatched with job requirements in local labor markets. The contention is that too many workers with relatively restricted human capital are chasing too few well-paying jobs. In addition, this position recognizes that local economies are dynamic and ever changing, and that the resulting restructuring profoundly affects opportunity and work structures, and the returns workers with modest levels of human capital can expect from their time, effort, education, training, and experience.

Structural explanations often highlight the effects of macro-level economic change on the poverty status of individuals and households. For example, the late 1970s and early 1980s were marked by a general trend of deindustrialization in the United States in which factories and plants began to shut down and globally relocate in response to cheaper production and labor costs overseas. In the first half of the 1980s nearly one million workers per year were dislocated because of plant closings (see chapter 8). A study by the Department of Labor found that five years after losing their jobs, one-third of laid-off workers were either still unemployed or had exited the labor market. Within the group of those who were employed, 40 percent of those workers were earning at least 20 percent *less* than they had previously (Ropers 1991). Rural economies were especially vulnerable to restructuring because of their lack of diversification, and their overrepresentation of low-skill jobs, which are the ones most easily displaced by globalization.

Regarding the structural reasons for high rates of rural poverty, this argument observes that many rural workers are left behind because newly restructured rural labor markets contain a disproportionate number of low-skill—low-wage–no benefit jobs, have a high prevalence of firms that offer little or no training and contain jobs with no career ladders, and are increasingly dependent on involuntary part-time and seasonal work. In other words, rural economies offer little protection from poverty even among persons with strong labor force attachment, and few pathways out of poverty. The restructuring of rural economies has replaced relatively well-paying, secure employment with marginal jobs. Rural workers are either over-qualified for the residual employment resulting from restructuring, and therefore underemployed, or they are under qualified, and therefore unemployable for new jobs in knowledge intensive producer services industries.

In addition, structuralists question whether labor markets actually match workers with jobs based on qualifications and merit. In rural economies, for example, numerous studies have shown that work and educational structures are embedded in rigidly stratified social systems (Duncan 1999; Billings & Blee 2000). As a result, access to education and job opportunities is controlled by deeply entrenched class interests, and qualified persons are excluded from jobs because of class, race, and/or family background. This negates the value of one's human capital and sends negative messages about education, employment, and the chances of escaping poverty. Structuralists observe that even though poor rural people tend to obey the rules of the game, they are still unlikely to improve their material situation (Shulman 2005).

The Cultural Explanation of Poverty in More Detail

In the most general sense, the individual explanation of poverty contends that people are poor because of behaviors and choices that keep them poor. The individual -level explanation quickly becomes cultural as it emphasizes shared sets of behaviors and preferences that reinforce and reproduce economic disadvantage. Perhaps the most widespread type of individual-level explanation is associated with the so called "culture of poverty" theory, the notion that people in poverty, and especially in generational cycles of poverty, share certain behavioral and personality traits that are simultaneously adaptations to life in poverty, *and* increase the chances of remaining in poverty.

The idea of the culture of poverty was first developed in the late 1950s and early 1960s by the anthropologist Oscar Lewis who was interested in patterns of international development and underdevelopment. Through extensive ethnographic research and psychological testing in Puerto Rico and Mexico, Lewis developed an inventory of traits he argued were common across people in long-term poverty, including social marginality, helplessness, dependency, powerlessness, present-time orientation and inability to delay gratification (Lewis 1959).

Although Lewis's work had an explicitly political-economic orientation and was deeply concerned with how particular learned sets of behaviors were adaptive mechanisms *in response to* conditions of systemic oppression and social and economic exclusion (O'Connor 2001), conservative researchers in the U.S. adopted this explanation of poverty, contending that poor people develop a culture of poverty which they internalize as their *preferred* way of life. According to this perspective, poor people reject behavior that will increase their chances of economic mobility (education, marriage, work, family planning) and behave in ways that hinder escape from poverty. As Jack Weller (1966) observed in his examination of Appalachian poverty, "The greatest challenge of Appalachia, and the most difficult, [was] its people" (p. 32). Similarly, Rupert Vance, a noted sociologist of the South, concluded that "to change the mountains was to change the mountain personality" (1966: ix).

Cultural explanations of poverty largely fell out of favor in academic circles in the 1970s because these explanations were thought to blame poor people for their own plight, and to indiscriminately label non-middle-class behavior as deviant (Morris 1989). In fact, some scholars contended that joblessness, out of wedlock childbearing, and criminal behavior had become normatively approved, preferred modes of behavior among populations with concentrated, intergenerational poverty. Moreover, it was argued that social welfare programs such as Aid to Families with Dependent Children (AFDC) provided perverse disincentives against work, marriage, and personal responsibility that perpetuated welfare dependence across generations (Murray 1984).

Rethinking Culture and Structure

Research during the 1980s by social scientists like William Julius Wilson (1987, 1997) and Ann Swidler (1986) attempted to *recast* cultural explanations of poverty in a less judgmental light, framing certain shared norms and behaviors as rational responses to structurally disadvantaged circumstances. Hence, a family that has a history of welfare dependency will be likely to raise children who are cynical about conventional labor market success, but who also learn behaviors that make sense in persistently poor environments, be they urban ghettos or underdeveloped rural areas.

This perspective has been strongly influenced by Swidler's (1986) concept of "culture as a tool kit." Swidler contended that culture is a set of skills and habits, not a set of preferences and wants. She observed that culture is not about what one wants, but about the skills and behaviors that are effective for negotiating the environment in which one lives. This tool kit is shaped by what people experience in their social world, by their social relationships. They use these "tools" to decide how to act. Many of the skills in the poor person's "tool kit" may seem inappropriate or deviant from a middle class perspective, and they may even be illegal,

Box 10.3 Professional Development for Educators and Ruby Payne's Culture of Poverty Framework

Despite a strong consensus among social scientists that the "culture of poverty" framework is fundamentally flawed as a means of understanding why some people are more likely to be poor than others, cultural explanations of poverty continue to be prevalent in popularly held attitudes and understandings of poverty (Rank 2005), as well as in public policy debates. The culture of poverty thesis contends that certain people are at high risk of being poor because they refuse to work or marry and have children out of wedlock, irresponsible behaviors that are passed down from generation to generation. The very title of welfare reform, *The Personal Responsibility and Work Opportunity Reconciliation Act of 1996*, signed by President Bill Clinton, stresses the use of public policy to encourage "personal responsibility" of the poor (Hays 2003). It attempts to do this through labor market integration of poor people (partially by imposing work mandates coupled with lifetime limits on eligibility for receiving benefits), by promoting two-parent families, and by discouraging out of wedlock births as a means of curtailing dependency upon social support programs. These provisions led one observer to describe the Act as "virtually a national revival movement calling for the restoration of moral compulsion to the lives of the poor" (Piven 2001: 135).

Culture of poverty frameworks are also found in the educational arena (Vernon-Feagans, Head-Reeves, & Kainz 2004). For example, Ruby Payne has sold over one million copies of her book, *A Framework for Understanding Poverty*, geared towards K-12 public educators. A former teacher with a Ph.D. in Educational Leadership and Policy Studies, Payne offers numerous workshops based on her work, has over fifty trainers on staff, and her business generates millions of dollars a year training educators how to teach children in poverty (Tough 2007).

Payne's argument is that academic success of economically disadvantaged children is constrained by a "mindset" and an array of behavioral patterns held in common by those in generational poverty, and markedly distinct from the beliefs and cultural practices of the middle and upper classes (2005). The key to teaching children coming from generational poverty backgrounds, argues Payne, is for teachers first to understand the "hidden rules" of poverty, and to teach poor children the cultural rules of the middle class. She argues that poor children will have heightened chances of success in school and beyond if they adopt language, behavior, and worldviews more closely aligned with middle-class values. In her book, Payne summarizes what she argues are the "hidden rules" of people in generational poverty, in the middle class and those among the wealthy.

These "hidden rules" enable Payne to make blanket assertions such as:

- "teachers want to get right to the point; parents, particularly those from poverty, need to beat around the bush first" (p. 30);
- "the poor simply see jail as a part of life and not necessarily always bad" (p. 22);
- "one pattern in poor communities is that virtually everyone has a VCR or DVD player because of the value placed on entertainment" (p. 73), and;
- "often the attitude in generational poverty is that society owes one a living" (p. 47).

While Payne has enjoyed enormous popularity as a leader of training workshops for teachers and educational administrators, critics maintain that her arguments have

Box 10.3 (continued)

little to no empirical support, ignore the significant disparities between wealthier and poorer schools and neighborhoods, and perpetuate demeaning and harmful stereotypes about people in poverty (Prins & Schafft 2009). Payne's approach, however, also illustrates how dramatically different policy implications flow from different approaches to understanding the nature of poverty and its causes. That is, from Payne's "deficit-approach" perspective, poverty is a consequence of cultural and individual-level deficiencies that are best addressed by changing the beliefs and behaviors of individuals rather than the structured inequalities that produce and reproduce poverty (Gorski 2006). Indeed, to refer back to Rank's metaphor of structural opportunities as a game of musical chairs, it is difficult to imagine how people could raise themselves out of poverty by changing their culture, unless the number of available well-paying jobs expanded dramatically. And yet, Payne's work continues to have wide currency among educators and educational administrators who find her explanation of poverty compelling and convincing.

but they are *not* dysfunctional insofar as they constitute adaptive behaviors for surviving in difficult environments.

Realistically there is significant interplay between individual and structural factors in the incidence of poverty. Earlier we read about Ann Lewis who lives in a trailer with her daughter and four grandchildren. Ann's oldest granddaughter, Megan, earlier expressed interest in becoming a veterinarian. However, at the time of the interview with Ann, Megan was contemplating dropping out of school. This is a "choice" that indeed she can make (at least the choice to drop out of school or not). Based on our discussion of the life course in Chapter 6, we know that as a high-school dropout her chances of poverty later in life are greatly increased. If, however, she is successful in becoming a veterinarian, her risk of living in poverty as an adult is slim. What must be taken into account, however, is that decisions are made within particular contexts. In the case of Megan, living in circumstances in which home life is continually disrupted, residential moves and school transfers have been the rule rather than the exception, and because her experiences with success at school have been marginal, her thoughts about dropping out begin to make much more sense.

How Relevant is the Inner City Story to Explaining Rural Poverty?

The answer to this question is that some aspects of the urban poverty model are relevant to explaining the causes of rural poverty while others are not. From the structural perspective, rural economies have been at least as adversely affected by deskilling and off-shoring as their urban counterparts As a result, job mismatch affects both types of areas, but joblessness is much less prevalent in rural areas. Rural persons seem more likely to accept low-wage jobs than their urban counterparts. In addition, restructuring has had differential impacts in urban and rural areas.

As Gibbs et al. (2005) showed, rural dependence on low-skill jobs has declined from about 49 percent to 42 percent between 1980 and 2000. The shift from goods production to services was accompanied by a shift to higher-skill occupations. Low-skill jobs in manufacturing tended to move off shore and be replaced by higher skill service occupations. This is good news for better-prepared workers, but not for persons who lack education and pertinent job experience. Gibbs's study showed that younger workers, workers with low education, and minorities failed to benefit from economic restructuring. In fact, workers with low human capital now face increasing competition for the remaining low-skill jobs, which exerts downward pressure on wages. As indicated earlier, rural workers are more likely to accept low-wage jobs while the urban poor are more likely to either refuse low-wage employment or to lack the necessary work skills for even these low-end jobs. Accordingly, rural poor persons are more likely to be underemployed while their urban counterparts are more likely to be unemployed or out of the workforce. High labor force attachment reduces the cultural model's credence as an explanation of long-term rural poverty. In contrast, lower urban labor force attachment and higher levels of joblessness seems consistent with cultural aspects of the explanation of urban poverty.

Social isolation, the other major aspect of Wilson's poverty theory, is expressed differently in urban and rural areas. While there are often racial and/or ethnic dimensions to rural poverty concentrations (Falk et al. 1993; Saenz & Ballejos 1993; Snipp et al. 1993; Snipp 1996) that isolate the poor from wider social opportunities and diminish the chances for mobility (Lichter & Parisi 2008; Pruitt 2010), it is not clear that the processes of exclusion that produced urban ghettos are also responsible for segregating poor persons in rural areas. As Duncan (1999) showed, poor people in areas of concentrated rural poverty like Appalachia or the Mississippi Delta tend to be socially isolated from the mainstream, but this is not necessarily the result of residential segregation. Rather, the causes seem to lie in rigid, hierarchical stratification systems with patron–client relationships that exclude poor persons from civic engagement, democratic influence, economic opportunities, and institutional resources like education.

Finally, social isolation in rural areas is likely to accompany *physical* isolation. Rural poor often have less access to transportation, and live in more physically remote areas which makes access to social services (including education, health and welfare-related services) more difficult, time-consuming and costly. They are often isolated from communication and informational resources that facilitate social mobility (Cushing 1999).

Conclusions

We began this chapter by observing that poverty is especially pernicious when poor people are concentrated in poor places. This is the case for the urban underclass and it is true of poor persons living in depressed rural regions as well. We have shown that rural poverty involves people left behind who tend to live in places left behind. While many of the same characteristics that predispose persons to be poor in urban environments – race, low education, being a single parent or the child of a single parent – are also associated with higher risks of rural

Box 10.4 Why Don't Poor People Leave Persistently Poor Rural Areas?

In Box 10.2 we discuss high levels of local residential mobility among many poor households, often occurring as a consequence of housing problems, coupled with a variety of social and economic crises at the household level. Given frequently high levels of local movement among poor households, and the relative lack of economic opportunity in persistently poor economies, why don't economically disadvantaged people leave economically disadvantaged areas, especially rural areas, for larger labor markets with higher levels of economic opportunity?

While many people *do* leave persistently poor rural areas, outmigration tends to favor those who are younger, have higher levels of education and training, and those who are relatively better off economically (Lichter et al. 1995). This makes sense when one considers that people with greater financial and human capital assets at their disposal are better able to afford the higher costs of a long-distance move, and are also better equipped to use their human capital to find and secure employment and other opportunities at the migration destination.

Poorer households are less able to afford the costs of long-distance moves (often to places where costs of living are also higher). Moreover, the returns to migration among low-income persons are apparently small. For example, research by Wilson and Tienda (1989) showed that migration among the unemployed failed to increase their likelihood of subsequent employment. Low-income families also tend to be highly dependent on the informal, but still critical, resources of local knowledge of housing and economic opportunities, and close access to family and community networks, in home communities. Last, and especially for many rural residents, one's personal identity is often firmly bound to place (Corbett 2007; Farmer et al. 2006; Fitchen 1991). Hence, a longer distance move may come with not only economic costs (and uncertain economic payoffs), but with psychic costs as well.

Jennifer Sherman's fascinating case study (2009) of a Northern California logging community provides an illustrative example. Golden Valley (a pseudonym) had been an active logging community with steady, if dangerous, work in the forests and mills. This changed drastically in the 1990s after legislation was passed protecting forest habitat of the spotted owl, legislation that effectively shut down the area's logging industry, and with it the area's primary economic base. Not only were almost all jobs lost in the local lumber industry, but almost half of businesses in the general community also closed in the 1990s, as they too were unable to weather the economic collapse.

Sherman found that after the sudden economic downturn, many residents did leave. Yet, far from the community disappearing, many residents stayed in Golden Valley, either refusing to leave, or finding themselves returning after attempting to leave. In some cases, men (who in the community had traditionally been the economic breadwinners within the household) left their families behind. Yet, as one resident explained to Sherman,

> One by one they ended up deciding that it wasn't worth it, and one by one they came back. And those particular people were go-getters. They would do like we did – they would've accepted any job just to keep going. And so they're not living on as much now, but they're here. (p. 127)

Box 10.4 (continued)

Many residents also harbored a deep mistrust of the city. A local teacher stated,

> There's a big pull back to Golden Valley. A lot of people leave and come back. There's something about staying in a safe community, even in poverty, that's easier for them than it is elsewhere. Some of them are generational poverty. It's easier to live poor than it is in the big cities. It's safer. (p. 130)

However, while the opportunity costs of relocating, and the alien urban environment of the city decreased permanent outmigration, the strong pull of local community and identity was equally significant in why people ultimately remained, and why the community managed to persist despite strongly negative economic conditions with little hope for turnaround. Another resident told Sherman:

> The people left here are survivors, not only from a traditional cultural standpoint. They're survivors for the lives that they've tried to build here and that they're still trying to hold onto. And those connections and those roots run really, really deep in rural communities. (p. 42)

As Sherman describes, Golden Valley persists despite serious local hardship because local residents are determined to hold fast to their community and way of life, their connection to place and community and its relationship to personal identity ultimately taking precedence over the possible economic benefits of moving, and the substantial hardships associated with remaining.

poverty, we have shown that rural poor are different in a number of critical ways. Most importantly, poor rural people are more likely to be employed and to be married. Accordingly, rural poverty is more likely to be working poverty, the result of insufficient well paying and secure employment. Also, while minorities have much higher poverty rates in both urban and rural areas, Whites account for the majority of the rural poor simply because rural populations outside of the South and Southwest are predominately White.

We also stated at the chapter's beginning that poor people suffer from a double jeopardy when they are concentrated in underdeveloped, economically lagging places. This is because the negative effects of personal and family deficits are magnified in resource poor communities while the returns to human capital and other kinds of investments are lower than in urban areas. What difference does college education make if local employers offer no jobs in which advanced knowledge can be utilized and rewarded?

As Grabher and Stark (1997) observed, places may be understood as *ecologies of social logic*. That is, local knowledge, culture, and historically embedded social networks, both formal and informal, fundamentally help to determine the shape of local institutions and social interaction. Duncan (1996; 1999) argues that the social ecologies of rural communities possess characteristics which make them distinct from urban communities. Because of this the dynamics of poverty and the maintenance of class structure also occurs differently:

> In rural communities we often find a kind of "micro social system," with actors from all the relevant social strata and organizations represented. Whereas in

> urban areas those with power over the allocation of resources are remote – in distant city halls, real estate agencies or banks – in rural communities the sources and effects of power are visible in everyday interaction. The whole class structure may be represented within the boundaries of a coherent place, and people have a tangible sense of the stratification system. They know who "runs things" and "whose father never did any good." (1996: 105)

For these reasons, the *local* political economy of many rural places may be much more rigidly stratified with far fewer possibilities for poor people to escape poverty. Local social structure militates against them and the rural dispossessed may not have the human or financial resources to leave the area. Rigidity of social structure and the division into "haves" and "have-nots" seems particularly prevalent in areas in which the economy lacks diversification, where there is a surplus of low-wage jobs and tight control over labor (Duncan 1996). In sum, rural poverty is widespread and persistent, and deserves higher visibility and more attention on the national policy agenda.

Notes

1 See also Rank (2005) for an excellent and in-depth discussion of these issues.
2 Since 1973, central city poverty rates have remained highest across the urban hierarchy, with the exception of 1986 when nonmetropolitan poverty rates, at 18.1 %, were slightly higher than central city rates.
3 All names used are pseudonyms. When appropriate, certain identifying details have been altered.

References

Adams, T.K. & Duncan, G. 1992. Long-Term Poverty in Rural Areas, pp. 63–83. In Duncan, C.M. (ed.) *Rural Poverty in America.* Auburn House, New York.

Albrecht, D.E., Mulford, C., & Albrecht, S.L. 2000. Poverty in Nonmetropolitan America: Impacts of Industrial, Employment, and Family Structural Variables. *Rural Sociology,* 65(1), 87–103.

Billings, D. & Blee, K. 2000. *The Road To Poverty: The Making of Wealth and Poverty in Appalachia.* Cambridge University Press, Cambridge.

Brown, D.L. & Hirschl, T.A. 1995. Household Poverty in Rural and Metropolitan-Core Areas of the United States. *Rural Sociology,* 60(1), 44–66.

Brown, D.L. & Kulcsar, L. 2001. Household Economic Behavior in Post-Socialist Rural Hungary. *Rural Sociology,* 66(2), 157–180.

Byrne, D. 1999. *Social Exclusion.* Open University Press, Buckingham.

Citro, C.F. & Michael, R.T. 1995. *Measuring Poverty: A New Approach.* National Academy Press, Washington D.C.

Corbett, M. 2007. *Learning to Leave: The Irony of Schooling in a Coastal Community.* Black Point, Nova Scotia, Fernwood Publishing.

Cushing, B. 1999. Migration and Economic Restructuring, pp. 13–36. In Pandit, K. & Davies Withers, S. (eds) *Migration and Restructuring in the United States.* Rowman and Littlefield, New York.

Duncan, C.M. 1996. Understanding Persistent Poverty: Social Class Context in Rural Communities. *Rural Sociology,* 61(1), 103–124.

Duncan, C. M. 1999. *Worlds Apart: Why Poverty Persists in Rural America.* Yale, New Haven, CT.

Falk, W.W., Talley, C.R., & Rankin, B. 1993. Life in the Forgotten South: The Black Belt, pp. 53–75. In Lyson, T.A. & Falk, W.W. (eds) *Forgotten Places: Uneven Development in Rural America.* University of Kansas Press, Lawrence, KS.

Farmer, T. W., Dadisman, K., Latendresse, S. J., Thompson, J., Irvin, M. J., & Zhang, L. 2006. Educating Out and Giving Back: Adults' Conceptions of Successful Outcomes of African American High School Students from Impoverished Rural Communities. *Journal of Research in Rural Education*, 21(10). Retrieved from http://jrre.psu.edu/articles/21-10.pdf

Feldman, S, & Ferretti, E. 1998. *Informal Work and Social Change: A Bibliographic Survey.* Cornell University Press, Ithaca, NY.

Fitchen, J.M. 1981. *Poverty in Rural America: A Case Study.* Westview, Boulder, CO.

Fitchen, J.M. 1991. *Endangered Spaces, Enduring Places: Change, Identity and Survival in Rural America.* Westview, Boulder, CO.

Fitchen, J.M. 1992. On the Edge of Homelessness: Rural Poverty and Housing Insecurity. *Rural Sociology*, 2(57), 173–193.

Fitchen, J.M. 1994. Residential Mobility among the Rural Poor. *Rural Sociology*, 59(3), 416–436.

Fitchen, J.M. 1995. Spatial Redistribution of Poverty through Migration of Poor People to Depressed Rural Communities. *Rural Sociology*, 60(2), 181–201.

Foulkes, M. & Newbold, K.B. 2005.. Geographic Mobility and Residential Instability in Impoverished Rural Illinois Places. *Environment & Planning A*, 37, 845–860.

Foulkes, M., & Newbold, K.B. 2008. Poverty Catchments: Migration, Residential Mobility, and Population Turnover in Impoverished Rural Illinois Communities. *Rural Sociology*, 73(3), 440–462.

Galston. W. 2008. The Politics of Fighting Poverty in Faltering Economies. *Pathways*, Summer, 26–28.

General Accounting Office. 1995. *Poverty Measurement: Adjusting for Geographic Cost-of-Living Difference.* GAO/GGD-95–64. U.S. General Accounting Office, Washington D.C.

Gibbs, R., Kusimin, L., & Cromartie, J. 2005. Low Skill Employment and the Changing Economy of Rural America. *Economic Research Report.* No. 10. USDA-ERS, Washington, D.C.

Gorski, P. 2006. The Classist Underpinnings of Ruby Payne's Framework. *Teachers College Record*, Published online: February 9, 2006 at http://www.tcrecord.org, ID Number: 12322.

Grabher, G.& Stark, D. 1997. Organizing Diversity: Evolutionary Theory, Network Analysis, and Post-Socialism, pp. 1–32. In Gasher, G. & Stark, D. *Restructuring Networks in Post-Socialism.* Oxford University Press, New York.

Harrington, M. 1962. *The Other America.* Macmillan, New York.

Hays, S. 2003. *Flat Broke With Children: Women in the Age of Welfare Reform.* Oxford, New York.

Hoppe, R. 1993. Poverty in Rural America: Trends and Demographic Characteristics, pp. 20–38. In Rural Sociological Society Task Force on Rural Poverty ((ed.) *Persistent Poverty in Rural America.* Westview, Boulder.

Jensen, L. & Jensen, E. 2008. Poverty, pp. 774–779. In Goreham, G. (ed.) *Encyclopedia of Rural America,* 2nd edn. Greyhouse Publishing, Millerton, NY.

Jensen, L. & McLaughlin, D.K. 1993. Human Capital and Nonmetropolitan Poverty, pp. 111–138. In Beaulieu, L.J. & Mulkey, D. (eds) *Investing in People: The Human Capital Needs of Rural America.* Westview, Boulder, CO..

Jensen, L., Cornwell, G., & Findeis, J. 1995. Informal Work in Nonmetropolitan Pennsylvania. *Rural Sociology*, 60(1), 91–107.

Jensen, L., Findeis, J.L., Hsu, W-L., & Schachter, J.P. 1999. Slipping Into and Out of Underemployment: Another Disadvantage for Nonmetropolitan Workers? *Rural Sociology*, 64(3), 417–438.

Jensen, L., McLaughlin, D., & Slack, T. 2003. Rural Poverty: The Persisting Challenge, pp. 118–134. In Brown, D.L. & Swanson, L.E. (eds) *Challenges for Rural America in the Twenty-First Century.* University Park, PA, Penn State Press.

Jollife, D. 2004. Rural Poverty at a Glance. *Rural Development Research Report.* July.

Jollife, D. 2006. Poverty, Process, and Place: How Sensitive is the Spatial Distribution of Poverty to Cost of Living Adjustments? *Economic Inquiry*, 44(2), 296–310.

Kaufman, P. & Lutz, S.M. 1997. Competing Forces Affect Food Prices for Low-Income Households. *Food Review*, 20, 8–12.

Killeen, K. & Schafft, K. A. 2008. The Organizational and Fiscal Implications of Transient Student Populations in Urban and Rural Areas, pp. 631–650. In Ladd, H.F. & Fiske, E.B. (eds), *Handbook of Research in Education Finance and Policy.* New York, Routledge.

Krauss, C. 2008. Rural U.S. Takes Worst Hit as Gas Tops $4 Average. *New York Times*. June 9.

Lewis, O. 1959. *Five Families: Mexican Case Study in the Culture of Poverty*. Basic Books, New York.

Lichter, D.T., & Jensen, L. 2002. Rural America in Transition: Poverty and Welfare at the Turn of the Twenty-First Century, pp. 77–112. In Weber, B.A., Duncan,G.J., & Whitener, L.A. (eds) *Rural Dimensions of Welfare Reform*. Kalamazoo, MI, W.E. Upjohn Institute for Employment Research.

Lichter, D. & Parisi, D. 2008. Concentrated Rural Poverty and the Geography of Exclusion. *Carsey Policy Brief*, Fall.

Lichter, D.T., McLaughlin, D.K., & Cornwell, G. 1995. Migration and the Loss of Human Resources in Rural America, pp. 235–256. In Beaulieu, L.J. & Mulkey, D. (eds) *Investing in People: The Human Capital Needs of Rural America*. Westview, Boulder, CO.

Massey, D.S., Gross, A.B., & Shibuya, K. 1994. Migration, Segregation, and the Geographic Concentration Of Poverty. *American Sociological Review*, 59, 425–445.

Mather, M. 2008. Higher Poverty Rates in 'Midsize' America. Population Reference Bureau, Washington, D.C. Accessed on December 19, 2008. From http://www.prb.org/Articles/2008/midsizeamericapoverty.aspx.

Moffatt, S. & Glasgow, N. 2009. How Useful is the Concept of Social Exclusion When Applied to Rural Older People in the U.K. and U.S.? *Regional Studies*, 43(10), 1291–1303

Molnár, E., & Schafft, K. A. 2003. Social Exclusion, Ethnic Political Mobilization, and Roma Minority Self Governance in Hungary. *East Central Europe/L'Europe Du Centre Est*, 30(1), 53–74.

Morris, M. 1989. From Culture of Poverty to the Underclass: An Analysis of a Shift in Public Language. *The American Sociologist*, 20(2), 123–133.

Murray, C. 1984. *Losing Ground: American Social Policy, 1950–80*. Basic Books, New York.

Nord, M. 2000. Does it Cost Less to Live in Rural Areas: Evidence from New Data on Food Security and Hunger. *Rural Sociology*, 65(1), 104–125.

O'Connor, A. 2001. *Poverty Knowledge: Social Science, Social Policy, and the Poor in Twentieth-Century U.S. History*. Princeton University Press, Princeton.

O'Hare, W.P. & Churilla, A. 2008. *Rural Children Now Less Likely to Live in Married-Couple Families*. Carsey Institute Fact Sheet, No. 13, Fall. Carsey Institute, Durham, NH.

Orshansky, M. 1965. Counting the Poor: Another Look at the Poverty Profile. *Social Security Bulletin*, 28(1), 2–29.

Payne, R. 2005. *A Framework for Understanding Poverty*. Aha! Process, Inc., Highlands, TX

Philip, L. & Schucksmith, M. 2003. Conceptualizing Social Exclusion. *European Planning Studies*, 11, 461–480.

Piven, F.F. 2001. Welfare Reform and the Economic and Cultural Reconstruction of Low Wage Labor Markets, pp. 135–151. In Goode, J. & Maskovsky, J. (eds) *The New Poverty Studies: The Ethnography of Power, Politics, and Impoverished People in the United States*. New York, New York University Press.

President's National Advisory Commission on Rural Poverty. 1968. *Rural Poverty in the United States*. USGPO, Washington, D.C.

Prins, E. S. & Schafft, K. S. 2009. Individual and Structural Attributions for Poverty and Persistence in Family Literacy Programs: The Resurgence of the Culture of Poverty. *Teachers College Record, 111*(9), 2280–2310.

Pruitt, L.R. 2010. Spatial Inequality as Constitutional Infirmity: Equal Protection, Child Poverty and Place. *Montana Law Review*, 71(1), 1–114.

Pucher, J. & Renne, J.L. 2004. Urban–Rural Differences in Mobility and Mode Choice: Evidence from the 2001 National Household Transportation Survey. Bloustein School of Planning and Public Policy, Rutgers University, New Brunswick, N.J.

Rank, M.R. 2005. *One Nation, Underprivileged: Why American Poverty Affects Us All*. Oxford University Press, New York.

Ropers, R.H. 1991. *Persistent Poverty: The American Dream Turned Nightmare*. Insight Books, New York.

Rural Sociological Society. 1993. *Persistent Poverty in Rural America*. Westview Press, Boulder, CO.

Saenz, R. & Bellejos, M. 1993. Industrial Development and Persistent Poverty in the Lower

Rio Grande Valley, pp. 102–124. In Lyson, T.A. & Falk, W.W. (eds) *Forgotten Places: Uneven Development in Rural America.* University of Kansas Press, Lawrence, KS.

Schafft, K. A. 2005. The Incidence and Impacts of Student Transiency in Upstate New York's Rural School Districts. *Journal of Research in Rural Education,* 20(15), 1–13.

Schafft, K. A. 2006. Poverty, Residential Mobility and Student Transiency Within a Rural New York School District. *Rural Sociology,* 71 (2), 212–231.

Schafft, K. A., Killeen, K., & Morrissey, J. 2010. The Challenges of Student Transiency for U.S. Rural Schools and Communities in the Era of No Child Left Behind, pp. 95–114. In Schafft, K.A. & Jackson, A. (eds), *Rural Education for the Twenty-First Century: Identity, Place, and Community in a Globalizing World.* University Park, PA, Penn State University Press (Rural Studies Series).

Schiller, B.R. 2001. *The Economics of Poverty and Discrimination,* 8th edn. Prentice Hall, Upper Saddle River, N.J.

Sherman, J. 2009. *Those Who Work, Those Who Don't: Poverty, Morality and Family in Rural America.* University of Minnesota Press, Minneapolis.

Shulman, B. 2005. *The Betrayal of Work: How Low-Wage Jobs Fail 30 Million Americans.* The New Press, New York.

Slack, T. 2007. The Contours and Correlates of Informal Work in Rural Pennsylvania. *Rural Sociology,* 72(1), 69–89.

Snipp, C.M. 1996. Understanding Race and Ethnicity in Rural America. *Rural Sociology,* 61(1), 125–142.

Snipp, C.M., Horton, H.D., Jensen, L., Nagel, J., & Rochin, R. 1993. Persistent Rural Poverty and Racial and Ethnic minorities, pp. 173–199. In Rural Sociological Society Task Force on Persistent Rural Poverty (ed.) *Persistent Poverty in Rural America.* Westview, Boulder, CO.

Snyder, A.R. & McLaughlin, R.K. 2004. Female-Headed Families and Poverty in Rural America. *Rural Sociology,* 69(1), 127–149.

Swidler, A. 1986. Culture in Action: Symbols and Strategies. *American Sociological Review,* 51(2), 273–286.

Tickamyer, A.R. &Wood, T.A. 2003. The Social and Economic Context of Informal Work , pp. 394–418. In Falk, W.W., Schulman, M.D., & Tickamyer, A.R. (eds) *Communities of Work: Rural Restructuring in Local and Global Contexts.* Athens, Ohio University Press, Athens.

U.S. American Community Servey, 2007. 1 year estimates. U.S. Census Bureau, Washington, D.C.

U.S.Bureau of Census. 2009. Poverty. Accessed on Nov. 1, 2010, at: http://www.census.gov/hhes/www/poverty/data/threshold/index.html.

Tough, P. 2007. The Class-Consciousness Raiser. *New York Times Magazine,* June 10, 52–56.

Vance, R. 1966. Introductory Note, p. ix. In Weller, J., *Yesterday's People: Life in Contemporary Appalachia.* University of Kentucky Press, Lexington.

Vernon-Feagans, L., Head-Reeves, D., & Kainz, K. 2004. An Ecocultural Perspective on Early Literacy: Avoiding the Perils of School for Nonmainstream Children, pp. 427–428. In Wasik, B.H. (ed.) *Handbook of Family Literacy.* Mahwah, N.J., Lawrence Erlbaum, Mahwah, N.J.

Walker, A. & Walker, C. (eds) 1997. *Britain Divided: The Growth of Social Exclusion in the 1980s and 1990s.* London, Child Poverty Action Group.

Weller, J. 1966. *Yesterday's People: Life in Contemporary Appalachia.* University of Kentucky Press, Lexington.

Wilson, W.J. 1987. *The Truly Disadvantaged.* University of Chicago Press, Chicago.

Wilson, W.J. 1997. *When Work Disappears.* Vintage Books, New York.

Wilson, F. & Tienda, M. 1989. Employment Returns to Migration. *Urban Geography,* 10, 540–561.

Zimmerman, J. N., Ham, S., & Frank, S.M. 2008. Does it or Doesn't it? Geographic Differences and the Cost of Living. *Rural Sociology,* 73(3), 463–486.

PART V

CONCLUSIONS

11 Rural Transformations and Policies for the Future

Rural society has been dramatically transformed over the past several decades. Population size and socioeconomic composition have been altered, rural economies have been restructured, social institutions, and people's relationships to them, have been transformed, and new environmental services are being expected of the natural environment. Moreover, all of these local and regional changes have taken place in a dramatically restructured global context that has significantly altered the relationship between the "global" and the "local." While each of these changes pose challenges for rural people and communities, many also bring potential opportunities. Current rural structures, and the legacy of the past, affect rural community prospects as places to live and work. In this chapter we will briefly review some of the major changes experienced by rural people and communities during the past several decades, indicating challenges and opportunities posed by these changes, as well as unresolved issues that persist as legacies of the past. In the course of this review, we will identify a number of "rural policy choices" that will affect the future of rural communities and the wellbeing of rural people.

A Changed Rural Demography

Changes in Rural Population Size and Percent Rural

As we noted early in this book, the United States is a highly urbanized nation, but with a significant rural population. While the number of rural people has held relatively constant at between 55–60 million persons during the last three decades, the share of the nation's total population represented by this population has been falling steadily from about 21 percent in 1990 to less than 17 percent in 2005 (Brown et al. 2004; USDA-ERS 2007). This is partly the result of slower relative rates of rural population growth since the mid 1990s, and partly a result of faster growing nonmetro counties being reclassified into the metropolitan category. It should be noted that urbanization and other demographic processes are often quite changeable from decade to decade. For example, as shown in Chapter 2, *internal* migration in the United States favored urban areas during most of the nineteenth and twentieth centuries only to switch toward rural areas during the 1970s, and from 1990 until the present time.[1] Since internal migration tends to respond to inter-area differences in economic fortunes, its direction typically reflects short-term differences in unemployment and other measures of economic wellbeing between areas. Hence, planning for changes in population size and distribution is difficult since migration's direction is unpredictable over time.

Changes in Population Composition

The rural population is becoming older as is true of the rest of the nation. Lower fertility rates drive this trend throughout the nation, while chronic out-migration of younger persons further amplifies the trend in rural areas. In addition to aging, the rural population is becoming more ethnically diverse. Hispanic population, in particular, is redistributing itself from the Southwest to the Midwest and South Atlantic regions. This redistribution reflects both interregional movement of Hispanics within the U.S., as well as immigration from Mexico and elsewhere in Latin America. While the reasons for this migration are complex, job opportunities in a number of industries such as meat packing, construction and food processing tend to be the main attractions.

Challenges and Opportunities Associated with Changing Demographics

As indicated above, many rural communities are contending with populations that have grown, declined, and/or become more diverse in ways that challenge local institutions such as schools, churches, health care, and local government, as well as social relationships more generally. More, fewer and/or different kinds of people affect the need and demand for various goods and services, thereby stressing institutional capacity, enhancing, or in the case of population decline, diminishing support of local businesses. New residents, especially when they differ in age, social class, or ethnic background can enhance creativity and other social resources, but increased diversity can also lead to social tensions and conflicts. However, even though demographic transformations induce changes in other aspects of society and economy, demography is not destiny (Brown 2009). Rather, as shown in Figure 11.1, the impacts of demographic changes are mediated by local social structure, and by the larger national and international environments in which localities are embedded. As Brown (2008: 242) observed,

> To assume that a unit change in population size or composition automatically and mechanistically results in a similar magnitude of change in economic activity, poverty reduction, farm land conversion, or public service utilization is to deny the agency of actors and the instrumentality of community institutions.

The translation of demographic changes into enhanced or diminished rural wellbeing is contingent on the effectiveness and responsiveness of local institutions, how rural communities position themselves with respect to external forces (national or supra-national), and as will be shown later in this chapter, whether national and regional policies are designed to promote rural wellbeing.

Transformed Rural Economies

Economic Restructuring

The restructuring of local economies involves three interdependent forms of social and economic transformation: (a) alterations in types of goods and services produced locally, (b) shifts in social relationships between employers, workers,

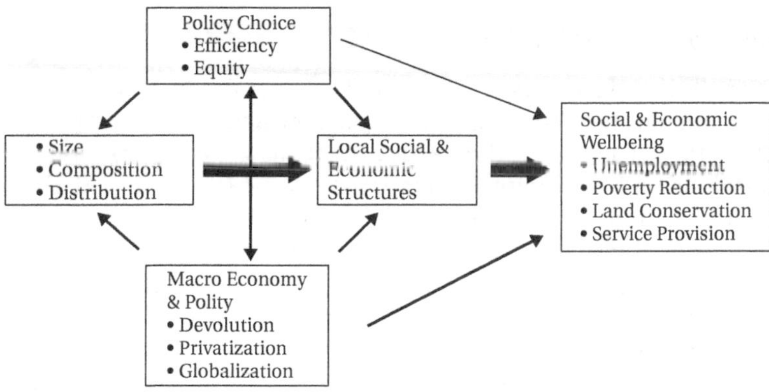

Source: Brown, 2008

Figure 11.1 Impacts of Population Change are Mediated by Social Structure

governments, and citizens, and (c) alterations in political–economic relationships between global, national, and local levels (Falk & Lobao 2003).

Industrial Restructuring

As was shown in Chapter 8, rural economies experienced two major transformations during the twentieth century that continue to produce both opportunities and challenges for rural workers and rural economies. In the early twentieth century, manufacturing replaced a heavy dependence on extractive industries such as mining, farming and forestry in rural economies. While factory jobs provided a mobility avenue for many rural workers, rural manufacturers often produced non-durable, resource-based products such as shoes, cigarettes, canned foods, and textiles. In contrast to the durable manufacturing concentrated in urban areas, rural manufacturing jobs paid lower wages, lacked benefits, and generally had only limited career mobility prospects.

Then, during the mid part of the twentieth century, in concert with urban areas, rural economies began to rely more on services and less on manufacturing. While this second industrial transformation concentrated on services in both urban and rural areas, urban economies captured most of the well-paying producer service jobs, and rural areas were left with low-paying employment in consumer and personal services. This distinction has adverse implications for both rural people and rural places. In the first instance, rural workers have less access to well-paying, secure, year-round jobs, and in the second instance, rural economies often specialize in non-basic services which circulate capital, but fail to attract it from the outside. As a result, many rural economies have bleak prospects for future growth and development, and rural workers are often *under*employed and in or near statistical poverty. While much current attention centers on services, it must be noted that manufacturing still comprises about one in five rural jobs, significantly higher than in urban economies, but since rural factories often produce non-durable products, they pay poorly and are the most vulnerable to global off-shoring.

Social Relationships of Production

The demise of manufacturing as the cornerstone of the nation's economy disrupted relationships between workers, employers, and government. As Falk and Lobao (2003:157) observed of the 1970s and 1980s "The institutional structure of capital/labor and state/citizen relationships, which regulated the Fordist economy and assured rising earnings, began to break down."[2] As a result, labor's bargaining power diminished, unionization declined, Keynesian demand management switched to supply side economics, and the national government devolved many social welfare functions to the states which were permitted to reduce the system's generosity.[3]

In other words, workers were now more likely to be responsible for their own wellbeing as employers and government re-negotiated the social contract in a manner that was more consistent with the conservative ideology ushered in during the Reagan administration in the 1980s. These transformations affected worker security and mobility adversely in both rural and urban areas, but they were especially severe in rural areas with their smaller and less diverse employment bases.

Rural Bright Spots

In the midst of this pessimistic picture, some types of rural economies have developed successful niches in the nation's spatial division of labor. For example, rural areas located within commuting distance to nearby metropolitan labor markets have succeeded in carving out a role as residential communities for part of the urban labor force. It is unclear, however, whether commuters spend the majority of their earnings where they live, or whether most of their income leaks out of the community as workers link shopping, service utilization, and recreation with their journey to work.[4] Moreover, long-distance commuting consumes large volumes of gasoline, and it contributes to global warming through exhaust emissions. Further, as fuel prices rise, as they inevitably will, given depleting supplies and exponentially increasing demands for gasoline in places like China, longer-distance commuting may be a luxury many will be unable to afford in the decades ahead. Therefore, while in the short term many rural areas on the metropolitan periphery have grown, in the absence of viable region-wide mass transit, rural commuting may involve as many challenges as opportunities in the century ahead.

Rural areas with amenity-based economies also appear to be succeeding. While many jobs in recreation and tourism are low skill, seasonal, and vulnerable to fluctuations in the business cycle, research shows that recreation-based economies attract income from outside, and have a positive multiplier, thereby contributing to further economic growth (Krannich & Petrzelka 2003). Moreover, recreation and tourism development has been shown to play a central role in the future development of rural retirement destinations (Brown et al. 2011f). While some longer-term residents are ambivalent about the in-migration of retirees, most agree that older in-migration brings economic resources, benefits the not-for-profit sector, and can invigorate public institutions (Brown & Glasgow 2008).

Accordingly, amenity based development appears to be a path toward rural opportunity.

Global–Local Connections

The industrial and institutional restructurings described above were strongly affected by the radical transformation in the world's political economy that has taken place under the label "globalization." Even though the "myth of rurality" promotes an image of rural autonomy and self reliance, rural communities and economies have never operated independently of regional, national, and international forces (Schafft & Jackson 2010). At present however, the degree of external influence on local affairs has heightened and the global–local power balance has become more asymmetrical. More than ever, rural economies occupy peripheral niches in the global economy, and are vulnerable to being undermined by the self-interested actions of trans-national corporations and other global actors. Rural communities with narrow economies dominated by a small number of economic activities and interests, and those that lack strong and responsive institutions are especially vulnerable to losing employment through global off-shoring. Moreover, global actors often force localities, both urban and rural, to participate in "beggar thy neighbor" competitions for economic development. Ironically, succeeding in such competition can be a pyrrhic victory, since communities are forced to make huge financial and other concessions and provide expensive infrastructure as a condition for attracting, expanding, and/or retaining global establishments.

Global linkages, however, are not necessarily deleterious, especially if local communities are strong enough to negotiate fair deals with regional, national, and/or global actors. As Young and Lyson (1993) showed, pluralistic rural communities with high levels of external penetration in the form of branch plants and franchises had higher quality of life measures than counterparts lacking externally owned enterprises. External linkages can bring control, manipulation, and exploitation, but they can also be a source of information, resources, and know how. Hence, the greater level of rural integration within national, regional, and global hierarchies can be challenging, but it can also bring opportunities for development.

Farming and the Food System

Except for in the Midwest, most rural economies do not depend on agriculture as a major source of employment and income. Yet, farming continues to be an extremely important contributor to national security and wellbeing. As we discussed in Chapter 9, this revelation derives from considering agriculture as one, but only one, integral part of a broader food system that involves social, economic, cultural, and natural processes, and spans from scientific research to manufactured inputs to production, marketing, and ultimately to consumption. Examined through this lens, agriculture contributes to numerous national goals, including human nutrition and human health, community development, international trade relations, land use, and environmental protection. Moreover, the food system spans numerous institutional domains from academia to the commercial sphere to the family and to public health. The food system perspective differs from the past when agriculture was treated as an independent economic sector that simply generated farm family employment and income, and supported regional economies where it was located.

The previous agri-centric view focused on the farm sector in isolation from the social, economic, and natural processes that sustained it. While some critics attempted to call attention to the social, economic, community, and health externalities associated with the industrialization of agriculture (Browne et al. 1992), most agricultural scientists and economists showed little concern as the sector became more and more concentrated in fewer and larger firms, as the sector's control passed from independent family farmers and local bankers to a relatively small number of transnational corporations, banks, institutional investors, and organizations, as monoculture and the factory farming of livestock came to dominate production, and as the regional distribution of agricultural production shifted, leaving many previous farming communities high and dry. Moreover, few seemed concerned as the sector promoted high-fat and high-carbohydrate diets that began to contribute to an epidemic of obesity, associated illnesses, and skyrocketing health-care costs.

As the nation entered the twenty-first century, social, economic, health, and environmental externalities of agriculture became undeniable, and critics began to propose alternatives to the industrial agriculture model (Allen 2004; Lyson & Guptill 2004; Pollan 2006; Schlosser 2001). They called for minimizing chemical inputs, carefully evaluating the direct and indirect, immediate and cumulative impacts of crop biotechnology, and raising and slaughtering meat animals more humanely. But more than anything else, critics promoted a re-localization of agriculture as a way to enhance healthful eating, local economic development, and the strengthening of local community institutions.

It is unlikely that the local foods movement will significantly diminish the industrial concentration of cash grain and meats production, nor the scale of international trade in these commodities. The sector is too well organized, too profitable, and has too many influential friends in strategic places where public policy is formulated and public monies appropriated to support the sector. However, as more and more people become concerned about nutrition-related illnesses, choose to buy locally, and resist purchasing and consuming highly processed foods, it is likely that smaller-scale, genuine family farms will survive as a sustainable mode of agricultural production for direct marketing.

As shown in Chapter 9, the data are clear that this is already happening at the peripheries of many large cities where direct marketing of fruits and vegetables, nursery products and dairy has gained a growing share of the consumer's dollar (Heimlich & Anderson 2001). Data on organic agriculture also show this trend. According to the USDA (2009), acreage in organic production increased from a little over 900,000 acres in 1992 to over four million acres in 2005.[5] Moreover, the rate of change in organic farming acreage increased dramatically between 2002 and 2005 compared with the previous decade. These same data show a steady increase in certified organic producers from around 3,500 in 1992 to almost 8,500 in 2005.

Poverty and Inequality

As shown in Chapter 10, poverty is concentrated in rural areas and in the central cities of large urban areas. In fact, the vast majority of persistently poor U.S. counties are rural. However, rural poverty is less visible than its urban counterpart, because while the rural poverty *rate* is relatively high, the rural *share* of the nation's poor population is relatively small, since rural areas only comprise 17 percent of the nation's total population. Moreover, rural poverty is often camouflaged by pleasant environments and picturesque landscapes. As a result, rural poverty seldom attracts policy attention commensurate with its depth and intractability.

Rural poverty is a particularly challenging social problem because many of its causes differ from the predominant urban model. As a result, urban-based welfare programs provide less assistance to the rural poor than to their urban counterparts. Most fundamentally, a high percentage of poor rural persons work full or part time, but fail to earn sufficient income to escape poverty. Since a substantial share of rural poor persons comprise the so-called "working poor," they receive little or no assistance from the nation's principal anti-poverty program, Temporary Aid to Needy Families (TANF), which is predicated on "welfare to work."[6] The high work effort among the rural poor also calls culture-based explanations of poverty into question to the extent that such explanations contend that people are poor because they do not want to work.

Similar to the situation in urban areas, rural poverty is disproportionately high among racial minorities. However, while urban minorities have reasonable access to a supply of jobs matched to their human capital, and relatively easy access to social services offices, job training, and other support services, rural minorities tend to be concentrated in regions of widespread underdevelopment such as the Mississippi Delta, Indian Country, and the lower Rio Grande Valley. Accordingly, rural poor minorities suffer from the double jeopardy of low human capital and a lack of access to jobs and supporting services. In addition , the legacy of slavery, and the influences of Jim Crow and the paternalistic plantation South remain strong in areas such as the Delta. As Duncan (1999) showed in *Worlds Apart* these legacies have produced rigid race and class structures in contemporary times constraining mobility for minorities living in many persistently poor rural areas.

Persistent net out-migration of better-educated young adults also contributes to high poverty rates in rural areas. Given the preponderance of low-wage, low-skill jobs lacking benefits and career ladders, educated youth have little choice but to move to urban areas upon high school graduation. Moreover, rural youth who attend college in urban areas seldom plan to return after obtaining their degrees. This chronic brain drain not only contributes to high rural poverty rates in a statistical sense, for example, by creaming off better prepared workers thereby leaving a residual population with low educational attainment, but also contributes to the very underdevelopment that is one of rural poverty's root causes. High labor quality is one of the principal factors used by employers to determine where to locate (and expand) establishments. Accordingly, employers tend to avoid locations with low educational attainment.

Persistently high rural poverty is one of America's most important challenges in the twenty-first century. This seemingly intractable problem reflects many of the other challenges discussed throughout this book: changing racial composition of rural populations, economic restructuring, loss of jobs matched to persons lacking higher education, rigid social stratification that diminishes community social capital, and lack of institutional capacity, especially in the context of devolution. However, as much as anything, rural poverty is intractable because of historical legacies that deny persons equal access to education, good jobs, social services, and the sense that they will be fairly rewarded for obtaining education, working hard, and playing by society's rules. A focus on root causes rather than contemporary symptoms is essential for ameliorating rural (or urban) poverty.

The Rural Policy Choice

Traditional rural jobs in extractive and manufacturing sectors have declined; job growth in well paying producer services is sluggish at best; wage rates, even within the same industries, pay less well than in urban labor markets; rural workers are less well prepared to obtain jobs in well paying sectors; and rural economies are especially vulnerable to global competition, a trend that seems unlikely to change in the near future. Some observers believe that these trends indicate that rural economies are simply experiencing a "natural" downsizing that is part and parcel of the process of capitalist economic development.

The economic transformations discussed above have distinct implications for rural America's social and economic wellbeing. While the contours of these economic transformations are indisputable, experts disagree on the most appropriate way to deal with the uneven development that is being produced (see Table 11.1). The rural economic policy choice can be understood as a debate between *equity advocates* who argue that state and national governments should play a key role in promoting rural economic development, and *efficiency advocates* who argue that rural economies are experiencing a "natural" transformation, and that public policy should not interfere with this process of change (Drabenstott et al. 1987).

Efficiency advocates believe that rural underdevelopment is an integral part of the process of capitalist economic development. They argue that rural economies are inefficient, and that capital is appropriately flowing from less-efficient rural locations to more efficient urban economies where returns on investment are higher. Workers are viewed as inputs in the production process who will gladly move to improve their material wellbeing. Communities, hence, are viewed as interchangeable sites of production not as valued social contexts. If one follows this line of reasoning, the appropriate rural policy choice is to enhance resource mobility by reducing regulations and providing readjustment assistance for displaced workers who must prepare for jobs in new, typically urban, economies. Equity advocates would argue that policies privileging economic growth over social wellbeing will inevitably result in structured inequality, the perpetuation of lagging economies in peripheral areas, and a form of development that treats people and landscapes as mere commodities to be exploited rather than as containing value in and of themselves (Polanyi 1944).

In contrast, equity advocates view communities as valued "hometowns." They believe that people have a right to live where they choose even if these choices may

Table 11.1 The Rural Economic Policy Choice

Policy Goal	**Instruments**	**Directed to:**
Equity	Developmental	
• Retain capital • Stem out migration • Stimulate economic growth	• Investment incentives: tax breaks, infrastructure, capital subsidy, land, relaxed regulations	**Private Sector Firms**
• Strengthen public management and civil society	• Technical assistance, information, leadership training, sub-state regionalism	**Public Sector, Civil Society**
Efficiency	Transitional	
• Reduce spatial misallocation of capital and labor (+mobility)	• Deregulation	**Specific Economic Sectors**
• Ease readjustment costs	• Work training/ retraining Labor market information, relocation assistance, temporary income support	**Individuals and/or Households**

Source: Author's own.

reduce the nation's overall rate of economic growth. Moreover, they embrace a role for public policy in equalizing economic growth rates and opportunity structures across space to facilitate these residential preferences. They promote a vision of rural development policy that seeks to stimulate economic development and community renewal by attracting and retaining capital in lagging regions, and by stemming out-migration. As shown in Table 11.1, development policy is directed toward private employers and features a set of investment incentives including tax breaks, capital subsidies, and infrastructure. In addition, efforts to strengthen local public management and the civic sector are seen as contributing to development. In fact, community development and local economic development are seen as two sides of the same coin. Efficiency advocates would argue that development programs such as these that attempt to retain labor and capital in lagging rural economies are wasteful, simply postponing the inevitable concentration that is a natural part of the capitalist accumulation process. Moreover, they observe that development efforts targeted to underperforming rural regions will fail as soon as protectionist subsidies and regulations are lifted.

Rural Community Capacity Reconsidered

The Inside and the Outside are Intertwined

Rural people's wellbeing depends on the internal organization of communities where they live and work, and on effective, mutually beneficial relationships linking their communities with the outside world. This mix of internal relationships and social structures on the one hand, and embeddedness in regional, national, and even global contexts on the other, is a critical ingredient of community sustainability. In other words, communities with an optimal mix of bonding and bridging social relationships and effective public institutions are less vulnerable to being undermined by external forces and, in fact, are more able to benefit from links with the outside (Etzioni 1996; Shucksmith 2010).

As we discussed in Chapters 3 and 4, internal community organization involves social relationships among people who live and work together as well as the presence of local institutions with sufficient capacity to provide essential services, manage public business, and plan for the future. Social relationships and social institutions are inextricably linked because people are more likely to mobilize in support of local government, education, public health, and other institutions if they are bound together in local relationships that they care about, e.g., relationships characterized by trust and norms of reciprocity, what many scholars characterize as "social capital" (Flora and Flora 2003). Conversely, part of the reason that people identify with their places of residence, and care about local social relationships, is because their residential communities produce valued public goods such as quality education, a social space where collective concerns can be openly discussed and contested, environmental protection, responsive and responsible government, and public health and safety.

Don't Blame the Victims

Unfortunately, simply recognizing that strong communities produce higher quality of life and are less vulnerable to outside forces is not particularly helpful unless one understands *why* some places are able to develop stronger social structures, and more effective social relationships, than others. Only then is it possible to propose inclusive and responsive policies for strengthening local society. Without such knowledge policy-makers are likely to blame less well-off places for their own underdevelopment, arguing that they would be better off if they could "only get along with each other." One problem in solving this dilemma is that ineffective, and often unequal, social relationships generally reflect a long history of social, political and economic exclusion based on race or other attributes that are difficult to overcome in the current situation (Duncan 1999; Schafft & Brown 2003). These persistent legacies poison contemporary social relationships, thereby constraining meaningful development (Harris & Worthen 2003). As Schafft and Brown (2003: 340) observed:

> by keeping the analytic focus on the characteristics of poor communities . . . a blind spot is created wherein it is all too easy to bypass or even disregard the underlying political, economic and social systems that shape and reproduce inequality.

Accordingly, strengthening rural community structure so that challenges are more likely to become opportunities is critically important, but doing so requires overcoming historical legacies as well as contemporary structural constraints (Duncan 1999). Producing more inclusive, civil, and democratic rural communities is a worthy goal that will contribute to improving the lives of rural people (Swanson and Brown 2003).

While it is undeniable that rural economies have become smaller and relatively less well off over time, and that they are especially vulnerable to globalization during the current era, some observers argue that this decline is not necessarily inevitable. As discussed in Chapter 2, rural areas have gained net migration from urban areas at various times since the 1970s reversing long, seemingly irreversible, trends of net migration loss. However, as shown in Box 8.1, research shows that many urban to rural migrants commute back to urban jobs. Hence, urban to rural migration may enhance a rural area's residential function, but it probably has little direct impact on employment possibilities or the prospects for non-residentially oriented economic development. This separation of work from home may be a perfectly reasonable economic niche for many rural areas, especially those located close to metropolitan centers.

Other observers argue that while many rural areas are declining, and will continue to do so in the future, some areas will be able to avoid this destiny. In some instances, this is because particular areas have natural endowments that will support future prosperity as energy producers, centers for tourism and recreation, and/or retirement destinations. However, even with such endowments economic development is not a certainty. Research by Brown and his colleagues (2011f) shows that places with attractive natural amenities only become retirement destinations if they develop these amenities for recreation and tourism at an earlier date. In other words, becoming a retirement destination is a two-step process that involves social networks that are built up between previous visitors and the places where they vacation. In some instances, these networks provide the social structure that guides previous vacationers to these locations in later life.

A more general observation is that rural places that have strong and effective social structure are more likely to prosper economically than their counterparts that lack effective institutions, organizations and social relationships (such as those discussed in Chapters 3 and 4). In particular, strong social structure is thought to be an effective buffer against the negative impacts of globalization. Communities with responsive and effective local governments, a high degree of civic engagement, a beneficial mix of bridging and bonding social relationships, a well prepared workforce and effective schools are better able to negotiate with global organizations to obtain sustainable economic opportunities. In contrast, communities with weak social structure and poorly prepared workers typically have to accept what global organizations offer, on the global organization's terms.

In conclusion, the prospects for rural economic prosperity depend on a complex mix of social, political, and economic factors. Community development and economic development are two sides of the same coin. Firms do not want to locate in communities with weak social institutions, and communities are seldom able to invest in institutions and organizations where economic opportunities are absent. Rural people and communities in highly urbanized societies such as the United States continue to play important roles as places to live and work and as stewards of natural resources. Moreover, Americans hold strong pro-rural attitudes even if they have little or no personal experience living, working, or even visiting rural communities. We have shown that rural society and economy has been dramatically transformed during recent decades, but we also emphasized that legacies of the past have powerful influences on the present society, economy, and culture. At times these legacies produce beneficial results as with the persistence of local agriculture, and sometimes these legacies have perverse effects, as with chronically underdeveloped, high poverty regions such as the Mississippi Delta and the stubborn inequalities that characterize race relations in certain parts of the rural South. Persistence and change, hence, is a major thematic characterizing rural America today. The rural challenge is to protect what is beneficial from the past while embracing change that reduces social, economic, and political exclusion and inequality. The rural policy choice is clear. We can either facilitate the transfer of remaining capital from rural to urban areas or we can choose to build sustainable rural communities and economies that provide a high standard of living and social wellbeing (see Box 11.1).

Box 11.1 Rural Digital Divide with a Focus on Indian Country

Access to information technology (IT) is an essential aspect of contemporary rural life. Lack of access to IT can negatively affect individuals, households, communities, and businesses. At the individual and household level, access to IT is necessary for finding jobs, maintaining important social relationships, making informed purchases, and obtaining public information. At the community level, access to IT is increasingly important for providing educational and health services, and for attracting and retaining businesses. Businesses depend on IT for direct sales and for business to business transactions such as obtaining legal, accounting, and other producer services.

Digital Divide

At the national level, 71 percent of U.S. households used the internet to access information in 2007 but access differs across population subgroups and between urban and rural areas. For example, according to the U.S. Bureau of the Census, 63 percent of rural households had at least one person going on-line in 2007 compared to 73 percent of their urban counterparts. [7] Moreover, this difference underestimates the true rural–urban "digital divide" because urban users are more likely to have access to high speed broadband services while many rural users still access the internet via slower dial-up services (Sternberg and Lowe 2009). Research shows that rural–urban differences in internet usage are a result of differences in access to internet infrastructure, and differences in demographic and socioeconomic composition, especially older age and lower educational attainment (Stern and Wellman 2010). In addition, as Boase (2010) has shown, rural persons have relatively few high prestige occupational connections and relatively numerous connections to persons with low occupational prestige which further limits their use of the internet in their homes.

Rural internet access, while still lagging urban access, is much higher than a decade ago when only about one-third of rural households had a computer, less than one-quarter ever went on-line or sent or received an e-mail message, and less than one in

Box 11.1 (continued)

ten went on line to view the news or to make a purchase (Hindman 2000). However, even though rural internet usage increased dramatically during the last decade, the urban–rural gap in usage has remained about the same. In other words, urban usage has increased at the same rate as rural, so rural areas are better off than they were, but still disadvantaged.[8]

Targeted Programs Have Enhanced Rural Access to IT

Public policies enacted during the last fifteen years have enhanced rural access to IT. In 1996, the Universal Service Program of the Telecommunications Act funded broadband access in the areas of telemedicine and secondary education. Telehealth has great promise to expand access to clinical specialists, reduce travel-related expenses, expand care options available locally for patients, facilitate electronic record keeping, and many other applications, yet research shows that despite its potential rural telehealth's adoption has lagged behind expectations. As Grigsby and Goetz (2004: 248) have observed, "Its adoption and diffusion are restricted by the very forces (e.g., low income, low density, insufficient government subsidy) that its proponents hoped its development would address." The 2008 Food, Conservation and Energy Act (aka the Farm Bill), also authorized loan and grant programs targeted to telemedicine, distance learning and rural broadband access, as did the 2009 Recovery and Reinvestment Act.

Other Dimensions of Unequal Access

At the individual and household levels, access to and use of IT is directly related to income, education, and other aspects of social inequality in the United States. Data from the Current Population Survey show that fewer than one in five households earning under $12,500 have at-home access to broadband while about 70 percent of households earning over $75,000 have access (U.S. Bureau of the Census 2007). This positive relationship between income and broadband access is present in both urban and rural areas, and rural households have markedly lower rates of access at each income level. As might be expected, internet access is decidedly lower among disadvantaged groups and racial and ethnic minorities.

IT Access in "Indian Country"

According to a 2010 study by the National Telecommunications and Information Administration, only 43 percent of American Indians used broadband in the home during 2007–2009 compared with 66 percent of non-Hispanic Whites and 67 percent of Asians.[9] Clearly, American Indians are digitally disadvantaged compared with Whites and Asians. This digital disadvantage is a result of low income and education, but also of living in low-density rural locales. In fact, American Indians are the most rural of America's racial minorities, with over fifty percent living in nonmetropolitan areas (Gonzales 2003) and about one-third on reservations or on other tribal trust lands (Sherson 2000).

While American Indian's relative lack of access to IT, especially in rural

Box 11.1 (continued)

environments, can be traced to their fundamental lack of economic development, to the low-density and sparse environments many live in, and to a lack of basic infrastructure be it roads, telephone service, or IT, culture also contributes to the American Indian digital divide. Some American Indians mistrust specific technologies. Progress is sometimes seen as a threat to culture, sovereignty, and self determination. This situation has been characterized as the "digital divide dilemma" (Bissel 2004). As Sherson (2000) has observed, lack of access to IT may be the result of internal cultural inertia on one hand, and on the other hand an historic lack of access to technology based on cultural difference.

In an article published in *EDUCAUSE review*, Davis and Trebian (2001: 38) observed that "Ending the digital divide in Indian Country requires allowing tribal communities to craft their own solutions . . . Close collaboration is necessary to avoid the imposition of 'solutions . . .'" Nobody disputes that access to IT is crucial for American Indian economic development, but some observers question whether the price of enhancing access is worth the benefit if the digital divide is narrowed in culturally inappropriate ways or in ways that sacrifice American Indian political sovereignty. Well-intentioned government policies may narrow the IT access gap, but at the risk of sacrificing cultural integrity. Surely, access to information technology on reservations can be accomplished in a culturally appropriate manner. In response to this need, the Bureau of Indian Education (2007) has launched major new initiatives to employ technology in education according with tribal needs and values. The BIE has launched a Master Plan that includes the Native American Student Information System, a unified BIE web portal, web-based collaboration tools, and increased training for teachers to improve the use of internet-based educational resources.

While developed nations throughout the world are debating this policy choice, the United States lacks a strategic view of the need for and impact of public actions to achieve broad societal goals and mitigate problems affecting rural people and communities; it lacks a rural policy. While numerous programs exist, the nation does not have a strategic vision of goals for rural people and communities, or how various programs might contribute to these goals. As Browne (2001) has observed, rural people and communities have suffered from historical institutional neglect.

Some would argue that agriculture policy is the United States' rural policy. However, as we showed in Chapter 8, only a small fraction of rural workers depends on agriculture for employment and income, and only one in five rural counties derives even 15 percent of earnings or employment from agriculture (USDA-ERS 2004). Accordingly, while farm policy may be important for the agricultural sector, it does not substitute for an integrated vision of goals and objectives to promote rural wellbeing across the nation's diverse rural space.

Other developed nations have made different rural policy choices (see Box 11.2). The European Union has an elaborate set of policy schemes focused on rural people and communities. Even though critics observe that the Common Agricultural Policy's (CAP) second pillar, where rural development policies reside,

Box 11.2 Rural Policy in the European Union: Supranational and Intergovernmental

U.S. and E.U.[10] Rural Policy in Brief Comparison

Rural policy in the U.S. and the E.U. presents an interesting study in contrasts. In particular, the U.S. lacks a comprehensive rural policy and tends to be mainly driven by economic considerations, while the E.U. has a well articulated, more comprehensive rural policy framework and is motivated by a broader array of issues including environmental management, landscape preservation, cultural heritage, social justice and social inclusion, and even defense (Brown 2008).[11] This broader policy agenda provides more space for equity considerations and for the value of "place" to shape policy as compared with the United States where resource mobility, market efficiency, and national economic growth dominate. Moreover, E.U. rural policy is clearly targeted to place and territory, while U.S. policies focus on the performance of particular industries such as farming, manufacturing, or energy extraction. One additional difference is important. Since the E.U. is an economic and political union of 27 member countries, its approach to rural development is both supranational and intergovernmental. The E.U. has a common rural development policy that is funded partly from the central E.U. budget, and partly by individual member states (European Commission 2010). In the United States, in contrast, policy may be intergovernmental in the sense that responsibility is sometimes shared between states and the national government, but it is seldom supranational.

What Constitutes Rural Policy in the E.U. ?

The E.U.'s rural policy aims at social and economic cohesion, adjustment of the agricultural sector to market circumstances, and protection and conservation of the environment. Rural issues are salient throughout the E.U. because about one-quarter to one-third of E.U. national populations live in rural areas, with higher percentages in Southern and Eastern Europe, and lower percentages in Northern and Western nations (Population Reference Bureau 2009).[12] Moreover, the majority of the E.U.'s territory is located in rural regions. Accordingly, from a policy perspective, rural development represents a critical aspect of regional integration both within and between nations.

Rural development falls under the E.U.'s Common Agriculture Policy (CAP). The CAP's original objectives, as set out in the 1957 Treaty of Rome, were almost entirely agricultural. However, the CAP was reformed in 2000, and again in 2003 to embrace environmental sustainability, rural community development, and other socially motivated goals such as food safety and animal welfare (Shucksmith et al. 2005). In addition, the "Agenda 2000" reforms featured a shift from away from supporting particular industries, such as agriculture, and towards territorial development.

Developing an Integrated Rural Development Framework: Agenda 2000

The desirability of moving toward a framework for sustainable and integrated rural development was first discussed at a 1996 Conference on Rural Development held in Cork, Ireland. The Conference declared that the E.U. should make a fresh start in rural

Box 11.2 (continued)

development policy. This ambitious declaration had a major impact on the CAP's Rural Development Regulation, as articulated in Agenda 2000. Agenda 2000 organized the CAP into two pillars. Pillar 1 is almost entirely focused on agricultural production while the second pillar includes a range of agri-environmental, economic development, and rural development programs.

The CAP's rural development policy seeks to build social cohesion through leadership and community development (Warner & Shortall 2008). Its LEADER program promotes local leadership development, and seeks to initiate bottom-up schemes of integrated rural development. At least in theory, LEADER provides a flexible program that can be adapted to the diversity of rural regions. It is oriented toward "development from below, towards a system of subsidiarity in which smaller and disadvantaged groups have more to say about their affairs" (Stohr 2004: xxv). As Lowe et al. (1998) have observed, the goals of sustainable and endogenous development are intertwined. The CAP's rural policy is to be geared to local requirements and initiatives and it places particular emphasis on making the most of local community leadership and organizations

Has E.U. Rural Policy Achieved its Goals?

Many observers believe that the CAP's Rural Development Regulation falls short of the objectives contained in the Cork Declaration. As Dwyer et al. (2002: 53) have commented, ". . . the potential effectiveness of the RDR is limited by the fact that in many countries it amounts to little more than an amalgamation of pre-existing measures to provide support for activities close to agriculture." Accordingly, it does not provide a coherent basis for integrated rural development. (Shucksmith et al. 2005). In addition, as Bryden and Hart (2004) have shown, the new Rural Development Regulation only accounts for about 10 percent of the CAP's budget with the other 90 percent continuing to go for production agriculture. They recommend that territorial rural development policy be separated from agricultural policy. Bryden and Hart (2004) believe that a separate rural development policy could promote a "framework of economic democracy that allows people who are affected by social and economic change to have real decision-making and fiscal power to change their futures" (342).

has been sidetracked by agricultural competitiveness and agri-environment schemes, they acknowledge that a wide range of rural development measures are possible within the CAP (Shucksmith et al. 2005). Moreover, European thinking on rural development features innovative ideas such as neo-endogenous development schemes which while strongly participatory, include a facilitative role for the state (Shucksmith 2010). While critics complain that bottoms-up programs such as LEADER are often controlled by social elites and fail to accomplish the program's democratic goals (Shortall 2004), the fact remains that rural policy is on the European policy agenda, and that efforts are being made to design and implement policies that involve genuine civic engagement and promote rural renewal. In comparison, rural policy is not on the policy agenda in United States. Since American public policy is shaped by urban agendas, resulting programs are often insensitive and poorly suited to the peculiar conditions found in rural America (Swanson and Brown 2003). Accordingly, we close our book with a call for a serious national dialog on the need for comprehensive and consistent rural policy shaped by clear goals and featuring strategic means for accomplishing these goals. The future of America's rural communities depends on it.

Notes

1 Note: During the last sixty years, rural areas have had net out-migration at young adult ages regardless of the overall rural–urban direction of net migration.
2 Fordism is the system of mass production and consumption characteristic of highly developed economies during the 1940s–1960s.
3 Keynesian economics is a macroeconomic theory based on the ideas of twentieth-century British economist John Maynard Keynes. Keynesian economics argues that private sector decisions sometimes lead to inefficient macroeconomic outcomes and therefore advocates active policy responses by the public sector, including monetary policy actions by the central bank and fiscal policy actions by the government to stabilize output over the business cycle.
4 This behavior is known as "trip chaining."
5 Congress passed the Organic Foods Production Act of 1990 which contributed to the growth of this agricultural sector.
6 However, they do benefit from Food Stamps and School Lunch (Smith & Savage 2007) and from the Earned Income Tax Credit (Mattingly 2009).
7 Corresponding figures for use in the home were 52% and 64% respectively (Sternberg & Lowe 2009).
8 The effect of metropolitan advantage in internet usage holds up after controls for income, education and age introduced in multivariate analysis (Hindman 2000)
9 Comparable figures for Black non-Hispanics and Hispanics are 46% and 40% respectively.
10 The E.U. was established by the Treaty of Maastricht in 1993 upon the foundations of the preceding European Communities.
11 Environmental protection and energy independence are gaining traction in rural policy in the United States.
12 According to the European Commission (2010), 56% of Europe's population is rural. This compares with from one-quarter to one-third according to the Population Reference Bureau, and illustrates the wide variation in statistical measurement of rural as described in Chapter 1.

References

Allen, P. 2004. *Together at the Table: Sustainability and Sustenance in the American Agrifood System.* University Park, PA, The Pennsylvania State University Press.

Bissel, T. 2004. The Digital Divide Dilemma: Preserving Native American Culture While Increasing Access to Information Technology on Reservations. *Journal of Law, Technology and Policy,* 2004(1), 129–150.

Boase, J. 2010. The Consequences of Personal Networks for Internet Use in Rural Areas.*American Behavioral Scientist,* 53(9), 1257–1267.

Brown, D.L. 2008. The Future of Rural America Through a Social-Demographic Lens, pp. 229–248. In Wu, J., Barkley, P., & Weber, B. (eds) *Frontiers in Resource and Rural Economics.* Washington, D.C., Resources for the Future.

Brown, D.L. 2009. Rethinking the OECD's New Rural Demography. Plenary presentation to the OECD Rural Policy Conference, Quebec, October 14.

Brown, D.L. & Glasgow, N. 2008. *Rural Retirement Migration.* Dordrecht, Springer.

Brown, D.L., Bolender, B., Kulcsar, L.J., Glasgow, N., & Sanders, S. 2011f. Inter-County Variability of Older Net Migration as a Path Dependent Process. *Rural Sociology*, 76(1).

Brown, D.L.,Cromartie, J., & Kulcsar, L.J. 2004. Micropolitan Areas and the Measurement of American Urbanization. *Population Research and Policy Review*, 23, 399–418.

Browne, W. 2001. *The Failure of National Rural Policy: Institutions and Interests*. Washington, D.C., Georgetown University Press.

Browne, W., Skees, J., Swanson, L., Thompson, P., & L. Unnevehr. 1992. *Sacred Cows and Hot Pototoes: Agrarian Myths in Agricultural Policy*. Boulder, Westview.

Bureau of Indian Education. 2007. Bureau of Indian Education Master Plan, 2007–2011. Washington, D.C., U.S. Department of Interior.

Bryden, J. & Hart, K. (eds) 2004. *A New Approach to Rural Development in Europe: Germany, Greece, Scotland and Sweden*. Lewiston, Edward Mellen Press.

Davis. T & Trebian, W.. 2001. Shaping the Destiny of Native People by Ending the Digital Divide. *EDUCAUSE Review*. January, 38–46.

Drabenstott, M., Henry, M., & Gibson, L. 1987. The Rural Economic Policy Choice. *Economic Review*, 72 (1), 41–58.

Duncan, C. 1999. *Worlds Apart: Why Poverty Persists in Rural America*.New Haven, Yale.

Dwyer, J., Baldock, D., Beaufoy, G., Bennett, H., Lowe, P., & Ward, N. 2002. Europe's Rural Futures the Nature of Rural Development: Rural Development in an Enlarging Europe. Land Use Policy Group of Great Britain and WWF Europe. London, Institute for European Environmental Policy, 52–54.

Etzioni, A. 1996. The Responsive Community, A Communitarian Perspective. *American Sociological Review*, 61(1), 1–11.

European Commission. 2010. Rural Development Policy, 2007–2013. *Agriculture and Rural Development*. Downloaded on May 18, 2010 at http://ec.europa.eu/agriculture/rurdev/.

Evans, C. 1999. The Native Digital Divide: A Review of On-Line Literature. *Native American Distance Communication Web*. Las Cruces, University of New Mexico.

Falk, W. & Lobao, L. 2003. Who Benefits from Economic Restructuring?, pp. 152–165. In Brown, D.L. & Swanson, L. (eds) *Challenges for Rural America in the 21st Century*. University Park, Penn State University Press.

Flora, C. & Flora, J. 2003. Social Capital, pp. 214–227. In Brown, D.L. & Swanson, L. (eds) *Challenges for Rural America in the 21st Century*. University Park, Penn State University Press.

Gonzales, A. 2003. American Indians: Their Contemporary Reality and Future Trajectory, pp. 43–56. In Brown, D.L. & Swanson, L. (eds) *Challenges for Rural America in the Twenty-First Century*. University Park, Penn State University Press.

Grigsby, W. & Goetz, S. 2004. Telehealth: What Promise Does it Hold For Rural Areas?, pp. 237–250. In Glasgow, N., Morton, L., & Johnson, N. (eds) *Critical Issues in Rural Health Care*. Ames, Iowa, Blackwell.

Harris, R. & Worthen, D. 2003. African Americans in Rural America, pp. 32–42. In Brown D.L. & Swanson, L. (eds) *Challenges for Rural America in the 21st Century*. University Park, Penn State University Press.

Heimlich, R. & W. Anderson. 2001. Development at the Urban Fringe and Beyond: Impacts on Agriculture and Rural Land. *Agriculture Economic Report*, No. 803. Washington, D.C., USDA-ERS.

Hindman, D. 2000. The Rural–Urban Digital Divide. *Journalism and Mass Communication Quarterly*, 77(3), 549–560.

Krannich, R. & P. Petrzelka. 2003. Tourism and Natural Amenity Development: Real Opportunities? pp. 190–202. In Brown, D.L. & Swanson, L. (eds) *Challenges for Rural America in the 21st Century*. University Park, Penn State University Press.

Lowe, P., Ray, C., Ward, N., Wood, D., and Woodward, R. 1998.Participation in Rural Development. A Review of European Experience, Research Report. Centre for Rural Economy, University of Newcastle upon Tyne.

Lyson, T.A. & Guptill, A. (2004). Commodity Agriculture, Civic Agriculture and the Future of U.S. Farming. *Rural Sociology*, 69(3), 370–385.

Mattingly, M. 2009. Forty-Three Percent of Eligible Rural Families Can Claim a Larger Credit with EITC Program. *Carsey Institute Policy Brief*, No. 12. Available at: www.carseyinstitute.edu.

National Telecommunications and Information Administration. 1999. Falling Through the Net: Defining the Digital Divide. Washington, D.C., U.S. Department of Commerce.

Polanyi, K. 1944. *The Great Transformation: The Political and Economic Origins of Our Times.* Boston, Beacon.

Pollan, M. 2006. *The Omnivore's Dilemma: A Natural History of Four Meals.* New York, Penguin.

Population Reference Bureau. 2009. *World Population Data Sheet.* Washington, D.C. Downloaded on May 26, 2010 at http://www.prb.org/pdf09/09wpds_eng.pdf.

Schafft, K. & Brown, D.L. 2003 Social Capital, Social Networks and Social Power. *Social Epistemology*, 17(4), 329–342.

Schafft, K.A., & Jackson, A. 2010. Rural Education and Community in the Twenty-First Century, pp. 1–13. In Schafft, K.A. & Jackson, A. (eds), *Rural Education for the Twenty-First Century: Identity, Place, and Community in a Globalizing World.* University Park, Penn State University Press.

Schlosser, E. 2001. *Fast Food Nation.* New York, Houghton Mifflin.

Sherson, G. 2000. Closing the Gaps: The Digital Divide and Native Americans. Thesis submitted in partial fulfillment for Master's degree in Communications. Victoria University of Wellington.

Shortall, S. 2004. Social or Economic Goals: Civic Inclusion or Exclusion? An Analysis of Rural Development Theory and Practice. *Sociologia Ruralis*, 44(1), 110–124.

Shucksmith, M. 2010. Disintegrated Rural Development? Neo-endogenous Rural Development, Planning and Place Shaping in Diffused Power Contexts. *Sociologia Ruralis*, 50(1), 1–14.

Shucksmith, M., Thompson, K., & Roberts, D. 2005 (eds) *The CAP and the Regions: The Territorial Impact of the Common Agricultural Policy.* Wallingford, U.K., CABI Publishing.

Smith, K. & Savage, S. 2007. Food Stamp and School Lunch Programs Alleviate Food Security in Rural America. *Carsey Institute Fact Sheet.* Available at: www.carseyinstitute.edu.

Stern, M. & Wellman, B. 2010. Rural and Urban Differences in the Internet Society – Real and Relatively Important. *American Behavioral Scientist*, S 53(9), 1251–1256.

Sternberg, P. & Lowe, S. 2009. Rural Broadband at a Glance. *Economic Information Bulletin.* No. 47. Washington, D.C., USDA Economic Research Service.

Stohr, W. 2004. Foreword, pp. xxiii-xxvi. In Bryden, J., & Hart, K. (eds) 2004. *A New Approach to Rural Development in Europe: Germany, Greece, Scotland and Sweden.* Lewiston, Edward Mellen Press.

Swanson, L. & Brown, D.L. 2003. Challenges Become Opportunities: Trends and Policies Shaping the Future, pp. 397–405. In Brown, D.L. & Swanson, L. (eds) *Challenges for Rural America in the 21st Century.* University Park, Penn State University Press.

U.S. Census Bureau. 2007. Internet and Computer Use Supplement. *Current Population Survey.* October. Washington, D.C., U.S. Department of Commerce.

USDA-ERS. 2009. Organic Production. *Data Sets.* Available at: www.ers.usda.gov/Data/Organic/.

USDA-ERS. 2007. Nonmetro Population Growth Slower Now Than During the 1990s. *Rural Population and Migration Briefing Room.* Washington, D.C., USDA-ERS.

Warner, M & Shortall, S.. 2008. Understanding E.U.–U.S. Rural Policy Differences. *Rural New York Minute.* Ithaca, NY, CaRDI.

Young, F. & Lyson, T. 1993. Branch Plants and Poverty in the American South. *Sociological Forum.* 8(3),433–450.

Index

Note: Page numbers in italics refer to figures. Those followed by t refer to tables; those followed by n refer to notes, with note number.